# On Scandal

Scandal is the quintessential public event. Here is the first general and comprehensive analysis of this ubiquitous moral phenomenon. Taking up wide-ranging cases in society, politics, and art, Ari Adut shows when wrongdoings generate scandals and when they do not. He focuses on the emotional and cognitive experience of scandals and the relationships among those who are involved in or exposed to them. This perspective explains variations in the effects, frequency, elicited reactions, outcomes, and strategic uses of scandals. *On Scandal* offers provocative accounts of the Oscar Wilde, Watergate, and Lewinsky affairs. Adut also employs the lens of scandal to address puzzles and questions regarding public life. Why is American politics plagued by sex scandals? What is the cause of the rise in political scandals in Western democracies? Why were Victorians sometimes accommodating and other times intolerant of homosexuality? What is the social logic of hypocrisy? Why has transgression been so central to modern art?

Ari Adut is Assistant Professor of Sociology at the University of Texas at Austin. He holds postgraduate degrees from École des Hautes Études en Sciences Sociales in Paris and the University of Chicago, where he has also taught. His research has received support from the Social Science Research Council and the American Council of Learned Societies.

# Structural Analysis in the Social Sciences

Mark Granovetter, editor

The series Structural Analysis in the Social Sciences presents approaches that explain social behavior and institutions by reference to relations among such concrete entities as persons and organizations. This contrasts with at least four other popular strategies: (a) reductionist attempts to explain by a focus on individuals alone; (b) explanations stressing the causal primacy of such abstract concepts as ideas, values, mental harmonies, and cognitive maps (thus, "structuralism" on the Continent should be distinguished from structural analysis in the present sense); (c) technological and material determination; and (d) explanation using "variables" as the main analytic concepts (as in the "structural equation" models that dominated much of the sociology of the 1970s), where structure is that connecting variables rather than actual social entities.

The social network approach is an important example of the strategy of structural analysis; the series also draws on social science theory and research that is not framed explicitly in network terms but stresses the importance of relations rather than the atomization of reduction or the determination of ideas, technology, or material conditions. Though the structural perspective has become extremely popular and influential in all the social sciences, it does not have a coherent identity, and no series yet pulls together such work under a single rubric. By bringing the achievements of structurally oriented scholars to a wider public, the Structural Analysis series hopes to encourage the use of this very fruitful approach.

## Recent Books in the Series

Philippe Bourgois, *In Search of Respect: Selling Crack in El Barrio (Second Edition)*

Nan Lin, *Social Capital: A Theory of Social Structure and Action*

Roberto Franzosi, *From Words to Numbers*

Sean O'Riain, *The Politics of High-Tech Growth*

James Lincoln and Michael Gerlach, *Japan's Network Economy*

Patrick Doreian, Vladimir Batagelj, and Anujka Ferligoj, *Generalized Blockmodeling*

Eiko Ikegami, *Bonds of Civility: Aesthetic Networks and Political Origins of Japanese Culture*

Wouter de Nooy, Andrej Mrvar, and Vladimir Batagelj, *Exploratory Social Network Analysis with Pajek*

Peter Carrington, John Scott, and Stanley Wasserman, *Models and Methods in Social Network Analysis*

Robert C. Feenstra and Gary G. Hamilton, *Emergent Economies, Divergent Paths*

Martin Kilduff and David Krackhardt, *Interpersonal Networks in Organizations*

# ON SCANDAL

*Moral Disturbances in Society, Politics, and Art*

**Ari Adut**

*University of Texas at Austin*

CAMBRIDGE UNIVERSITY PRESS
Cambridge, New York, Melbourne, Madrid, Cape Town, Singapore, São Paulo, Delhi

Cambridge University Press
32 Avenue of the Americas, New York, NY 10013-2473, USA

www.cambridge.org
Information on this title: www.cambridge.org/9780521895897

First published 2008

Printed in the United States of America

*A catalog record for this publication is available from the British Library.*

*Library of Congress Cataloging in Publication Data*
Adut, Ari, 1971–
On scandal : moral disturbances in society, politics, and art / Ari Adut.
p.   cm. – (Structural analysis in the social sciences)
Includes bibliographical references and index.
ISBN 978-0-521-89589-7 (hardback)
1. Deviant behavior.   2. Scandals.   3. Sex scandals – Case studies.
4. Scandals – History – Case studies.   I. Title.   II. Series.
HM811.A38    2008
302.5'42–dc22        2008005084

ISBN 978-0-521-89589-7 hardback

*To Elyo and İkbal Adut*

And if your quarrels should rip up old stories,
And help them with a lie or two additional,
I'm not to blame, as you well know – no more is
Any one else – they were become traditional;
Besides, their resurrection aids our glories
By contrast, which is what we just were wishing all:
And science profits by this resurrection –
Dead scandals form good subjects for dissection.

Lord Byron, *Don Juan*, Canto I. St. 31

# Contents

# List of Figures

# Acknowledgments

I am grateful to Andy Abbott for his continuous, unstinting support since the late 1990s. I am extremely lucky to have worked with someone with such boundless intellectual scope and curiosity during my doctorate. I would also like to express my gratitude to Bill Sewell, who has helped me out in so many ways and from whom I have learned so much in Chicago and afterward. Andreas Glaeser and the late Roger Gould gave generously of their time and knowledge while I was in graduate school. I am indebted as well to Faruk Birtek, Nilüfer Göle, and Michel Wieviorka for initiating me to sociological thinking and research.

Randy Collins, Mark Granovetter, James Jasper, Michael Schudson, Christine Williams, and several anonymous reviewers provided munificent, detailed, and extremely helpful feedback on the entire book manuscript. Jack Katz and Charles Tilly generously made many incisive and useful comments on several chapters. I have tried to address most of the issues that they raised, and wherever I was successful in this enterprise, the book significantly improved. I should also like to thank Viviana Zelizer for her warm encouragement over the years. Thanks are due as well to Ed Parsons, my resourceful in-house editor at Cambridge University Press.

I profited quite a bit from exchanges with Damien de Blic, Luc Boltanski, Bruno Fay, Willie Jasso, Steven Lukes, Laurent Thévenot, Loïc Wacquant, and Ezra Zuckerman. The sociology departments of the University of Chicago and the University of Texas at Austin provided wonderful environments for research and writing. Parts of the book were presented at the various meetings of the American Sociological Association and the Social Science History Association, as well as at the University of Chicago, University of Texas at Austin, Princeton University, University of California at Berkeley, University of Pennsylvania, New York University, and Columbia University Graduate School of Journalism. I benefited much from the responses of these audiences. The Social Science Research Council, the American Council of Learned Societies, Andrew Mellon Foundation, the University of Chicago, and the University of Texas at Austin furnished funds at various stages during this project. I was able to include artwork in this book only thanks to a University Co-Operative Society Subvention Grant generously awarded by the University of Texas. I am also grateful to Matt Valentine for the author photograph. The first, second, and fourth chapters of this book adapt some material that I have already published elsewhere: "A Theory of Scandal: Victorians, Homosexuality, and the Fall of Oscar Wilde" *American Journal of Sociology* 111 (1): 213–48; "Scandal as Norm Entrepreneurship Strategy: Corruption and the French Investigating Magistrates," *Theory and Society* 33 (5): 529–578.

What I owe to the following people combines the personal with the intellectual. Ödül Bozkurt, Marc Breviglieri, Ozan Erözden, Diana Fleischman, Robert Hogg, Harris Kim, Jim Leitzel, Ali Hakan Muştu, Michael Reinhard, Atila Sezen, Diego von Vacano, Brooke Wexler, and Levent Yılmaz helped me in myriad ways impossible to express here. I am indebted as well to my dear University of Texas colleagues Maya Charad, Andrés Villarreal, Michael Young, and Wei-Hsin Yu for their both cerebral and bighearted friendship, which aided me immensely while writing. The ideas that are proposed in this book started to take form in graduate school, mostly through conversations with fellow sufferers. Of the latter I am particularly thankful to Deborah Boucoyannis, Dorothee Brantz, Dave Grazian, Nicole Greene, Gülriz Kurban, Haydar Kurban, Paul Manning, Jacqueline Mraz, Esra Özyürek, Devin Pendas, Michael Rosenfeld, and Joan Stavo-Debauge.

I would not have been able to write this book without the moral support of my family. My greatest debt is thus to all the members of my family, and especially to my parents, Elyo and İkbal Adut, to whom this book is dedicated.

# Introduction

- Notorious adulterers such as Franklin D. Roosevelt and John F. Kennedy had no difficulty getting away with their sexual shenanigans in a fairly straitlaced America. So how did Bill Clinton get impeached in the times of *Sex and the City*? Why is carnal wrongdoing such a common theme in contemporary public and political life even though Americans have lost much of their puritanism since the sixties and even though empirical evidence shows little difference in sexual practices and attitudes between the United States and other Western countries? What underlies the rise of sexual politics?
- Most French politicians of the twentieth century relied on illegal funds. This was no secret, but the issue was scarcely raised until the late 1980s. Then, all of a sudden, things changed; the hitherto common and tolerated finance schemes became unbearable. At least nine hundred elected officials, including fifty-three former or sitting ministers and one former prime minister, were placed under examination for corruption during the 1990s. Moreover, the formerly untouchable grandees were brought down mostly by a group of legal officials who had traditionally occupied one of the lowest rungs in the French judiciary. By the end of the decade, the French judiciary, which had long been subordinate to the other branches of government, had snatched relative independence from executive authority and enhanced its status for the first time since the Revolution. How does ordinary, largely accommodated behavior by political magnates suddenly become outrageous and subject to pursuits by nobodies?

- One can hardly think of a more perfect victim of nineteenth-century English puritanism than Oscar Wilde. The famous dramatist was tried twice and convicted in 1895 with legally inferior evidence, as a result of which he served two years in prison for consensual sexual acts. He passed away in exile, a penniless pariah. But Victorians had not always been this cruel on Wilde, whose sexual inclinations were no secret in London for a long time before his demise. In fact, although he was the subject of much badmouthing, Wilde was also the star of the literary and social scene, winning praise from all quarters. It was not just him. Homosexuality laws were rarely enforced in nineteenth-century England, and many Victorian men known to have the same predilections as Wilde not only evaded social scorn but often reached the highest positions in society. Why would Victorians be seemingly so inconsistent vis-à-vis homosexuals? What is the logic of their notorious hypocrisy?
- Disgrace has come to hover over American presidents in the recent decades. Nixon was forced to step down. Clinton was impeached. Reagan was not, but came close. Legion are cabinet members and White House staffers who have been harried by the media and the law with accusations of misbehavior. Yet isn't common wisdom on the modern presidency that it is an imperial office with ever-swelling powers and freedom from oversight? Has the imperial presidency molted into the imperiled presidency?
- Manet's *Le Déjeuner sur l'herbe* was bashed by most critics for being both ugly and immoral when it was exhibited in 1863, but the famous painting brought modernism to prominence. Why has transgression, both aesthetic and moral, been so central to the development of modern art and the self-definition of the modern artist? What is the strategic and moral logic of artistic provocation? Under which conditions is it more likely to be successful? How and why do aesthetic decisions become moral ones both for artists and their audiences? Has the transition from modernism to postmodernism changed transgression in art?

This book develops a theory of scandal to address these puzzles and problems. The cases just described might seem very different, and much ink has been spilled over them. I will show here, however, that they all have to do with transgression and public reactions to it and that thus none of them can be resolved without a proper understanding of scandal. The theory I propose will allow us to explain wide-ranging phenomena such as Victorian attitudes toward homosexuals, corruption and the fight against it in France, sexual politics in the contemporary United States, artistic modernism, and the American presidency. While doing so, I will also be able to address in a nonnormative fashion central questions regarding morality: Why do we find so much inconsistency in social and legal reactions to wrongdoing? How does publicity alter the meaning and effects of transgression and shape our response to it? How can those with low rank subject those with high status to their ethical aggression? How can transgression as well as outrage be deployed to self-aggrandize? How can morality and publicity be used as successful weapons in social, political, and artistic conflict? Why are conservative cultures often more tolerant of sexual wrongdoing? When and how do transgression and public reactions to it become transformative? This book will show that the set of behavior that we encounter in scandals of all kinds – behavior that engages in various ways with transgression – is a large yet ignored part of our moral repertoire.

In the pages that follow, I consider when wrongdoings generate scandals and when they do not. This will require us to understand scandal as lived experience – more specifically, as the disruptive publicity of transgression. The logic of this phenomenon can only be captured by analyzing when and how publicized transgressions contaminate, provoke, normalize, and tempt. But, as I will show, the cognitive and emotional experience of scandals is shaped by the structure of relationships among those who are involved in or exposed to them. My approach explains variations in the effects, frequency, elicited reactions, outcomes, and strategic uses of scandals. It also allows us to examine how scandals are dealt with and the various arrangements to prevent them from happening.

*On Scandal* is a study in morality. It is mostly about norm work –
a set of actions that encompass committing, publicizing, sanctioning,
and responding to transgression – by artists, politicians, legal officials, as well as private citizens. Such practices have a moral character
not in the sense of being right according to some absolute standard
but rather because they either come with or seem to require some
kind of moral justification. Study of scandal reveals that norm work
is profoundly shaped by the anticipated and actual effects of publicity – and not simply by the values in society. In particular, I will
show how publicity accounts for the significant and otherwise inex-
plicable variations in legal and social reactions to wrongdoing. A
good deal of hypocrisy in the world – alas obviously not all of it –
will thereby be explained. Scandal derives an important part of its
force from publicity, an emergent and transformative social form that
radically alters the meaning and import of wrongdoing. By thinking
about scandal, we will acquire insights into the nature of publicity,
the role of morality in political conflict and art, the strategic use of
transgression, and the conditions for successfully attacking elites.

Scandals are salient social phenomena with singular dramatic
intensity. They are also ubiquitous. It is difficult to browse a newspaper, trace the history of a nation or organization, think about
the development of modern art, engage in gossip among friends and
relatives, or read a novel without coming across these key events.
Scandals may seem ephemeral and frivolous. But they come in small
and big sizes, ludic and grave modes: compare the routine reporting
of the assorted inanities of Britney Spears on American television
with the repercussions of the horrors of the Abu Ghraib prison in
Iraq. Furthermore, what might start out as a minor incident – a third-
rate burglary, as in the Watergate scandal, or the court-martial of
an obscure captain of the French army, as in the Dreyfus affair –
might eventually bring down a president or galvanize a nation. In
effect, scandals can mobilize much emotional energy, at times with
momentous consequences.

We come across scandal in all areas of life. It has come to occupy
the center stage in Western democracies during the recent decades,
especially by contributing to the decline in public confidence. Since

the rise of modernism, scandal is intricately linked to artistic activity; it has been in effect an engine of aesthetic dynamism. More generally, scandal plays a pivotal part in the implementation, solidification, and transformation of norms in all domains of life. And since scandal is the public event par excellence, any account of the public sphere and its contemporary transformations is sorely lacking without a grasp of its essence.

Scandal is a disruptive, profane thing. But it also opens up various opportunities for some, who may decide to participate in it. Scandal is the very stuff that much of conflict is made of in society, politics, and art. In all these sectors, consequential challenges against and among elites often take the form of scandal-generating provocations and denunciations. A good deal of moral conflict in the public sphere is actualized in scandals, even though it is mostly high-profile, heavily scripted, drawn-out, and widely reported instances that are identified as such. This book, then, does not simply consider rare events such as presidential impeachments but covers a wide and seemingly heterogeneous array of social phenomena. A protean form, scandal underlies all kinds of events and processes in public that have to do with actual, alleged, or apparent transgressions: a high-profile trial, a scene at a wedding, a political purge, a gallery opening, a cause célèbre, a catastrophe that instigates recriminations, a heretical act in the open, an organizational wrangle spun out of control, a witch hunt, an instance of civil disobedience, an anticorruption campaign, a publicity stunt, or a congressional hearing. Scandals are not only significant in terms of their actual effects. Insofar as their intended or unintended effects on third parties are anticipated, there will be individual and collective efforts to prevent or defuse them. Dealing with scandal, which may require sizeable resources, is an ongoing activity of individuals, groups, and organizations.

Scandal matters also in terms of what it reveals. As the most salient public occurrence, it throws into full relief the social dynamics of publicity. And the royal road – or, in any case, one royal road – to understanding the social organization and cultural code of a specific time and place is paved by its scandals, both actual and averted. I believe that the analyses of scandals in this book will illuminate previously misunderstood aspects of the contexts in which they have erupted. I will attempt to rectify or improve, with the aid of my theory of scandal, our grasp of things as disparate as Victorian England, the modern American presidency, contemporary sexual politics, modern art, legalization of politics, and moral crusades.

Here is a quick overview of what is to come. In the first chapter, I propose a general account of scandal. I study the lived experience, strategic use, and interactional character of scandals, but I also underline the structural factors that underlie and affect their making. The rest of the book fleshes out the empirical implications of the model laid out in the first chapter by considering all kinds of scandals, big or small, in different social and historical contexts.

The second chapter analyzes the seemingly inconsistent Victorian attitudes toward homosexuality (one of the most scandalous sins of the period) and the unfolding of the Oscar Wilde affair. I show here how scandal reveals the dramaturgical dimension of the public sphere and the central yet often ignored effects of publicity on the legal and societal reactions to wrong doing.

The third and the fourth chapters are about the incidence and effects of political scandal in Western democracies. One overarching issue in this book is the role of scandal in elite conflict and competition. These two chapters reveal how scandal is often used strategically by political, legal, and media elites in their struggles with each other and among themselves. I focus on the American presidency in the third chapter. I investigate the structural and conjunctural factors that render a given president vulnerable or immune to moral attack, as well as those that have a bearing on the likelihood and success of scandalmongering against the White House. This also enables me to consider the contradictions of the modern presidency and the developments that have undermined presidential power since the late sixties. I examine the strategic use of political scandal and the conditions for undertaking successful ethical assaults against the high and mighty in the fourth chapter. The case is the corruption investigations in France during the 1990s and 2000s.

The fifth chapter treats the escalation of sex scandals in the United States since the seventies, which, I argue, was paradoxically made possible only by the sexual liberalization of the sixties. Here, I explore the intimate connection between sex and scandal and explicate the rise of sexual politics in the United States since the 1970s.

The sixth chapter is on artistic transgression and the reactions it generates. I expound in this section on the strategic logic of provocation in modern and contemporary art. I also maintain that art scandals unveil the moral aspect of artistic production and reception.

The conclusion points to some of the moral ambiguities of scandal.

# ONE

# The Disruptive Publicity of Transgression

"SCANDAL is gossip made tedious by morality," wrote Oscar Wilde in *Lady Windermere's Fan*. The Victorian wit had a capital point. Scandals are intensely moral phenomena, and they do generate a goodly sprinkling of unoriginal, sanctimonious cant. I am not only referring to punitive narrow-mindedness about minor private sins – the kind that Wilde had in mind. It is through scandal that all inquisitional moralizers, from Maximilien de Robespierre to Joe McCarthy, make their mark in history.

Yet Wilde was decidedly understating the difference between gossip and scandal. The former is private, the latter public. However toothsome and trifling, gossip usually has a moral core, whereas scandals are hardly all dull. In fact, they can be tragic. When he was gossiped about, Wilde was the star of London. In the wake of his scandalous trials, he became a convict – and later a reviled outcast. Since scandals can at times be quite grave affairs, often having to do with the common good, they can spark serious public discourse. Two distinct yet implicit views underlie such thinking. Let us start by considering them, so that I can then propose my own approach to scandal.

The first perspective focuses on significant transgressions such as political or corporate corruption that elicit (or should elicit) reaction once publicized.[1] We can call this the objectivist view, for it is primarily concerned with real misconduct. Watergate would thus be a case study of – or would be explained by – the organizational pathologies of the Nixon White House and its imperial leanings. Similarly, the Enron affair of 2001 would be the ineluctable culmination of the irrational stock market exuberance of the 1990s or an illustration of the unchecked corporate greed of the same decade. The objectivist approach treats scandals as the proverbial iceberg tip – as events in which the usually concealed corrupt components of social systems are revealed to the public. One is to disregard the brouhaha surrounding the exposure so that the deep structures that have enabled the deviance can be dispassionately dissected.

The other position regards scandals as socially construted phenomena and thus puts the stress on the public reactions to transgressions. Let us call this the constructivist view.[2] Scandal can take on different guises here. Watergate could be seen as a grand ritual of renewal through which Americans asserted their core values.[3] In an analogous fashion, scandals that give rise to national controversies (for example, the Lewinsky affair) could be understood as events revealing or reenacting the cultural divisions in society. Or, in more general terms, scandal can function as a social control mechanism, through which public opinion, for better or worse, reigns supreme and discourages us from acting up. Finally, for more cynical constructivists, scandal is a moral panic fashioned or exploited by elites to manipulate mass perceptions.

The two views are not simply academic or intellectual fancies. Journalists, as well as those embroiled in scandals themselves, use them, too. One is not always an objectivist or a constructivist, however. A given person will tend to go back and forth between focusing on a real transgression and on the reactions to it, depending on the specific scandal. Denouncers usually adopt an objectivist perspective. The denouncees and their advocates, on the other hand, subscribe to a moralistic version of constructivism. Hence, Republicans regarded the Lewinsky affair as the result of Bill Clinton's outrageous conduct. In contrast, for the Democrats the scandal was created out of whole cloth by the president's enemies to destroy him. Media are often grilled for superficially covering only sensational transgressions and personalizing them, instead of discussing the ostensibly much more important structural and impersonal issues that lay underneath them. This is, of course, objectivist thinking. Yet the same critics can also be, in a constructivist fashion, censorious of journalists for blowing things out of proportion, for creating "pseudo-events."[4] An extreme

example of the latter would be the celebrity scandal, a genre specializing in the trivial trespasses of famous people, suspected of being
little more than publicity stunts.

Sociologists indulge in a high dose of constructivism when they
label mobilization around causes such as obesity or drunk-driving as
moral panics. There is often a debunking, if not a denunciatory, spirit
at work here: from a constructivist perspective, scandals can be quite
consequential with sundry nefarious results. They can distort reality.
Substituting popular justice for legal justice, giving free rein to pent-
up resentments, and creating scapegoats, they can bring about witch
hunts. Or more insidiously, scandal, or the presentation of news
as such, can bestow dignity to what is vacuous, shamelessly expose
what should remain private, corrode privacy norms, and pollute the
public sphere. A distinction is therefore frequently made between
news and scandal – especially by respectable journalists. Hence, the
winner of the 1896 contest organized by Adolph Ochs, the owner of
the *New York Times*, for the journal masthead logo: "All the World's
News, but not a School for Scandal."[5]

The objectivist and constructivist views say important things about
scandal. Yet they are also marred by problems, and they miss the
underlying logic of the phenomenon. Despite its valuable insights
into the making of transgressive behavior, the objectivist position,
ironically, often suffers from a normative streak: it reproduces the
grievances of the victims or denouncers of misbehavior. Treating
scandals as the epiphenomena of transgressions, it ignores that the
latter need not be authenticated to occasion the former. Think of
all the ramifications of the Whitewater affair of the nineties, including the impeachment of the president, which had little to do with
the unproved charges of real estate fraud attributed to the Clintons.
Sometimes mere allegations can elicit more reaction than uncontested
revelations. And, as we will see time and again in this book, unpublicized yet well-known transgressions do not occasion scandals at all.
There is no correlation, no direct relationship between rule breaking
and scandal.

As for constructivism, it rightfully reminds us that reactions to
transgressions cannot be derived from the transgressions themselves.

But it has not put forth a general model that would account for the conditions, incidence, dynamics, and effects of scandals with different contents and publics. What is more, constructivism is unduly voluntaristic: it has difficulty explaining variations in public responses to misbehavior, which do not necessarily reflect the strength of the violated values. Scandals, however, frequently involve violent condemnations of transgressions that were widely known and tolerated before. Besides, reactions may well morph after a scandal breaks – the knowledge or suspicion of the transgression remaining constant. For instance, Nixon clearly saw in the last months of Watergate (but before the incriminating tapes surfaced) that the growing persuasion among the Republican electorate that he would be impeached led many of his supporters to withdraw their support from him.[6] Finally, scandals rarely renew or purify. On the contrary, they often yield profane phenomena prone to pollute all those who come into any contact with them. The Lewinsky affair stained not only Bill Clinton but also his office, the Democratic Party, Independent Counsel Kenneth Starr, and Speaker of the House Bob Livingston. Scandals can be disruptive for all. When Gerald Ford said, "Our national nightmare is over," upon taking office, most Americans concurred with the new president's characterization of Watergate.[7]

## What Is Scandal?

Scandal is a polysemic word.[8] A significant transgression, the forceful reaction that a transgression elicits, the discredit heaped on persons and institutions as a result of a transgression or its denunciation, and an episode during which a transgression is publicized and condemned are all referred to as "scandal" in everyday parlance. My concern in this book is mainly sociological, so I am primarily interested in scandal as a public event, as opposed to a subjective assessment of an action.

In this sense, a scandal is an event of varying duration that starts with the publicization of a real, apparent, or alleged transgression to a negatively oriented audience and lasts as long as there is significant and sustained public interest in it. Scandals usually include not only public attention but reactions to the publicized transgression as well. They are therefore usually not single events but episodes. Some of them are very short affairs. The publicized transgression may simply embarrass or offend an audience without eliciting a fully articulated reaction. In this case, the scandal will be relatively brief, coterminous with the emotional state of the audience. In other instances, the transgressor can anticipate reaction and preemptively make an apology or expiate before the public, or those who act in its name, has had an opportunity to act. An example is the resignation of House Speaker Bob Livingston in late 1998, shortly after it became public that *Hustler* magazine was about to go to press with a story divulging the politician's adulterous past. Many scandals are not this brief, though. The publicization will often meet with a denunciation of some kind by the aggrieved party, his or her advocates, authorities, or opinion leaders. The scandal will be even lengthier if this reaction is followed by a denial – or by some kind of defense.

And there are scandals that are truly long lasting. They will grow before they end: the original publicization will give rise to further revelations or allegations that may be more damning or significant. These developments will accompany wider and more intense attention and possibly further action by the offender. Various authorities and opinion leaders may intervene with their words and deeds; so can the allies, associates, and opponents of the alleged offender. The scandal will thus be an episode of interaction around a publicized transgression played out in front of a negatively oriented audience. The duration of a scandal is a function of public interest. It may be as brief as a minute (a scene at a wedding) or as long as a year (the Lewinsky affair). The importance of a scandal may change, too. Watergate started with the revelation of a third-rate burglary committed by some minor unsavory characters before becoming a presidential affair. Reactions run the whole gamut from silent shunning to public disapproval to legal sanctions to rioting to lynching, and they may transform in the course of a given scandal.

Let us consider the three basic elements of scandal: a transgression, someone who will publicize this transgression, and an interested public.

## The Transgression

A transgression is necessary for a scandal to occur. But it need not be real. An apparent or even simply alleged transgression can cause a scandal as long as it generates a negatively oriented interest or even curiosity from a public. So I don't necessarily refer to a real occurrence but only to a seeming or effectively claimed one when I use the term "transgression" (or similar terms like "offense") in this book. The same applies to the term "transgressor" and its synonyms. And even though the notion of transgression assumes some social or legal standard, the transgressor may disagree with others' moral assessment of the act in question.

Equally important is the fact that privately tolerable behavior can become unacceptable once publicized. This may reflect a normative incongruity between a subculture and the larger society. The discrepancy between the high costs of the enforcement of a norm and the cheapness of lip service can also account for social hypocrisy. Frequently, however, the contradiction between private tolerance and public wrath has to do with how publicity transforms and magnifies the sense of all acts, including transgressions. I expound on this point shortly.

Scandalous transgressions are often willful wrongdoings that, when made public, make the transgressor look like a bad person. Yet exceptional acts that reveal gross incompetence by those we trust (such as politicians or doctors) can also set off scandals – but usually when they are particularly harmful and when the opinion leaders loudly and successfully frame the matter in moral terms. In effect, anything that will bring about shame or that will embarrass or provoke when made public can trigger a scandal. A transgressive intent is neither sufficient nor necessary. Some artists attempt to scandalize without success; others scandalize without meaning to. Nonliberal publics will in particular not require transgressive intent to see something as scandalous. If a public believes, for instance, that only those of a certain race can fill the upper echelons of government, revelations or allegations about the impure (and thus transgressive) origins of a high-ranking official will cause a scandal, even if the person in question were in the dark about his or her pedigree.

The publicity of things sexual is particularly scandalous – again, often independent of intent. When Paris Hilton's sex tape was put on the Internet by her malevolent ex-boyfriend in 2004, it did cause a minor scandal, which, if the entertainment channel can be trusted, mortified even the usually unflappable heiress. Further, certain acts are objectively shameful, and their publicity automatically eventuates in a scandal. Oedipus had good reasons to kill the man he killed and to marry the woman married; no one in Thebes said he should have inquired beforehand about his biological ties to the two. Yet he still stabbed his eyes out in horror and was forced into exile when it turned out that his acts, however unknowingly committed, were all the same transgressive and in need of expiation. We moderns tend to emphasize responsibility when making normative judgments;[9] it is nevertheless not hard to understand Oedipus's reaction to the moral extremity that befell him.

## The Publicizer

Scandals usually break by someone publicizing a transgression. I will thus often refer to this act as causing or creating a scandal. The publicizer can be the author of a transgression already committed, as is the case in a public confession or challenge. Or one can publicize a transgression by provocatively committing it in front of a real or virtual audience. Think of Martin Luther burning a papal bull and a copy of the canon law in 1520 or Salman Rushdie publishing his *Satanic Verses* in 1988. Or imagine someone proposing an offensive idea or uttering a racial epithet at a meeting.

One can also, more commonly, create a scandal by publicizing the real or alleged transgression of someone else. This can be done in a normatively neutral way, as in a news report or an official release, or by an explicitly moral act, usually in the form of a public denunciation. The most famous example of the latter is Émile Zola's legendary *J'accuse*, his condemnation of the general staff of the French army in 1898 in the newspaper *L'Aurore* for having framed Captain Alfred

Dreyfus with treason charges.[10] The eyewitnesses or the victims of the transgression as well as the advocates of the victims can accuse in public, just as those who claim to (or are institutionally entitled to) speak in the name of those who are offended can.

The alleged perpetrator may well cry breach of privacy, but implicit in a public denunciation is the pretension that the transgression is a matter worthy of general attention.[11] When private actors publicly denounce, they are usually trying to mobilize others by a compelling definition of the situation. Authorities such as prosecutors and judges accuse openly as a matter of course.[12] Since a denunciation can be met with retaliation, one can resort to anonymity as well. A corporate slave can reveal his firm's monkey business in an anonymous blog. An aggrieved girl can expose a promiscuous classmate, deemed a danger to all respectable female students with corruptible boyfriends, on the walls of the high school bathroom. One can leak compromising information about one's superiors to journalists or legal officials and thereby have someone else do the publicizing. However, a public denunciation does not have to include new or true information to engender a scandal; it is sufficient that it generates negative and sustained interest.

When it is undertaken intentionally by the transgressor or the denouncer, the publicization of a transgression is often a moral attack. Structural factors, which I analyze later, however, make scandal-generating denunciations and provocations more or less likely and effective. But a scandal need not be occasioned deliberately; it can come about unintentionally. One can offend one's audiences without meaning to. One can unwittingly divulge a fact that was meant to remain secret, the disclosure of which could not but be tumultuous. A scandal can break due to an accident, as in the botched Watergate break-in. Or consider an involuntary yet revelatory act such as an embarrassing lapse in a wedding ceremony by the bride, who, by mixing up the names of the groom and her former boyfriend, betrays her real object of desire to those attending.[13] A spectacular catastrophe such as the Enron bankruptcy or the Katrina disaster – which either clearly springs from a wrongdoing or, given the extent of suffering, urges a hunt for one – might also eventuate in a scandal. Nevertheless, the transformation usually necessitates a public denunciation in such cases.

## The Public

For a scandal to break, a transgression must be communicated to an audience that is negatively oriented to it. The information that is publicized need not be apodictic, however. Even when there is doubt about the veracity of a transgression, the public (or many members of it) may still act on the assumption that it is true if nonresponse is risky; if shunning the alleged offender is cheap; or if the allegations hew too well to the settled beliefs about the offender or to the stereotypes about his or her group. Yet a scandal does not require an unequivocal general reaction once it breaks. This might come about eventually at the end of an interactional process. It is enough that there is a strong possibility from the public's perspective that the alleged transgression might be true. The journalist Christopher Hitchens's longtime accusations that Mother Teresa is a fraud did not cause a scandal for this reason.[14] Again, for most Americans, the charges that the cyclist Lance Armstrong owed his record-breaking string of Tour de France triumphs to dope did not stick. The French were predictably more skeptical.

The public of a scandal can be as small and contextual as the guests at a wedding or as large and permanent as a nation. Whatever its size, however, the public is a collectivity that has reasons to be interested in the event. It may have a stake in reacting to the offender or, more often, in legitimating reaction taken in its name by authorities or opinion leaders. But a scandal does not require a fully participating public; it is enough that the public simply watch. This is why the public of a scandal mostly consists of the nonintimates of the transgressor – that is, those who can remain spectators to the event, those who are basically outsiders. It is difficult to conceive of a scandal breaking solely within the nuclear family: one cannot legitimately be a distant and disinterested spectator to another member's sin or grievance in such an intimate unit where there are no outsiders.

### More Complex Forms

Scandal in its bare form involves a transgression, a publicizer, and a public. But actual scandals usually display a more complex structure with additional parties, especially if they are of long duration. In many instances, the publicizer and the transgressor are not the same person: one publicizes the transgression of another. Media play a role when the public is not physically co-present. A transgressor is often denounced by an opponent, and transgressions often have identifiable victims. When the violated norm is not a social rule of conduct but a law or an organizational code, reactions can come not only from the public but also from authorities. And even in the case of a scandal with a small public that does not involve unlawfulness, it is typically the opinion leaders and not the public as a whole who respond directly to the transgressor. Transgressors in major scandals tend to be relatively powerful people, and, especially if charges against them are not verified, they will usually find defenders. In effect, some national scandals, such as the Dreyfus affair, can even sunder an entire society into two: those who react against the transgressor and those who support him or her (and think that the real culprit is someone else, frequently the denouncer). To the extent that they can be affected by the scandal, the associates of the transgressor can be significant actors as well. One can be an associate as a result of common group membership or institutional connection, or, at times, simply because one belongs to the same social category. Associates of transgressors or victims may also serve as their advocates. But an advocate does not have to be linked to the transgressor or the victim.

All scandal publics display some level of heterogeneity. More-over, a scandal can obtain differentiated subpublics varying in terms of their identification with the norm that is violated or of their relationship to the transgressor. The electric Bob Dylan was scandalous solely to his folk fans. Interpretations within a public can also vary. The Democrats' take on allegations of wrongdoing by a fellow congressman will tend to be different from the Republican attitudes. Subpublics will not necessarily have the same incentives to voice reaction. They can disagree on the significance of the transgression and have divergent ideas on the veracity of the charges. An obvious example is the O. J. Simpson case in which American blacks and whites disagreed vehemently on the guilt of the former football player – as well as on the meaning of the event. Whites saw it mainly as a celebrity scandal, whereas for blacks the affair was all about racism. Here is an example from the Old Regime France. Prior to the Revolution, puritans and closet republicans were scandalized by the peccadilloes of great lords, which, to them, confirmed the corruption of the social and political order. Still this assessment was not sufficient to generate significant general reaction. Aristocrats got in serious trouble only when they challenged royal authority or brought international discredit on the regime.[15]

The public of a scandal can progressively expand, and reactions may change as a result. Consider the following scenario. A political science professor is accused of plagiarism by a colleague in a mass e-mail sent to the members of her department. The issue remains a departmental matter. Most faculty members have incentives to keep it this way. Some think that the infraction is not established or is minor, while others deem the transgressor crucial to the welfare of the department. Most believe that publicity will make everybody look bad. But then an enterprising journalism student publishes the charge in the campus newspaper. Soon after, the school being a prestigious institution with national visibility, the *Washington Post* decides to do a story on the event. In the meantime, political scientists from other universities have entered into the melee, taking sides and offering different interpretations of what happened for all kinds of reasons, avowed or not. We see here a scandal that is expanding. Note that the final public is heterogeneous and that its components are differentiated by their degree of outsiderness toward the incident. The distance from the main characters in the drama and the amount of publicity the issue gets will have significant effects on attitudes. Those who were critical of the alleged perpetrator in the first stage can change position once the scandal acquires a wider or novel audience.[16]

Those who want to create consequential scandals may need to try several audiences or reach out to an expanded public before they get the result they want. The Don Imus incident of 2007 is a case in point.

His original listening audience was not all that outraged by the radio host's characterization of the members of Rutgers University's female basketball team as "nappy-headed hos." Imus's detractors therefore had to publicize the act to a wider audience, whose spokespersons proved much less accommodating.

## *Publicity*

Unless effectively publicized, a transgression will not generate a scandal. No publicity, no scandal. But publicity is not an obvious concept. A transgression may be widely known. This may, however, well fall short of generating collective and focused attention – which is what publicity involves. Those, including authorities, who know of a transgression may nevertheless ignore it to avoid the undesirable consequences that would ensue if it were to come unavoidably into the open. Publicity is usually achieved when we are exposed simultaneously to a transgression, either actually or discursively, from the same source(s) of communication. Each recipient of the discreditable information (or each spectator of the transgression itself) thus knows and cannot pretend not to know the position of the others. Everyone knows that everyone knows that everyone knows . . . , ad infinitum – the technical definition of common knowledge.[17]

Sometimes a scandal involves the publicization of a transgression to those who have already formed a public many times – for instance, the American nation. A transgression can also be communicated to an existing public in an ongoing performance. Consider someone saying something offensive during a televised event. Other times publicity may create a new public out of common spectatorship. Yet in all these instances, publicity decreases the coordination costs among those who know of or suspect a transgression.

Coordination can be especially elusive in the case of word-of-mouth communications. Gossip tends to keep information within bounds; participation in it is dependent on membership in small groups and insider networks.[18] Its logic is different from that of scandal. There are social dictates against publicizing discreditable information that can nevertheless be legitimately gossiped about.

For example, although it is on the whole acceptable to gossip about the adultery of a colleague dyadically, it would be thoroughly inadmissible to bring it up in a gathering, thus making the issue a public matter – even if the adulterer is absent and the attendees are aware of each other's knowledge of the adultery. Rumor, the serial transmission of unverified information typically through weak social ties,[19] does a better job than gossip in spreading allegations. But it also creates ambiguities by generating reformulations and, at times, multiple accounts.[20] Thus, receivers of a rumor can find it hard to coordinate their behavior vis-à-vis the transgressor. Unless nonaction is immediately consequential, as in emergencies and disasters, rumor and gossip might not be acted on when dealing with the transgression would be risky or when attitudes toward it are either discrepant or unclear. Even if they result in sanctions against the transgressor, such communications usually don't lead to scandals unless they are followed by a public denunciation or revelation. In contrast, publicity, as I define it, almost imposes the transgression on the audience. Malinowski provides us with an example from the Trobriand Islands:

> I have found that the breach of exogamy – as regards intercourse and not marriage – is by no means a rare occurrence, and public opinion is lenient, though decidedly hypocritical. If the affair is carried on sub rosa with a certain amount of decorum, and if no one in particular stirs up trouble – "public opinion" will gossip, but not demand any harsh punishment. If, on the contrary, scandal breaks out – every one turns against the guilty pair and by ostracism and insults one or the other may be driven to suicide.[21]

Here, the scandal broke only after the discarded lover of the aberrant girl (who was having an affair with a relative) denounced his rival in public, thereby making it impossible for the community to continue to close its eyes to the transgression. The reaction was conditioned not by endogamy, which was previously abided in part to eschew trouble, but by its publicization. That large numbers within the French political elite had collaborated in one way or another with the Germans during the Occupation was again well known but only ignited a scandal when asserted loud and clear in the documentary *Sorrow and Pity* by Marcel Ophüls in 1969.[22]

These cases show that a public denunciation does not necessarily provide new information regarding a transgression but can nevertheless generate a scandal by imposing it on the public. And if executed well, a public denunciation can function as a humiliating sanction in itself, regardless of its veracity. An accusation is an act of "ethical aggression."[23] It can make, in a Nietzschean manner, might out of morality, especially when enunciated in the name of a physically present public.

## Scandal as Lived Experience

I have defined scandal as an episodic event, but we have yet to uncover its basic logic, the thing that underlies public interest and reaction. At first blush, we might think that the cultural offensiveness, objective harmfulness, physical disruptiveness, social costs, or sheer extraordinariness of a transgression will determine whether it will be seen as scandalous. These obviously matter.[24] The social status of the offender is, however, usually a much more important factor. The publicity of the transgressions of low-status people can only create small scandals – if any scandal at all. If they ever obtain attention, it is from a smaller public. The publicity of the deviant sexual practices of a single priest can occasion a scandal. Yet a much bigger one will break – with a larger public and more intense reaction – if the offender is a cardinal. Low-status offenders get little or no attention unless their transgressions are in some way exceptional or successfully presented by opinion leaders as symptomatic of social problems that should implicate high-status individuals or organizations. It is even more common to link elites to the sins of low-status people. All journalists know that you will have a much better story – a bigger scandal – if you can show how the munchkins are taking the rap for the satraps.

Transgressions of the elite are scandal generating in part because many high-status people are also well known; their acts are readily salient when publicized. The most atrocious acts by ciphers can go unnoticed. The mere fame of someone who has purportedly perpetrated a peccadillo will, in contrast, often be sufficient to spur massive publicity. Prior renown is not obligatory, however; with or without fame, high status draws forth an unfixed farrago of fascination, identification, and resentment from others.[25] This explosive mix is given full force when elites fall. The high and mighty will by and large find some supporters when things go wrong, but their riveting scandals also vindicate the uneasy resentment they provoke in us.[26] Outrage at washed-up elites is thus frequently fused with schadenfreude – an all-too-human satisfaction that often comes from cutting down to size those whose prominence used to comparatively degrade us. The transgressions of high-status actors elicit interest also because elites usually have opponents standing to gain from their scandals. In any case, fall from grace is a compelling, gripping story line for audiences. Shakespeare saw well the affinity between scandal and high status in *Rape of Lucrece*:

> The baser is he, coming from a king,
> To shame his hope with deeds degenerate:
> The mightier man, the mightier is the thing
> That makes him honour'd, or begets him hate;
> For greatest scandal waits on greatest state.
> The moon being clouded presently is miss'd,
> But little stars may hide them when they list.[27]

We are positively drawn to scandal. But most scandals are often more than amusing episodes eliciting fleeting interest; they also involve something disturbing. The transgressions of elites can lead to scandals in great part because their publicity generates various disruptive, negative effects on the institutions or values they stand for, on their associates, or on their audiences. A genuine scandal usually requires that a publicized transgression does in a significant fashion one or both of these things:

- Demoralize or shame one or more of the following entities: the public to whom the transgression is communicated or the individuals, groups, or institutions that hold high status in the eyes of this public
- Challenge the public, authorities, or both

I will call the first main effect of scandal contamination, and the second, provocation. Both are simultaneously cognitive, moral, and emotional: they produce meaning, alter the moral standing and well-being of those they touch, and place them in an unbidden affective state. On the whole, the more widespread and intense the contamination and provocation, the larger the public interest and the bigger the scandal will be. Publicity is a key variable here. It is only when they are effectively publicized that transgressions acquire contaminating and provocative powers. And not all transgressions contaminate or challenge, or to the same extent, when they are made public. As I argue shortly, factors such as the nature of the transgression, the status of the transgressor, the structure of the transgressor's group or organization, and his or her relationship to the audiences and authorities will have a bearing on this issue. The high status of the transgressor, for example, will not simply make a publicized transgression salient but also highly contaminating.

A scandal is an episode of moral disturbance, marked by an interaction around an actual, apparent, or alleged transgression that draws sustained and negative attention from a public. What governs attitudes and behaviors during a scandal is mostly the contamination or provocation (or both) that is experienced when a transgression is publicized. Scandal is experienced differentially by different parties. And it is not a discrete variable, an all-or-nothing thing, but always a matter of degree; hence, the language of size (big, small, growing) that one uses to talk about scandal.

My approach to scandal combines phenomenology (study of lived experience) with strategic and structural analysis. In this chapter, I am mostly interested in studying the nature and determinants of the emotional, cognitive, and moral effects of scandals on those who experience them. The rest of the book will consider in detailed case studies how these effects are managed and manipulated through strategic interaction. I will also (i) focus on the incentives and opportunities to publicize transgressions in society, politics, and art and (ii) consider how supraindividual factors affect the likelihood and success of moral attacks in public.

23

As lived experience, scandal is the disruptive publicity of trans-gression. Let us consider in detail the main disruptions that scandals entail.

## Contamination

A mere public allegation, even if it is not true and even if it does not meet with any visible immediate reaction, can besmirch the character of the putative offender. Time and repair work will be necessary for the person to decontaminate. This is not all, however. All those associated personally, institutionally, or even categorically with the suspect can also be contaminated. The recent pedophilia allegations implicating some clergymen smeared their families as well as the Roman Catholic Church. The Enron bankruptcy slashed the standing of numerous actors and institutions of American capitalism.

### Associative Contamination

I pointed out that for a scandal to break, the alleged offender should usually be of high status or that the event should somehow implicate a prominent individual or institution. This is not just because elites command attention. More important, elites represent groups, insti-tutions, and values; the publicity of their sins has significant contam-inating effects. A full professor is a better synecdoche of an academic department than an assistant professor, and the publicized transgres-sions of the former will damage the institution more than those of the latter. The semiotic association will be particularly robust – and the resultant scandal proportionately disruptive – if the high status of an elite is the consequence or the condition of the trust vested in his or her person, as is the case with politicians and profession-als. Transgressions by such persons are magnified to the extent that they reveal hypocrisy: the greater the discrepancy between the moral claims embodied by the offender[28] and the act that is publicized, the bigger the scandal.

Even when high status does not officially entail exigent ethical standards, elites are frequently deemed to be role models and may be held accountable for the conduct of others on whom they (are thought to) exert influence or power. For instance, the Lewinsky scandal brought home the fact that American presidents are saddled with exemplary duties in addition to their executive responsibilities – but also that the weight of the former is declining.[29] Finally, groups are more dependent on their high-status members than they are on their lower-status members; any sanctions on elites thus carry consequential externalities on others.

Its contaminating effects distinguish scandal from law in terms of social control. Legal justice regards its subjects as autonomous individuals and demands exacting criteria of proof to establish wrongdoing. Scandal, in contrast, has a collectivistic nature and entails the exercise of popular justice: associates of offenders are often compromised with mere allegations. The logic of scandal combines guilt by suspicion and guilt by association. These two characteristics explain the strenuous efforts expended by groups and organizations to resolve their issues and discipline their members internally with as little publicity as possible – and sweep a great number of things under the rug.

The nature of contamination derives largely from that of shame. One might feel ashamed simply because one is exposed, symbolically or physically. Shame can also come about as the result of nonmoral failures such as poverty or even because of physical deformity.[30] The intensity of this emotion is usually multiplied to the degree that one's vulnerability is communicated to strangers. Hence, contamination does not ipso facto imply wrongdoing and can often contradict rationality. When publicized, the sins of the father will defile the son. We frequently feel embarrassed about our close associates, even when their shortcomings or indulgences cannot be reasonably extended to us. Magical thinking and cultural codes shape the dynamics of contamination.

## Audience Contamination

Certain transgressions can contaminate everyone to whom they are publicized. Take an everyday scene, a miniature scandal: a couple starts to fight at a dinner party and soon ends up divulging discreditable details of their intimate life. The most immediate effect is usually on the audience. Even before the sparring parties feel ashamed of themselves – this may well come later, especially if they are drunk – the attendees will be overcome by a contagion of embarrassment,[31] which is a situational and milder form of shame. Defacement is infectious, and one is not always immune to the polluting power of what one denounces in public, either. Consider how the Lewinsky scandal contaminated Independent Counsel Kenneth Starr, widely suspected of being a prurient zealot obsessed with sex, as much as it did President Clinton.[32]

Taboo objects are particularly contaminating. It is a striking characteristic of taboo that it can encompass the most sacred as well as the most profane. And taboo violations pollute those who are simply exposed to them. Here is an example showing how desecration contaminates. In 1941, the invading Nazis corralled a pack of stray dogs and massacred them in a yeshiva in Kovno, Lithuania.[33] Looking for something to cover the decaying canine corpses, and no doubt also to mortify the local Jews, they coerced the rabbis to tear up a Torah scroll. Jews from all over town were brought in under threat of violence to watch the desecration. The event was traumatic for the community, and a high rabbi was consulted for the procedures of penance. He proposed a schedule based on the degree of exposure to the horrible transgression even though, of course, the Jews were not in any way responsible for it. The rabbi decreed that those who saw the scroll being ripped had to rend their clothes; it was enough for those who had simply heard about the event from someone else to give alms. Albeit in varying degrees, all the Jews in the city were contaminated, so everybody was ordered to repent the following Shabbat.

Desecration, which refers to the defilement of any sacred thing properly religious or not, is polluting. But what is already profane can be equally contaminating. In many societies, things sexual, and a fortiori sexual transgressions, tend to have a polluting "viscosity,"[34] which is magnified when they are made public. This is why we find sex at the center of otherwise very different scandals – and not only because sex is intrinsically titillating for audiences.

Hence, almost all societies attempt to restrict what can appear in the public sphere through propriety norms and ascribe taboo status to certain things and words to prevent audience contamination. These social arrangements are shored up internally by shame and embarrassment.

Scandal in general, and not just sex scandals, revolves around the double meaning of transgression. Transgression is not simple wrongdoing but has the larger sense of a trespass or an intrusion – a violation of boundaries. Something that is perfectly appropriate in a private setting can be disruptive if exercised or simply placed in the public realm. Some scandalous transgressions can in effect be only committed in public; there is nothing wrong about urinating in the bathroom. A scene is often embarrassing for an audience not because what is exposed is an infraction in itself but because what is publicized is something that should have remained private. And in almost all interactional contretemps, the misbehavior or the untowardness of another has the potential to put us in shame through an affective mechanism that Adam Smith called sympathy.[35]

Transgressions (or even accidents) involving bodily things or acts are unusually salient. Creating informational overloads for audiences, they stick irrationally and sometimes interminably to their authors. People usually prefer not to know about the bodily functions of others, much less the norm violations regarding them. Such information automatically elicits a visceral reaction and upsets social interaction with no benefits. Violation of biological privacy either by the self or others is contagiously embarrassing and is potentially scandal generating. For some time, it was difficult to think of Bill Clinton independently of his sexual acts graphically itemized in the Starr Report. Civility requires a collective ignorance of our biological selves.

## Aggravating Elements

The contamination that is unleashed in a scandal can be compounded by the high status of the offender and the taboo properties of the transgression. Here are some other factors that determine its intensity. If the public experiences a steep information asymmetry with the transgressor's group, there will be a natural inclination to generalize the guilt to the collectivity to reduce risks. If outsiders lack the resources to differentiate the offender from others filling the same social role, they may well see the occurrence as typical. In the absence of evidence pointing to the contrary, a scandal about some pedophile priests can make it reasonable for us to suppose that many other Catholic priests must be sinful, too. In the Enron scandal, allegations about some employees at Arthur Andersen illegally shredding compromising documents smeared first the audit firm and then the accounting sector.

Contamination is exacerbated when the scandal gives away a deficiency of internal control within the transgressor's group. In patriarchal societies, in which female chastity is a signal asset, the publicized sexual looseness of a young girl disgraces her whole family because it bespeaks of lack of moral regulation within the household. Not only the father but also all the daughters (who will be seen as fungible and therefore equally ineligible in the eyes of the outsiders) will be contaminated by the scandal. Among some Middle Eastern groups the contamination can be so severe that the attainted family may need to slay the strayed daughter to salvage its honor.[36]

A similar mechanism, one that thankfully is not always lethal, can be observed operating among professionals. Doctors are, for instance, ambivalent with respect to misbehavior by colleagues. To outsiders, all doctors, save the ones they know personally, are largely interchangeable: a malpractice suit implicating a doctor discredits other doctors as well, albeit to a lesser extent. And as insiders, such professionals might have a more accurate – but also a more self-serving – interpretation of what happened. They might assume that anyone can make a mistake. The usual reflex is therefore to keep the matter private. But should the issue become dangerously public and if it looks like outside authorities and audiences have a robust consensus on the guilt of the accused member, then the professional group will resort to draconian measures to signal rectitude.

It matters whether the offender's group is tightly closed. Such groups enjoy freedom from constant scrutiny by outsiders[37] and retain autonomy in the way that they offer accounts. The price they pay for privacy is that they are responsible for their own monitoring, and a scandal apparently linked to a member will pollute the whole entity. Consider the rapid and comprehensive contamination of the Catholic Church by the sexual abuse scandals of the early 2000s. Its organizational closure prevented the clerical authorities from convincing outsiders that the publicized incidents were isolated events.

Background information about the denouncee will have a bearing on whether an accusation will stick on him or her. It obviously matters whether, for instance, the denouncee has been denounced or found guilty of a similar transgression before. Cultural frames about the denouncee's group or category are also important. Negative stereotypes that are held in some circles about male athletes in elite colleges – that they are pampered brutes – tragically gave some currency to the trumped-up rape accusations made by a stripper against the Duke lacrosse players in 2006. Bias, well founded or not, can also determine whether an allegation will damage not just the offender but also his or her associates. The Catholic Church again provides a good example. Philip Jenkins has controversially contended that despite the lack of evidence that Catholic clergymen abuse children more frequently than the officials of other congregations, there exists a perennial anti-Catholic slant in contemporary America, which made it easier for some opinion leaders to extend successfully the disgrace of some reprobate priests to the Church as a whole.[38]

Another case in point is the David Baltimore affair. Appointed president of Rockefeller University in 1990, the Nobel Prize–winning biologist Baltimore resigned the next year in the wake of a scientific fraud scandal, which whirled around the charges brought against a colleague for having doctored data in a paper coauthored with him.[39] Baltimore was blistered for his unconditional defense of the paper, and a congressional inquiry followed with immense media attention. A major scandal erupted, but only because the charges emerged against a backdrop of general malaise about misuse of public funds in science; the paper was a minor one, and the charges against it seemed hyperbolic to many scientists. The affair contaminated the whole scientific community, and not just those who were directly involved or implicated. Some well-known biologists turned against Baltimore as a result to prevent the reduction of federal monies to research, and Rockefeller University was impelled to ask its president to step down.[40]

Or take a historical example, again revealing the importance of cultural frames. Most of the political scandals of the French Third Republic – especially the Panama, Dreyfus, and Stavisky affairs – broke and unfolded in a deeply anti-Semitic climate.[41] In all of these scandals, the trope of the Jew as the greedy yet craven traitor working behind the scenes allowed allegations about individual Jews to contaminate all French Jewry. Anti-Semitism both enabled the scandals and was strengthened by them in a self-fulfilling fashion.

Contaminations suffuse more swiftly in puritanical societies, in which the publicity of certain (particularly sexual) transgressions is perceived as odious as the transgressions themselves. The Oscar Wilde case will bear out this proposition in the next chapter. Scandals will also have acute polluting powers in groups with strong emotional solidarity and collective liability. Military organizations have both of these characteristics, which explains why they will be so wary of scandals and why court-martials are not open to the public.

Consider the case of the French army, which was disgraced and demoralized as it came under fire in the Dreyfus affair at the end of the nineteenth century. The scandal broke with the conviction of a Jewish captain, Alfred Dreyfus, in a court-martial for espionage and grew when more and more evidence suggested that the officer had in fact been framed and that the army was willfully covering up the incident. The scandal split France into two camps. Dreyfusards denounced the miscarriage of justice and the vast conspiracy they thought had concocted it. Many of the anti-Dreyfusards were thoroughly anti-Semitic and refused to see anything other than a traitor in the figure of the Jewish captain – even in the face of mounting evidence against the army. But even those anti-Dreyfusards who thought that the captain might indeed be innocent opposed a retrial. They maintained that the Dreyfusards had hurt the army as a whole with their crusade. The issue for them was no longer a man's private plight but the reputation of the army, and they felt that a public retrial would damage the whole nation. And some French did eventually put the blame for the subpar military performance in the First World War on the scandal.[42]

Finally, the more offensive, hurtful, or salient the offense is (or successfully represented as such), the more there will be a collective appetency to generalize culpability to the higher-status associates of the offender – especially if the rank of the latter is unsatisfactorily low. Too big a disproportion between the amount of harm caused and the social status of the offender will make the event absurd and the ensuing suffering insufferable. The public or opinion leaders will try to come up with a transgressor equivalent to the transgression. This mechanism applies to devastating occurrences like catastrophes as well. Even when there is no one directly and obviously responsible in such a calamity, there will usually be a call for the officials at the top to take the blame. In the case of transgressions that are unambiguously or ostensibly of collective or institutional authorship, we observe a somewhat analogous tendency. Here, the reflex is to find scapegoats who would personify the wrongdoing. But, again, the greater the transgression, the higher the rank of the sacrificial lamb should ideally be.[43]

## Provocation

A scandal does not only or always contaminate. It can also transform a transgression, however minor, into a challenge. It can thus provoke. This other main emergent effect of scandal is engendered when the offender makes the transgression public either by defiantly communicating it or by committing it in front of others – as in public heresy, art scandals, or civil disobedience. The violator both breaks the norm and challenges the public by flaunting the transgression.[44] In all societies the public transgression of a norm is a far graver, more scandalous matter than its violation in private.[45] Tartuffe was only half-hypocritical when he said,

> And there's no evil till the act is known;
> It's scandal, Madam, which makes it an offense,
> And it's no sin to sin in confidence.[46]

This position is cherished not solely by cynical offenders but also frequently by audiences and authorities – albeit in an unacknowledged way. Strict repression of public misbehavior can go hand in hand with an extensive lenience vis-à-vis the same transgression in private; drinking during Prohibition is an example. Publicity can multiply or even create the offense. Public transgressions are potentially disruptive because the offender, by making others spectators to the act, sinuously urges imitation. At any rate, it can seem that way. If the legitimacy of the norm is shaky and if adherence to it stems at least partially from strategic misrepresentation of one's real preferences to avoid social censure, well-publicized violations can set off motivational cascades and inspirit others to breach.

Such public transgressions were central to the collapse of communism in the former Eastern bloc.[47] There is also some empirical evidence suggesting that repeated and open rule breaking might have accelerated the repeal of Prohibition, and it seems that in regions where there was no public drinking, the taboo regarding alcohol outlived the ban for a long time.[48] Similarly, the likelihood of the enforcement of a professional norm is positively correlated with the visibility of its violation.[49] Visible transgressions can publicize incongruities in private sentiments and embolden some in the audience, and even among the authorities, to flout the norm. A publicized transgression can thus deviously transmute into a litmus test of the vigor of the violated norm – a discomfiting and even dangerous ordeal for the authorities.

Social status is central to effective provocation. The degree to which a publicized transgression will provoke is largely a function of the status of the offender. Other things being equal, low-status individuals will find it arduous to provoke unless others imitate them – and they are much less likely to be imitated than high-status persons.

Elites will have an easier time: their stature will impart salience and significance to their offense. And because attention is a sign of status, authorities and audiences will be indisposed to publicly denounce, or even punish, provocateurs who are nonentities lest they be consecrated negatively as worthy of interest. Such thinking is particularly relevant when authorities are not duty bound to react and norm enforcement befalls on the public.

Unknown provocateurs will thus need to compensate for their lowliness by increasing the offensiveness of their transgression. One method, perfected by the English punks during the seventies, is to be maximally obstreperous.[50] Another way is to engage in a public act that could not fail to meet with punishment. The offender could thereby signal grit and become a martyr in the eyes of those who don't identify with the violated norm. And since honor is usually acquired through display of courage or by a willingness to discount negative consequences, such provocateurs can receive prestige even from those who are provoked.

In addition to contaminating and provoking, scandals can also exert secondary, indirect effects. They can unwittingly normalize transgressions and tempt susceptible souls by the lure of the forbidden.[51] They can, at times, even inform some members of the public of the very existence of a type of transgression. Scandals are phenomena that easily lend themselves to exploitation by all kinds of moralizers. They nevertheless also give salience to transgressors and their transgressions, which can be quite a boon to them. Thus, the notion of a succès de scandale. This contradiction lies at the heart of art scandals. There is undoubtedly such a thing as bad publicity: reputations are often irrevocably, unjustly ruined in scandals. But for those working in highly competitive sectors with low level of normative consensus, where being noticed by multitudes is both hard and essential to success, any publicity, however obtained, can be good – especially if there are no objective measures to differentiate the top runners. The supermodel Kate Moss, for example, not only survived her recent cocaine use scandal but successfully made hay of her public battle with addiction to regain her prominence in the fashion world. When she came back, she did so stronger, the dramatic story of recovery giving an edge to Moss over her listless rivals in the modeling world.

## What Follows

This book is about when and how publicity endows actual, apparent, or alleged transgressions with significant effects. Regardless of whether they are fully conscious of this fact, those who create, prevent, and react to scandals are dealing with these effects. The key to understanding scandal is thus the lived experience of its disruptions. But, in the chapters that follow, I also study the interactions that scandals generate. The effects of a scandal (and hence its meaning) are many times equivocal and open to strategic manipulation. The veracity of an allegation, the degree to which it contaminates third parties, whether it will lead to further revelations, and the way that it will be managed are all, to a certain extent, determined by a path-dependent interaction. The tragic end of Oscar Wilde will provide an illustration in the next chapter.

I began this chapter by pointing out that scandals are moral phenomena. They involve making and contesting moral claims in public, often aggressively. They are shot through with moral language, and they produce moral sentiments. Such language is used and such sentiments are generated strategically by all kinds of people, including journalists, artists, politicians, revolutionaries, celebrities, and prosecutors. As I argued, the higher the status of the denouncer or the denouncee, the more likely a public denunciation will elicit general interest and engender a scandal. This principle also applies to public provocation. Scandals are thus often created or exploited by elites to attack other elites with whom they are in conflict or competition. Lower-ranking elites often mix morality with publicity to discredit their higher-ranking brethren. Generally speaking, that one can attack collectivities with substandard evidence through scandal makes it an attractive (albeit also risky) weapon for many.

The moral and the strategic are fused in scandal. Strategic behavior can't, however, be understood independent of constraints and opportunities. A main point of this book is that structural factors affect the capability and incentives of people for creating and caring about scandals in society, politics, and art. These factors comprise both organizational and cultural characteristics, and it is by taking them into account that I will explain things such as variations in media hostility toward presidents, zeal and accommodation in law enforcement, and the logic of aesthetic transgression. The vulnerability of elites to moral attack will prove to be an important factor, which, I argue, often has a lot to do with the anticipated third-party effects of a scandal. The phenomenological, structural, and strategic perspectives in social science are often seen as incommensurable. I hope to show in this book that this need not be so. Scandals are at once cognitive, moral, and emotional phenomena. Strategy nevertheless plays an important role in their creation, development, and dénouement. Further, structural variables influence both the particular effects of a scandal and the likelihood of its happening.

Scandals may have merely short-term effects. Yet, as we will see in various contexts, scandals frequently come in waves. They can also have long-term consequences, especially when they articulate to deep structures and ongoing trends. Watergate both fed from the dormant contradictions of the modern presidency and helped deepen them. Luther's open heresy was a founding moment in the history of Protestant Reformation. It was with Le Déjeuner sur l'herbe that artistic modernism was unleashed. Combining disruptiveness with salience, scandals such as the Dreyfus affair can rouse popular passions, become central references in the collective consciousness of societies,[52] and function as "historical events" transforming social structures.[53] By provoking, normalizing, or tempting, scandals can transform norms and spawn social change. At the same time, their potentially disruptive power explains why individuals and collectivities of all kinds are constantly, if only surreptitiously, regulating themselves and each other to avert scandals.

Scandal is almost routinized in certain realms of life. Chapters 3 and 6 will illustrate how it became an integral part of political conflict in post-Watergate America and an engine of change in modern art. Competition came to be played out in these contexts more and more through this social form. But I will also show that the high incidence of scandal in politics and art correlates negatively with its disruptiveness: a decrease in the anticipated negative effects of a certain kind of scandal will make it more affordable and thus increase its frequency. In a similar fashion, a given scandal will make a subsequent one with similar content or denouncee easier to break, and a rapid succession of such events will end up making us blasé. At the same time, somewhat paradoxically, the more it is routinized, the more scandal will be revelatory of the world in which it erupts. This is why its logic is essential to understanding modern art or contemporary presidential politics. Even though they have their autonomous interactional dynamics, it is still through scandals that which is hidden, unsaid, yet crucial in a society is thrust into the open. It is thanks to what is exposed in these episodes that we can go beyond the official view of things in a given time and place.

The term "scandal" may suggest an extraordinary, even fringe, occurrence. Events with the magnitude of Watergate, Oscar Wilde's conviction, or the exhibition of Manet's *Le Déjeuner sur l'herbe* are obviously rare. But my theory of scandal can explain the making of all kinds of public happenings, big or small, provided that they revolve around a wrongdoing – real, apparent, or alleged. A large number of the episodes I analyze here are those that have been narrated and recalled as scandals. Yet there is no sharp break between scandal and other forms of moral conflict in public. Any moral attack or any moral failure in public, in front of a public liable to be interested in the event, can create a scandal. Much of social, political, and artistic conflict takes place in public and is verbalized through moral attacks; it thus feeds on scandal or takes on its overall characteristics. Any happening in public can turn into a scandal if it is not handled well. Hence, my model has wide applicability. Note, however, that not all conflict or interaction over transgression is scandal. Publicity, which transforms the meanings of transgressions, is an essential condition of scandal: there is a qualitative difference between gossip and other kinds of private moral discourse on one side and scandal on the other.

My approach to scandal should improve our understanding of all kinds of publicized transgressions and the reactions they elicit.

Take terrorism. Terrorist acts are usually not experienced as scandals. There are two reasons for this. First, terrorists are located to an extraordinary extent outside the moral universe of the audiences they target: they can't contaminate any significant entity dear to the public, unless they turn out to be high-status members of the community or connected to them. Second, terrorist acts are oriented more to scaring civilian populations than to offending them. Nevertheless, terrorism does mix publicity with transgression, and its authors do exploit the status-enhancing characteristics of public norm breaking – very much like heretics using scandal to provoke. Terrorists will, of course, find themselves condemned for treating civilians the same as soldiers, but their main constituencies may well not care much about the norm that is violated. In any case, terrorists may see the condemnation as a small price to pay for the profitable publicity they get as a result of their transgression. The attacks on the Twin Towers on September 11, 2001, for instance, instilled fear in American audiences, revealed the United States in the eyes of hostile Muslims to be a government that cannot protect its citizens, and established an equivalency between the superpower and an obscure terror organization.

I will show in this book that the logic of scandal shapes a broad range of phenomena from presidential politics to moral campaigns to the development of modern art. We will also see how and when scandals can have long-term consequences and consider their role in society, politics, and art. The cases I use vary widely in terms of content, but many of them are high-profile legal cases. The Oscar Wilde affair, one of the most spectacular trials of nineteenth-century Europe, is the object of the following chapter in which I put my theory of scandal into practice and analyze how publicity affects the legal process as well as the social attitudes toward wrongdoing.

# TWO

# The Fall of Oscar Wilde

PITILESSLY PUNISHED by the English homosexuality laws in 1895, Oscar Wilde is commonly considered to be the iconic victim of Victorian puritanism.[1] A typical evaluation is provided by one of his recent biographers: "The motive behind the 'rough justice' meted out to [Wilde] lay solely in the obsessive homophobia of the Victorian public."[2] A historian points to the "moral panic over homosexuality and decadence which developed in the last decade and a half of the nineteenth century, and whose high point was the trial and imprisonment of Oscar Wilde."[3] Victorians did, in effect, hold homosexuality in horror, and Britain stood out at the turn of the twentieth century as the only country in Western Europe that criminalized all male homosexual acts with draconian penalties. Wilde was prosecuted and condemned to the fullest extent of the law even though the evidence against him was circumstantial, uncorroborated, and tainted. Legal officials demonstrated fierce fervor in securing a conviction in a second trial, when the first one terminated with a hung jury. Oscar Wilde was vehemently vilified during his trials and was transformed into a pariah in the wake of his two-year prison-with-hard-labor sentence for gross indecency.

The wrath directed at the dramatist stands in contrast, however, with the rare and reluctant enforcement of the homosexuality laws in Victorian England.[4] During the 1840s, for instance, the annual number of sentences for sodomy ranged between twelve and eighteen, and high-status individuals rarely figured among the convicts.[5] The police looked the other way.[6] The proclivities of Wilde were, moreover, well known in London for a long time before his tribulations began. Homosexuality was implied in some of his writings and in his public persona. Yet he was the darling of London society. Even though Wilde's art was later to be branded as corrupt, his works received considerable critical acclaim and remained popular across all social classes until the day of his arrest.

Why would audiences and authorities accommodate those who are widely known to commit a transgression deemed repulsive by society and criminal by law? And why would such a transgression suddenly elicit very harsh reactions after being overlooked for a long time?

Norm underenforcement, the first part of the puzzle, obtains three, not necessarily incompatible, accounts in sociology: weakness of the norms, high status of the offender, and practical impediments to enforcement. One argument is that norms are underenforced when they are weak. Norms deteriorate either with rapid social change[7] or as a result of the breakdown of regulatory processes in society.[8] There is also some unsurprising evidence indicating that norms are underenforced when the offenders are high-status people who can get away with deviance either because they can evade monitoring or by the virtue of their clout over the enforcers.[9] Some have pointed out that insomuch as many people are dependent on elites, the latter are more apt to transgress with impunity.[10] The risk of reprisals could translate into underenforcement, too. Finally, it seems self-evident that norms would be underenforced if evidence is hard to get, and this practical problem will be aggravated if the violations are of a victimless variety.[11]

Although these accounts have surface validity, they prove unsatisfactory in elucidating the ordinary underenforcement of homosexuality norms in Victorian England, much less the ostensibly inconsistent treatment that Oscar Wilde received. There is no indication that disgust of homosexuality significantly declined during the Victorian period. A proposal to abolish the capital punishment for sodomy ran into parliamentary resistance in 1841 and was aborted, even though there were no executions after the 1830s.[12] This law was eventually abrogated in 1861, but only to be supplanted with life imprisonment. Historians have documented incidents in which those convicted of homosexuality have been prey to mob violence.[13] It is true that the law enforcers ran into snags in substantiating guilt. Prosecutors had to rely on accomplice witnesses who were either unlikely to cooperate or who were deemed noncredible according to the English law of evidence. The severity of the sentences might also have made juries loath to convict and prosecutors unenthusiastic about bringing charges. And the high status of Oscar Wilde might have enabled him to get away with his well-known deviance. But why then did the Victorian law later turn so suddenly and heavy-handedly against the dramatist despite substandard legal evidence, and why did society ostracize him so mercilessly for something that was hardly news?

The publicity of homosexuality – in particular the publicity of elite homosexuality – generated major scandals in nineteenth-century England, and my scandal theory can explain both the habitual Victorian underenforcement and Wilde's harrowing fate. We saw that a scandal does not only affect the apparent offender but that it contaminates those related to him, audiences, and at times even authorities. We can basically think of these effects as costs on the parties involved. Of course, other parties could stand to gain from inflicting such costs on the transgressors, their associates, and the things they represent. This is usually why one may strategically resort to scandal. And there are various collective benefits to enforcing norms as well as ingrained emotional impulses underpinning punitiveness. Nevertheless, these factors may well be counteracted or even offset by the anticipated costs of a potential scandal on third parties (defined in this book as those who are neither the perpetrators nor the victims of transgressions) especially when the transgression does not entail an immediate and identifiable victim. As a result, one may be discouraged from sanctioning offenders. The norm will then be underenforced as long as its transgressions are committed in, or remain, private. Indeed, homosexuality norms were underenforced by the nineteenth-century English law and society, even when transgressions were well known, to prevent scandals. Homosexuality went unsanctioned because its publicity, which would be unavoidably concomitant to the punishment process particularly in the case of elite offenders, would contaminate a wide array of third parties.

Once a scandal breaks, however, the externalities that are put in motion will prod polluted or provoked third parties into showing extraordinary zeal vis-à-vis the offender to signal rectitude or resolve. This is exactly what happened to Oscar Wilde. We will see in this chapter that many inconsistencies in norm enforcement cannot be understood unless we take into account the effects that are unleashed on third parties when transgressions are publicized – as opposed to when they are simply known – in scandals. In the first chapter, I studied the nature of these effects. Here, by focusing on a fairly complex scandal, I offer a detailed empirical analysis of how contamination and provocation bring about an episode characterized by strategic interaction.

## The Scandal of Homosexuality in Victorian England

Attitudes toward sex were fraught with a fundamental ambivalence in nineteenth-century England. Victorians did not deny or repress sexual pleasure as long as it was sought within the confines of the nuclear family.[14] They even condoned a fairly developed underground pornography for men.[15] The representation of sexuality in the public sphere, however, was altogether a different affair.

Modesty and reticence were the paramount principles of the nineteenth-century English public culture: they were, in effect, the prime requisites of respectability. The two dispositions are related but also somewhat different. Modesty refers to the negative attitude vis-à-vis the discursive or visual public representations of sexuality. The unwillingness to talk about sex in public is captured by the notion of reticence. For the Victorians, any open discussion or representation of sexuality debased the public sphere and defiled its principle participants, the members of the middle and upper classes. The nineteenth century was a time when Shakespeare, Gibbon, and the Bible alike had to be bowdlerized of their indelicacies for public consumption.[16] Hence, the arresting absence of adultery – the bread and butter of French and Russian literatures – in the Victorian novel.[17] Physical well-being of national populations became a vital issue in Europe during the nineteenth century with the ascendancy of mass circumscription and industrial capitalism; unregulated sex was thus seen as a multiple hazard. It was nevertheless mostly through sanitized technocratic language, which focused on the health effects of promiscuity among the lower classes, that sexuality could legitimately become a public matter. And even then the publicity of sexual issues remained problematic. It made little difference if the intention behind it was honorable. In 1885, many newspapers castigated William Thomas Stead's *Pall Mall Gazette* and its crusade against prostitution as shameless.[18] The publicized sexuality of specific individuals was particularly anathema. After the Divorce Act of 1857, divorce cases by upper-class couples, often involving adultery, were narrated in the pages of the *Divorce Court Reporter* and the *Illustrated Police Reporter*. Yet these newspapers targeted lower-class audiences; respectable Victorians were very uncomfortable with such accounts.[19]

Modesty was a protection against the corrupting and contaminating influences of sexuality. One way to check the evils of prostitution, pornography, and masturbation was to ensure that children and women would not hear about them. Reticence and modesty also served as diacritical markers to differentiate the elite from the far less priggish rough masses. And what mattered was not so much actual sexual righteousness as appearing proper:

> The Victorians thought it no small virtue to maintain the appearance, the manners, of good conduct even while violating some moral principle, for in their demeanor they affirmed the legitimacy of the principle itself... George Eliot, living with a man whom she could not marry because he could not legally be divorced from his wife, reproduced in their relationship all the forms of propriety... [She] assumed the forms and manners of marriage and respectability.[20]

The publicity of homosexuality, regarded as infinitely more heinous than that of most other sexual sins, was naturally very disruptive. It contaminated not only audiences but also those who named it in public even in a denunciatory mode. Michel Foucault and others deploying his constructivist perspective on sex have contended that the nineteenth century was marked not by repression but rather by a proliferation of discourses on sexuality and that homosexuality itself, at least as a category, was a Victorian creation.[21] Both claims are questionable at best – especially the second one. Pace Foucault, homosexuality was largely absent from the Victorian public moral universe – even as a foil. Neither the scientific and medical discourse on sex nor the publicized divorce cases of the nineteenth century concerned homosexuality. Havelock Ellis was prosecuted in 1898 for the first volume of his book *Studies in the Psychology of Sex*, which investigated homosexuality; the rest had to be published in the United States. The medicalization of homosexuality, which contributed much to the decontamination of its publicity, is a twentieth-century phenomenon.

Sodomy was an "unmentionable" or "nameless" crime for Victorians. Here is what Sir William Blackstone, who cast a long shadow on nineteenth-century legal thought, wrote on buggery in his *Commentaries on the Laws of England*: "I will not act so disagreeable a part, to my readers as well as to myself, as to dwell longer upon a subject the very mention of which is a disgrace to the human nature. It will be more eligible to imitate . . . the delicacy of our English law, which treats it in its very indictments as a crime not fit to be named."[22] When the home secretary recommended the closing of parks to halt their use by homosexuals in 1808, he requested that these measures be taken "without divulging to the Public the disgraceful occasion of them."[23]

The publicity of homosexuality was thought to corrupt or tempt young and female audiences, too. At a homosexuality trial in Lancaster, the judge pointed out that "the untaught and unsuspecting minds of youth should be liable to be tainted by hearing such horrid facts" and prohibited note taking as well as the presence of young people in the courtroom.[24] Lesbianism was never criminalized in England lest young females, who were perceived to be more susceptible than males, be inadvertently recruited to the sexual practice. Consider how Lord Desart successfully countered a proposed provision against female homosexuality in 1921: "You are going to tell the whole world that there is such an offence, to bring it to the notice of women who have never heard of it, never thought of it, never dreamt of it. I think this is a very great mischief."[25]

The publicity of homosexuality, and not homosexuality itself, was then the principal preoccupation of the authorities. Public homosexuality was not countenanced and often implacably punished because it challenged the audiences and authorities. In contrast, the director of public prosecutions commanded in 1889 that no "unnecessary publicity" be given to cases of gross indecency.[26] Restraint with regard to enforcing the homosexuality laws was particularly patent in the case of elite offenders. Prosecutions would make for sensational trials, endowing the transgression with inordinate salience. Trials risked traducing the good names of reputable families. They would provide for public consumption the sordid spectacle of the internecine hostilities within the English upper crust. The insularity of the upper classes closely connected by tight-knit networks would allow individual scandals to disgrace the whole elite. Hence, many instances of homosexuality within the high echelons of English society, though frequently open secrets, were hushed up. In 1889, a male brothel, the clientele of which included several aristocrats, including Lord Arthur Somerset and Prince Albert Victor, was fortuitously discovered on Cleveland Street.[27] Timorous of scandal, the lord chancellor advised inaction in a memorandum: "The social position of some of the parties will make a great sensation and this will give very wide publicity and consequently will spread very extensively written matter of the most revolting and mischievous kind, the spread of which I am satisfied will produce enormous evil."[28] Merely two minor figures were apprehended; they later got off with light sentences.

The society was disinclined to sanction homosexuals for similar reasons. Discretion was exercised above all about incidents in prestigious single-sex public schools, which mushroomed during the second half of the nineteenth century.[29] Potential scandals would not only be embarrassing for the elite of the nation; the publicized to-dos, by bestowing visibility to homosexuality, could also perversely normalize and multiply the deviance in such propitious settings. Hence, when William Johnson and Oscar Browning, both masters at Eton, were shown the door after allegations of homosexual deportment in the 1870s, the real reason for their departures was never made public.[30] Browning was actually made a Cambridge don and could carry on with his notorious debaucheries. Victorians grandees such as Edward Fitzgerald, John Addington Symonds, Cardinal Newman, Frederic Lord Leighton, and Walter Pater, who were well-known homosexuals, all evaded social scorn.[31] Take the unfettered professional ascent of a similar figure, Reverend Charles John Vaughan, who held the exalted titles of the headmaster at Harrow school, the bishop of Rochester, the vicar of Doncaster, the master of the temple, and the dean of Llandaff during the second half of the nineteenth century. Vaughan's homosexuality was well known among the Victorian elite. Even the archbishop of Canterbury and the prime minister knew about it.[32]

Reputational imperatives dissuaded parents who believed their sons to have been initiated into homosexuality by older men from taking legal action. And there were further disincentives to making charges. The English common law, the product of a society heavy with aristocratic heritage in which family name is one's most prized possession, has a stringent libel tort. Historical semantics suggests that defamation jurisprudence in England originated to forestall scandal as much as possible: in early modern English, the words "scandal" and "slander" were synonymous, referring to "malicious or defamatory gossip" or "general comment injurious to reputation."[33] According to the law, it is sufficient for the libel to be communicated in print form to the person libeled for the crime to be constituted; publication to a third person is not necessary. To be acquitted, the defendant must prove that the assertion is true and that its publication is in the public interest.[34] The *North London Press*, on November 16, 1889, named Lord Euston as a habitué of the Cleveland Street brothel. The peer sued the newspaper for libel and won, for the judge did not consider the male prostitute witnesses against Euston to be credible. The reporter who wrote the article was sentenced to 12 months' imprisonment.

There were a few high-profile homosexuality prosecutions during the late-Victorian era. Suspects in these cases were mostly, however, either those caught flagrante delicto in public places[35] or politicians who were pursued only after their professional competitors chided the government with cover-up charges. Politics, being mostly a zero-sum game, was the main arena that offered direct individual profits for accusing rivals of sexual misbehavior. Nevertheless, such incidents were rare and legal authorities reluctant to move. In the Cleveland Street scandal, the opposition, relying on leaks, accused the government of sheltering eminent names. Arthur Somerset was issued an arrest warrant – but not before the lord had been notified and given sufficient time to flee. The sole political homosexuality scandal of the period that culminated in some legal sanctions was the Dublin Castle affair of 1884, which was kicked up by the home rule supporters' attack on the British administration in Ireland. All the compromised officers were exculpated in the ensuing lawsuit, however, with the exception of the country police inspector. Prosecutions for sodomy increased slightly during the Napoleonic wars. Most of these cases, however, involved members of the military forces and served foremost to secure naval discipline.[36] At any rate, nonmilitary suspects were allowed to leave the country.[37] And even when cases went to trial, convictions were often undesirable on the score of their disruptive effects. Criminal statistics of 1856 show that only 28 percent of those tried for sodomy were convicted as opposed to 77 percent for all offenses.[38]

A good example of the Victorian disinclination is the Boulton and Park trial of 1871.[39] Two transvestite homosexuals were detained when they were spotted in feminine outfit in front of the Strand Theater. These two were the sons of prominent Londoners. Love letters turned up in their lodgings pointing to carnal relations with the MP Lord Arthur Clinton, the son of the duke of Newcastle. The defense averred meagerly that Boulton and Park, who occasionally took female parts in amateur theatricals, were given to playacting in public. Few entertained doubts about the sexuality of those embroiled in the scandal. The general opinion was bluntly articulated in this lewd limerick that circulated among the London lower classes, who were decidedly less genteel than their social superiors:

> There was an old person of Sark
> Who buggered a pig in the dark;
> The swine, in surprise,
> Murmured, "God blast your eyes,"
> Do you take me for Boulton or Park?[40]

The two were absolved. Both the authorities and the opinion leaders thought it better not to convict. The *Times* of May 16, 1871, wrote approvingly of the acquittal and adduced that a guilty verdict "would have been felt at home, and received abroad, as a reflection of our national morals."

## Victorians and Oscar Wilde before His Trials

Victorians were thus reluctant to sanction homosexuals, especially when the latter had high status. The case of Oscar Wilde, whose homosexuality was well known long before his trials, is no exception. His effeminate public persona fit fully the Victorian stereotype of the homosexual. From the late 1870s to the mid-1880s, a central figure of London society cutting a wide swath with his sharp wit and extravagancies, Wilde sported a flamboyant look with flowing locks, colossal flopping collars, colorful scarves, velvet frock coats, and knee-length stockings. The editorialists of *Punch*, the bastion of middle-class morality, called him a "Mary-Ann." He was regularly caricatured by George du Maurier, who mocked his epicene preciosity, in the satirical magazine.[41] Gilbert and Sullivan's comic opera *Patience* (1881), a pungent portrait of Wilde as a sham aesthete, ventured vague sexual suggestions:

> Then a sentimental passion of a vegetable fashion must excite your
>     languid spleen,
> An attachment à la Plato for a bashful young potato or a not-too-
>     French French bean.[42]

In the early 1880s, Wilde, the quintessential poseur, put his audiences in a state of uncertainty. His homosexuality was mostly a matter of conjecture in London except in circles proximate to the author. He married in 1884 and took up the traditional dandy garb. He got a haircut. The widespread scuttlebutt about his sexuality subsided for a while after the birth of his two children. Some thought that his effete ways were merely part of his ostentatious aestheticism. Their sexual allusions notwithstanding, the public satires of Wilde, including those in *Punch*, were equivocal. One could always pretend that they merely spoofed his effeminacy.

Although these parodies hatched suspicions, they turned him into a curiosity, too. Wilde astutely exploited the liminal public image fashioned, as though in a collusion, by the press and himself to the point of peeving James Whistler, his rival for the position of the chief Victorian aesthete: "[Wilde] made a point of greeting du Maurier graciously. Whistler was jealous and, at a showing of his work, walked up to du Maurier and Wilde talking together and asked, 'Which of you discovered the other?'"[43] The success of *Patience* prompted a publicist to hire Wilde to travel across the United States to lecture on art. But Wilde could afford to shock only so much. Hence, he staved off the talk about his homosexuality with his marriage. Mixing respectability and eccentricity, he kept his audiences guessing. The name recognition that he acquired this way served him well in the 1890s when he produced his literary works. Wilde's art, and especially his plays, reproduced his public persona. Many deemed his dandy dramatis personae with dubious desires indistinguishable from the dramatist himself.

The uncertainty about the sexuality of Oscar Wilde gradually waned. By the end of the 1880s, he was already going around in public with a green carnation boutonnière – the badge of French homosexuals. His short story "The Portrait of Mr. W. H." (1889) queried the sex of the addressee of Shakespeare's sonnets. Homoerotic tension was palpable in *The Picture of Dorian Gray* (1890), a novel that flirted with decadent themes imported from France. Although Wilde never unambiguously paraded his homosexuality, he was becoming indiscrete about his goings-on. He prated imprudently in London society on the delights of male beauty. He surrounded himself with fetching young men in fashionable restaurants and lectured them about Socratic love. He partied with prostitutes in posh hotels and rented houses with upper-class paramours.

Consequently, Wilde's homosexuality became well known in various quarters. The press reported his vacations with male companions. Among these, Lord Douglas, a student at Oxford and the third son of the marquess of Queensberry, was the most prominent. Wilde was riding high when he met Lord Douglas in 1891. He had already become a major writer and dramatist with the publication of *The Picture of Dorian Gray* the year before and the recent opening of the huge hit *Lady Windermere's Fan*. Although the relationship between the two men was sexual in the beginning, it seems that it soon assumed a predominantly romantic nature. This did not, however, stop the two from cruising the London netherworld swarming with working-class male prostitutes.

Wilde's relationship with Lord Alfred Douglas was a society item even though its veritable nature was, of course, never named. The *Pall Mall Gazette* reported that the lord followed the famous dramatist like his shadow.[44] People in cultural, aristocratic, political, and intellectual milieus talked.[45] As early as 1891, the marquess of Queensberry was derided behind his back within his own circles for letting his son "go about with a bugger."[46] Some gossip was apocryphal. Queensberry had, for instance, heard that Wilde's wife was asking him for a divorce on the grounds of sodomy. A pornographic novel was also erroneously credited to him. But a good deal of the backbiting was accurate. It seems that law enforcement was in the swim, too. Sir Edward Hamilton, the confidant of the prime minister, noted in his diary during the trials that the word in London was that the police were long cognizant of the dramatist's dalliances.[47] "The wonder is not that the gossip should have reached Lord Queensberry's ears, but that, after it was known, this man Wilde should have been tolerated in society in London for the length of time he has," the peer's lawyer would later cry out during the libel trial, as much as in incredulity as in indignation.[48]

Oscar Wilde's wife worried about their reputation after the publication of *Dorian Gray*. She remained, however, a high-flying socialite active in the Women's Liberal Foundation. The *Pall Mall Gazette* wrote that Constance Wilde was on her way to becoming "one of the most popular among 'platform ladies.'"[49] The Prince of Wales commended Wilde lavishly and publicly in the première of *Lady Windermere's Fan* in 1891. Prior to his legal travails, the dramatist was an indispensable fixture in the country abodes of the Victorian beau monde and hobnobbed with political nabobs such as William Gladstone, Herbert Henry Asquith, and Charles Parnell.

Wilde's well-known homosexuality did not instigate a scandal until his trials simply because it was not publicly denounced. People prattled – much and maliciously – but always in private. The polluting publicity of the transgression, strict libel laws, and the high status of Wilde all led to reticence from the Victorians. Those who perceived themselves to be victims and would have legally superior evidence about his homosexuality (for instance, the families of his lovers) had reputational disincentives to take on the dramatist. They would themselves be contaminated by the resultant scandal. Private shunning of Wilde was costly as well. One would be deprived of the company of a beguiling, witty, and very famous man connected to everybody who mattered in London. Furthermore, a private crusade against him could eventuate in a public contestation – a chancy proposition in the light of the tough libel laws. Finally, even though Wilde was the subject of gossip within various milieus, without a public denunciation, it would be difficult to coordinate attitudes vis-à-vis the deviant dramatist within the larger society. Those with low tolerence of homosexuality would find it costly to sanction him; those with higher tolerance (like many in the cultured elite) would not have to at all.

The middle classes also partook in this virtual conspiracy of tolerance. Even though he would posthumously be hailed as the hapless victim of hidebound Victorian morality, Wilde actually weathered ethical onslaughts, after his homosexuality became an open secret in London, not from straitlaced pundits but from artistic competitors with unconventional lifestyles akin to his own. André Raffalovich's *A Willing Exile* (1890) and Henry James's *Tragic Muse* (1890) lampooned him and his coterie with thinly disguised innuendos, even though they did not name names. A mordant roman à clef titled

*The Green Carnation* (1894), written by Robert Hichens, a former member of Wilde's clique, was based recognizably on the dramatist's affair with Lord Douglas. The anonymously published book was attributed to Wilde before he denied the allegation in a letter to the *Pall Mall Gazette*.

Such sniping parodies were in fact relatively less covert than *Punch*'s allusions of the former decade. Ironically, it was thanks to their outsider status that these authors could afford to be less mindful of the Victorian reticence norms and publicly insinuate Wilde's homosexuality during the first half of the 1890s. On the one hand, the literary representations furnished fodder for gossip. Their deliberate obliqueness, on the other hand, provided everybody the possibility to pretend in public as if they did not mean what they meant. As long as Wilde did not respond – and the studied equivocalness of the insinuations permitted him this option – his well-known homosexuality would not become an unavoidably public matter. What is more, the intimations were not picked up by the mainstream press for the already cited reasons.

*Punch*'s position toward Wilde in the 1890s until his trials was indeed complimentary, in part because his plays were then all the rage across the board in Victorian society.[50] The higher classes delighted in his playful fetishization of the aristocratic habitus, and the biting undertones of his work were often relished by the middle-class audiences. The melodramatic strains in plays such as *A Woman of No Importance* resonated with the lower social groups. Even though the premières of Wilde's plays were major events for the Victorian upper crust, the middle and lower-middle classes packed the pit and the gallery of the theaters. A critic called Wilde, "perhaps the most popular middle-class wit at present before the public."[51] A few reviewers did pan *Dorian Gray*, the sole work of his ever to be impugned for immorality; but they did so not because of its decadent themes, for several of his other writings were shot through with similar motifs as well, but rather because of its aristocratic settings.[52] In effect, Wilde paid much heed to the expectations of his middle-class reviewers.[53] On the whole, he was assailed much more for self-advertisement and superficiality than for turpitude.

## The Impending Scandal

Given the individual and collective costs that well-mannered Victorians faced in denouncing homosexuality, it was ineluctable that the nemesis of the eccentric dramatist could only be another eccentric, the marquess of Queensberry. Refusing to take the religious oath of allegiance to the queen, which he dubbed as "Christian tomfoolery," the marquess had forfeited his seat in the House of Lords for his ardent atheism. A former prizefighter and the formulator of the eponymous boxing rules, Queensberry was a pugnacious spirit with a penchant for attacking prominent people in public, often through litigation. As a provocateur, he liked to stand up for unpopular causes.[54] For instance, he championed Charles Bradlaugh, a fellow atheist – though one with a working-class origin – who published in 1876 a pamphlet advocating birth control, for which he was prosecuted and found guilty in a tumultuous trial. Universally disliked, the marquess had no reputation to lose. Being a divorcé on very bad terms with his children, he cared even less for his family name.

Sometime after he heard about Lord Douglas's affair with Wilde, Queensberry ordered his son to cease all contact with the dramatist. Lord Douglas was contemptuous of such meddling in his life; he continued his relationship with redoubled recklessness. The marquess menaced his son in a missive in 1894: "If I catch you again with that man, I will make a public scandal in a way you little dream of."[55] Assisted by his band of bruisers, the peer was soon hounding Wilde in fancy restaurants. He arrived at the opening of *The Importance of Being Earnest* on February 14, 1895, with the purpose of perturbing the performance. The police, instructed by Wilde to guard the theater, did not let him on the premises. Queensberry nevertheless deposited a bouquet of vegetables at the entrance of the theater to declare his disdain for the dramatist.

On February 18, 1895, Queensberry showed up at the Albermarle Club to which Wilde belonged. Not finding him, he left a calling card with an insulting, in part illegible, and misspelled message. When Wilde picked it up ten days later, he read the note as, "To Oscar Wilde, ponce and sondomite." The marquess would later maintain that he had scribbled, "To Oscar Wilde posing as a Somdomite," a phrase easier to justify in a libel case. Surmising that there was nothing that he could do to eschew the looming scandal, Wilde set out to preempt Queensberry by suing him. This is how the dramatist described his dilemma in *De Profundis*, the doleful diatribe against Lord Douglas that he would later pen in prison:

> So the next time [Queensberry] attacks me, no longer in a private letter and as your private friend, but in public as a public man. I have to expel him from my house. He goes from restaurant to restaurant looking for me, in order to insult me before the whole world, and in such a manner that if I retaliated I would be ruined, and if I did not retaliate I would be ruined also.[56]

Wilde seems to have reckoned that he would fare better in court than in a public fracas, given the high standard of evidence required in libel cases. He understandably did not foresee that Queensberry could deliver any witnesses; they were all partners in crime. In any case, the judge would not consider their testimony reliable; most of them were prostitutes. Under these circumstances, the trial would surely devolve into a popularity contest between the beloved of London society and the black sheep of the English peerage, abhorred even by his own family. And the critical acclaim and commercial success of *The Importance of Being Earnest*, which had just opened, only boosted Oscar Wilde's self-confidence.

## The Dynamics of the Oscar Wilde Affair

We saw in the first chapter that a transgression usually generates a scandal by contaminating and provoking various parties with its publicity. A scandal will usually not simply elicit attention but also pique reactions from parties who are directly affected by it and from authorities who are institutionally expected to sanction offenders. Those who are implicated by and exposed to scandals don't simply suffer them but often strategically manipulate and manage them. But response to a scandal may be risky. It may only prolong the episode by furthering public interest so that, as a result, the transgression may be dignified with consequentiality and the transgressor be granted with gratis publicity. One may thus calculatingly refrain from reacting. At the same time, once it breaks, a scandal can furnish fillips for the foes of the offenders or of their associates to intervene for exploitative purposes.

A scandal tends to take the form of an episode. An existing institutionalized means to deal with transgressions – for instance, a legal investigation or a trial – can shape its trajectory. When the offense is perpetrated by a group, the morphology of the conspiracy can overdetermine the sequencing of the exposures.[57] Yet more than anything else, the development of a scandal has to do with how parties react to its contamination or challenge in an episode marked by strategic interaction. This process will generally comprise struggles around the veracity of the transgression in cases in which this is in doubt. Here, the apparent offender can deny the transgression, minimize its importance, offer a convenient account to the public, render an apology, or accuse the accuser. Denouncers and their allies could attempt to establish the transgression in the eyes of the public. There might be all kinds of further denunciations about the offender, his associates, or his opponents strategically undertaken to shift or localize blame. The dialectics of cover-up and exposure greatly structure the scandal process. But even if there is little question about the veracity of the allegations, or after the veracity is established at some point, we may find another, and at times more vicious, discursive battle around the significance, real authorship, and implications of the transgression.

Scandals are emotional episodes. We already saw that the logic of contamination transcends rationality. Anger does not always make sense post facto, either: even when it is feigned (for example, to prop up a denunciation), it can soon become only too real and overwhelm the denouncer. Public fury is worse, for it can self-feed through collective effervescence. There is nevertheless a strong cognitive aspect to emotions – they involve certain understandings of the world.[58] Nor are the emotional and the strategic opposed. As a rule, one denounces or provokes to elicit certain emotional states in others. In turn, emotional states themselves instigate strategic responses. Those

54

who are contaminated in a scandal will often have to do things that would signal rectitude to others. Similarly, those who are challenged by public transgressions may have to signal resolve. At the same time, audiences and authorities can be tolerant of or even indifferent to allegations about transgressors if they are highly dependent on them – in other words, if the transgressors' fall would be costly for them. But the wider the publicity, the harder the indifference.

Scandals are fast-paced episodes with difficult-to-predict outcomes. It is hard to foresee what will be revealed, which parties those revelations will affect, and what those parties will do in responding to or anticipating them. In their temporal course, scandals frequently implicate more and more people and obtain increasingly larger publics. This is why, as we'll see shortly, they can easily get out of hand. Their effects can be hard to foresee or contain. Scandals tend to turn into dramas of disclosure with no natural limits to what can be divulged or alleged about the associates of those snarled in them. Charges about associates often follow each other seriatim.

All this goes to show that scandals are not rituals of cohesion but moral disturbances. They entail strategic and emotional entanglements with public pollutions and challenges rather than the affirmation of core values.[59] But scandal also shares some characteristics with "interaction ritual,"[60] because it is an episode involving collective emotional entrainment on a common focus of attention. Just like such events, a scandal is not meant to last forever; however uproarious, its emotional intensity will eventually flag, and amnesia will hollow out its content. All scandals die off with or without a resolution regarding the veracity of the offense, the culpability of the transgressor, or the accountability of the latter's associates. The dynamics of scandal are dependent on spectatorship, and public interest will not fail to fade eventually. Fatigue will take its toll, something new will capture our attention, or the matter will satisfactorily come to a close with appropriate sanctions.

The theory of scandal proposed in this book has implications on how we should think about the public sphere. Following the German philosopher Jürgen Habermas, the recent literature tends to see this domain, through normative and rosy lenses, as a deliberative order in which citizenship is exercised.[61] Yet few phenomena engage the public as much as scandal, the nature of which blatantly contradicts this paradigm. In fact, the dynamics of scandal reveal that the public sphere is the domain not only of collective communication and action but also, and more importantly, of appearances. It is the way that apparent transgressions appear in public that endow them with disruptive effects, and it is the impressions that offenders, denouncers, authorities, and even audience members foster to each other in public that govern their interaction in the scandal process. The implicit logic of the public sphere, which equates being with appearance,[62] is fully actualized in scandals.

This is why high-status individuals, and especially elite public officials, should avoid the appearance of impropriety.[63] The publicity of their apparent offenses will make it arduous for them to stabilize the signification of their act to others, especially when the act gives rise to uncontrollable externalities for which they will be held liable because of their indiscretion or recklessness. Such a rebuke was recurrently leveled at Clinton during and after the Lewinsky crisis by those who otherwise did not mind his sexual escapades and related evasions. Surely it matters whether the transgression was willfully made public by the offender. But one is also expected to ensure that one's transgressions, in the case of norms that can be tolerably violated in private, would not become public through carelessness.

The public sphere is therefore primarily a dramaturgical order, and scandals are an extreme illustration of this principle. Reactions to them are conditioned by the fact (or to the extent) that they are reactions undertaken in public, in front of others. Authorities or associates of offenders often sanction transgressions that they would otherwise accommodate only because the publicity of the transgression challenges or contaminates them in the eyes of the public. Sanctions function more as signals of resolve or rectitude to the audience than as direct reactions to the offender. The censorious Republican reactions toward Trent Lott in December 2002 were, for instance, conditioned by the general obloquy heaped on the senator in the wake of his public panegyric of the politics of the young late

Strom Thurmond, who had run on a pro-segregation presidential campaign in 1952. Audiences by and large remain bystanders in scandals. Yet this does not mean they don't matter. They shape the course of scandals and the behaviors of their participants significantly by the reality or assumption of their spectatorship.

Members of a public can find themselves in an analogous predicament vis-à-vis each other when not shunning an offender can be interpreted as a sign of moral shortcoming. Reactions in scandals are then governed by the way that publicity transforms the meaning and import of apparent transgressions. An implication of this principle is that an individual reaction to a scandalous transgression is largely conditioned by anticipations about how the others will react, especially when such reactions have immediate repercussions on one's life chances. In the Enron scandal, for instance, the allegations of misconduct by the company executives contaminated all other similar firms in the eyes of the public, which faced steep information costs in gauging whether the publicized transgressions were isolated incidents. The general pollution influenced even the actions of buyers who could distinguish fraudulent firms from upright ones and who distrusted the stock market only because one could not trust that others would trust it. Hence, discredit was generalized through a self-fulfilling prophecy.

All of these dynamics are readily discernable in the unfolding and dénouement of the Wilde affair.

### The Libel Trial

The Wilde affair took off with the libel trial that opened with immense publicity in the Old Bailey on April 3, 1895, and during which the dramatist's homosexuality was finally openly denounced by Queensberry's lawyer, Edward Carson. In the course of the proceedings, Wilde's chief lawyer, Sir Edward Clarke, withdrew the charges against Queensberry even before testimony could be heard against his client. This act was not, as it might seem, primarily motivated by Clarke's fear of the marquess' witnesses – youthful hustlers who were cowed and compensated to give evidence.[64] Before the trial Clarke had already perused Queensberry's plea of justification itemizing the occasions on which Wilde had allegedly solicited the prostitutes to commit sodomy. This evidence struck some of the dramatist's less sanguine friends, who pleaded with him to drop the case, as substantial, but he settled on proceeding. His lawyers, including the veteran Clarke, the former solicitor-general who was at the time the president of the English Bar, did not demur. Queensberry's lawyer Carson faced strict evidence standards. The male prostitutes who were to testify against Wilde were all self-confessed accomplices with records of blackmailing. Their testimony would be considered tainted. In effect, the marquess himself had briefly toyed with the idea of initiating legal proceedings against the dramatist but had decided not to go ahead for this very reason. Even though in retrospect it turned out to have been a misstep, Wilde and his lawyers' gambit was a calculated one.

Oscar Wilde lost his libel trial because of the way his publicly alleged homosexuality provoked and contaminated. Queensberry's lawyer highlighted his homosexual writings as well as those of young men held to be within his orbit in *Chameleon*, an undergraduate magazine published at Oxford. Carson pressured the dramatist to abjure these works and acknowledge his depraved influence over their authors. Refusing to judge his own or his acolytes' writings by moral standards, Wilde said, "I do not believe that any book or work of art ever had any effect whatever on morality."[65] When Carson presented *Dorian Gray* as perverted, he said, "it could only be so to brutes and illiterates."[66] Carson then read the following epigram taken from a piece titled "Phrases and Philosophies for the Use of the Young" that Wilde had published in *Chameleon*: "There is something tragic about the enormous number of young men there are in England at the present moment who start life with perfect profiles, and end by adopting some useful profession."

The wisecrack was in fact not all that different from the *Punch* send-ups of the 1880s. Take the following dialogue from a cartoon by de Maurier published on February 12, 1881. In it we find the aesthete Maudle, the obvious stand-in for Wilde, chattering with a provincial woman about her son's prospects:

*MAUDLE:* How consummately lovely your son is Mrs. Brown?

*Mrs. BROWN (a philistine from the country):* What? He is a nice, manly boy, if you mean that Mr. Maudle. He has just left school, you know, and he wishes to be an artist.

*MAUDLE:* Why should he be an artist?

*Mrs. BROWN:* Well, he must be something.

*MAUDLE:* Why should he be anything? Why not let him remain for ever content to exist beautifully?

The caption under the caricature reads: "Mrs. Brown determines that at all events her son shall not study art under Maudle."

The *Punch* cartoon is typical of the many others that had turned Wilde into a celebrity a decade earlier. Yet, in the context of open, frontal, and ineludible allegations about his homosexuality, this kind of witticism now could not but sound outrageous. Thus, Wilde appeared during his cross-examination not as someone privately indulging in his unnatural tastes but as an elite who was abusing his high status (and the artistic license that such status conferred on him) by impudently, bare facedly debauching the youth. Even though all the men suspected of improprieties with the dramatist were over the statutory age of consent, Carson underscored throughout the trial the class disparity between Wilde and the male prostitutes and the age difference between him and Lord Douglas. In his opening speech for the defense, Carson recited a homosexual poem written by the lord as probative of his moral corruption and asked rhetorically:

Is it not a terrible thing that a young man on the threshold of life, who has for several years been dominated by Oscar Wilde and has been "adored and loved" by Oscar Wilde, as the two letters prove, should thus show the tendency of his mind upon this frightful subject? What would be the horror of any man whose son wrote such a poem?[67]

But more important, Wilde came across as a provocateur defying society through his words and persona even as he denied his transgression. To Carson's question, "The majority of persons would come under your definition of Philistines and illiterates?" the illustrious homme d'esprit rejoined, "I have found wonderful exceptions."[68]

When Carson asked him to comment on whether his aphorism, "Wickedness is a myth invented by good people to account for the curious attractiveness of others," was true, he dismissively retorted, "I rarely think that anything I say is true."[69] Flippant quips did not help his case, either. Upon being interrogated about whether he kissed a servant boy, the dramatist snapped back, "Oh dear no. He was a peculiarly plain boy. He was unfortunately extremely ugly. I pitied him for it."[70] The *Star* accused "the aesthete" on April 3, 1895, of giving "characteristically cynical evidence." It was when juxtaposed with such an impervious performance that the witnesses against Wilde became perilous. His lawyers, facing a hostile public opinion, dropped the charges against the marquess.

## The Prosecution and Conviction of Wilde

The outcome of the libel trial posed a challenge to the authorities. Prosecutorial apathy at this point could be read as a want of steadfastness in upholding the homosexuality laws. Yet, the legal case against Wilde was far from adequate. Losing a libel trial involving homosexuality did not inevitably lead to criminal action in Victorian England, either. The trials imposed high costs on third parties; the authorities were averse to act.

The libel case of Robert Ross, one of Wilde's former lovers, is a case in point. From 1911 to 1914, after he renounced homosexuality, Lord Douglas composed epistles to the prime minister, several judges, and the public prosecutor accusing Robert Ross of being a sodomite, blackmailer, and pedophile. He even betook himself in person to Scotland Yard with a man who signed a statement confessing to physical relations with Ross. The private crusade was futile; the authorities were immovable. But Douglas's harassment would not cease, so Ross finally sued him for libel in 1914. Douglas produced a string of witnesses in court. Like Wilde, Ross entered a plea of nolle prosequi, which meant that he admitted to the charge made in the libel. The authorities, however, disregarded Douglas's plea of justification; Ross was thus not prosecuted. The contrast between Ross and Wilde is all the more glaring because the evidence against the former was much more devastating than that against the latter. It came from nonprostitutes, and, unlike in the Wilde case, the witnesses testified in court.[71]

It is the different third-party effects of their scandals that account for the divergent destinies of Ross and Wilde. Ross, unlike Wilde, was nonconfrontational in court and hence did not come across as a provocateur. He was much less famous, so his case got much less publicity. His lower status also rendered the outcome of the libel trial less disruptive. More important, the pollution produced by the publicity of Ross's homosexuality was relatively contained. The ill-starred Wilde, in contrast, was tried, and truculently so, because the libel trial exposed the dirty linen of the Victorian elite, contaminated the authorities, and thereby drastically increased the costs of not punishing Wilde.

Queensberry cultivated a long-lasting rancor for the current prime minister, Lord Rosebery. The marquess' oldest son, Viscount Drumlanrig, had worked as the private secretary of the lord when he was the foreign minister. Queensberry, persuaded that Rosebery had a homosexual entanglement with his son, chased the former with a dog whip in August 1893 at Homburg. The incensed peer could be ejected from the scene and the pandemonium prevented only thanks to the intervention of Prince of Wales.[72] Drumlanrig died shortly after – apparently, in a shooting accident. The marquess believed, along with some others, however, that his son was threatened with exposure over his affair with Lord Rosebery and had killed himself to protect the latter.[73]

Queensberry had stated his detestation of Rosebery in numerous letters that were now in the possession of Wilde's counsel. Clarke had already referred to, but not read, these letters in the police court proceedings. The grand jury deliberations were, nonetheless, leaked to the continental press. The English press did not print the prime minister's name, but the news traveled around the country.[74] In the libel trial, after Wilde's provocative, self-destructive performance, Clarke read the marquess' letters to show that Queensberry was an unhinged man whose accusations could not be taken seriously. In one of his letters to his former father-in-law in which he grumbled about his ex-wife, the marquess called Wilde "damned cur and coward of the Rosebery type" and blamed the prime minister for the bad blood between him and his son.

> I don't believe that Wilde will now dare defy me. He plainly showed the white feather the other day when I tackled him – damned cur and coward of the Rosebery type. Your daughter must be mad by the way she is behaving.... I am now fully convinced that the Rosebery-Gladstone-Royal insult that came through me from my other son, that she worked that. It shall be known some day by all that Rosebery not only insulted me by lying to the Queen, which makes her as bad as him and Gladstone, but also has made a lifelong quarrel between my son and I.[75]

The name of the prime minister, once enunciated in court, spawned insidious suspicions – some of which were pronounced obliquely in public. Wild rumors, some founded in truth others not, sprouted apace during the trials in London about the Queensberry-Rosebery-Wilde link. Many were whispering, correctly, that Rosebery was a homosexual. There had already been some bad-mouthing of the prime minister in some circles; the scandal now refueled the ignominious bruits and disseminated them to larger publics. It was said that Rosebery was pressuring the prosecution to drop charges against Wilde, who was his friend. Some falsely suggested that the dramatist was blackmailing the government.[76]

As we saw, the Victorian authorities balked at trying homosexuality cases involving elites in part because London society was a very small world connecting anybody with everybody: scandals could stain entire elite networks and reveal all kinds of skeletons in their closets. This is, of course, precisely what transpired during the Wilde affair. Thoroughly contaminated, the authorities were thereby compelled to pursue the dramatist relentlessly, so as to dampen the talk about Rosebery and the prosecution and prevent the scandal from possibly growing bigger. Sir Edward Hamilton, the assistant financial secretary, noted in his diary, "A verdict of guilty would remove what appears to be a wide-felt impression that the Judge & Jury were on the last occasion got at, in order to shield others of a higher status in life."[77] After the first criminal trial, Carson asked Solicitor-General Frank Lockwood if the crown could not cut Wilde loose given that he had already gone through so much. Lockwood replied ruefully, "I would, but we cannot; we dare not; it would at once be said, both in England and abroad, that owing to the names mentioned in Queensberry's letters we were forced to abandon it."[78] When T. M. Healy, the Irish Home Rule MP, beseeched him not to pursue his compatriot, Lockwood put forth the identical rationale for the prosecutorial intransigence: "I would not but for the abominable rumors against [Rosebery]."[79] The Liberals lacked a majority in Parliament, and Chief Secretary Arthur Balfour cautioned Lord Rosebery that succoring Wilde would cost them the upcoming elections.

The strategic interaction in a scandal is conducted through signaling, and it is usually this interaction, not the consensus in a society regarding the offensiveness of a transgression, that determines the unfolding of the episode. The Wilde affair generated such a process that aggravated the antagonism toward the dramatist. As Wilde appeared as a public provocateur, the courtroom audience turned against him. The public gallery cheered when Queensberry was acquitted, and the popular reaction was officially endorsed when the judge refrained from silencing the crowd.[80] The press was, in turn, encouraged by this uncustomary forbearance and cudgeled Wilde without clemency. The *National Observer* expressed gratitude to the marquess in the name of those with "wholesome minds" "for destroying the High Priest of the Decadents," "an obscene impostor whose prominence has been a social outrage ever since he transferred from Trinity Dublin to Oxford his vices, his follies and his vanities." The *Daily Telegraph* berated Wilde for "shameless disavowal of all morality" and for having established "a cult of degeneracy." He was also held accountable for having contaminated the English public by bringing the libel case. "We have had enough of Oscar Wilde, who has been the means of inflicting on the public during this recent episode as much moral damage of the most hideous and repulsive kind as no single individual could well cause," declared the same newspaper. Some exhorted legal action against Wilde. "[Wilde] may now change places with Lord Queensberry and go into the dock himself," wrote *The Echo*.[81] *The Importance of Being Earnest* and *An Ideal Husband* were shortly after cancelled at St. James Theatre and the Haymarket.

The growing public opinion against Wilde made inaction by the authorities seem like lack of resolve. More damningly, however, the press smelled a cover-up. In its coverage of the police court hearings, the *Evening News* questioned on March 9 the probity of the legal officials. Reporting the private interview that the judge had with the counsels of the defendant and the plaintiff after the mentioning of the Queensberry letters, a journalist voiced the doubts of many: "What was the reason for the retirement, was the case to be nipped in the bud in the interest of 'exalted personages'?"

Risking discredit, the authorities resorted to zealous prosecution and adjudication. Sir Justice John Bridge declaimed after the libel trial, "I think there is no worse crime than that which the prisoners are charged." Wilde was thus refused bail. This gratuitous denunciation was legally tenuous and the incarceration irregular: Wilde was arraigned not with a felony (sodomy) but only with a misdemeanor (gross indecency), the maximum sentence for which was just two years. In the first criminal trial, the male prostitutes were promised immunity for their word against Wilde. In addition to being uncorroborated accomplices, however, several of these eyewitnesses were self-avowed blackmailers, and one of them perjured himself on the stand. One of the two nonprostitute eyewitnesses gainsaid indecencies between him and the dramatist. The other one's testimony was muddled. The eyewitnesses from the hotels were contradictory and unreliable. The trial terminated with a deadlocked jury.

London was now aflutter with rumors regarding Rosebery's homosexuality[82] and his putative efforts to save Wilde. Some testimony in the trials hinted, furthermore, that some of the young men Oscar Wilde had slept with were the relatives of Victorian dignitaries. The *Morning* suspected illegitimate interference with justice on May 2, 1895:

> Society feels that a gross public scandal has not yet been probed to its depths; and that a great mass of loathsome evidence must once more be heard in open court. . . . Ought the prosecution stop

there? That is a very grave question. Whatever may be truth as regards Wilde and Taylor, the evidence given at the Old Bailey seems to affect more reputations than those that have been openly impugned.... What are these mysterious names written on slips of paper and passed between counsels' table, the witness-box and the Bench? If there is a widespread canker in our midst, as the authorities seem to believe, it cannot too soon be thoroughly cauterized.[83]

The vortex of the scandal, threatening to tarnish more and more prominent names,[84] forced the hands of the authorities to convict the dramatist. Nevertheless, the authorities wanted to forefend the publicity of his sin as much as possible. When the judge of the libel trial congratulated Carson for his impeccable cross-examination, he also thanked him for sparing the court of "the filth" of Wilde's deeds. The press was urged to censor its coverage: the *Evening Standard* edited Queensberry's note as "Oscar Wilde posing as —."[85] Other papers simply referred to it as "words unfit for publication." Some in the press debated the pros and cons of prosecuting with such publicity. The editors of the *Pall Mall Gazette* wrote on April 6: "It is a difficult question to decide whether in such cases absolute reticence or modified publicity is the better in the interests of public morality." After the jury disagreed in Wilde's first trial, some worried that more harm "would be done to the public morals" if the case were renewed.[86] The press almost unanimously supported the prosecution of Wilde, but not without acknowledging its cost. "It is at a terrible cost that society has purged itself of these loathsome importers of exotic vice, but the gain is worth the price," wrote the *News of the World* on May 26, 1895, after Wilde was sentenced.[87]

And as they would rather not try Wilde, the powers that be implicitly extended him several opportunities to flee the country. He was notified forthwith after the libel trial through informal channels of his imminent arrest. The magistrate who had denied Wilde bail and repudiated him in the most impassioned terms issued his warrant with sufficient delay for him to catch the last train for Dover. His friends implored him to leave. Even Queensberry thought it would be better for him to go abroad. "If the country allows you to leave, all the better for the country," wrote the jubilant peer in a message dispatched to him.[88] But he stayed – or rather shilly-shallied. After the first criminal trial, Wilde was accorded another chance to abscond. He spurned this opportunity as well and had to be prosecuted with a vengeance.

The prosecution proffered, albeit without success, to withdraw charges against Wilde's procurer on the condition that he turn state's evidence. In a decision that was particularly detrimental to the dramatist, the director of public prosecutions instructed Solicitor-General Lockwood to take the helm at the second criminal trial. Lockwood was famous for his ferocity and retained, thanks to his rank, the customary right to make the final address to the jury. This was the second important case in which he was detailed to exploit this prerogative. Moreover, as the *Star* reported on May 20, Justice Sir Alfred Wills was appointed by special arrangement to preside.[89] He proved unduly tendentious. Prejudicing Wilde in the eyes of the jury, he permitted his trial to follow immediately that of his procurer, against whom the evidence was much more solid.[90] He admitted all the evidence that the judge of the first criminal trial had barred in the absence of independent validation. The testimony of the sole nonprostitute witness teemed with so many inconsistencies that the prosecution had to relinquish the complaint regarding him. Nevertheless, in his summation to the jury, the judge presumed Wilde's culpability by playing up his supposedly noxious sway over Lord Douglas, as manifested in the billets-doux exchanged between the two men.

Over and above reacting to Wilde's homosexuality, the authorities were endeavoring hammer and tongs to ward off the contamination of his publicized sin. Their asperity, however, unwittingly authorized the press's ire against the dramatist, which, in turn, only spurred the authorities to be more fervent. The feverishly self-feeding fury could not but have unfavorable effects on the jury: Wilde was finally convicted to the severest sentence that the law allowed for gross indecency with the uncorroborated testimonies of accomplices – a rare occurrence in the English criminal practice of the time. The witnesses had blackmailing records to boot. Even the prosecution privately conceded the paucity of legally pertinent evidence against the accused. As the jury was deliberating, Lockwood reassured Wilde's counsel Clarke, "You'll dine with your man in Paris tomorrow."[91] But Justice Wills scathingly upbraided Wilde and called the standard sentence for the crime he was accused of, two years in prison with hard labor, to be "totally inadequate for such a case as this."[92] Taking its cues from the authorities, the English press was unstinting in its en masse assault. "Open the windows. Let in the fresh air!" cried the *Evening News* on May 27, calling him "a social pest." The *Daily Telegraph* proclaimed, "The grave of contemptuous oblivion may rest on his foolish ostentation, his empty paradoxes, his insufferable posing, his incurable vanity."

This reciprocal reinforcement of rage not only contributed in large part to Wilde's conviction but also forced the members of the different sections of the Victorian public to signal rectitude to each other by shunning him after his sentence.[93] The dynamics of the scandal made it progressively dear for those who would rather not punish the dramatist not to do so, while minimizing the sanctioning costs faced by those who rather would. If Wilde were acquitted or if the prosecution had not retried him, he would have suffered much less social ostracism. During the late Victorian period, many high-status individuals who were widely held to be homosexuals but were nevertheless legally vindicated, or were not prosecuted in the first place, encountered restricted opprobrium. The aforementioned acquittal of Boulton and Park absolved them for the press. None of the elites embroiled in the Cleveland scandal, except Lord Somerset, who was allowed to decamp, were seriously touched. Prince Eddy, widely assumed to be a homosexual, was made duke of Clarence in May 1890.[94] Even though Lord Euston had confessed in his libel trial to having been in the male brothel on Cleveland Street – with the feeble pretext that he had stumbled into it under the impression that it was a regular striptease club – the peer was soon elevated to the rank of the grand master of the Mark Masons and later nominated an aide-de-camp by King Edward VII.

The contrast between the Wilde and Ross cases is again telling and attests to how it frequently took legal verdicts for Victorian society to censure elite homosexuals consistently and forcefully, even in instances when the transgression was already well known. After he lost the aforementioned libel trial against Lord Douglas in 1914, and hence acceded to the charge of being a sodomite, Robert Ross had to resign from his post as "assessor of picture valuations to the Board of Trade." But because he was not prosecuted, he survived his scandal, for all intents and purposes, unscathed. After the verdict, 300 members of the Victorian crème de la crème issued a testimonial to the good character of Ross. He was made a trustee of the National Gallery two years later.[95]

Only because (and only after) Wilde was prosecuted and sentenced, on the other hand, did society prove much less obliging to its former favorite. His conviction imposed a unity on the different sections of the Victorian public against him, and he abruptly became an untouchable. Even though Oscar Wilde's homosexuality was much talked about in various circles, it was only with his trials that it was effectively and inescapably publicized. The sentence now forced the various subpublics, especially the higher and cultured ones, to take a stance against Wilde lest they be stained in the eyes of the others. His plays were hence banished from the theater scene, his books pulled from bookstore shelves. No one but an obscure pornographer would publish *The Ballad of Reading Gaol*, which Wilde wrote in exile. And it was in the seventh printing of the plaintive poem in June 1899 that the expatriate would finally dare insert his name in brackets on the title page. Most reviewers overlooked the work. In accordance with the logic of scandal, his high status, which had hitherto safeguarded Wilde, now exacerbated reactions to him.[96] With his homosexuality public, he was now a synecdoche of the innovative segments of the art community, demonized as a baneful influence on the English youth. The scandal also offered a chance to some middle-class opinion leaders to vent their class resentment. Wilde was thus represented as the avatar of the degenerate elite. The London *Evening News* of May 26, 1895, excoriated him and others of his ilk:

> England has tolerated the man Wilde and others of his kind too long. Before he broke the law of his country and outraged human decency he was a social pest, a center of intellectual corruption.

He was one of the high priests of a school which attacks all the wholesome, manly, simple ideals of English life, and sets ups false gods of decadent culture and intellectual debauchery. The man himself was a perfect type of his class, a gross sensualist veneered with the affectation of artistic feeling too delicate for the appreciation of common clay. To him and such as him we owe the spread of moral degeneration amongst young men with abilities sufficient to make them a credit to their country. At the feet of Wilde, they have learned to gain notoriety by blatant conceit, by despising the emotions of a healthy humanity and the achievements of a wholesome talent.

The contamination compelled the denizens of the art world along with the cultured elite of the country to signal rectitude to the larger community as well as to each other by shunning Wilde. Most of his fellow artists who were well privy all along to his sexual habits snubbed him in France after his release – when they did not bluntly convey their contempt.[97] A close friend, the painter Edward Coley Burne-Jones, hoped that he would commit suicide. Few signed a petition drafted by Bernard Shaw to have his sentence reduced. Many illustrious names – including Henry James, Holman Hunt, Victorien Sardou, and George Meredith – refused. Aubrey Beardsley, who had illustrated *Salomé*, declined to draw for the *Yellow Book,* the chief journal of the aestheticism movement, as long as Wilde was published there. To parry stigma, his wife changed their sons' names and in her will forbade him to ever see them again. His few remaining years in France were of solitude and penury.

A scandal may leave few traces and may be fast forgotten even after intense effects on those it touched. It is essential to differentiate between the coeval and long-term effects of a scandal. For a scandal to be consequential in an enduring way, it usually has to operate as a catalyst and activate dormant social processes. Or it should start off a wave of scandals. Watergate, for instance, had direct effects on Nixon and the Republicans during its course, but it transformed the American political process as well. As I argue in the next chapter, Watergate unleashed the implicit contradictions of the modern presidency and spurred scandal activity in its wake. It furnished a general template and script for dealing with all kinds of political wrongdoing, and numerous institutional reforms were undertaken in its aftermath.

The Wilde affair had long-term consequences too, and the dramatist was not its only victim. Lawrence Stone has suggested that the traditional Victorian morality was loosening up in some circles during the last decade of the century.[98] Exploited by the conservative forces in English society, the Wilde scandal thus put an end to "the naughty nineties." His fellow artists tried to limit the contaminations of the scandal on them by shunning Wilde. All this was unavailing, however. The affair was far too salient. And, unlike its modernist French counterpart,[99] the English avant-garde had not effectuated a rupture with bourgeois society and was very much reliant on it. Aestheticism, tarred in toto by the scandal, petered out soon after Wilde's conviction.[100]

The unfolding of scandals is, in part, structurally determined. The cultural attitudes of the Victorians toward the publicity of sex; the fame and high status of the dramatist; and the dense networks within the Victorian elite that connected Queensberry, Wilde, and Rosebery molded the third-party effects that would be generated when the scandal broke. But scandals also give rise to a strategic interaction, in which parties respond to and attempt to manipulate such externalities. During such episodes, one responds more to others' prior public handling of disgrace than to the underlying transgression. Hence, the unfolding of scandals cannot be reduced to sociological variables: the strategic and sequential wielding and warding off of disgrace renders them path-dependent.[101]

The piteous fortune of Wilde was particularly path-dependent. Wilde would most probably not have been tried if he had not himself initiated the legal process by suing Queensberry – even though he would have nevertheless been attacked in public by the peer, which would have brought upon him some social censure. Wilde's deviance was already well known in London. It was the allegations in the libel trial that granted unavoidable publicity to his sexuality by imposing it simultaneously onto the audiences and authorities who had until then reasons for ignoring it and who would have incurred costs for denouncing it. Still, Wilde could have possibly won his libel trial if he had not appeared as a provocateur during his cross-examination. He would at least have been exempt from the moral blitz of the opinion leaders and thereby would have later elided the repercussions of their collective fury on the judicial process. It was the confluence of Wilde's legal rout with the contamination of the Victorian elite in the libel trial that eventuated in the criminal prosecution of the author. Here, contingency played a part. Many Victorian libel cases bared the seamy doings and dealings of elite families to the general public. Yet it was not inevitable that the Queensberry letters would be read in court; Clarke did not foresee the consequences of this fateful act. Once Lord Rosebery was tied to the affair, this externality compelled the authorities to distance themselves from it through perfervid prosecution and adjudication. Finally, had Wilde not been prosecuted or sentenced, or had he left the country during his trials, the reactions he would have had to endure would have been much more temperate. It was, in large part, the legal process that adversely altered the incentives of various Victorian groups and prompted their turnabout.

Let's recapitulate. For the Victorians, the publicity of homosexuality contaminated third parties along with the public sphere as a whole and was thought to have enormous provocative and normalizing effects. Punishing homosexuality would entail its publicity and thereby create scandals. Homosexual acts committed in private were thus tolerated by authorities and audiences even when such acts were well known. This was especially the case with elite offenders, for high status exacerbated the third-party effects of the publicity of homosexuality. And audiences and authorities were contaminated – as well as provoked – when Wilde's well-known homosexuality was unavoidably made public in the course of his legal ordeals. These externalities gave rise to a strategic interaction among those affected. During this process, the authorities were prodded to signal resolve and rectitude to the public through extraordinary zeal. The official acts, in turn, united the already provoked public against the author. Hence, the very dynamics that underlie the underenforcement of the homosexuality norms in Victorian England bred overenforcement once Wilde's transgression became inescapably public.

I showed in this chapter to what extent norm work and reactions to wrongdoing are profoundly molded by publicity, a sui generis social force that radically transforms the meanings and effects of transgressions. Equally important, we saw that the public sphere is a dramaturgical domain governed by the logic of appearances. Finally, the Wilde case allowed us to empirically study the temporal dynamics of the scandal process. The unfolding of a scandal is partly an interactional, a contingent affair. But I also pointed out some structural factors that underlie both the usual underenforcement of homosexuality norms in Victorian England and the dénouement of the Wilde affair. I extend this structural perspective in the next chapter to political scandals in general and to presidential scandals in the United States in particular.

# THREE

# The Presidency, Imperial and Imperiled

AMERICAN PRESIDENTS have been blighted by scandal since the seventies. We have seen one president toppled. Another was impeached, and a third came close. Countless White House staffers and cabinet members have been impugned of wrongdoing in the media, charges contaminating the presidency and disrupting its functioning. The first term of Bush fils was relatively scandal-free. Yet his second term, scourged by a slew of damning allegations about his administration, signals that the trend has not quite changed. Not long ago, however, scholars considered the modern presidency to be an imperial office.

I will show in this chapter that there are general processes and factors that affect the likelihood and efficacy of public allegations about high-status politicians. I focus on presidential scandals in the United States, this also allowing me to address the internal contradictions of the modern presidency – in particular, the vulnerabilities underneath its imperial façade.

## Political Scandal

A scandal is political to the extent that it affects the exercise of political power. Such events are almost always about high-status politicians, whose real or alleged transgressions pollute themselves and those they represent: their offices, parties, associates as well as the values they are supposed to stand for. The trust vested in these entities is thereby vitiated and the political process disrupted. The most common offenses that might give rise to political scandals are various uses of public office for private financial gain, abuse of power, and treason.[1] Yet other transgressions, like sexual misconduct by politicians, can occasion political scandals as well by blotting the public persona of the offender as well as the office they represent. Although reaction will obviously depend on the gravity and credibility of the charges, the status of the denouncees matter a great deal, too. The higher up the accused politician, the bigger the scandal and its audience, and the likelier the episode may actuate a significant redistribution of power.

Democratic politics is by nature contentious: moral opposition is systemically encouraged, for there are direct profits to be made out of scandal. In addition, the public denunciation of a political actor might be at times difficult to differentiate from ordinary critique. Consider, for instance, a senator skewering the president for having kowtowed to private interests in the determination of the energy policy of the executive branch. There is thus no sharp break between scandal and politics as usual. Rather we are presented with a continuum, at the one end of which we will find picayune, unexceptional bickering about morals and policy and on the other events such as Watergate with seismic effects. Most scandals are somewhere in between. Nevertheless, we should say that a political phenomenon is more of a scandal (or becomes a bigger scandal) to the extent that it does not look like and is not experienced as politics as usual. Also, a significant political scandal will typically involve identifiable transgressions with specific offenders – not simply abstract criticisms – and require some kind of institutional reaction.

Political scandals are recounted in the media in the form of bounded stories. They are often given names – for example, the Abu Ghraib scandal or the Iran-Contra affair. Christening is not inconsequential. A name grants the episode a high level of narrative coherence and enables, if not magnifies, collective focus. It makes it easier to coordinate responses. The authoritative definition of a political event as a scandal can engender scripted responses. In the United States, successfully affixing the "-gate" suffix to a real or alleged event involving the executive branch serves to differentiate it from politics as usual and to legitimate the appointing of a special counsel and the launching of congressional hearings. But not all scandals get proper names; many events, to the extent that they revolve around alleged wrongdoings by political actors, take the scandal form even if they are not denoted as such. The impeachment of Andrew Johnson is an example. But controversial policies (such as the Vietnam War) don't constitute scandals. Nor does low performance in office. Given our fiduciary relationship with politicians and their widespread visibility, politics is a fecund site for scandal. Depending on the context, a routine moral attack can morph into a scandal or can remain an isolated act.[2] Similarly, as the interest in the event wears, a scandal can dissolve into politics as usual.

## Democracy and Political Scandal

Some scholars see a close relationship between scandal and liberal democracy. It is "after all" only in such a political regime that the pursuit of power is constrained by a panoply of rules and procedures, the breaching of which is qualified as abuse. Free speech and separation of powers permit the publicization and sanctioning of transgressions by political actors. Within this framework, one could even argue that scandals are healthy symptoms, proof that politicians are not sacred cows and that they have to render accounts when they (seem to) violate the trust accorded to them.[3]

Yet, it is far from clear that democracy and scandal have to go together. Take the Moscow show trials of the 1930s. Public accusations and confessions were the essential tools of Stalinism. The French Jacobins routinely resorted to scandal during the Terror as well. Purges in all regimes consist of a sequence of scandals in which conspiracies of all sorts supposedly engineered by treacherous elites are "uncovered" by their competitors. Scandal is not restricted to modern times, either. Much of the internecine politicking in pre-revolutionary France was put into practice by scandalous libels scribed by lowly pamphleteers under the pay of rival aristocrats.[4] Political scandal is possible to the extent that the publicity of a transgression has political effects, especially those that undermine legitimacy or prestige. Whether the public that the transgression is communicated to has democratic controls over the exercise of power is irrelevant. Consider, for example, the Diamond Necklace affair,

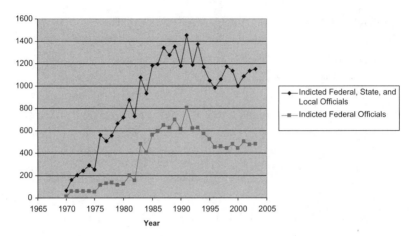

Figure 3.1. Federal Prosecutions of Public Corruption in the United States.

which exploded during the reign of Louis XVI, shortly before the French Revolution. The scandal redounded to the unpopularity of the monarchy at a critical moment and sapped the traditional sources of legitimacy that French absolutism was built on.[5]

Democracy and liberal institutions make adverse publicity about politicians more possible and effective. They are not necessary to a political scandal, however. Authoritarian regimes stifle or even criminalize moral attacks on high-status public officials because such assaults are deemed, not without reason, to be disruptive. It is not a coincidence that for the seventeenth-century Star Chamber, "scandal" meant "sedition," and "scandalous" qualified criticisms of public figures by private men. The truth of the utterance only aggravated the crime.[6]

Nevertheless, political scandals seem to be on the rise in many Western democracies. Not all federal prosecutions generate full-fledged scandals in the United States, but it is difficult not to be impressed by their high incidence in the recent decades (Figure 3.1).[7] Corruption scandal waves have also engulfed European countries such as France, Italy, and Spain.[8] As we will see in the next chapter, the French elite were particularly hard hit in the 1990s. What would affect the frequency of scandals in a political system? The objectivist paradigm perceives political scandal as the manifestation of

76

corruption and puts the blame on the growing dependence of politicians on money and on the languishing internal controls on their comportment. Draconian measures along with more transparency are proposed. The constructivist perspective, in contrast, points the finger to media and elite activism. Some have decried the emergence of an "attack journalism" in the United States during the sixties and seventies,[9] but journalists are not the only actors who can create scandals. Scholars have pointed to collusions among publicity-hungry prosecutors, belligerent investigative bodies of Congress, and the scoop-oriented press.[10] Regardless of their differences, both objectivist and constructivists bemoan that political scandals erode public trust in government.

Since it conflates political scandal with political wrongdoing, the objectivist account is problematic. A lot of corruption goes unpublicized; arguments about its rise or decline are difficult to substantiate. By the same token, a rise in the frequency of political scandals does not necessarily reflect a corresponding growth in misconduct. Much of what was kept private and abided before (such as illegal party finance in Italy and France and sexual misconduct in the United States) now risks getting publicized and punished. Moreover, many scandals involve charges that do not get legally confirmed. Finally, it seems that increasing transparency in Western politics has only been accompanied by more scandals.

## The Media

The objectivist position ignores that political scandals are mostly strategically created or capitalized on. But constructivists tend to affix too grand a part to the media in the making of scandals. Journalists receive boundless kudos for their role in events such as Watergate or unstinted criticism for their behavior in those such as the Lewinsky affair. And when journalists themselves join in the chorus, whether self-adulating as the fearless fighters of corruption or self-flagellating as the corruptor of public morals, they are simply confirming their supposed social power and relevancy, if not indulging in self-aggrandizement. The overall significance of the media seems, however, more modest. The European countries in which we observe the most spirited political scandal activity in the past two decades are Latin countries such as Italy, France, and Spain, which don't boast of a tradition of investigative journalism. In the United States, a large number of exposures are made by audacious and enterprising journalists. The latter are nevertheless very much dependent on their legal or political sources, which frequently use them for their own purposes. Deep Throat allied with the *Washington Post* journalist Bob Woodward during Watergate mainly to jockey for power within the FBI. Judith Miller's excessive reliance on manipulative government insiders in the reporting on Iraq impaired the *New York Times* coverage during the run-up to the war.

Furthermore, journalists, at least partially, respond to social demand, and they are constricted by social and legal norms determining what news is publishable – such as standards of decency and good taste, privacy and defamation laws, as well as notions of public interest and newsworthiness. Journalists can hype events, but only as long as what they say strikes a chord in us. Some believe that the media exercise disproportionate powers in shaping our perception of scandals, but American journalists often go out of their way to present the perspectives of both the accusers and the accused in these episodes. This narrative configuration serves dramatic purposes and allows for an appearance of impartiality. Moreover, those who think of scandals as media concoctions tend to ascribe a unitary character to news organizations. Yet, the American media reflect already-existing political and cultural rifts in society, and decades of communications research have found that people are not passive recipients of the information relayed by journalists and that to a large extent they use it to confirm their beliefs and not to acquire new ones.[11] Besides, although "what the public wants" cannot be objectively determined, it is nevertheless the case that, in many instances, media follow public opinion rather than lead it. Vietnam is a good example of such temporizing. According to a 1967 poll, half of Americans thought the war was a mistake,[12] despite the positive press coverage of Vietnam, until the Tet Offensive of early 1968. It was only then, after the war effort hit a major roadblock, that the media ran more and more athwart the administration's policy, beginning on television with Walter Cronkite calling, at the end of February 1968, Vietnam a stalemate.[13]

Naturally, media do matter in the making of scandals. What journalists choose to communicate and the way they define the transgressive act – all the more so if there is a strong consensus on the matter – can have an amplificatory and homogenizing impact on public perceptions. The recent allegations of sexual abuse by Catholic clergymen were thus seen by Americans as constituting a pedophilia scandal even though most of the ensnared priests were actually accused of having sex with postpubescent boys. It is also true that the more dominant members of the media will have more power in interpreting scandals, even though status hierarchies and discursive monopolies have been seriously attenuated since the mid-1990s – think of the rise of Fox News.

The media are nevertheless mostly crucial not as ideological apparatuses but insofar as they ensure publicity to things. As Michael Schudson has convincingly argued, their power resides not in telling us what to think but in their ability to "publicly include."[14] That we all read the same thing in the newspaper knowing that others are reading the same thing creates common knowledge about events. Even if not everyone is reading, it is the assumption or the myth that they are doing so that structures our behaviors and attitudes as private citizens, celebrities, or politicians to scandals and other events. The public of news, and hence the public of a national scandal, is, to a certain extent, a fiction, but it is a forceful, performative one that is fashioned in part by the media.

Of course there is publicity, and there is publicity. The authoritativeness of the source of communication augments the power and extent of the publicity of a scandal – especially when the transgression is merely alleged and ascribed to a high-status person. Elites are likely to be judged as more credible by both audiences and authorities, and they have better access to channels of publicity; low-status whistleblowers will usually need high-status allies.[15] The status of the denouncer is particularly important if there is an uncertainty about the meaning of a transgression.

The same principle applies to the medium of communication as well. Often allegations aired by low-status papers do not occasion genuine scandals before prestigious newspapers pick up these news items. Even in the age of bloggers, who have started to dent the monopoly of the print media in defining what is newsworthy, the status of the news source remains central. Matt Drudge, a seedy Internet gossipmonger at the time, could only break the Lewinsky scandal in 1998 by publicizing how an elite media actor, *Newsweek* magazine, had spiked a story about the president's affair with an intern. And many items in blogosphere need to be picked up, and sanctified, by more traditional outlets to achieve widespread publicity.

Nevertheless, it cannot be denied that the proliferation of the media sources and the establishment of the round-the-clock cable news cycle have stoked the demand for scandal and facilitated its publicization process. The effects of the citizen-journalism of YouTube, which allows almost anyone to put any kind of compromising images about elites into the public domain, are obvious. These trends are reinforced by heightening competitive pressures on journalists, which tend to encourage vociferous political reporting. The exigency to find material needles pundits to rely heavily on scandal and controversy in news coverage.

Journalistic scandalmongering is constrained and enabled by structural factors. Without those able and willing to pass along discreditable information, reporters would have a hard time writing compromising things about politicians. Without a public attuned to political wrongdoing, journalists would be greatly hampered in their attacks. Media astringency toward powers that be is, in large measure, a function of the vulnerability of the latter. Allegations against high-status politicians become more fulsome, more frequent, more convincing, and more consequential after the political elite have already suffered a prestige decline. As I argue here, the tropism to negativity in the American media has in large part fed from such a process since the late sixties. The upshot is a higher incidence of scandals, but each with fewer effects and reduced air life, and a blurring of the difference between them and politics as usual.

## Moral Attack and Vulnerability

Chance plays an important role in the making of political scandals: if Nixon had destroyed the Watergate tapes, he probably would not have come to a sticky end. And there is no reason to assume that all politicians are morally equivalent. The conditions and processes that encourage, lead to, or facilitate more or less wrongdoing matter as well. Nevertheless, since transgression is not equivalent to scandal, we also need to consider two additional elements that affect political scandal frequency: (1) incentives and capability to engage in moral attacks against high-status political actors and (2) vulnerability to such attacks.

Vulnerability, always a question of degree, refers to the lack of protections against moral attacks. Moral attacks in politics are public denunciations that can originate from law, society, and the political elite; we can thus differentiate among legal, social, and political vulnerability. These types are relatively autonomous from each other. A president who can easily be taken to court may nevertheless be very popular and thus immune to media attacks. Vulnerability can also spill over, however. For instance, low approval ratings tend to bring on congressional assaults on presidents and make them more efficacious than they would otherwise be. At the same time, we should bear in mind that even though vulnerable presidents will be relatively easier to attack, this does not mean that they will not survive their scandals. Contingency and strategic acuity will be important in how things turn out.

There is a link between vulnerability and moral attack. Vulnerability encourages public denunciations and lowers the evidence threshold necessary for them to be successful.[16] A politician's immunity to (and capacity to deal with) normative aggression naturally has a lot to do with credibility and actual power – formal or informal. But this is not all. Another important factor is the anticipated public costs should a scandal involving the politician break. These costs are contaminations or real disruptions, and their perception can be manipulated to a certain extent. If a political scandal seems to have high collective costs, there will be incentives to overlook the matter – just as it was the case in elite homosexuality in Victorian England. If these costs are lowered, then politicians would have less immunity, and we should expect a higher incidence of scandal. Let us see how these mechanisms play out in the case of American presidents.

## The Vulnerabilities of Presidents

Founded on a deep distrust of centralized authority, a fairly expansive right to criticize the public officialdom, and the separation of powers, the United States has been a fertile ground for political scandal. Yet we also observe significant historical variations in scandal activity, especially insofar as the presidency is concerned, partly because the branches of government have not been in stable equipoise throughout American history.

Congress of course retains oversight powers, but it has not always had the incentives and opportunities to exercise them aggressively. Its powers are limited: it can hold hearings but cannot prosecute executive officials for misconduct or remove them save through impeachment – an extraordinary procedure not possible without an exceptional amount of unity. The presidential capability to cite executive privilege effectively in the face of watchdog activism in the Capitol also varies as does the degree of presidential control over law enforcement. Nixon received much flak when he had a special prosecutor, investigating executive malfeasance, fired; Grant and Truman, who did the same, were spared. Another issue is the changes in judicial attitudes toward presidential power: if the Supreme Court had decided that Clinton could not be the subject of a sexual harassment lawsuit during his tenure, we would not have had the Lewinsky scandal. Finally, immunity comes in extra legal forms as well. One is less vulnerable if one's potential attackers fear effective (however illegal) ripostes. The public prestige of a president can erect a protective halo that could also make assaults costly or flimsy.

Variability as to what constitutes scandalous presidential conduct further complicates things. A presidential scandal can originate from the violation of a clear legal or social norm by the president, but the constitutional, statutory, and traditional rules that constrain the behavior of the White House incumbents are on the whole indefinite and elastic. Some presidents found it easy to assert executive privilege; others like John Tyler risked impeachment for it. Such issues are rarely legal puzzles that can be solved by cool ratiocination; they are always passionately politicized and moralized. Finally, the extent to which a president is seen as responsible for the actions of his or her subordinates is also variable.

The likelihood of an effective moral attack against a sitting president and the latter's vulnerability to it are affected by (1) the institutional characteristics of the office of the presidency and its structural relationship to the political environment and society at large and (2) the specific context in which individual presidents find themselves. I will refer to these two factors as the mode of governance and the sociopolitical conjuncture. The first has a deep, *longue durée* logic. The second is much more temporary. The two factors interact, but they are nevertheless autonomous.

First, the mode of governance and sociopolitical conjuncture combine to mold inducements or disincentives for engaging in moral attacks against the White House. Second, they shape the capabilities (legal or otherwise) of a president to quash and deter attacks, cover up compromising events, shift or resist blame in the case of scandal, and prevent incompetence from transforming into moral culpability.[17] Third, they are particularly important in determining the anticipated effects (costs or benefits) of presidential scandals on various third parties. These externalities affect a sitting president's freedom from scrutiny and level of immunity. Finally, the mode of governance and the sociopolitical conjuncture can allow or prod presidents into undertaking actions that will be seen as scandalous when they are later exposed.

### Sociopolitical Conjuncture

The domestic context is the first conjunctural element. Divided government will make presidential scandal more likely by enabling Congress to investigate and publicize discreditable actions linked to the president and frame them in the most deleterious ways. Consider how the rising hostility between Clinton and the Republican Congress from 1994 onward climaxed in the impeachment of the president in 1998 as a result of the Lewinsky scandal. Congressional resistance to executive action in times of divided government can, furthermore, motivate the president into surreptitious action, which, when unearthed, can look like illegality. Take the Iran-Contra affair. It was in the face of unbending opposition from the Capitol to the administration's policy in Nicaragua that the conservatives in the administration built an alternative intelligence apparatus attached to the National Security Council that bypassed congressional surveillance.[18] The operations of this organization – money-for-hostages deal, covert operations, and arms sales to Iran – eventually came into the open in a major scandal.

Presidents can also be distrustful of their parties, which can have their own fissures that would exacerbate scandal creation. American political parties are ridden by cross-cutting issue cleavages.[19] There is limited party discipline in the legislative branch, with politicians keyed in on their personal political future; a majority in Congress of the president's party does not guarantee immunity. Consider the series of Truman administration scandals, most of which took the form of combative hearings by the Democratic Congress.[20]

Finally, presidents may have to contend with a whole array of antagonistic political and social actors, including the media, interest groups, civil society organizations, and state elites. The coalitions that these actors can forge can at times be resilient and robust. Presidents who are at loggerheads with them will be particularly scandal prone.[21] In contrast, presidents such as Franklin D. Roosevelt facing a coalition that represents an order that is bankrupt or ailing in the eyes of the public will prevail against attacks, however virulent.

The international situation constitutes the second conjunctural element. Foreign affairs, as Tocqueville saw clearly, augment the presidency's resources, which can be used against detractors.[22] International crises will push things that can be embarrassing for the administration off the agenda. It will be much easier to justify executive secrecy, and the public will coalesce around the president. As the real or perceived dependency of the public on the leader increases, so will the collective costs of a presidential scandal and thus the White House's immunity from attack.[23] In such times, legal and social tolerance for dissent drastically declines.[24] Those who dare to speak publicly against the president will more likely be ignored, ridiculed, or reviled. If, however, such presidents eventually prove to be inept to deal with the crisis – or appear that way – their immunity will be significantly impaired, and their detractors will soon rummage for depravity underneath the incompetence. Compare George W. Bush's first and second terms, the former marked by September 11 and the latter by the Iraqi imbroglio.

The third factor is the charisma of the president. The more charismatic a president is, the more accommodating the public and the more hamstrung the critics of the White House will be. Franklin D. Roosevelt and John F. Kennedy found it easier to define authoritatively moot events and acts in terms advantageous to themselves, unlike their uncharismatic brethren Richard Nixon and Andrew Johnson. Presidential charisma is, however, an elusive thing, a hodgepodge of personal characteristics and social attitudes. It might even sometimes be a fiction. Michael Schudson and Elliot King have compellingly argued that the image of Reagan as the charismatic communicator is bereft of empirical support. Yet this myth, fabricated by the media and the political elite, was nonetheless quite consequential because it frustrated the normative blows against the president.[25]

The final conjunctural element is the internal, temporal dynamics of a given presidential term. Presidents who are struck early with effective allegations of wrongdoing or incompetence can suffer from the self-reproducing and self-fulfilling logic of the distrust generated by these scandals. This principle explains in part the blizzard of scandals that beset the administrations of Grant, Truman, Reagan, and Clinton.

## Mode of Presidential Governance

By mode of presidential governance, I mean the long-term institutional characteristics of the office of the presidency: its administrative apparatus, its de jure or de facto prerogatives, its general relationship to other political institutions and the media, the normative constraints that it is subject to, and its visibility. American history provides us with two modes that we can call traditional and modern.[26] The nature of governance has an important bearing both on the likelihood of effective attacks against presidents from law, society, and Washington and on the presidential vulnerability against them. To the extent the office becomes the central symbol of the nation and its political core, the moral integrity of the presidency, whether real or imagined, will become an essential public good. Unthinking deference, semiconscious hypocrisy, collective collusions, and formal or informal arrangements will come together to protect presidential aura. As presidency comes to be the focus of government, presidents will be armed with various legal and extra legal resources against moral detractors. But the ascendancy of the presidency is a mixed blessing for presidents; it is accompanied by a high level of visibility and expectations, which can prove detrimental if they lose the control over the way they appear.

## The Traditional Presidency and Its Scandals

Washington, Jefferson, Jackson, and Lincoln exercised significant autonomy at critical junctures. Nevertheless, the presidency was a relatively weak office from the early republic until the early decades of the twentieth century. Most governing was conducted at the state level, and the functions of the national government were restricted to patronage politics. Presidents had small administrative staffs, and executive departments were obliged to report to Congress. Theodore Lowi has argued that the premodern president was merely an appendage to the legislature.[27] Since the United States was not one of the main players in the international arena, foreign affairs were only sporadically in the foreground, and the role of the president in the general polity was proportionately limited. Last but not least, the presidency was not a very visible office; most of the press coverage focused on Congress. Presidents were distant figures. The founding ideology enjoined a rhetorical relationship between them and the public to prevent the creation of demagogues.[28]

These institutional features meant that no great symbolism or centrality bulwarked the presidents against attacks at themselves or their administrations in times of trouble. And nineteenth-century American politics was indeed characterized by a high incidence of moral attacks in public, some of which caused scandals of various sizes. Political conflict was thus often difficult to differentiate from routine scandalmongering. However common, scandals still at times riled reputations; they must have surely macerated morale.

The presidency was often pummeled by a cantankerous press. The American media were unabashedly partisan until the late nineteenth century: journalists were raucous hacks whose salaries were shelled out by politicians. With the Jacksonian democracy, newspapers became party organs featuring vitriolic editorials, which did not spare the presidents. In *Democracy in America*, Tocqueville gave an example of the general timbre of the journalistic discourse of the 1830s in a quote from *Vincenne's Gazette*, a contemporaneous newspaper.

> In this whole affair, the language of Jackson [the president] was that of a heartless despot exclusively concerned with preserving his own power. Ambition is his crime, and that will be his punishment. Intrigue is his vocation and intrigue will confound his plans and snatch his power from him. He governs by corruption, and his guilty maneuvers will turn to his shame and confusion. He has shown himself in the political arena as a gambler without shame or restraint. He has succeeded, but the hour of justice draws near; soon he will have to give up what he has won, throw his false dice away, and end his days in some retreat where he will be free to blaspheme against his folly, for repentance is not a virtue that has ever been given to his heart to know.[29]

To make things even more fractious, American culture had little patience for formalities and false politeness, both of which were associated with affected Europe. Neither journalists nor politicians shied away from below-the-belt attacks. From Washington to Cleveland, many presidents were accused in public – at times with a great deal of noise – of sexual transgressions. At the same time, journalists' openly tendentious nature meant that they had limited prestige, this softening the impact of their low blows. More of this in the fifth chapter when I study sex scandals in American history.

The early republic was stamped by a thick boundary between the patrician elite and the masses. Restricted suffrage and relatively low levels of literacy bolstered social hierarchy. Since America did not have a natural aristocracy, the right to rule had to be justified by the obligations attached to one's high position in society. Character thus being a capital asset, one standard way to score points in political battles was to ravage the good name of one's rival.[30]

Inchoate party formation, springing in part from the Founding Fathers' mistrust of factions,[31] contributed to the personalistic tenor of political conflict as well. It is common to recount the history of the Revolutionary period as a narrative of factional strife between the Federalists and the Republican Democrats. These alignments had, however, limited substance, especially after the Federalists were shellacked with the election of Jefferson. At any rate, it is crucial not to overstate the unity and coherence of the camps. Consider how Alexander Hamilton, a leading Federalist, supported Thomas Jefferson against John Adams in 1800. The fact that organizational and ideological identities did not clearly differentiate politicians further added to the weight of moral reputation in political life.

Social hierarchy and political atomism thus moralized the conflicts within the patrician elite. The reverence that Americans now show to their founders was not shared by the founders themselves; scandal, in the form of attacks by denunciatory pamphlets, was an essential tool by which the patrician elite jockeyed for power. As we will see in the fifth chapter, the period is awash with allegations of sexual depravity. Charges of financial corruption and treason were also rife, hurled about almost indiscriminately.

The legitimate claims of early presidents to power were predicated on appearing super partes over private interests and factions. Jefferson famously said, "We are all Federalists and all Republicans," when he moved into office. The presidency was nevertheless routinely subject to ad hominem attacks that questioned the pretensions of its incumbents. A general distrust of centralized authority meant that those who had power could always be reasonably suspected of abusing it. Hence, Washington and Adams found themselves many times dressed down for their grandiosity. The newspapers, according to Gail Collins, wrote about Washington's "courtly levees" and "queenly drawing rooms."[32] Some called him "a usurper with dark schemes of ambition." Jefferson and his allies roasted the first president for planning to establish a monarchy after the adoption of the Jay Treaty in 1794, which, in their eyes, bespoke of a perfidious favoritism toward England. Some even demanded his impeachment.

Domestic turbulences such as the Whiskey Rebellion and hesitations in the international arena – both the birth pains of the fledgling state – allowed opportunities in spades to accuse one's political rivals of being traitors. Executive officials were fair game: Edmund Randolph, the secretary of state under Washington, was charged with accepting bribes from France to spark the Whiskey Rebellion. No conclusive proof could be mustered, but the scandal undid his reputation all the same. Campaigns were exceptionally rough. The *New England Courant* wrote that if Jefferson became president, "murder, robbery, rape and adultery and incest will be openly taught and practiced, the air will be rent with cries of distress, the soil soaked with blood, and the nation black with crimes."[33]

The Jacksonian democracy extended suffrage to white males, democratized the Electoral College, and opened the era of the all-powerful political parties. These organizations integrated the unwashed masses into the political process, dominated the presidential selection system, and made Congress the chief branch of government. In this system, which would later be called "congressional government" by Woodrow Wilson,[34] the main function of the presidency was the distribution of federal patronage to party factions and local machines. Parties did try hard to seize the presidency. And, owing much of their authority to their parties, presidents remained, on the whole, subordinate to them once elected. Not all the incumbents were equally pliable, however. Some attempted to transgress the implicit limits set on them by the traditional mode of governance, but such acts were easily qualified as beyond the pale. It is not an accident that the two nineteenth-century presidents who came close to being removed from office had both locked horns with a legislature dominated by the party that had put them in the White House: Andrew Johnson, who was impeached, and John Tyler, who became the first president against whom articles of impeachment were drafted by Congress. Besides, both presidents were bereft of the legitimacy that comes from being elected and were therefore even more susceptible. "High crimes and misdemeanors," the constitutional standard for impeachment, is a nebulous concept that has set off acrid exegetic skirmishes in the history of American politics. In the cases of both Tyler and Johnson, the motivations were unambiguously political.

In 1841, Tyler succeeded William Harrison, who died in office.[35] Early in Tyler's term, Henry Clay, the leader of the Whigs, proposed a bill that would establish a national bank with branches in several states. This was one of the most important policy objectives of the Whig Party, but Tyler vetoed it on states' rights grounds, whereupon his party expelled him and his cabinet collectively resigned. The president formed a new cabinet staffed by southern conservatives along with a commission headed by private citizens to ferret out venality in the New York customhouse. In a time when governing was indistinguishable from distributing office and other perks to party loyalists, the report of the presidential commission unsurprisingly unearthed massive graft by both the Democrats and Whigs. Congress struck back and quickly passed a law forbidding the president to pay private agents to undertake investigations without congressional consent. It also took on the executive branch for its own praetorian practices and asked for information regarding jobs distributed among the president's political supporters. Citing privilege, Tyler refused to comply.

In this all-out war between the two branches of the government, Congress requested the president's secretary of war to release information about army fraud against the Cherokees. Tyler simply instructed his secretary not to testify. In addition, the Whigs attempted to introduce an amendment that would have made a simple majority of Congress capable of overriding a veto. The move ended in smoke, however. The Whigs did not give in. Even though they had relinquished control of Congress in midterm elections, a sizeable group in the Whig Party considered impeachment, hoping that enough Democrats would support the motion. A House select committee promptly charged that Tyler had committed impeachable offenses as a president. Soon articles of impeachment – six charges of abuse of power and three charges of misconduct of office – were drafted against him. The president was taken to task for abusing his veto power and prevaricating to the American public. The House voted down the articles, however, because the Democrats did not find it expedient to rally to the Whig cause.

An even more tempestuous episode, albeit with similar dynamics, was the confrontation between Andrew Johnson and Congress.[36] Like Tyler, Johnson succeeded a deceased president. A Southern Democrat attached to states' rights, he had been nominated as Lincoln's vice president in 1864 by those who wanted to signal that their novel platform, the National Union Party, encompassed wide-ranging interests and not just those of the Radical Republicans. Johnson was under fire right out of the chute. The *New York World* lacerated the bibulous president for his inebriated performance during his inauguration and called him "the person who defiled our chief council-chamber on Saturday with the spewings of a drunken boor." Not only did Johnson face a hard-shell Republican majority in Congress, but he also proved restive by displaying independence from the party that had put him in the White House. He vetoed the Civil Rights Act of 1866, which had declared blacks as citizens and denied states the power to restrict their rights, to slow down the Reconstruction process. In effect, the president vetoed twenty-nine bills and was overridden fifteen times during his tenure, more than any other who had held the same office until that time.

In August 1867, Johnson fired the disloyal secretary of war, Edwin M. Stanton, an ally of the Radical Republicans, without the Senate's assent. The move was in defiance with the Tenure of Office Act, a measure passed on March 2, 1867, by Congress over the veto of the president. The act had been proposed to prevent any interference from the White House with the military occupation of the South. Johnson protested the impingement and reiterated his right to dismiss anyone he wanted in his cabinet, but the Supreme Court, intimidated by the Radicals, refused to pass on the case. General Grant, whom Johnson appointed secretary ad interim, turned the office back to Stanton when the Senate refused to approve his dismissal.

Johnson's arrogation stirred up a political hornet's nest. Congress, pushing a capacious view of impeachable offenses, took on the president. In response, Johnson decided to circumvent the Washington elite. But his barnstorming as he traveled around the country for support only drew more maledictions and was universally regarded as overstepping.[37] This was not a time when presidents could reach out to the masses for backing in their scrimmages with Congress. Eventually, Johnson was impeached. The witnesses that appeared before the House Judiciary Committee during the Senate trial made wild and racy incriminations against the president. Placatory in his defense, Johnson pledged to cease meddling with the reconstruction. Still, he came within an ace (one vote) of being convicted.

Even wartime presidents were assailable in the nineteenth century. It is often pointed out that Lincoln expanded presidential prerogatives, throttled civil liberties, and suspended the writ of habeas corpus. What is less frequently noted is the amount of opposition that Lincoln received during the Civil War not only from the Democrats, who routinely called him a dictator and war criminal, but also from his own party, which castigated him for corruption in the appointment of generals. Republican congressmen proclaimed to be the "arbiter and regulator of the War Powers" and set up a pesky special committee to oversee the president's conduct of the war. Lincoln's secretary of war was whacked by Congress for being wasteful and incompetent. His wife was pilloried in the press for her spending sprees and flashy fêtes. Slurred of being a Confederate spy, she was even investigated for treason by a joint committee. Lincoln was elected twice – mostly because he was such a consummate operator in the patronage game[38] – but the attacks did nick his authority. Had he had less fortitude, he could have crumbled. Had he not been assassinated, he certainly would have run into difficulties in pushing his Reconstruction agenda. And whatever powers Lincoln achieved in war for the presidency were impermanent. The Supreme

Court rejected his wartime measures in 1886 and affirmed that the Constitution should be operative in war and peace alike.

## The Modern Presidency and Its Protections

The resources of the American president expanded gradually at the expense of the political parties and Congress during the first half of the twentieth century, especially with the New Deal and later with the Cold War. The White House became the fulcrum of the U.S. government, its chief resident transformed in the process from a clerk of congressional rule to a full-fledged leader.

The presidency crescent had multiple causes. The first one is the mounting importance of foreign affairs. The United States rose to become a world power in the aftermath of the First World War, and Congress effectively relinquished its war-making rights with Korea.[39] Second, economic modernization boosted the regulatory functions of the executive branch. Third, political parties saw their power weakened. Primaries destroyed the clout of the machines in the selection of presidential candidates. Civil service reform undercut their patronage operations. Identification with parties declined, and ticket-splitting became the norm after the Second World War. Presidents grew autonomous from their parties and augmented their role in the shaping of legislation, a process that originated with the passing of the 1921 Budget and Accounting Act.

The administrative resources of the White House expanded. Wilson had seven aides; Franklin D. Roosevelt's staff numbered over 150.[40] The presidents furthermore acquired full control over the executive departments. Beginning with Eisenhower, they ran campaigns with their own political apparatus, separate from their parties. Paralleling their autonomization, they were now more visible to the public and established a rhetorical relationship with the public over the heads of Washington elites.[41] The presidency evolved into a plebiscitary institution, and the president emerged as the unifying figure of American politics. Presidents' positive public image – now measured and publicized periodically by polls – became the main spring of executive power, something indispensable to their leadership postures as well as to their ability to negotiate with the political and social elite.

The accretion of its functions granted a real and symbolic centrality to the presidency. This also meant that normative attacks on presidents would have collective costs. Thus the media and the other branches of government often colluded in protecting the presidential mystique as much as possible from the inevitable degradation that routine political competition brings. The institution gained an aura. Its activities now shrouded by rituals, the presidency had to be treated with respect. Since the modern presidency is a highly personalized office, presidents partook much of the institutional nimbus in the form of charisma. Even though not all presidents were equally gifted in this regard, charisma became to be more and more expected from those who wanted to be an incumbent.

The relative inviolability of the presidency not only ensured substantial immunity for presidents, it also armed them with redoubtable resources of deterrence – resources that could be legitimate as well as illegitimate – against those such as administration insiders or journalists who would have access to discreditable information about them. Of course, attacks on presidents tend to be justified by the claim that they are unworthy of their office. All the same, it is not that easy to differentiate the person from the office. Just as presidents deploy the powers of their office, their acts reflect on the presidency. A profaned president will profane the presidency. Immunity that presidents occupying an elevated presidency have is far from absolute. It will nevertheless be enough to deter or neutralize many attacks, all the more so if the charges are mere allegations and if the public and media are equipped with incentives to assume that the emperor has clothes.

Presidents captured the limelight in the twentieth century. In the nineteenth century, the presidency was the topic of 20 percent of all political reporting in Washington; this figure climbed to 80 percent in the twentieth century.[42] More important, presidents had tight control over the way they appeared. General coverage was usually positive until the late 1960s. The private lives of politicians, and especially of presidents, were only presented in a flattering light.[43] The press

94

showed much discretion and self-censorship about the mistresses of Harding, Franklin D. Roosevelt, Kennedy, and Lyndon Johnson. The media proved tractable – at times prostrate. Journalists had a private stake in this as well. Trying to establish journalism as a respectable profession, late-nineteenth and early-twentieth-century media corps elevated what they covered, this divesting them with the high purpose they craved.

Scandals did, of course, occur occasionally that ruffled the executive branch and the presidency in particular. Contingency did play its part. Congress did not altogether abnegate its oversight functions. Some terms were marked by heightened wrongdoing and partisanship, and presidential campaigns could get stormy. Some conjunctures were more prone to scandal than others. For example, various executive agencies were placed under congressional probes during Truman's tenure, and an assistant attorney general was jailed for a bribe. Scandals mostly had limited effects on the presidents themselves, however, especially if they were popular.[44] Even though Congress was at times scrappy against Franklin D. Roosevelt, who was hated by business interests and some populists like Father Coughlin, a good deal of the grumbling was private or ineffectual – except when the president overreached in his attempt to pack the Supreme Court. There was much public support for the president; first the Depression (even though he was unable to cure it, policies proposed by his opponents looked worse), and then the war (which did cure the Depression) protected him.

Until the 1970s, most dirt about modern presidents came out either during campaigns or after the incumbent was no longer in office. For instance, the Teapot Dome scandal broke and was investigated after Harding died in office of a cerebral hemorrhage in 1923. The same applies to the president's White House mistress and illegitimate child, which were again made public much later. Now thought to be one of the worst presidents, Harding was actually quite popular during his tenure.[45] Even when presidents became unpopular, as in the case of Truman whose approval ratings dropped down to twenties at the end of his second term, the institution of presidency itself still commanded respect. Korea undermined the president, and some cried treason during his feud with General MacArthur. But, as the presidential scholar Richard Neustadt points out, confidence in the institution and its prerogatives were not touched.[46]

Of the latter, perhaps the most important is executive privilege. It was in the course of the twentieth century (until the seventies) that presidential withholding of information became increasingly frequent. The Constitution does not make clear stipulations regarding the confidentiality of executive documents. Congress retains a right to ask for information, but the president can well not honor the request. The issue is hence more political than legal.[47] Some nineteenth-century presidents had occasionally claimed privilege: in 1807, Jefferson successfully waved off congressional pressures to provide information about the Aaron Burr controversy. Although in the nineteenth century Congress saw such moves mostly as provocative infringements, twentieth-century presidents acquired more and more leeway in defining the boundaries of their authority. On several occasions, the information they withheld had to do with foreign affairs, the paradigmatic locus of justified *arcana imperii*. McKinley, for instance, refused to cooperate with the Senate during an investigation about Cuban funds.[48] International matters were not the only domain, however. Theodore Roosevelt effectively rebuffed a Senate request to release information regarding an apparent violation of the Sherman Antitrust Act by United States Steel.[49]

Presidents routinely claimed executive privilege after the Second World War. Even during the McCarthy years, they could refuse, without much public fuss, to disclose information that could embarrass them. Truman was harpooned by the Capitol for harboring communists in his administration, and his popularity eventually dropped. But the president successfully retained control over what to make public. Truman thus withheld security files throughout his administration from the House Un-American Activities Committee. In 1948, the California congressman Richard Nixon remonstrated in vain to the president's refusal to release an FBI letter concerning a prominent scientist accused of disloyalty by the same committee. In 1952, Truman extended his aegis even to those seen as security risks by his own administration.[50]

Immunity from scrutiny reached a high-water mark in the 1950s during the Eisenhower presidency. In effect, the very term "executive privilege" was first enunciated then. Although the president faced a Democratic Congress, there was much comity in the relations between the two branches of government. Like Truman, Eisenhower asserted privilege against the House Un-American Activities Committee on the issue of congressional access to executive information regarding the security files of government employees. Arguing that disclosure would impede free debate within the administration, the president claimed that internal deliberations had to remain confidential. The *New York Times* of May 18, 1954, concurred: "The committee has no more right to know the details of what went on in these inner Administration councils than the Administration would have the right to know what went on in an executive session of a Committee of Congress."[51] Such deference to presidential privacy would become unthinkable after Watergate. From June 1955 to June 1960, there were at least forty-four instances when officials in the executive branch denied information to Congress on the directives of president.[52] There were more such cases in those five years than in the entire nineteenth century.[53] The prerogative covered virtually any executive branch officer.

The Eisenhower years did witness one significant corruption scandal within the administration. Sherman Adams, the White House chief of staff, resigned in 1958 over a vicuna coat and an oriental rug received from a woolen manufacturer whose troubles with a federal regulatory agency evaporated with phone calls from the presidential aide. The scandal was enabled by the crevices within the Republican Party. Adams was under attack by the press and had already alienated a good number of congressional Republicans, who did not feel compelled to come to his aid in his dire straits. The president was very much saddened personally; he could nonetheless easily extricate himself from his disgraced aide. In any case, Adams evaded legal punishment. And when it came out that he was deeply in the soup with the Internal Revenue Service in 1961, the new president, John F. Kennedy, checked with Eisenhower, who innervated the old boys' network to raise money to bail him out. No prosecution was undertaken, and the story did not come out until the 1970s.[54] Adams was not the only one who accepted items from private persons. The president was himself given a vicuna coat, a $4,000 tractor, a $1,000 bull, and $40,000 worth of agricultural equipment and livestock for his Gettysburg farm from various political backers. But there was no scandal. In a news conference on July 31, 1957, Eisenhower could regally slap down a journalist who was so bold as to mention these presents: "Conflict-of-interest law does not apply to me."[55] The matter was closed.

The White House became progressively untouchable during the two decades following the Second World War. The presidency of John F. Kennedy should be seen as the apotheosis of this process.[56] The institution had reached such empyrean heights by then that the Bay of Pigs fiasco roused no grumblings. The American people rallied around their president, whose approval rating shot up to 83 percent. Kennedy peremptorily stated in a press conference held on April 21, 1961, four days after the debacle, "I don't think any useful national purpose would be served by my going further into the Cuban question this morning." Everybody was satisfied. The president addressed the American Newspaper Publishers Association a few days after and noted: "A newspaper should not only ask the question 'is it news?' but also the question 'is it in the interest of the national security?'"

Kennedy was able to dissemble from the nation both the true import of the Cuban missile crisis and the backstairs settlement that concluded it. According to the official version, the Soviets backed out for an explicit American commitment never to invade the island. The actual quid pro quo, however, required the U.S.S.R. to pull out the nuclear weapons from Cuba only in exchange for the United States doing the same for the Jupiter missiles based in Turkey.[57] Kennedy's countless dalliances with prostitutes, Hollywood stars and starlets, and women connected to the mob are not only all well documented, but it seems that many around him, as well as journalists, knew about them. No one whispered a word in public. Mixing personal pizzazz and presidential power, Kennedy could both seduce and strong-arm journalists. He invited some of them to his White House orgies. He could get less winsome, too. In the last year of his time in office,

Kennedy browbeat the *New York Times* to change its Hanoi correspondent, who had riled up the president with his uncomplimentary Vietnam coverage.

Collusion was extensive to safeguard the presidential mystique. Even J. Edgar Hoover, who personally and politically loathed Kennedy, took part in it. The FBI chief was a stalwart believer in the presidency and could be counted on to help avert the publicity of Kennedy's innumerable sexual shenanigans. One of these was a fling with the wife of a military attaché at the West German embassy, Ellen Rometsch, who was believed by some to be an agent of the East German intelligence. The Kennedys were able to whisk her off the country to avoid a major scandal. The Republicans got wind of the affair, however, and a Senate committee started to investigate Rometsch as she had a long track record of bedding Washington big shots. Alarmed, the White House made sure that she would not be able to get an American visa and come back to testify. In addition, Hoover, at the behest of Robert Kennedy, quelled the concerns of key Republicans in the House by reassuring them that there was no link between Rometsch and the president. That the attorney general was the president's brother helped – something that would be inconceivable in the post-Watergate context.

## The Making of Watergate

The famous scandal broke with the arrest of five men, including a former FBI agent, in a bungled burglary of the Democratic National Committee at the Watergate complex in Washington, D.C., on June 17, 1972. The purpose of the break-in was to bug the Democratic National Committee and steal documents regarding its electoral campaign strategy. Two former White House aides, Gordon Liddy and Howard Hunt, were also detained in relation to the crime, and it was soon found that they worked for the Committee to Re-elect the President – an organization that would thereafter be referred to sardonically as "CREEP." The seven men implicated in the break-in were indicted on September 15, and on July 1, 1972, former Attorney General John Mitchell resigned from the position of the campaign manager of the CREEP. Bob Woodward and Carl Bernstein of the *Washington Post* had been writing on Watergate since August 1972. The two gadflies revealed in autumn that a $25,000 check donated to the president's reelection campaign had been deposited in the Florida Bank account of one of the Watergate burglars, and they thereby linked the White House Chief of Staff H. R. Haldeman to the scandal.

Nevertheless, Watergate was not yet a major presidential affair. Some Democrats harped on it during the 1972 campaign, but the issue had little traction. The interested public was small and the reaction faint. Few journalists worked on it. An October 1972 Gallup poll showed that less than half of Americans had heard of the incident, and Nixon was elected by a landslide in November. The scandal would not go away, however; it would only metastasize. The Watergate jury returned a guilty verdict in January 1973, and Judge John Sirica meted out conditional sentences of twenty to forty years to each of the defendants for breaking and entering, wiretapping, and conspiracy. One of the defendants, James McCord, agreed to cooperate and wrote a letter on March 27 to the judge in which he divulged the political pressures that the suspects were under. He also fingered the former attorney general as the mastermind of the Watergate operation.

Every week there was something new. The acting director of the FBI stepped down on April 20 after admitting that he had annihilated evidence about Watergate on the advice of Nixon's aides. Ten days later it was the turn of the White House chief of staff and two other presidential liegemen to offer their resignations. It was soon revealed that Hunt and Liddy had broken into the office of the psychiatrist of Daniel Ellsberg, a former Defense Department analyst who had slipped classified Pentagon documents on Vietnam to the *New York Times* in 1969. The two operatives, under directions from White House staffers, were trying to purloin compromising personal information to wreck the credibility of the Vietnam dissenter.

The Senate approved a probe on February 7, 1973, and the televised Erwin Committee Hearings began on May 17. The next day,

Archibald Cox was appointed as the special Watergate prosecutor by the Department of Justice. On June 25, John Dean, the presidential counsel who had resigned on April 30, accused Nixon during the hearings for covering up Watergate and for channeling hush money to those arrested in the burglary. More minatory to the administration, another aide divulged on July 16 the existence of a taping system in the White House. The mystery of the presidential involvement in Watergate could now perhaps be brought to light.

Archibald Cox subpoenaed the White House tapes in early October 1973. Nixon was incompliant; he cited executive privilege. Cox was adamant; he had to have the tapes. John Sirica, the judge presiding over the Watergate trial, intervened and ordered the tapes to be turned over to him so he could examine in camera to decide whether the presidential claim was indeed warranted. Nixon went to court, but his appeal was vanquished as a higher court upheld Sirica's decision on October 12. The president proposed a compromise; he agreed to issue a typed synopsis of the tapes. Cox would not budge and ventilated his disgruntlement at a news conference, whereupon Nixon ventured a more radical way out. On October 20, he instructed Attorney General Elliot Richardson to fire Cox. Richardson refused to carry out the president's order and resigned. His replacement was equally recalcitrant. However, Solicitor General Robert Bork, third in the justice department chain of command, obliged the president.

Cox was out. Yet it was unclear whether Nixon had won more than a Pyrrhic victory. The series of events regarding the firing of the special prosecutor, immediately dubbed as the "Saturday Night Massacre," touched off a paroxysm of protest. Anger was not restricted to Washington. A difficult-to-ascertain number of letters – possibly in the hundreds of thousands – were sent from all around the country to members of Congress and to the White House condemning the presidential fiat. On October 23, the House Judiciary Committee announced an investigation into impeachment charges. In response, Nixon agreed a week later to turn over the tapes. Two of the tapes were missing, however, and an eighteen-and-a-half-minute gap was revealed in one of them on November 21. The White House maintained untenably that Nixon's secretary had inadvertently erased a part of the tape while transcribing it.

In the meantime, the Watergate trial came to an end; six of the defendants were convicted with stiff jail sentences on November 9. Gordon Liddy, who had declined to cooperate with the prosecution, got twenty years. Nixon's morass was deepening. Allegations of wrongdoing of all kinds – some serious, others garden variety – were slung at him daily in the press and the courts. He was blindsided on October 10, 1973, with the resignation of his vice president, Spiro Agnew, who soon pleaded guilty to tax evasion and money laundering. On November 13, the representatives of two oil companies admitted in court to making illegal contributions to Nixon's election campaign. Other firms would later report similar donations. Much more incommodious for the president, on March 17, 1974, the grand jury investigating the Watergate affair indicted seven former Nixon administration officials for conspiracy to obstruct justice. The president himself was named as an unindicted coconspirator. In June, John Ehrlichman, a presidential aide, confessed to his role in the Ellsberg case and was convicted the following month.

And the tape trouble would not go away, either. The Senate Watergate Committee had subpoenaed more tapes and documents from Nixon in late December 1973; Nixon declined to surrender the material on January 4, 1974. In April, the House Judiciary Committee again subpoenaed forty-two tapes. On April 29, 1974, well-nigh two years after the break-in and hard-pressed to hold out any longer, the president offered a 1,200-page edited transcript of the White House tapes. The materials contained no evidence of illegality by the president, but they were flush with foul language and sinister scheming; their release in paperback edition by the major newspapers was a bombshell.

Nevertheless, the new special prosecutor Leon Jaworski and the House Judiciary Committee were not propitiated. They needed the actual tapes – all of them. The issue of executive privilege regarding the tapes had been sitting at the Supreme Court, which eventually ruled on July 24 against the president. The House Judiciary Committee approved two articles of impeachment against Nixon, charging him with obstruction of justice and violating his oath of office. Nixon could no longer stonewall, and, on August 5, he finally released the transcripts of a conversation with his chief of staff, which revealed that six days after the break-in he had ordered the CIA to derail the FBI investigation of Watergate with the pretext that it would interfere with a sensitive intelligence operation. This was the smoking gun, establishing the presidential hand in the cover-up. Nixon's remaining support in the Capitol tailspinned; he resigned on August 9, 1974. Sworn in the same day as the next president, Ford granted Nixon a complete pardon on September 8.

The Watergate scandal was a watershed in U.S. political history. Its very title instantly entered the contemporary political nomenclature as a metonymy of the murky underbelly of Washington. It was in its wake that presidential scandal activity escalated, and it was equally after Watergate that a host of institutional reforms were implemented to clip the abusive potential of the executive branch. Yet this tremendously transformative scandal was not the simple outcome of Nixon's personal sins. The Watergate transgressions, their progressive publicization, and the effects of the scandal as well as the reactions to it were in significant part conditioned by the dormant contradictions of the modern presidency. The modern presidency – with its plescibitary, personalized, and highly visible nature – had always harbored potentially self-undermining tendencies, which both in part enabled Watergate and grew more active in its aftermath. The social and political developments of the 1960s, the implicit contradictions of the modern presidential governance, and the autonomous logic of the scandal process combined to seal Nixon's fate.

## The Transgressions

To understand is not to pardon. There was nevertheless a rhyme and reason to the Watergate transgressions; they were not simply a matter of poor morals or paranoid politics. They were, in part, geared to deal with the problems that the modern presidency ran into with Vietnam. Image became vital to the White House in the twentieth century. As long as presidents could control the way they appeared, their visibility

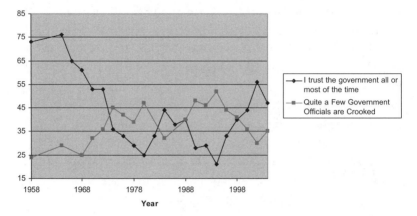

Figure 3.2. Trust in Government – National Election Study Polls.

redounded to their grandeur and only made them more untouchable. And various parties – including the media and even many in the Washington elite – often had incentives to have the presidency appear in a favorable light and keep embarrassing matters out of view. The sixties changed things, however. First, Vietnam exerted direct public costs that were impossible to paper over or spin. Unlike the Korean War, it seemed more and more geopolitically unnecessary and was perceived by the counter-establishment as a veritable moral debacle. Second, this was a time of surging individualism with respect for institutional authority on the decline.

As a result, the percentage of those who reported trusting the government officials all or most of the time declined from 76 percent in 1964 to 53 percent in 1972 (Figure 3.2). The executive branch experienced a similar freefall (Figure 3.3), and Congress and the media lost in part their former discretion and deference to the presidency. Distrust induced presidents to invest more in impression management both in legal and illegal ways.

Nixon had already created in his first term the White House Office of Communications, which tracked the media coverage of the president and his day-to-day standing in the polls and disseminated a line-of-the-day.[58] This development curdled the White House's relationship with journalists, for it also limited access. In any case, the office

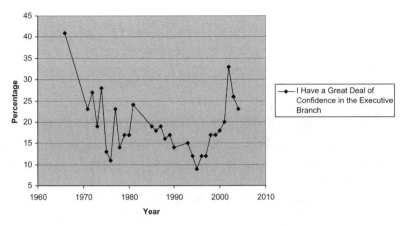

Figure 3.3. Trust in the Executive Branch – Harris Polls.

was an inadequate solution to the public relations problem. What Nixon was mostly concerned – and eventually obsessed – with were leaks, which could easily sabotage the presidential image. The burgeoning public disaffection with Vietnam and negative media attitudes were emboldening disaffected army and state officials, who slipped compromising information about military incompetence, executive duplicity, or war monstrosities to reporters. The publication of the leaked Pentagon Papers by the *New York Times* in 1969 showed that the Nixon administration could check neither the Defense Department nor the media, even when the publicized information was top secret. Despite the fact that the disclosure mainly exposed wrong-headedness in the Johnson administration, the president and his national security advisor Henry Kissinger nevertheless felt that it also crippled their public relations capabilities. Nixon sought an injunction against the *New York Times* on the basis of threat to national security, but the Supreme Court lent its imprimatur to the publication.[59]

The president was resolved not to leave Vietnam with the semblance of debility to Hanoi, but this meant the continuation of an unpopular war. What is more, Nixon was deeply suspicious of career bureaucrats and fumed at the Democratic entrenchment in many executive agencies and departments, particularly at the high levels.

"Every effort is met with resistance, delay, and the threat of deroga-
tory exposure," wrote the rankled president in his *Memoirs*.[60] As
a solution, Nixon put together a counter-bureaucracy that circumvented cabinet secretaries and officials in the control of the main
executive agencies. Leaks would not desist, however. Little was, for
instance, secret about the secret bombings of Cambodia in 1970.
Progressively paranoid and his paranoia either proving partially
founded or bearing its own bugaboos in a self-fulfilling fashion,
Nixon switched to the war mode. The embattled president formed
a unit called the "plumbers" that would be responsible for stanch-
ing leaks and riding herd on confirmed enemies and suspicious aides
alike through wiretapping.

Vietnam encouraged leaks, but the problem is not specific to
Nixon. As we saw, the twentieth-century mode of governance was
built on an expanding presidential staff. On one hand, this aggran-
dizes the presidency. On the other hand, it can make governing a
parlous endeavor. The bigger the White House bureaucracy gets, the
more likely it will leak when things don't go well. In effect, all presidents from Lyndon Johnson during his second term onward would
share Clinton's complaint: "The White House leaked worse than a
tar-paper shack with holes in the roof and gaps in the walls."[61] And
a larger staff not only increases the wherewithal of presidents but
also expands their web of accountability, for the modern presidency
is based on the notion that the incumbent personifies the executive
branch.[62] The tension between the bureaucratic and personal logics
of the presidency is perilous for the incumbents. It is not certain that
Nixon would have given the green light to the Watergate break-in
had he known about it before, but the Oval Office tapes reveal that
even a paranoid president like him had difficulty keeping the actions
of his underlings under check.

The contradictions of the modern presidency, the vulnerabilities
that lurk under its imperial crust, required a cataclysmic event like
Vietnam to come into full play. But one can maybe argue even further:
the very decision to go to war may have had to do with the mode of
governance. Being the leader of the free world, in Cold War parlance,
taxed presidents with quasi-infinite responsibilities and could prompt

them to overplay their hand in the international arena. Some blame Kennedy for having dragged America into the Vietnam quagmire. This may be true. We should bear in mind, however, that there was a strong consensus around the issue at the time. It was none other than the editorial page of the *New York Times* who corrected Kennedy on September 6, 1963, after the president called Vietnam the war of the Vietnamese, and gently goaded him: "But [it is] also our war – a war from which we cannot retreat and which we dare not lose."[63] Hence, the overreach that the United States displayed in Vietnam – as well as the difficulty it experienced in getting out of it – was not altogether independent of the high expectations that Americans have of their modern presidents.

## The Unfolding of Watergate

Let us now consider the publicization of the Watergate crimes, their effects, and the reactions to them. There is no denying that Nixon was unlucky: it was sheer happenstance that the Watergate burglars were caught. And without the revelation of the taping system, Nixon would have ridden out the storm. It is nevertheless impossible to explain his meltdown if we give short shrift to the conjunctural factors that were stacked against him and to the contradictions of modern presidency that were given free rein in the post-Vietnam context. These elements underlie both the revelations against the White House and the public reactions to them.

The flubbed burglary was not at first tied to the president. Most journalists were dismissive of Watergate, which had little effect on the 1972 elections. The whole thing looked like politics as usual and did not immediately affect Nixon, who was fairly popular with his domestic and foreign policies among the "silent majority." Further disclosures began to hurt him, however, and it is necessary to consider the tensions within the administration to understand how they came about. Despite the indubitable intrepidity and tenacity of the *Post* journalists, it is equally clear that they would not have gone far without tips from Mark Felt, a.k.a. Deep Throat, who linked the burglary to the president's men. Felt was the number two man at the

FBI and used Bob Woodward and Carl Bernstein as a cat's paw in the infighting within the organization that broke as a result of Hoover's death.[64] It was therefore in part Nixon's loosened control over this hitherto amenable agency that allowed the scandal progressively to implicate the president.

The president was, of course, the author of egregious wrongdoings. Still, one should not forget that much of what Nixon did had already been done by Kennedy and Johnson. Once Kennedy was in office, Nixon was subjected to an extensive audit by the IRS, and the justice department launched an investigation of his brother. The Kennedy administration had wiretapped reporters, political opponents, and businessmen. Martin Luther King was placed under close electronic surveillance. Hoover had gone along when the Johnson aides asked for certain reporters to be wiretapped.[65] Nixon may have been worse than his predecessors in terms of abuse of presidential power, but this was perhaps because they were not as beleaguered as he was. The presidency was, however, now defanged in part because of Vietnam, and the broad coalition against Nixon would exploit his vulnerability. What had remained secret yesterday – often thanks to an implicit yet widespread collusion – would more likely become public. Charges that would have been brushed aside would now look credible. What had gone accommodated would now look unacceptable.

Nixon endured fierce opposition from the counter-establishment and its allies in the government, all dead opposed to his Vietnam policy. There was significant antagonism from the civil society as well, despite his moderate – liberal by our standards – domestic policies. And Nixon was the first president in 120 years to take office with both houses of Congress controlled by the opposition. Worse, he was not always conciliatory. His attempt to check congressional power with the doctrine of the unlimited impoundment of appropriated funds in 1973 put Democrats in high dudgeon. Besides, the ornery president was now, like all his second-term post-FDR brethrens, a lame duck. A committee in Congress had already tried to mount a probe into Watergate during Nixon's first term, but a majority to vote for subpoena power could not be had. As the president lost part of his bargaining power with the legislative branch after reelection, it became much easier to get the sufficient number for the hearings.[66]

Vietnam does not only underlie the presidential transgressions; it also had an indirect bearing on the attitudes toward them. The failure of the Johnson administration to carry out successfully the Vietnam War, as well as the mounting casualties and widening draft, cankered confidence in public institutions. The civil rights movement and the rising young demographics of the United States[67] fed cynicism about political authority.[68] The percentage of those who trusted the government lapsed from 76 in 1964 to 53 in 1972. In 1958, 24 percent of American believed that the government was run by crooks. This figure rose to 32 percent in 1970 and had reached 36 percent by 1972. Watergate would bring the statistic up to 45 percent (Figure 3.2) – even though there had been no annual increase in the number of indicted federal officials (Figure 3.1). We observe a similar trend in confidence in the executive branch (Figure 3.3).

Declining trust impaired the symbolic armor of the presidency and made Nixon vulnerable. A very high number of Americans from early in the scandal thought that the president was not only lying about the cover-up but that he had actually ordered the break-in. A Gallup poll undertaken near Easter 1973 found that 40 percent of the national sample was of the belief that Nixon knew about the Watergate bugging in advance.[69] The percentage of Americans who believed in some kind of presidential guilt rose from 56 percent on May 11–14 to 76 percent on August 3–6.[70] Arguably, if the government had not already suffered a prestige decline, Nixon's public assurances during the scandal could have been more credible.[71]

Judicial acts were decisive in Nixon's demise; the growing independence of the judiciary, which refused to treat White House as a sacred cow, was an important factor in the unfolding of Watergate.[72] The scandal would have stalled, if not ended, early on had it not been for the uncommonly intemperate twenty-year sentences that Judge Sirica gave to the convicts in January 1973, thereby forcing them to implicate the higher-ups involved in the cover-up in exchange for leniency in the final sentencing. It was only thanks to this extraordinary act that the Watergate conspiracy was exposed. And without the Supreme Court's unanimous decision that Nixon had to release the Oval Office tapes, there would have been no smoking gun.

It is difficult to put forth evidence showing that these judicial moves were conditioned by cynicism about political authority. Yet the Supreme Court had been much more respectful of the privacy of the executive branch earlier in the twentieth century, and it is important to remember that its decision against Nixon was made at a time when the president had little support left in Washington or the nation. In any case, it is clear that the antiauthority climate made it difficult for Nixon to impede the legal process. A ruckus broke out when he fired the special prosecutor investigating Watergate, and a Gallup poll taken at that time found 44 percent of its national respondents favoring impeachment.[73] Yet however ill-advised and cavalier his action was, Nixon was within his legal rights: the special prosecutor was a subordinate member of the executive branch. The act was not unprecedented either. As a matter of fact, two of the four special prosecutors who were assigned to investigate executive wrongdoing prior to Watergate had been dismissed without much ado. In 1875, Grant appointed the first outside prosecutor to look into the St. Louis Whiskey Ring. The result was 253 indictments, including a confidant of the president; Grant sent the prosecutor packing. Similarly in 1952, Truman's attorney general named a Republican special prosecutor to probe misconduct in tax collections. Two months later, the prosecutor was bagged by the attorney general, who was soon replaced by the president with another one who simply shelved the investigation with no public outcry.[74] Nixon's similar assertion of executive authority over law enforcement, in contrast, looked outrageous.

Structural and conjunctural factors did militate against Nixon. Still, things did not have to be divulged the way they did. There was a chance that Nixon could have prevailed. The Oscar Wilde case showed us that scandals have their own internal, path-dependent logic, and accounts of Watergate tend to understate Nixon's buoyancy. The president's support did fluctuate considerably during the scandal. The Erwin committee hearings, in the course of which John

Dean accused Nixon in the Watergate cover-up, had been pernicious to the president, and his job approval ratings dropped from 57 to 32 percent.[75] Yet only a few had impeachment or resignation on their minds when they were over. And the vox populi was far from settled. Immediately after the hearings, 52 percent of those polled reported thinking that they had been beneficial, whereas 41 percent had a negative view of them. The latter thought that the hearings had either been a waste of time or were bad for the morale of the country.[76] There was a rift in the country on the issue of presidential veracity: 38 percent of those polled believed John Dean's denunciation of the president, whereas 25 percent reported not knowing who was truthful.[77]

Nixon had wanted to disassociate himself from the polluting effects of the hearings, so he had declined to testify. However, he addressed the nation afterward in a televised speech on August 15, denying all connection to Watergate. It is unclear whether Americans changed their opinions about the credibility of the president, but the move was nevertheless not bootless. An August 18–20 Opinion Research Corporation survey found that now 54 percent of the public thought that the Senate hearings had hurt the country, and only 29 percent had a favorable view of them. A majority considered the costs of the scandal to outweigh its benefits. In addition, more people sided with Nixon in his refusal to release the White House tapes than against him. The same survey found that 49 percent of those polled believed that the confidentiality between the president and his aides was absolute, against 33 percent who did not. Forty-six percent of Americans thought that forcing the release of the tapes might damage the office of the presidency and the country against the 39 percent who discounted this possibility.[78]

Such figures are striking because at the same time most Americans believed the president was lying. As I mentioned earlier, an Easter 1973 Gallup poll had found 40 percent of Americans thinking that Nixon was responsible for the burglary. The result of another poll conducted in August was that 76 percent of the public believed that the president was guilty in one way or another. However, according to the August 18–20 Harris poll, only 17 percent of Americans wanted him to resign.[79] Around the same time, another Harris poll found that fewer than 50 percent of Americans thought that Nixon should resign "if it were proven that he knew about the bugging."[80] More arrestingly, another survey recorded similar results even when the question's wording was changed to "Nixon should resign if it were proven that he ordered the cover-up."[81] The decline in public confidence made Nixon unbelievable but not impeachable.

The outcome of Watergate had much to do with the scandal's perceived public costs. Congress waited for the general opinion to turn against Nixon before moving to impeach him: behavior in Watergate was influenced by opinion polls, a consequence of the plescibitary legitimacy of modern presidents. And Americans (or rather the Independents and the moderates in both parties) shifted against the president not when they started to think that he was lying but later. The president's stock fell after he had Cox fired. The effects of the Saturday Night Massacre were transitory, however. Five days later, things improved for Nixon. Support for impeachment slid to 28 percent on October 26, and his job approval rating went up to 40 percent[82] – not that bad compared with, say, George W. Bush's approval ratings during his second term, which hovered in the twenties after the 2006 midterm elections.

As long as Nixon could successfully paint his opponents as partisan zealots and as long as he could convince the public of the high costs of the scandal, he could perhaps tough out Watergate. Two-thirds of the national sample simply did not believe Nixon when he claimed that the two critical tapes that the judge demanded never existed. Still, only 10 percent wanted him impeached around the same time.[83] Restraint was not restricted to the public. A poll of House members in November 1973 found the percentage of those supporting impeachment to be 20.[84] Things somewhat worsened for the president after his widely derided November 21 claim that his secretary had erased by mistake some 18 minutes of a crucial conversation on one of the subpoenaed tapes. Yet the end of the year polls showed 56 percent of the Independents and 79 percent of the Republicans opposing impeachment.[85] The situation was definitely not rosy for the president; his credibility was in tethers both among the public and the Washington elite. Nevertheless, this did not translate into a consensus on impeachment.

When did the tide irrevocably turn against Nixon? The stalemate over the tapes paralyzed the government in the first months of 1974. It seemed more and more that the scandal had to be resolved one way or another, and deferring to legal authority would be the simplest solution. Moreover, the economic situation deteriorated in 1974 and adversely affected Nixon's approval ratings. Here, too, Nixon was a victim of the modern mode of presidential governance, which makes presidents' popularity contingent on things – especially economic factors and dramatic international events – that are often beyond their control.[86] Time was working against Nixon with a growing number of Republicans becoming convinced that it might after all be better for the country and their party if the president stepped down. Realizing this and to assuage his opponents, Nixon released the White House transcripts. The material did not reveal any specific legal transgressions, but their underworld tenor and shabby content – ironically put in bold relief by the ubiquitous editorial note "expletive deleted" – imposed on the public all the specifics of the way executive sausage is made in the Oval Office.

There is no reason to think that most Americans were really surprised at what they read. Politics is assumed to be dirty. The unavoidable publicity of how business is done in the White House, however, made the pretense of the dignity of the presidency impossible to uphold – even by those (Independents and moderate Republicans) who would have preferred to be able to subscribe to this useful myth. Nixon was now not only expendable, but an albatross. A Harris poll taken in the aftermath of the release of the transcripts found that, for the first time, a plurality of Americans supported impeachment and removal.[87] Congress intensified its demands as popular support for Nixon fell. The House Judiciary Committee steeled its resolve in the battle over evidence, and Congress moved against Nixon after the release of the transcripts by starting the formal impeachment procedure. In the last week of July, the House Judiciary Committee voted to recommend three articles of impeachment against the president (obstruction of justice, abuse of power, and contempt of

Congress). The coup de grace was fired by the Supreme Court, which came down 8–0 on the side of the Watergate prosecutor Jaworski in his demands for the tapes. Nixon had no choice but to succumb and produce the smoking gun. Tapped out of his remaining support in Washington, the president tendered his resignation to prevent his inescapable ouster.

In retrospect, for many, Watergate looked like a legal matter: Nixon resigned when the damning evidence surfaced. Yet, as I have argued, without his vulnerabilities and the opposition he faced, things could have turned out very differently for Nixon. It is far from inconceivable that faced with the same issue in a different time, Eisenhower or Kennedy would be able to claim executive privilege successfully. In any case, the president had already decisively lost support from both Washington and the public with the release of the White House transcripts, and Congress had already moved against him, with a majority wanting his head, before he produced the tapes.

## The Presidency after Watergate

The relative degradation of the presidency, which made it vulnerable to moral attack, was an enabling condition of Watergate. Yet once it broke and ended the way it did, Watergate profaned the White House even further and contributed to the ensuing scandal culture. There are three main factors that can degrade political authority. The first is the waning prestige of the political elite. Sanctioning a politician will be costly for the public or deemed unnecessary if the citizen feels that the one who is being accused is rendering a useful service. Or, because scandals often do not entail full proof of wrongdoing, the citizen might be more inclined to give the politician under fire the benefit of the doubt. If the political elite in general are performing poorly, however, or if they are stricken by rising and difficult-to-meet expectations, the reverence that the public will have for political institutions will suffer as well – thereby decreasing the immunity of those who represent them. Besides, the declining performance of political actors will make audiences less tolerant of their transgressions, minor or major. Finally, the lower the prestige of the political elite, the less credible are the defenses of politicians ensnared in scandals. We already saw these mechanisms at work in the case of American presidents, and the next chapter provides another illustration in the French context.

Degradation can also result from the decline of the real or perceived public dependence on political institutions. Italy provides us with a good example. High levels of clientelist corruption were condoned for decades until a deluge of corruption scandals swamped the country in the early nineties and decimated the political elite. Five hundred and twenty members of the parliament and the heads of all the major parties were indicted. The anticorruption campaign called the *Mani pulite*, during which scandals broke one after another, was not the simply consequence of financial wrongdoing by politicians. Corruption had been high all along in the postwar Italian political system, which pitted a coalition headed by the Christian Democrats against a powerful Communist Party in the opposition. Financial skullduggery by the mainstream parties was long abided, for its exposure would only help the extreme left. With the fall of the Berlin Wall, however, the tolerance lost its raison d'être and the sociopolitical conditions for prosecutorial activism were met.[88] Scandals, just like revolutions, are more likely to plague institutions that are either already ailing or have lost their former importance for their constituencies.

The third factor is increasing transparency. There are several ways in which surveillance can either undermine political authority or boost scandal activity in a more direct fashion. Even though beefed-up surveillance can discourage wrongdoing, it also makes it easier to make public a great deal of suspect behavior. It can be difficult to verify whether what is publicized is criminal or even immoral, but this will not necessarily prevent scandals from happening in a context in which the implicated institutions have low prestige – hence low credibility – in the public eye. Furthermore, increased transparency makes political actors and institutions more assailable because the control that an entity has over its self-representation is positively correlated with the sacredness that is accorded by the others to it.[89] Transparency levels political institutions and renders politicians

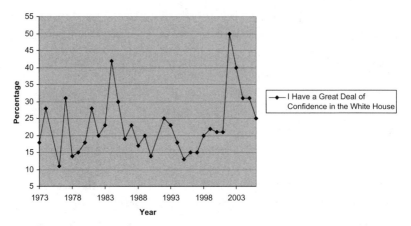

Figure 3.4. Trust in the Presidency after Watergate – Harris Poll.

familiar – worthy of contempt. Finally, heightened surveillance will expand the capabilities of actors with vested interests to sustain scandal activity, such as congressional investigative committees, special prosecutors, advocacy groups, and watchdog organizations.[90]

The three processes underlying the degradation of political authority can interact. Low confidence after Vietnam and Watergate justified surveillance on the presidency, and the combination of these two factors greatly enhanced scandal activity. Let us empirically consider the degradation-scandal relationship in the post-Watergate context.

Obviously, the presidency did not lose all its imperial capabilities – far from it. These could be unleashed full throttle in conjunctures marked by real or perceived foreign threat. And expectations from presidents remained high. Yet on the whole the declining public confidence in the institution encouraged normative aggression on presidents and made allegations against them more credible.[91] In 1959, 61 percent of Americans believed the presidency to be the part of government that knew best, and only 17 percent wanted to accord Congress this honor. In 1977, the public favored Congress 58 percent to 26 percent – but the legislative glory was short-lived as confidence in Congress fell sharply in the eighties and started to do worse than the White House.[92] The graphs charting trust in the presidency (see Figure 3.4), executive branch (see Figure 3.3), and government in general (see Figure 3.2) show the low prestige with which post-Watergate state institutions had to grapple. There are two significant upturns, in the early 1980s and in 2001. Yet they are both temporary, and they both have to do with some kind of international security matter, which usually generates a passing rally-around-the-flag effect.

Of course, not all post-Watergate presidents have been unpopular, all the time. Presidents usually take office with very high approval ratings, which in any case tend to be higher than the trust in the White House. Nevertheless, the office came to be distrusted, and presidents found that they were no longer protected by the institutional aura of the presidency. The low confidence in the White House drove down the threshold of the amount of evidence required to make an efficient allegation, even in the case of a popular president like Clinton. Consider the disruptive effects of a scandal like Whitewater – it ultimately led to the Lewinsky affair after Senate hearings and many years of independent counsel investigation – that was based on little legal evidence.[93] Low confidence magnified the significance of the peccadilloes of all executive branch officials. An example is the case of Carter's chief of staff, Hamilton Jordan, who was pursued by a special prosecutor in 1978 for a single alleged incident of cocaine use on the sole basis of the testimony of a shady character already convicted for tax fraud and drug dealing.[94]

Presidents came to be routinely second-guessed in the new context of suspicion. Take the case of Gerald Ford, who pardoned Nixon after he took office. This was apparently not an easy decision. Ford seems to have believed that Nixon's conviction would undermine the image of the nation; it would be better if the county moved on. Even Bob Woodward, the Watergate sleuth, would later come to agree that Ford acted sagaciously.[95] But it was hard for the president to signal the purity of his motivation; it was widely suspected that he had promised Nixon a pardon before his resignation in exchange for the presidency. The pardon was seen as yet another scandal, and Ford never recovered from it. Watergate weakened the new president's authority over his cabinet, too. One of its consequences was that, in April 1975, his defense secretary James Schlesinger could openly disobey Ford in a foreign policy crisis when the president commanded him to send aircrafts for strikes against Cambodia as retaliation for the seizure of a commercial vessel.[96]

Presidents found themselves deprived of some of their formal prerogatives. The War Powers Resolution of 1973 forbade presidents to commit American troops anywhere abroad for more than thirty days without congressional approval. The Hughes-Ryan Amendment of 1974 required the executive branch to inform Congress of covert operations. The Budget and Impounding Act of the same year decreased presidential power in the legislative process. It was in part due to their diminished capacities that some presidents resorted to illegality in the realm of foreign affairs in the post-Watergate era. When such acts were exposed, as in the Iran-Contra affair, they created major scandals.

The low confidence in the presidency imposed unparalleled moral correctness on presidents. Jimmy Carter ran his presidential campaign in 1976 by setting an unprecedented standard that could not be but scandalously fallen short of: he promised never to lie to the public. The president also supported a stringent conflict of interest legislation, which required his cabinet members to make full public financial disclosures and divest themselves of holdings liable to pose potential conflicts of interest. The Ethics in Government Statute passed in 1978 limited campaign contributions and regulated the jobs that ex-public officials could take as well as the government lobbying they could do. The establishment of the Public Integrity Section made it easier to prosecute public officials by the new inspectors general who report directly to Congress. The first victim of Carter's defensive moralization was the administration itself. Bert Lance, the director of the Office of Management and Budget and a former banker, had to resign after Senate hearings and the special prosecutor investigation of an alleged financial indiscretion. Lance was eventually absolved, but the scandal impaired the Carter presidency: one legacy of Watergate was that the alleged transgressions of cabinet members and aides bore heavy on the president. The president's poll numbers fell thirteen points.

By enveloping the presidency in a miasma of suspicion, Watergate revved up scandal activity by spawning novel surveillance institutions. Presidents became obliged to render detailed accounts to the law, to various political and societal agencies, and to the press. Transparency, the putative panacea to corruption, however, only augmented the frequency of scandals by pushing into the open all kinds of dubious (but not necessarily criminal) activity among those connected to the president and by further profaning the White House. Transparency also gave rise to and bolstered entities that thrive on scandal.

It is difficult to overstate the last point. Perhaps the most consequential surveillance reform of the post-Watergate era was the Special Prosecutor Provision of the Ethics in Government Act of 1978, which remained operative until 1999. According to this provision, in the event of an allegation of misconduct against an executive official, the attorney general, so as to preclude the appearance of a conflict of interest, had to ask a panel of senior federal judges to appoint a special prosecutor (after 1982, an independent counsel) to continue the investigation. These judges, picked by the chief of the Supreme Court, did not have to account publicly for their decisions.[97] The prosecutors could be removed from their inquiries only for grossly improper behavior and only with the permission of the panel that appointed them. The provision gave free rein and expansive berth to these legal officials, who could determine how long their investigations would take, had access to unlimited resources, and dispensed with the accountability problems and financial constraints of regular prosecutors. With such action capabilities, they could undertake cases normal prosecutors would not touch. The Lewinsky scandal, which I analyze in Chapter 5, revealed that there were few limits to what they could probe.

The investigations undertaken by these legal actors were much more public than the usual pursuits by regular prosecutors: whereas the latter take most of their decisions in private, all independent counsel reports had to be publicized. The media could thus pick up items in their reports that did not later become part of indictments. The investigations also tended to last a long time, and their high-profile status pressed these legal officials to come up with something lest they be seen as irresponsible. In any case, early ends to probes were often seen by clamorous pundits in the media as cover-ups or derelictions of duty. Consider how the *New York Times* editorial page railed against Kenneth Starr for "selfish indifference to his important civic obligations" when the independent counsel announced on February 17, 1997, that he would terminate the Whitewater investigation, which had been going on for four years with no results, to become the dean of the law school at Pepperdine University. The scolding was effective. Starr went back to work and helped unleash the Lewinsky affair onto the American public sphere the following year.

These freewheeling prosecutors were appointed for twenty investigations from 1978 to 1999.[98] One could have terminated Reagan's presidency; his secretary of defense was eventually indicted. Another investigation ended in the impeachment of Clinton. Few executive officials implicated in the probes were convicted, but reputations were nevertheless traduced, at least temporarily. Here is the tally of those investigated or targeted: three presidents, one first lady, one attorney general, a former assistant attorney general, several chiefs of staff, and six cabinet secretaries. The probes took progressively longer; some lasted as long as eight years. Although the first ones focused on targets set by the justice department, the later ones tended to rove, both in terms of charges and suspects. The independent counsel staff size also ballooned and reached 100 in Kenneth Starr's investigation of the Lewinsky affair in 1998. Investigations disrupted the political process but also increasingly became a regular feature of it.

The new act had its provenance in the disgrace of the executive branch (and in particular, the presidency), which was no longer entrusted with its own monitoring. Its intention was to depoliticize law enforcement, but it had a contrary effect. There were no protections in the law against the politically motivated decisions by the counsels and the judges who selected them. So paradoxically the law widened the field of politics by allowing judges and prosecutors into it and contributed to the legalization of political life, as well as to the politicization of the judiciary.[99] Even when the prosecutors and the judges who picked them acted with pure legal motives, since these were usually actors with a political identity or past, they had difficulty convincing the public of the legitimacy of their acts.

Congress stoked up its oversight activity in the wake of Watergate as well. The 1970s witnessed staffs in the House triple in size, and those in the Senate doubled.[100] Hearings in 1975–6 dredged up all sorts of unsavory executive operations including CIA assassination plans, involuntary drug testing, and domestic spying. Congressional surveillance went unabated in the 1980s and 1990s, especially with the routinization of divided government, which allowed the legislature to micromanage the executive agencies.[101] The two most disruptive presidential scandals of the post-Watergate era occurred in a time of divided government. I analyze the Lewinsky case in the fifth chapter, but briefly consider the Iran-Contra affair. It was only after the Democratic victory in 1986 that Congress took action on claims regarding secret shipments of weapons from Israel to Iran. The Iran-Contra hearings, modeled on Watergate, were very much geared to implicate the president directly. The emphasis was therefore placed on the diversion of funds to the Contras and not on the sales to Iran for hostage trade.[102]

The polarization in American politics aggravated the presidential plight. Partisan roll calls (votes in which a majority of Republicans in Congress line up against a majority of Democrats) rose from 37 percent in the 1970s to 61 percent in the 1990s and reached 67 percent in 2006 for the Senate.[103] Even though polarization began its ascent in the mid-1960s, in a time marked by race riots, the free speech movement, and Vietnam,[104] it is not altogether independent of the modern presidential governance. The binding presidential primaries that were established after 1968, which flowed from the plescibitary logic of the presidency, not only furthered the autonomy of presidents from their parties. They also split parties into factions and cliques dominated by radicals and hence were a factor in polarization.[105] But it is important to note that political and cultural polarization is an elite phenomenon; there seems to be no evidence of a parallel process at the mass level.[106]

Presidential capability to assert executive privilege was significantly curtailed after Watergate. Congress successfully demeaned all such claims as ruses to conceal wrongdoing. Presidents had to disclose even personal documents if need be. Reagan, for instance, turned in his diaries during the Iran-Contra investigations, even though the 1974 Supreme Court decision in *United States v. Nixon* had not compelled presidents to comply with congressional subpoenas. Transparency extended to all the members of the executive branch as the administrations were forced to make their internal records available to the public. The Freedom of Information Act of 1974 required agencies to respond to citizen requests for information within ten working days. The Government in the Sunshine Act, passed in 1976, opened federal agency deliberations to public scrutiny.

The modern presidency, given its plescibitary dimension, had always been heavily reliant on public relations. The declining trust in their office prodded presidents to invest even more in impression management. A substantial part of post-Watergate White House activity therefore has to do with presentational rather than substantive functions. During the Carter administration, it was estimated that more than 30 percent of the forty-nine White House assistants were dedicated to dealing with the media.[107] Constant polling to monitor the image of the presidency and its incumbent became an integral part of governance; Clinton reportedly spent $2 million on it in 1993.[108] The imperative to damage control while being second-guessed at every turn can, however, both draw resources from presidents and make them prey to accusations of inauthenticity.[109]

Since the seventies, journalists have lost their former reverence for presidential authority, especially during campaigns or when the economy is doing poorly. A recent study that focused on the coverage of the Reagan, Clinton, and Bush administrations in 1981, 1993, and 2001, respectively, found that the percentage of positive coverage by the *New York Times* and *Washington Post* has been 40, 39, and 36 percent, respectively.[110] These figures are lower for the White House and its staff (26, 39, and 37 percent) and even worse for the executive branch (24, 22, and 24 percent).[111] The positive coverage of presidential aspirants slumped from the sixties onward.[112] In 1960, 75 percent of coverage was positive; this statistic dropped to 40 percent in 1992. These figures are highly relevant because the sitting president is often one of the presidential candidates and because the campaigning period has lengthened in recent years.

Advances in communication technology have also had important consequences. The pullulating news sources and the establishment of the twenty-four-hour news-cycle boost competitive impulses and encourage ideological coverage with lessened concern to appeal to the center of the political spectrum. Demand for scandal stories, the production costs of which are usually low, thus hikes. Another signal development is the blogosphere, which has decreased the cost of and the decency threshold for publicizing discreditable information about high-status politicians, including presidents.

All of these factors combined in the 1980s and 1990s to yield high levels of executive branch scandal activity, which affected the presidency in varying degrees. More than 100 administration officials were accused of criminal or ethical misconduct during the two terms of the Reagan's presidency. Attorney General Edwin Meese was investigated in connection with the Wedtech scandal by an independent counsel and resigned in July 1988. The secretary of interior was convicted in the Department of Housing and Urban Development's grant-rigging affair for defrauding the government out of money intended for low-income housing. In the Iran-Contra affair, many staffers, including two national security advisors, were convicted with a host of charges including conspiracy and lying to Congress. Independent Counsel Lawrence Walsh indicted Caspar Weinberger, Reagan's secretary of defense, five and a half years after the investigation began. There was a good possibility that Walsh could have also indicted Reagan had he not been very ill.[113] The scandal contributed to Bush's electoral defeat in 1992. The president was slightly ahead in the polls until the Weinberger indictment, which occurred days before the 1992 elections, spawning suspicions about the truthfulness of Bush's own Iran-Contra account.

The Clinton years were remarkably rocky. The post-Watergate legal degradation of the White House touched its nadir with the Supreme Court's unanimous 1997 ruling in the Paula Jones sexual harassment case, which made the president answerable to a civil suit while in office, just like any other citizen. The outcome of this judicial demotion – blessed by the *New York Times*, *Nation*, and Fox News alike – was the Lewinsky scandal, which had Clinton impeached. In addition, the president found himself ensnared in (1) Whitewater, which revolved around allegations of real estate fraud; (2) Cattlegate, which involved the first lady's cattle futures that earned questionably high returns; (3) Travelgate, in which the administration was battered for firing the members of the White House travel office; (4) Filegate, which broke with the charges that the White House had improperly obtained FBI files on more than 900 individuals, some of them prominent Republicans; (5) the Paula Jones sexual harassment case, in which the president was the defendant; and (6) the campaign finance scandal, during which the White House was accused of receiving illegal donations from foreign operatives and Asian-American donors. These scandals gave rise to hostile congressional hearings and probes by independent counsels. Clinton was routinely pounded in the media for all kinds of misconduct. Not all the charges were run-of-the-mill: the editorial page of the *Wall Street Journal* linked Clinton to the suicide of his former lawyer Vince Foster.

Clinton was legally assailable, but this did not mean he could not survive his scandals. Despite the general assumption of guilt in most of these affairs and despite the fact that the presidency itself did not inspire much confidence, the public ratings of Clinton's job performance, mainly thanks to the healthy economy, stayed high. Scandals could easily break against him and disrupt governance, but Clinton had the gumption, luck, and popular accommodation to fight them.

## Imperial Tendencies in the 2000s

The declining trust in government and intensifying surveillance relatively profaned the modern presidency and rendered it more scandal-prone after the seventies. Yet, as I pointed out, there is another factor affecting presidential vulnerability: the perceived public dependency on the president. The higher the dependency, the more immune the president. Dependency is higher when foreign affairs come to fore, and this is why even after Watergate presidents retained most of their imperial prerogatives in this domain. The War Powers Resolution of 1973 remained a dead letter. Even though the relationship between the presidents and the press became frostier after Vietnam and Watergate, journalists are inclined put on kid gloves in White House press conferences about foreign policy issues.[114] Presidential immunity is relatively high in times of war – as long as things are not going too badly. Reagan during the invasion of Granada and his successor during the first Gulf War were both granted a high level of latitude in controlling and framing media coverage.[115] Both presidents enjoyed soaring approval ratings during these times, this giving especially Reagan much-needed respite and protection from moral attacks on the White House staff and his administration.

It is thus clear why scandal activity regarding the presidency flagged during the first term of George W. Bush. The attacks on the Twin Towers on September 11, 2001, afforded the president significant exemption against congressional and media oversight during his first term because they increased the public's perceived dependence on its leader. Trust in the White House, according to the Harris poll, went from 21 percent in 2001 to 50 percent in 2002, and the president's job approval figures reached the high 80s. Fifty percent might not seem high, but it is nevertheless a striking lift with no equal in the previous forty years. September 11 and the "War on Terror" made everything else trifling in comparison, and the president, transformed into the commander-in-chief, was consistently given the benefit of the doubt in the response to the event. Congress and the media were again complaisant in the run-up to the Iraq War; few consequentially contested the official casus belli, the alleged weapons of mass destruction in Iraq.

Presidential privacy expanded after September 11. Shortly after the attack on the Twin Towers, on November 1, 2001, President George W. Bush issued an executive order to extend vastly the purlieu of communication privileges available to sitting and former presidents. Under the new regime, former presidents may claim executive privilege over their own papers, even if the current incumbent disagrees. Contrariwise, sitting presidents are given the right to assert executive privilege over the papers of a past administration, regardless of the former incumbent's wishes. The order requires those who seek access to presidential records to show a "demonstrated, specific need." Thanks to the Executive Order 13233, the Bush White House was able to overturn the Presidential Records Act of 1978, which had stipulated that the records of former presidents are federal property and need to be made accessible to the public within twelve years after leaving office.

September 11 also provided the president with an ability to undertake a sizeable executive "power grab."[116] Bush found it much easier to resort to secrecy and to ignore congressional intent in the execution of laws. He used signing statements to curb the powers of the inspectors general who report to Congress on the Iraqi occupation. In all this, the president was greatly aided by the end of divided government in the first six years of his presidency and by the fact that the independent counsel provision was left to expire in 1999. The pressure on the executive branch was significantly alleviated.

But as most Americans began to see the Iraq War as a fiasco in the second term (with the Middle Eastern country imploding into a civil war), imperial acts by the executive branch that could formerly be justified and those that remained secret are increasingly made public and condemned. The Democratic capture of Congress in 2006 obviously made things worse for the president. The resumption of scandal activity in the second term – the fallout from the Abu Ghraib affair, the revelations about warrantless wiretapping of domestic calls by the government, the Katrina debacle, and the donnybrook over the firing of federal prosecutors, among others – should not come as a surprise. There is reason to think that the leak scandal, which led to the conviction of the chief of staff to Vice President Dick Cheney and eventually to the resignation of presidential counsel Karl Rove, would not have reached the intensity it did if the war were going better in Iraq. Even though Scooter Libby was convicted only for lying, in the eyes of much of the media and the Democrats, the investigation and the trial were a moral indictment of the administration's decision to go to war in Iraq on false premises. These executive scandals did not all have to do directly with the White House but still undermined the president in various ways. Bush fils has been luckier than his predecessors, but the presidency is far from having shed its susceptibilities to scandal.

An important question that arises out of the analysis offered in this chapter is whether the low trust in the presidency and the multiplication of presidential scandals reveal a legitimacy crisis in the American political system. I don't think so. Degradation of their institutional authority makes life more difficult for presidents and renders governing harder. And a certain level of trust in public institutions is a public good. But the profanation of the presidency, which is always a question of degree, has some positive effects as well. The inviolability that sheathed Kennedy's Camelot had symbolic benefits for the public, but it also enabled a great deal of reckless behavior by the president, which could have easily resulted in a major calamity. If the American public had been more cynical about the presidency earlier on in the 1960s, Vietnam might have been averted – or at least fought differently.

In any case, cynicism about government was the norm in much of U.S. history, and a return to this attitude hardly signifies a loss of legitimacy. Presidents may have lost certain legal and institutional protections, but their approval ratings are not always low. In fact, presidents tend to start out with very high poll numbers, which tend to fall gradually, the process reflecting the extent of popular expectations from presidents. A 1996 ABC News poll found that 83 percent of Americas believe that "Whatever its faults, United States has the best system of government in the world."[117] Some political scientists have argued that government has suffered a decline in confidence during the past forty years even as it has become more efficient in almost every aspect.[118] Hence, one cause for the declining prestige of the governmental institutions may be the unrealistic public expectations as to what they can accomplish.[119]

Finally, the fact that presidential scandals break easily does not mean that they always end in sanctions. In fact, as allegations about presidents become more and more a routine element of political life, their impact tends to decline. There is in fact a trade-off, a negative relationship between the intensity and the frequency of political scandals. One reason why there are more scandals is because they are less intense. If the anticipated collective costs of presidential scandals were very high (as it was the case at the height of the imperial presidency during the Cold War), we would have fewer of them.

# FOUR

# Investigating Corruption in France

POLITICAL SCANDAL activity spiked to record highs during the 1990s in France. According to the statistics of the ministry of justice, the number of annual convictions in corruption cases more than doubled between 1990 and 1999 from 133 to 286.[1] At least 900 elected officials were placed under investigation for corruption and related charges from 1992 to 2002.[2] This figure includes fifty-three former or sitting ministers; one former prime minister; the presidents of the Constitutional Council and the National Assembly; more than 100 members of the parliament; a quarter of all the big city mayors; and six former or current leaders of political parties. Hundreds of top executives, including ten CEOs of the forty largest companies in France, found themselves as the targets of high-profile legal pursuits. The scandals of the nineties ensnared all the major parties and rooted out the illegal ways in which political life has been financed during the Fifth Republic (1958–).

Despite this explosion, there is little reason to think that French politicians grew more corrupt in the 1990s. The illegal financial practices that were exposed had in effect been hitherto very common, tolerated, and rarely subject to judicial pursuits. Many of the illegal activities that were made public dated from the 1980s. The investigation, exposure, and public allegation of political corruption are often risky acts with anticipated returns. The corruption affairs of the 1990s erupted from the high-profile investigations by the French investigating magistrates, and I analyze here how and why these low-level legal officials resorted to scandal as well as the conditions that enabled them.[3] This will require an examination of the relationship between the judiciary and the political elite in France. The French case will also provide us with another case of the increasing vulnerability of Western politicians to legal attacks. But I have a more general objective, too: to study the strategic use of scandal, the logic of which strongly shapes moral crusades and political purges. I am particularly concerned with the conditions for undertaking successful normative attacks against the high and mighty – an issue that has obvious importance if we want to understand social conflict and political contention.

## Norm Entrepreneurship

Howard Becker coined the term "moral entrepreneurs" to refer to those who make, promote, and enforce norms. He differentiated between two types within this category: those who create and champion new rules and those who are assigned to enforce them once they have been established. It was, however, the first type who was for him the quintessential moral entrepreneur.[4] Becker suggested that rule-enforcers (which he equated mainly with police officers) maintain a dispassionate professional attitude toward their work and are interested in practical issues. Subsequent sociological work has similarly studied the motivations, class bases, and activities of moral crusaders in civil society who advocate novel norms.[5]

Moral entrepreneurs, rebaptized as "norm entrepreneurs" by Cass Sunstein, have in recent years captured the attention of legal scholars as well.[6] Defining these agents as those "who are interested in changing social norms,"[7] jurists have focused on their incentives and impact. This literature, like recent sociological studies,[8] has a tendency to treat social norms separately from laws. For legal scholars and sociologists alike, norm entrepreneurs are usually either charismatic individuals (e.g., Martin Luther King or Catherine MacKinnon) or social movements (e.g., the Temperance movement).

Enterprising norm work in society is, however, not restricted to the generation of new rules. In fact, it often revolves around legal or social norms that are already established (codified or discursively upheld) but underenforced. Pushing for heightened enforcement can be seen as entrepreneurship not only because the potency of a norm is a function of actual adherence to it but also to the extent that the crusade presents risks as well as potential benefits for its instigators. And this kind of entrepreneurship is not solely embarked on by political or civil society actors but also by legal officials. Prosecutors, for example, act as norm entrepreneurs seeking political profit and taking variable levels of risk when they set up enforcement priorities – when, for instance, they decide to allocate more resources to combat certain crimes at the expense of others. Such acts are justified by the democratic legitimacy of their authors and balanced with their political accountability. Lower-level enforcement actors, who are neither elected officials nor political appointees, on the other hand, are, in principle, expected merely to do their well-circumscribed jobs, render accounts to superiors, observe due process, and apply the laws made by others without zeal.

But this does not always happen. In this chapter I present a case where relatively low-status legal officials engage in norm entrepreneurship through scandal. Journalists, politicians, advocacy groups, watchdog organizations, social movements, individual whistleblowers, and artists often resort to scandal. If they are presented with an auspicious incentive and opportunity structure, legal officials may do the same as well – even if the integrity of the judicial process itself may have to be sacrificed along the way.

## Scandal and Norm Entrepreneurship

Two main properties of scandal differentiate it from law as social control and underlie its strategic use. First, in a scandal, the denouncer of a transgressor appeals directly to the public: popular, and not legal, justice is frequently exercised in scandals.[9] Lawful yet immoral behavior as well as illegal yet difficult-to-prove infractions can be chastised by an effective public denunciation. A consequential scandal about an unlawful act takes much less evidence than is required in a court of law. A forceful denunciation can be enough provided that the public is receptive, and the ensuing discredit and social sanctions heaped on the alleged offender can, in many instances, be more devastating than legal punishment. Appealing directly to the public can also skirt the exigencies and fastidious technicalities of criminal procedure. This is why scandal can prove serviceable to punish offenses such as corruption that evade prosecution due to practical and political reasons.

Second, as against the individualism of law, the logic of scandal is collectivistic. The publicized transgressions of elites are not only salient but strongly implicate the groups and institutions they represent. The effects of such scandals are further boosted when the accused party is deeply embedded in the group that the violated norm targets, especially if this collective bears the onus for its own monitoring. These factors result in high information costs for outsiders in verifying and localizing blame, making it arduous to winnow the wayward members of the target group from its scrupulous ones. Hence, the discredit that is generated by a single yet effective allegation can be extended to associates. A rapid concatenation of such allegations can set off a bandwagon effect as well, making subsequent charges at once cheaper to make and more credible. The general discredit engendered by similar scandals cropping up seriatim might compel the group of the accused to adopt novel measures to signal trustworthiness.

The collectivist logic of scandals then makes them a good strategy both for attacking groups and organizations. At the same time, a string of scandals with similar themes will obey the rule of diminishing returns. A moral crusade will suffer even more if the scandals that it comprises start to exert high costs on the public and if the norm entrepreneurs run into hurdles in signaling impartiality. The dynamics described in this paragraph hold exceptionally for political scandals.

Here, I first study the underenforcement of anticorruption laws in France during the Fifth Republic. Then I discuss the relationship between the French judiciary and the executive as well as the role of the investigating magistrates within the legal system. Third, I show how these legal actors, by taking advantage of the tanking prestige of the political elite, zeroed in on high-status politicians and publicized their corruption investigations during the nineties through leaks and other scandal-generating techniques. The use of scandal helped the investigating magistrates circumvent the political pressures on the judicial process and the niceties of criminal procedure, discredited the political elite as a whole, and forced the latter to adopt anticorruption measures. Fourth, I consider the effects of the scandals on the political elite and the judiciary. Traditionally subordinate to the executive branch, the French judiciary mobilized around the corruption scandals and, for the first time since the Revolution, acquired relative independence and enhanced status. Finally, I consider how the crusade lost much of its force in the 2000s, in great part due to the rising public costs of the scandals and the declining capability of the judges to appear unbiased.

## Corruption in France

A good deal of political finance in twentieth-century France was illegal.[10] Most mainstream politicians and parties relied on sub rosa cash donations from corporations and wealthy individual financiers, whereas Communists enjoyed munificent assistance from the Soviet Union. One common monetary source for all were kickbacks from procurement contracts, funneled usually through consulting firms issuing bogus or inflated invoices or through municipal public service offices headed by party officials. Some local officials used the publicly funded voluntary associations that they controlled to subsidize their political activities. In addition, many politicians and parties were the recipients of clandestine payments from state-owned corporations. Even the Matignon (the prime minister's office) was not exempt from questionable practices. Secret cash funds have been traditionally doled out to the members of the cabinet. Not intended for election or private purposes, there has been virtually no control over the use of such monies.

Norm underenforcement stems from practical, political, or ideological factors – or from their combination, as was in the case of anticorruption laws in France before the 1990s. It is simply hard to prosecute a corruption case successfully, for it consists of a consensual exchange, often extended in time, between a public official and a private citizen. There are no or few witnesses. And the generalization of illegality within the political elite decreases the likelihood that insiders would come forth with evidence. Sophisticated techniques such as the use of intermediaries, counterfeit invoices, and offshore accounts make venal exchanges all the more difficult to track down. Finally, corruption has indirect victims, and the cost that each citizen incurs individually from it is a modicum; there are few incentives to do something about it. Its victims are diffuse, and, until the nineties, there were few civil society associations in France to represent them.

The underenforcement of anticorruption laws in France was also a solution to the contradictions between the official values and practical realities of French democracy.[11] Jacobinism, the warp and woof of Gallic political culture and organization, is characterized by a strong state and a distrust of all private interests and groups, including parties.[12] The presidential system that France adopted in 1958 further devalued the standing of political parties, which could claim no real legal status until 1990 and were subjected to the 1901 law on associations. Public support was nominal: all private donations unlawful.[13] With the exception of the Communist Party, the frequently impermanent French political parties have been feeble organizations with few civil society moorings. So membership dues, their main legal source of revenue, were always inadequate.[14]

Not surprisingly, from Clemenceau to de Gaulle to Mitterrand, the French political parties and candidates made do with illegal funds. The problem was worsened in the seventies and eighties when politics grew prohibitively expensive with the accelerated electoral cycle and expanded reliance on media. The mimetic normalization of illegal practices within the political system was the outcome. But French corruption was mostly "gray corruption:"[15] it incorporated a host of practices that were not deemed uniformly reprehensible. When allegations of wrongdoing were made, the public, which was not altogether unaware of the financial foundation of their democracy but was nevertheless loath to support political parties with its taxes, by and large, looked away.

The underenforcement of anticorruption laws in France had properly political causes as well. The mechanisms of corruption control were otiose in the Fifth Republic until the late nineties. Surveillance agencies such as the Cour des Comptes or the Inspection des Finances had little independence from the executive. Nor did they have much muscle to monitor the members of the National Assembly. There was almost no public inspection of party finances before the reforms of the nineties. Devoid of a legal identity, parties did not have to disclose their sources of revenue or expenses.

The French legislative has had restricted oversight capabilities over the executive branch; fishy financial practices by governments have thus been ensconced from public scrutiny under the cloak of raison d'État. In the French political system, the cabinet is accountable only to the president and not to the National Assembly.[16] Nor do the parliamentarians have strong incentives to keep tabs on the executive branch. Most of them hold multiple offices. It is not uncommon for a deputy to be a mayor as well as the president of a local association such as the housing commission. The main goal of the members of the parliament has been to consolidate their mandate through favors from the executive branch, and a good deal of financial legerdemain transpires at the municipal level where funds necessary for reelection to the National Assembly can be illegally procured.[17]

Finally, the executive dominion over the judicial process was perhaps the key enabler of the underenforcement of anticorruption laws during the Fifth Republic until the last decade of the twentieth century. In the Jacobin tradition, law is merely one of the modalities and instruments of state action.[18] The principle of the separation of powers applies only to the executive and legislative branches. Magistrates, bereft of democratic legitimacy, were long considered "the mouth of the laws made by the legislature." The history of the French judiciary is punctuated by purges and characterized by a general subservience to executive authority.[19] Corresponding to this dependence is their relative low status. Constituting a unitary corps comprising both the prosecutors and judges, magistrates are recruited by examination from the graduates of the École Nationale de la Magistrature, a decidedly less exalted educational establishment than any of the grandes écoles that produce the political, administrative, and economic elite of the nation.[20]

The French judiciary has two branches: the prosecution (*le parquet*) and the bench (*le siège*). Until the reforms of the nineties, the hierarchically organized prosecution received directives from the ministry of justice, responsible for determining and implementing penal policy. Whereas the upper echelons of the public prosecutor's department are occupied by political appointees, the bench judges are irremovable and have traditionally enjoyed more independence. Nevertheless, legal careers involve considerable toggle back and forth between the prosecution and the bench. Besides, the advancement of all magistrates has been subject to the same system of evaluations by superiors. Conseil Supérieur de la Magistrature (hereafter CSM) is the chief authority of the magistrates. It makes recommendations for appointments to the bench and wields plenipotentiary disciplinary power over the magistrates. This body, however, convenes under the direction of the president of the republic, who, until the 1993 reform, selected all its members. Before 1993, the CSM had no say in the nomination of prosecutors, and its input in the appointments to the bench was restricted.

## Transformations in the Eighties

Scandals involving financial skullduggery by political actors broke only sporadically until the mid-eighties during the Fifth Republic. When they did occur, they did so on allegations of misconduct by individual politicians and did not bear on party finance. Scandals rarely led to political or legal sanctions on those embroiled in them. Unlike the affairs of the nineties, they remained isolated incidents with negligible impact. The electorate was, by and large, forgiving. An example is the Bokassa Diamonds scandal of 1979, during which President Valéry Giscard d'Estaing was accused of accepting valuable diamonds from the president of the Central African Republic when he was the finance minister in 1973. Although some of the charges seemed well founded, opinion polls failed to record any decline in confidence.

Corruption scandals multiplied in the second half of the eighties at the executive, legislative, and local levels. Entangled in them were institutional and high-status actors. What were publicized were the cavernous finance systems of all the major political parties. Most important, the charges roiled the public opinion, and the implicated politicians incurred significant sanctions.

Munitions sales from a prominent arms manufacturer to Iran were exposed in the Luchaire affair of 1986. The transactions had violated the existing embargo, and it was alleged that commissions were paid to the Socialists for their connivance. Another major scandal of the period, the Carrefour du développement affair, broke by the revelation of the fraudulent financial practices of the eponymous agency that had been set up in 1983, under the auspices of the ministry of development, to aid third world countries. The new minister of the recently elected right-wing government proclaimed in 1986 that 10 million francs had been despoiled from the accounts of the association. Soon it was revealed that part of this amount had gone to disburse the costs of the electoral campaign of a socialist minister, Christian Nucci.[21] Businessmen known for their propinquity to the Socialists and the principal advisor to Finance Minister Pierre Bérégovoy were indicted in the two insider trading scandals that erupted in 1988 and 1989.

The corruption scandals of this period were not confined to the executive branch. Assorted false invoice affairs, which aired the squalid inner workings of illegal finance at the local level, afflicted French politics in the second half of the eighties. The mayors of Nice, Toul, and Angoulême were eventually convicted. Discoveries in Marseille and Lyon in 1989 suggested that a major public works company was relaying contributions to municipal party officials across the political spectrum in return for preferential treatment in procurement contracts. The investigation ended in May 1990 with thirty-six indictments. Seven members of the legislature from the political left were indicted, as were eight from the right. During the investigation, a company executive confessed to a wide system of kickbacks arranged through URBA, a consultancy close to the Socialist Party that allegedly took care of election-related bills. The claim was combustible: evidence suggested that the consultancy distributed the plums at the national level. If the investigation were to be broadened, it could easily wend its way up to the magnates of the Socialist Party, including the treasurer and the general secretary. Some facts even indicated that URBA might have partially bankrolled the presidential campaign of François Mitterrand in 1988.

As we saw in the last chapter, accounting for political scandal frequency requires us to consider three factors: amount of wrongdoing, incentives and opportunities to attack high-status politicians, and the vulnerability of these actors. I also contended that it was the declining prestige of the presidency during the 1960s and the heightening surveillance on the executive branch that rendered American presidents legally and politically vulnerable to scandal in recent decades. Something similar happened to the French political elite during the eighties. The relative relaxation of étatism and the shrinking trust in the political elite combined to decrease immunity to scandal and acetified competition. The resultant scandals of the late 1980s rendered politicians even more susceptible to disparagement and set the stage for the ferocious anticorruption drive of the 1990s.

Let us first consider the 1980s. The three developments of this decade – administrative decentralization, push toward liberalizing the economy, and "cohabitation" – all undermined French étatism. Shortly after their ascent to power in 1981, the Socialists set out to dismantle administrative centralization, which was at once inefficient and in variance with democratic governance. The decentralization reforms extricated elected local officials from the tutelage of Paris.[22] By increasing the number of elections at the municipal, cantonal, and European levels, however, the reforms intensified political competition as well, so now politics both required more money and offered more occasions for moral squabbling. More important, mayors and other elected officials grew more attackable with decentralization. The reforms did not only eliminated the a priori controls that the prefects had exercised over the mayors. In the same movement, mayors' contract allocation decisions were also shorn of the protections they had antecedently been blessed with as a result of them being undertaken conjointly with prefects, who could be tried solely in administrative courts. The powers of elected local officials were enhanced in the eighties. But simultaneously their official actions were made more transparent and subject to scrutiny by third parties in the newly founded regional finance courts, which, despite having blunt penal teeth, could serve as public fora to voice allegations. These administrative developments brought about a blizzard of local scandals in the late eighties.

The gradual liberalization of the economy unintentionally invigorated scandal activity in France as well. The relative weakening of the pampered monopolies in the public works sector led some of the newcomers, whose tenders were not accepted, to denounce old crony practices, openly contest bidding decisions, and pursue rivals in court. Some of the losers in privatizations, which frequently took the form of bidding wars between economic actors with ties to the political elite, resorted to public denunciations and legal action. And as television was freed from government control, the media became yet another site of competition and scandal a lucrative news item.

Finally, cohabitation (power sharing between the president and the prime minister when they come from opposing parties) further soured political conflict. The fierce rivalry between the Elysée and the Matignon translated into a high incidence of scandal as the Socialists relinquished control over the judiciary and the police in 1986 when they lost the legislative elections. First practiced in 1986–8, cohabitation was normalized in the nineties (1993–5, 1997–2001) and would be an essential enabler of the anticorruption crusade.

In sum, liberalization, decentralization, and cohabitation decreased the costs and augmented the profits of scandalmongering. By reducing and fragmenting the power of central authority, accentuating conflict, and making administrative and political decisions more transparent, these processes also relatively degraded the state apparatus. As a result, the political elite were more vulnerable, and the number of annual convictions in corruption cases quintupled from 25 to 133 between 1984 and 1990.

Moreover, the prestige of the political elite plummeted in the course of the 1980s with the failure of consecutive governments to deal effectively with the soaring unemployment rate, which reached 10.7 percent in 1987. The public and the press grew more attentive to corruption allegations and less accommodating of illegality in the

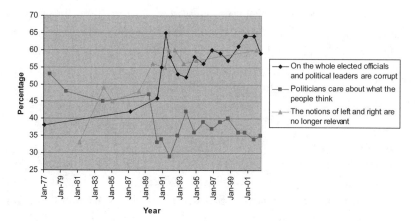

Figure 4.1. Vulnerability of French Politicians to Scandal – TNS Sofres Poll.

eighties to the extent that they found the governments incompetent as well as unresponsive. Fifty-three percent of the French population polled in September 1977 thought that politicians were concerned with the problems of the people, as opposed to the 42 percent who were of the opinion that that they were not. In November 1991, the percentage of those polled who believed that politicians were indifferent to their concerns had catapulted to 69 percent, and only 29 percent maintained a positive image of them (Figure 4.1). As class politics and the relevance of the categories of right and left in electoral behavior declined in this period, morality rose to be a key weapon in political conflict, used especially by antiestablishment forces such as the extreme-right National Front and the Ecologists. Decentralization, liberalization, cohabitation, and decline in confidence set the stage for the scandals of the late 1980s.

The political elite's reaction to the scandals of the 1980s was complex. On the one hand, governments wielded their influence over the judiciary to shelve or soft pedal many of the investigations. The aforementioned bogus invoices probe was discontinued by the public prosecutor of Marseille in 1989. The investigation into the Luchaire affair marked time. The relevant magistrate was not allowed access to the documents, which were classified as military secrets. The matter was soon stifled, for it turned out that the export of arms had continued under the new right-wing government. Legal inquiries into the two major insider trading scandals met the same fate before they could incriminate the bigwigs of the Socialist Party.

On the other hand, in an effort to stem the tide of scandal and to authorize legitimate ways of financing political life, the National Assembly passed several laws in 1988 and 1990. These laws allowed for private donations, established expenditure ceilings, limited campaigns periods, and ensured some public funding to parties and candidates. In addition, a pardon was maladroitly granted in 1990 to those who had engaged in unlawful financial operations for political, as opposed to personal, gain. Although the amnesty did not extend to the members of the National Assembly, it did cover Christian Nucci, the socialist politician indicted in the Carrefour affair, who happened to be a minister without portfolio at the time of the offense.

### The French Penal Procedure and the Investigating Magistrates

In spite of the 1988 and 1990 legislations, scandals exploded relentlessly in the nineties. Parties, needing much more than the 500,000 francs set for corporate contributions, scrambled for funds in the early nineties. But the escalation of the corruption affairs was in large part due to the publicized probes of the French investigating magistrates, who often focused on alleged infractions dating from the 1980s. Before studying their strategic use of scandal, it is necessary to give an overview of the French penal procedure and the role of the investigating magistrates in it.

The French penal procedure is inquisitorial. With an absolutist pedigree, it has been one of the most important repressive resources of the state.[23] In this system, it is a bench judge, the investigating magistrate (*le juge d'instruction*), who investigates criminal infractions and determines whether there is a prima facie case. There are around 600 territorially assigned investigating magistrates in France in a judicial corps of 6,000 members. The position is often occupied by the recent graduates of the magistrate school and is poorly paid (approximately $2,500 per month after tax in the 1990s). The expression *le petit juge,* which distinguishes these legal actors from regular bench judges and captures their low status within the hierarchy, is commonly employed to designate the investigating magistrate (hereafter IM). At the same time, these judges cannot be directly transferred by political actors and are equipped with formidable prerogatives against suspects. They direct the judiciary police, collect evidence, question witnesses and suspect(s), conduct searches, and seize objects and documents. The suspect does not have full access to the magistrate's dossier and may not have an attending lawyer during questioning before being officially "indicted" or "placed under investigation."[24]

Indicting or placing under investigation is one of the main decisions left to the discretion of the IMs. The act implies that there is evidence that would lead one to presume that the person in question has participated as a perpetrator or an accomplice to the acts to which the judge is referred by the prosecution. The intervention of defense lawyers is delayed and limited during the investigative process. Until 2001, the IMs could remand suspects in custody at will. Their extensive prerogatives have been conventionally justified by the assumption that, unlike the police or prosecutors, they will not investigate with a tilt to incriminate.[25]

But the IMs are not, of course, the sole actors in the judicial process, and they are subject to a series of inbuilt institutional safeguards. First, they cannot initiate legal proceedings. Only the public prosecutor's department can refer them to cases. The prosecutors of the republic have almost total discretion over whether to open investigations. They can very well decide for various justifiable reasons – such as the penal policy of the government, envisioned hurdles in conviction, or caseload – to discontinue action. The prosecutors can do the same also with shady motives – for instance, to squelch the investigation of a deputy in the National Assembly at the behest of the minister of justice. Unless there is an identifiable victim, who can act as a plaintiff by obtaining the legal capacity of *partie civile* and bring charges independently, the case can be closed. Or the prosecutor can bypass the IM by ordering a preliminary inquest to the police. Second, this judge has to inform the prosecutor's office of his or her findings and needs authorization to extend the field of investigation to new facts. The prosecution follows the investigation closely, has access to the dossier, and can appeal the decisions of the IM.[26] Third, the latter's control over the police, which is under the authority of the minister of interior, is far from complete. Finally, the IMs are obligated to keep their investigations confidential.

There are usually no particular victims in corruption cases who can take their grievances directly to the IMs. Hence, the prosecutors, under the directives of the ministry of justice, can very well not launch legal proceedings at all. Or in the case of already open inquests, they can legitimately refuse to extend the investigatory fields of the IMs. They can constantly appeal their decisions. With disobliging prosecutors, the IMs could be thoroughly shackled. In addition, the ministry of interior can make the police unhelpful. Recalcitrant IMs can have their careers hobbled by negative appraisals from their superiors and the CSM; this is especially true if these judges aspire to careers in the prosecution. Such incidents might be devastating for the ambitious among them because upward mobility in the French judiciary more often than not requires alternation between the bench and the prosecution.[27]

In sum, the IM is a contradictory figure. Although the inquisitorial penal procedure accords these legal officials redoubtable powers, they are also subject to checks and even pressures. The system envisions that they can exercise their full prerogatives only on common criminals or luckless private citizens. As the repressive face of the state in its relationship with civil society, the IMs are mighty beings. Vis-à-vis the other members of the state elite, they have low status. Balzac once said of these judges, "No human force, neither the king, nor the minister of justice, nor the prime minister can encroach on the powers of an investigating magistrate; nothing can stop him, nobody can order him. He is a sovereign, subject only to his conscience and the law."[28] This is a hyperbole. The IMs have been sovereign mainly against private citizens and to the extent that they represent the state.

## The Mobilization of the Investigating Magistrates

The amnesty of 1990 enraged many in the French judiciary, who believed that it was tailor-made to exonerate the former minister

Nucci. Indignation was publicly expressed for the first time in the decision reached on April 4, 1990 by a panel of senior magistrates responsible for investigating the Carrefour case. In an unprecedented press conference, they stated acerbically that, although the terms of the amnesty meant that Nucci could not be brought to trial, it was the first time in the history of the republic that politicians were pardoning themselves. Such a public reproach, which violated the magistrates' professional obligation of reserve, would previously have been inconceivable. The opinion polls, however, found 76 percent of the population to be shocked by Nucci's pardon. A 1990 *CSA – Journal du Dimanche* survey revealed that two out of three Frenchmen believed that most politicians across the spectrum were dishonest.[29] Public opinion was on the side of the magistrates.

The rebuke by the senior magistrates heartened young IMs across the country to engage in acts of protest. Three of them liberated with much fanfare petty crime suspects whom they had earlier imprisoned with burglary charges. Here is how Thierry Jean-Pierre, one of these trailblazing magistrates, later vindicated himself:

> When an IM remands someone into custody, the official justification is maintaining public order. But what one really takes into account is the actual gravity of the offense. Does the application of the amnesty law in the Nucci affair modify this notion of public order? Our answer was yes. Look at the psychological and moral earthquake that it provoked. The amnesty law did not hesitate to trouble the public order.... When one pardons someone who misappropriated twenty million francs, how can one, with the sole reference to public order, lock up someone who only stole a car?[30]

This was merely the beginning. Throughout the nineties, the IMs undertook high-profile corruption probes. They were not merely "doing their jobs." Not only did they defy political and hierarchical pressures, but they also tended to focus on high-ranking politicians. Furthermore, allegations were publicized in full detail well before the trials, such events betraying a novel judicial activism at times bordering on illegality. The scandals triggered by the investigations were therefore not simply an inevitable by-product of the legal process.

The capability to create effective political scandals is contingent on various conditions. First, denouncers need incriminating evidence. Second, they require access to channels of publicity. Third, the risks should not be too high; one can be dissuaded from publicizing the transgressions of the high and mighty if one strongly anticipates overwhelming retaliation. Fourth, significant reaction should follow the denunciation: there will not be much of a scandal if the public or opinion leaders prove apathetic to the allegations.

The social status of the denouncer is not independent of the capability to generate a scandal. Elites' accusations are both more salient and credible with less of a chance of being met with a crushing retribution. Low-status whistleblowers will then often need high-status advocates to take on elites. And the higher in status the denouncee is to the denouncer, the more incriminating evidence the denunciation should include. The denouncee usually needs to have high status for a scandal to be occasioned. Yet politicians' institutional status (their constitutionally bestowed rights) might be at odds with their prestige (the esteem they command from the public). It is the widening discrepancy between their rank and prestige that makes politicians vulnerable to allegations of wrongdoing.

These factors apply to scandalmongering legal officials too. Such actors will, nevertheless, be trammeled by the hard-and-fast rules of the judicial procedure. Although justice does entail openness at the trial stage, resorting to publicity during the investigation phase can impair due process and subvert judicial hierarchy.

The relative weakening of French étatism during the eighties decreased the risks of the IMs to undertake publicized probes during the following decade. These legal officials also capitalized on the intense competition within the political elite, which continued into the nineties with quick alternations of power, the normalization of cohabitation, and the emergence of new parties. Politicians intriguing to do away with rivals were used as informants and plaintiffs in the inquests. Politically appointed prosecutors could at times be counted on as enablers or facilitators when those investigated did not belong to the parties in power. The perpetuation of the low job performance of the political elite kept them susceptible, and the discredit with which they were plagued made it difficult for them to make reprisals against the magistrates.

But the astonishing animus of the IMs during the nineties would remain enigmatic if we ignored their incentives. Scandal is seldom deployed merely for civic purposes. A common motivation on the part of the denouncers is to enhance their standing. If the denouncee is already well known, scandal presents the denouncer with a chance to attain renown by association: one can appropriate – or leach onto – the fame of the famous by successfully attacking them in public. And fame, a most desirable asset in itself, can be parlayed into other forms of power with relative ease. Scandals offer other opportunities for self-aggrandizement as well. A successful public denunciation, just like a provocation, is a challenge in public: it actuates an honor contest.[31] Such contests, which derive from the duel form, construct an equivalency between the opposed parties.[32] This is why when the accused is of substantially higher status than the denouncer, the former would be well advised to dismiss the challenge lest the latter be validated as an equal in the eyes of the audience. Nevertheless, lower-status actors can gain prestige by successfully challenging higher-status actors in public when their provocations are interpreted by or successfully presented to the public as worthy of attention or simply when the denouncers can strike humiliating and difficult-to-ignore blows at the accused in front of others. To the extent that such confrontations are also ideal occasions for public displays of rectitude and courage, they make it possible for denouncers to claim honor.

The effects of scandals are subject to atrophy. The denouncers can, however, convert the temporary prestige they acquire in them into a permanent status upgrade. Even if norm entrepreneurship is not undertaken to self-aggrandize, its success can almost impose prestige on the entrepreneur and can corrupt. The success of individual denouncers can also stir others, especially those who belong to the same group, to imitate them. Groups may coalesce through and around scandals with the aim of boosting their standing in society. Legal officials, who have a vested and not necessarily an impartial interest in justice, can successfully stipulate their status promotion as the sine qua non condition of the enforcement of the norms in question. In any case, sinewed enforcement would in itself beef up the role and visibility of the enforcers.

These dynamics were put in motion in the course of the anticorruption drive in France during the nineties. To the extent that they appeared as solitary, unswerving soldiers of virtue, the IMs gained much fame and prestige in the public eye by denouncing prominent politicians. And as the scandals successfully demeaned the political elite, other legal officials imitated and abetted their courageous colleagues. Interventions from the ministry of justice, feverish flak from the politicians, and kudos showered on some of the IMs drew many into the ranks of the mutinous. The 1990 amnesty had already functioned as a founding moment in the making of a contentious judicial identity, which superseded the bench-prosecution divide as well as union affiliations. During the nineties, the IMs, and later the magistrate unions and the judiciary as a whole, saw in anticorruption activities a golden opportunity for status upgrade. By arguing that they needed independence to investigate wrongdoing by the political elite, they pushed for more resources and greater autonomy in determining their careers. The discredit they heaped on the politicians legitimated their demands. Since their main argument for independence was the crookedness of the political elite, whose control of the judiciary could not be but scandalous, the magistrates used the investigations to drive this point home and often denounced systemic cover-up. The upsurge in scandal activity during the 1990s gave rise to a polarization between the legal officials and the political elite, and by the end of the decade the crusade had culminated in the redistribution of power within the state apparatus.

Resentment was a potent force propelling the anticorruption campaign. The standing of the French magistrates among public officials had always been relatively low. In the early nineties, a recent graduate of the magistrates school earned 14,000 francs per month after tax (about $2,500); the monthly wage only went up to 20,000 francs after twelve years of service. In an interview given to two *Le Monde* journalists in 1993, President of the Commerce Court of Paris Pierre Bézart groused about the magistrates' miserable working conditions:

"The general prosecutor of Paris is not even provided with an official residence. Visit the prefects, look at their offices.... Look at the military where the lowliest colonel is given a car."[33] Being bestowed with none of the perks that come with being an elite state functionary or politician, even high judges such as the counselors to the Court of Cassation had to take the subway to work.

The eighties had been marked by a further *déclassement* of the judiciary corps, which was mortifyingly clinched by the reorganization of the ceremony protocol on September 13, 1989, that relegated the presidents of departmental courts to the twenty-second rank – after the subprefects, local officials, and military personnel. The status diminution was exacerbated by the languishing odds for advancement for junior magistrates, whose numbers multiplied during the eighties. Stasis deepened the rift within the hierarchy between the lower strata and the higher-ups and encouraged activism by the former. To the extent that their mobility prospects dimmed, lower-level magistrates paid less and less allegiance to the executive branch. Among these, the deputy prosecutors and the IMs[34] would discern a commonality in their life chances and antiestablishment sentiments and would league together during corruption investigations. But there is reason to think that without the prestige slump of the political elite, which made both their extensive prerogatives intolerable and individual politicians easier to attack, judiciary jaundice would not have metamorphosized into righteous indignation and eventually into legal action.

## The Scandal Strategies

Contestation became the constitutive element of the French judiciary habitus during the nineties, thanks in large part to the activities of the IMs. As I pointed out, these officials cannot refer themselves to cases but can only examine the preliminary charges handed down by prosecutors. High-profile corruption probes thus often involved reinterpreting these charges; extending inquiries to actions by high-status political actors; disregarding directives from superiors; colluding with deputy prosecutors behind the backs of other law enforcement officials; incarcerating suspects; and, most important, publicizing various elements of the investigations.

## Techniques of Insubordination

We can observe many of these techniques in the 1991 raid conducted by the IM of Sarthe Thierry Jean-Pierre on URBA, the aforementioned consultancy firm staffed by Socialist Party militants and responsible for collecting kickbacks for procurement contracts from businesses. The incident served as a template for the other IMs. It is therefore worth recounting in detail. The thirty-two-year-old Jean-Pierre was referred to a case in Sarthe involving a work accident. Soon after he allegedly received an anonymous telephone call[35] denouncing that the firm he was investigating had been making payments to URBA. Not briefing the Mans prosecutor, as he was technically duty-bound to do, but colluding with a deputy, Jean-Pierre broadened the ambit of his investigation to corruption and misuse of corporate assets with the rationalization that such illegal activities prevented the firm from improving the work conditions of its employees. The deputy qualified the charges as fraud – this allowing Jean-Pierre to subpoena and remand a Socialist Party official, who made a clean breast of the illicit operations of URBA in Marseille.

The case was thus no longer about simple fraud but corruption and influence peddling. To be able to exploit the confessions he had obtained, however, the IM needed another authorization from the prosecutor's department. Knowing that he would never acquire the assent of the relevant prosecutor, a Socialist appointee, the judge stealthily betook himself to another deputy, who was a member of the anticorruption association that he had founded a couple of years previously, Forum de la Justice. The deputy was not on duty at the time, so Jean-Pierre patiently waited for a week and had him reestablish the charges as corruption, extortion, and forgery.

Armed with preliminary indictments, Jean-Pierre incarcerated a high-level URBA official without his lawyer present. He also took the testimony of a former police inspector named Antoine Gaudino, another friend and fellow founding member of the Forum de la

Justice. Gaudino had raided the Marseille offices of URBA in 1989 and published his findings in a best-selling screed against the Socialist Party in 1990,[36] as a result of which he was cashiered from the police force the following year. In effect, nothing that the IM learned from his informants had not already been made public the year before by the former cop. He was nevertheless resolute about resuming the kickbacks investigation that had been dropped two years earlier in Marseille even though it had little to do with the case to which he was assigned by the Mans prosecutor.

Jean-Pierre was promptly informed by the judiciary police of his removal from the case by the president of Mans Court for having "acted partially and according to purely personal considerations." Abandoned by the police, but after, apparently, alerting some journalists, the IM repaired to Paris, raided the Paris headquarters of URBA on a Sunday under a phalanx of cameras, and stayed the night there after a locksmith had changed the locks to avoid meddling from the government lawyers who were yelling outside. In the morning, Jean-Pierre left the building carting fives boxes of documents with him. The URBA pell-mell was an above-the-fold item for the press. The IM defended himself on television against the minister of justice, who accused him of vigilantism. Jean-Pierre, however, won plaudits from his colleagues and found boosters in the press. The public was supportive as well. Although soon after he was taken off the case, the Appeals Court of Anger upheld his procedurally problematic acts in a controversial decision. As a result of the raid on URBA and the publicity it bred, the probe into the finances of the Socialist Party was reopened. Henri Emmanuelli, the former treasurer, was indicted the next year by another IM.

### Targeting Higher-ups

At any time, a typical IM has close to a hundred cases, an infinitesimal fraction of which would have a political content. The French judges, however, prioritized corruption investigations in the nineties. The targets rose in stature. The president of the National Assembly was indicted in 1992. The other casualties of the same year included one sitting and several former ministers, many deputies and senators, and miscellaneous elected officials.

Leaks from an investigation by Thierry Jean-Pierre into the financier of the Socialist Party, Roger-Patrice Pelat, exposed in February 1993 an unpaid interest-free loan of a million francs to the Socialist Prime Minister Pierre Bérégovoy. Pelat, who had died in 1991, had been indicted in an insider trading scandal in 1989 when Bérégovoy was the minister of finance. The ignominious suspicions led Bérégovoy to commit suicide on May 1, 1993,[37] shortly after the Socialist smackdown in the legislative elections that started another bout of cohabitation. The finances of the Socialist and Republican parties were canvassed with numerous indictments in this period. The Balladur government well-nigh outdid its predecessor in terms of corruption scandals, and three sitting ministers were forced to resign. One of these ministers, Alain Carignon, was eventually convicted. Badly bruised, Édouard Balladur could not make it to the presidential runoff, and the cohabitation ended in 1995 with the ascent of Jacques Chirac to the Elysée.

There was little respite, though. The second half of the nineties began with a controversy regarding the low rents paid by the prime minister and former municipal officer Alain Juppé and his son for apartments owned by the city of Paris. The finance mechanisms of the Gaullist party Rally for the Republic, the largest party on the right, were probed by several judges from 1994 onward. Many party officials, including the mayor of Paris, the prime minister, and a former minister, were placed under investigation. The accounts of the Center of Social Democrats, Center of Liberals, the Communist Party, and the Socialist Party were also scrutinized. Magistrates placed the leaders and treasurers of these parties, most of them deputies or former ministers, under investigation. The inquiry into Socialist Party finances terminated with the conviction of president of the National Assembly Henri Emmanuelli in 1996.

The Elf scandal erupted during the same period.[38] The first IM of Paris Eva Joly (other judges would join her later) alleged a raft of schemes used to rifle the formerly public oil company Elf-Aquitaine to fund political parties and candidates. An estimated 300 million

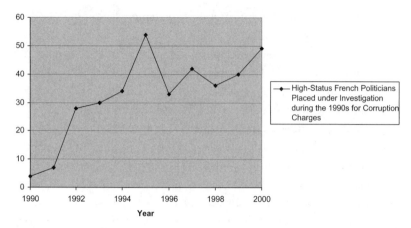

Figure 4.2. French Politicians and the Corruption Investigations.

francs had been spirited away from Elf's accounts in the form of commissions on big oil deals or property investments. Loïk Le Floch-Prigent, the former head of Elf during the eighties and the head of the French railways at the time, was incarcerated by Joly. The long roster of the *mis en examen* of the Elf saga, which stretched into the 2000s, included the former foreign affairs minister and president of the Constitutional Council Roland Dumas; several deputies in the National Assembly; former ministers, including Charles Pasqua; and former Prime Minister Édith Cresson.[39] In another major scandal, the rising star of the Socialist Party, Minister of Finance Dominique Strauss-Kahn, was placed under investigation of forgery and back-dating lawyer's fees in a property deal and was compelled to resign in 1999.[40] The IMs spared no one. The trail of a kickback investigation dating from the late nineties finally reached President Chirac in 2001 (Figure 4.2).[41]

Prosecuting corruption or related crimes such as influence ped-dling is tough if the IM approaches the matter from the politician's angle. Evidence that would corroborate corruption is hard to obtain. Proof of intent is elusive. Witnesses, if any, are unlikely to be coop-erative, and there are usually few traces of the unlawful transaction. There might be a time delay between the payment and the favor. The arrangement between the parties might be tacit rather than explicit.

The IMs thus started pursuing corruption through the infraction of *abus de biens sociaux,* the misuse of corporate assets.

The original intention of the law was to prevent the malicious misappropriation of funds from a company against the interests of its poorly represented and poorly organized stockholders.[42] In the nineties, however, the IMs habitually applied the law to go after suspect investment decisions by CEOs, as well as illegal actions that actually benefited companies, such as commissions and bribes to win contracts, so that the political actors on the receiving end of the circuit could be pursued with the infraction of the receipt of misused corporate funds. The legal category served as a catch-all infraction in the hands of the IMs. Its use facilitated access to discreditable information and decreased IM dependence on the prosecutor's department. By pursuing misuse of corporate assets, the judges could obtain full entrée to the accounts of the firms that were suspected of greasing the palms of politicians. They exploited a particularity of the law as well. The statute of limitations for corruption and related crimes starts three years after a crime is committed. The time ban for misuse of corporate assets, in contrast, takes effect three years after the transgression is unearthed. The legal impediments to coercing political actors during the probes encouraged employing this angle further. Even though there is no plea-bargaining in France, the IMs routinely placed high-level business executives under investigation for misuse of corporate assets and detained them until they went back on the politicians with whom they had been in cahoots.

## Publicizing the Transgression

The high-profile probes of the IMs, especially when the politicians with fingers in the pie hailed from the parties in power, naturally alarmed the government. For reasons legitimate as well as illegitimate, the ministers of justice and the prosecutors under their yolk tried to hinder or shelve the inquests. Ministers sent directives to prosecutors to appeal the decisions of IMs, and some transferred those who did not heed them. Prosecutors were pressured to slow down ongoing investigations. Many of them refused requests to extend probes from corporate fraud to political corruption or from small fry to famous names. Some others circumvented judicial investigations and assigned the police to do innocuous preliminary inquests when they received denunciations of corruption. Still others divided cases among IMs or chose those not technically adept to investigate financial crimes or infractions. A few ministers of interior instructed the judiciary police not to cooperate with the IMs when they acted up. In a bollixed sting operation, an interior minister even used the police to discredit an IM in 1994.[43]

Many IMs still resisted instructions coming from the prosecutors. In 1992, the ministry of justice sent a directive to the public prosecutor's department, and the latter to the IMs, to drop cases involving practices undertaken not for private but for party benefit. Although this was consonant with the spirit of the amnesty law of 1990, several judges declined to comply saying that they still needed to make inquiries to ensure that there really was no private enrichment, and others proclaimed that the difference itself was specious.

But it was publicity, transforming investigations into full-fledged scandals, that was the main weapon of the IMs. Some of the latter made public statements regarding their cases. Several wrote best-selling books with blow-by-blow accounts of the political and prosecutorial pressures they endured. A few became standard fixtures on television, debating corruption and judicial matters with the leading members of the government. More commonly, many IMs publicized the contents of their dossiers as well as the political pressures on them through leaks. Such publicity, of course, spawned a spate of scandals, related not only to financial corruption but also to abuse of power by the executive branch. As a result "substantive scandals" morphed into "procedural scandals,"[44] and the public attention moved from "first-order transgressions" into "second-order transgressions."[45] The resultant discredit delegitimated the hierarchies in the French judiciary, hog-tied the executive branch and its prosecutors, and made it progressively easier for the IMs to undertake high-profile investigations. Above all, the publicity of the investigations and of the dissensions in the public prosecutor's department helped them in their attempt to dominate the judicial process. The prosecutors and the members of the Appeals Courts were thereby discouraged from appealing and overturning decisions by the IMs lest they be seen as shielding scofflaws.

In the nineties, detailed leaks about ongoing corruption investigations crammed the front pages of the French newspapers on a daily basis. The unfolding of the probes could be followed in the media in real time. IM decisions were frequently made public weeks before they actually were put into effect.[46] Thanks to leaks, such acts were rendered uncontestable, the investigations irreversible, and their political repercussions amplified. As a matter of fact, it was only thanks to leaks that a large number of the major corruption inquiries of the decade could be launched.

A case in point is the publication of a report authored by the IM of Rennes Renaud Van Ruymbeke in *Libération* and *Le Monde* on the finances of the Republican Party and its leader Gérard Longuet.[47] On March 24, 1994, Ruymbeke addressed a note to the general prosecutor of Rennes pointing to the fishy cash flows in the accounts of the political party. He had detected that a total of 28 million francs had been deposited between 1987 and 1991. The memorandum was forthwith communicated to the ministry of justice, and the general prosecutor halfheartedly initiated a preliminary inquest, which dispensed with the services of Ruymbeke and not surprisingly was soon stalled. On September 19, 1994, the IM drafted a second report to the general prosecutor in which he claimed that funds from a public works company were funneled to the Republican Party. He also adduced receipt of misused corporate assets on the part of Longuet. The minister was accused of having had repair work done on his Saint-Tropez villa by a corporation that was then allegedly awarded contracts in Meuse.

Ruymbeke was at the time charged only with the inquiry into the Socialist Party finances. He was thus not authorized to investigate the Republican Party and needed prosecutorial authorization. The tone of his second report was much more strident, but the prosecutors were naturally still unenthusiastic. Longuet was Balladur's favorite minister, and the evidence against him seemed sketchy. Yet when the report found its way on September 20 to *Libération* and on

21 September to *Le Monde*, the minister of justice had to instruct the prosecutor of republic to open a judiciary probe, during which Ruymbeke would place Longuet under investigation, thereby causing his ouster from the cabinet – even though the probe was inconclusive and eventually ended with a nonsuit.

Publicity served as a severe sanction as well. The first IM of Paris Édith Boizette was candid in a 1992 interview: "*Médiatisation* is an essential component of the sanction." Discreditable public allegations annihilated all presumption of innocence. The use of publicity for punitive purposes was central to the anticorruption objectives of the judges. The corruption investigations last from three to seven years in France. The conviction rate is low, and prison sentences rare. The trials take place several years after the investigations, are anticlimatic, and produce little new evidence. The probes of the nineties frequently ended in acquittals or suspended prison sentences, which obtained as puny attention from the media as the dismissal decisions. The moment of placing a suspect under investigation emerged as the most important public event in the judicial process during this decade.[48]

As a public official responsible for determining whether evidence against a suspect warrants a trial, the IM is empowered to accuse. The findings, acts, and decisions of this judge can be passed on, however, only to other legal officials. More than any other judicial actor, the IM is constrained by an obligation of reserve and confidentiality and cannot accuse suspects in public – unlike the prosecutors who are authorized to do so in court in the name of the French Republic. The IM, unlike a regular bench judge, does not have the right to decide on the guilt of a suspect and has to respect the presumption of innocence of the person placed under investigation. Moreover, being neither elected nor directly appointed by elected officials, the IM lacks the democratic legitimacy and political accountability of prosecutors.

To avoid the professional danger associated with directly addressing the public, many IMs transmitted the contents of their cases to a journalist or some other party[49] who publicized the material for them. This division of labor not only protected the concerned parties from legal action. The IMs were also buffered from the inevitable symbolic pollution that could spring from any direct public contact with the outsiders of the judicial process.[50] Leaking of information by the judge to the press violates the "confidentiality of investigation" and is actionable. The investigation is to be held in secret to ensure that it is not hampered by publicity and to protect the presumption of innocence of the accused.[51] A quick glance at any French daily during the nineties suggests that the norm of the confidentiality of investigations was a dead letter. The infraction is, however, painstakingly difficult to establish because the other parties to the probes, such as the witnesses or suspects, could publicize what they know with impunity. Besides, reporters are not obligated to reveal their sources in France, so few incidents were prosecuted. In any case, the Conseil Supérieur de la Magistrature, sympathizing with the IMs, was averse to chasten its own. And at times it seemed that other enforcement officials (such as police officers) were the sources of the leaks. Given the details that were made public, however, it is hard to avoid the conclusion that the IMs were doing substantial leaking to the press. Many of them even came to concede this. In the words of one who, unsurprisingly, wished to remain anonymous,

> Of course, in theory, we have to observe this damned confidentiality of investigation. But I'll say that this is one of those things we deal with case by case, and everybody knows that. Everybody says that of course we never violate confidentiality, but everybody does it all the time. That is all.[52]

François Guichard, the first IM of Colmar, justified violation as a last resort:

> In a situation of judiciary blockage, the final resort of the judge is to appeal to public opinion. The institution has the means to paralyze us. Let's take an example. I discover in a case that a protected person has committed a serious crime. What do I do? I stop investigating and demand that the prosecutor of the republic refer the issue to the Criminal Chamber of the Court of Cassation. But what if the prosecutor replies: I am sorry. I won't do that. In that case, I, the investigating magistrate, can do nothing. Nothing.[53]

Some magistrates defended the publicity of the investigative process as an end in itself by an ideology of transparency. According to the prominent IM Eva Joly, "But it is legitimate that public opinion should be informed why the president of the regional council is in prison. We simply cannot maintain secrecy." Another one, Philippe Courroye, put it bluntly: "As a citizen, I would like to know what there is against Mr. Strauss-Kahn. What he is accused of."[54] The first IM of Paris Édith Boizette said similarly, "In important cases, the public has a right to know."[55] The French judges regarded the public sphere as their natural terrain. In the words of Jean-Louis Bruguire, a leading IM,

> If the executive branch refuses to help and blocks a case, one should then consider the problem in political terms. I would not hesitate, if the executive branch acted completely contrary to my principles, to bring the issue to the public.[56]

### Challenging the Political Elite

Leaking was not the only way that the IMs created scandals. What occasions a scandal is the reaction-eliciting communication of a transgression to an audience; all publicized acts in investigations could acquire this semiotic function. High-profile raids, arrests under cameras, and photo shoots with handcuffed deputies in front of the Palace of Justice made the transgressions that the judges were alleging as salient and believable as possible. Like leaks, these acts were timed to draw maximum media coverage.[57] They were public challenges – or rather, challenges in public – where the relatively low-status magistrates, by using publicity both as protection and as instrument, abased high-status politicians in order to enhance their own prestige.[58] What was communicated to the public was not solely the moral deficiency of the political elite as opposed to the uprightness and courage of the judges. The acts also produced and presented simultaneously the humiliating vulnerability of these erstwhile impregnable potentates, who were habituated to holding the magistrates in contempt because of their lowly educational credentials. Their abasement to the level of petty criminals through publicized legal duress was a theatrical display of power by the judges before the public and the associates of the accused.[59]

The IMs stepped up the legal blitzkrieg during the 1990s. They first stormed party-affiliated consultancies, then party headquarters, and later personal residences. Each sensational punch normalized similar subsequent offensives by others and inspirited more radical ones. When the incoercible IM of Lyon Philippe Courroye, while exploring the links between arms trafficking and party finance, descended on the ministry of foreign affairs in 2001, few found the move to be extraordinary. In the same vein, the IMs imprisoned suspects with vanishing levels of restraint. The official rationales for remanding into custody in France are to secure public order, ensure the continuation of the investigation in cases in which the suspect is considered a flight risk, and prevent him or her from pressuring witnesses. But during the nineties, businesspeople implicated in corruption investigations were routinely put in prison for months – at times before even being formally charged. Relatively more shielded, high-status politicians were not spared either. On October 13, 1994, Philippe Courroye locked up Minister of Communications Alain Carignon for eight months. The French political establishment was aghast. This was the first time since King Charles X that a sitting minister found himself behind bars for corruption – before he even stood trial.

A good example of how the probes were transformed into challenges through publicity is the presidential witness summons sent by the IM of Créteil Éric Halphen to President Jacques Chirac on April 4, 2001. Halphen had been looking into the kickbacks received in exchange for public housing contracts in Paris in the late 1980s and early 1990s, during the time the president had been the city mayor. Following the publication of a posthumous tape recorded by a Gaullist official averring that Chirac was on the ball about the payoffs dished out among different political parties, the IM sent the president a summons letter, which was leaked to the press with dispatch, even though the Constitutional Council of France had already ruled that he possessed immunity during his term in the Elysée. Never in French history had a judge summoned a president prior to this incident. Moreover, the IM floutingly posted the notice to Mr. Chirac, "at his last known address, the Presidency of the Republic, Rue du Faubourg Saint Honoré, Paris 75008." The publicized letter contained the standard warning that recusant summons witnesses could be coerced to appear before the judge.

Chirac cited separation of powers and asserted that the executive branch could not be truckled to judiciary authority, much less at the whim of a bumptious IM. In a letter to the prime minister, the apoplectic president called for disciplinary action against Halphen for suggesting that he could drag the president to his office. The Elysée Palace also slammed the magistrate for leaking the summons. But as the French public overwhelmingly thought that Chirac should testify and as the Socialist government did not mind the spectacle of the right-wing president in the lurch (despite the fact that the investigation implicated them as well), the ministry of justice refrained from admonishing the rogue magistrate. Although Chirac held out and did not testify, his popularity dipped in the upturn of the summons episode.

## The Consequences of the Scandals

Alleging corruption is easier than proving it. Of the fifty-three highest-status politicians (sitting or former prime ministers, ministers, presidents of the National Assembly and the Constitutional Council, and general secretaries of political parties) placed under investigation since 1992, only sixteen were convicted, and of these merely three received prison sentences. Numerous top-ranking political actors – including Ministers Dominique Strauss-Kahn and Gérard Longuet; the head of the Communist Party, Robert Hue; and the president of the Constitutional Court, Roland Dumas – were legally exonerated. Nevertheless, in the public eye, the probes disgraced the entire French political elite. Opinion polls consistently found that most of the electorate thought their politicians to be praetorian across the board.

The insular character of the political elite and its sway over the judiciary had not only facilitated financial malfeasance but had also left it normalized, unpublicized, and underprosecuted before the late eighties. In the nineties, however, once the IMs were supplied with the incentives and opportunity to pursue high-status politicians in publicized investigations, these very factors reinforced the sentiment that corruption was rife. The lack of transparency in the political system made the public generalize the blame arising out of individual scandals and hold the party apparatchiks accountable when low-status officials were the targets of probes. Multiple office holding by political actors made it possible for investigations about local graft to be easily tied to the legislative and, at times, executive levels.

The scandals set off a self-feeding momentum. The IMs found themselves less and less crimped by the prosecutor's department, and the dissemination of discredit progressively lowered the threshold of evidence required to make an effective public allegation leading to judiciary investigation and resignation. A casualty was Socialist Minister of Finance Dominique Strauss-Kahn, who was ousted from his post in December 1999 following a leak based on a dubious police report.[60] The scandals prodded the politicians to institute sanctions on colleagues who had brushes with the law. Socialist Prime Minister Pierre Bérégovoy established in 1992 the rule that a minister facing indictment should resign. This measure was adopted to dam the contaminating effects of allegations and appease the hostile press. Yet it also involuntarily confirmed the muscle of the magistrates. The subsequent governments espoused willy-nilly the same principle: ministers placed under investigation were out. The members of the National Assembly were impelled to lift the immunity of those under investigation, and party organizations often called for their resignations. In 1995, the parliamentary protections that the members of the National Assembly had enjoyed thus far were curtailed.[61]

The French political elite implemented stringent monitoring measures to signal righteousness to the public. Financial disclosure requirements were established. Novel legislation necessitated that the wealth and income of the deputies in the National Assembly be declared. In 1993, the Bérégovoy government created a central agency responsible for gleaning data on corruption.[62] Better procedures for assessing tenders and awarding public contracts were instituted. Ever more restrictive finance laws were passed by the National

Assembly from 1990 to 1995. Political funding was made more transparent by new legislation in 1993, and strict caps were placed on electoral spending. Parties gained legal status, and their books were submitted to scrutiny. A ceiling was placed on private donations in 1993. But all donations seemed shady and provoked probes; corporate contributions were finally banned in 1995.

The scandals did not simply strengthen the corruption norms and intensify surveillance. They also ended up reconfiguring the relationship between the judiciary and the executive branch. Their high-profile cases made the IMs celebrity judges and created an equivalency between them and the prominent politicians they attacked. Flattering biographical portraits and comments on investigative styles larded the reporting of the probes. Their habits, hobbies, nocturnal outings, idiosyncrasies, and even sartorial tastes achieved newsworthiness. Laurent Davenas, the prosecutor of the Republic of Évry, said in 1994, "Everybody in the École Nationale de la Magistrature now dreams of becoming an investigating magistrate."[63] Some IMs capitalized on their fame by giving television and press interviews, writing books, and calling for additional resources to cleanse the Augean stables of French politics.

Acquiring prestige from a scandal requires the denouncer to communicate effectively the costs of his or her normative enterprise. The IMs probing corruption therefore took care to dramatize the risks that they were taking in the course of their investigations, which were framed either by themselves or their champions in the press as heroic uphill battles. Some IMs publicized the death threats they allegedly received. The televised sight of these paladins of probity surrounded with bodyguards filled the evening news. Prestige packed this way was parlayed into institutional capital in 1999 with the opening of a special branch for financial crimes within the Paris prosecutor's department, which brought together judges and prosecutors, in the spacious former headquarters of *Le Monde*. Divisions focusing on other kinds of crimes followed suit. By the end of the 1990s, many magistrates were organized in semi-autonomous units analogous to the prestigious *grands corps d'État* forming the French high bureaucracy.

Only 7 percent of all legal cases are referred to the IMs, and crimes committed by politicians constitute a minute fraction of this percentage. Fight against corruption, however, symbolized French justice in the nineties with the pursuit of independence becoming the overriding judicial preoccupation. The two unions, the centrist l'Union Syndicale des Magistrats and the left-wing Le Syndicat de la Magistrature, which ran with independence as the primary item on their platform, together corralled 92 percent of the votes in the 1995 union elections. The corruption scandals led, for the first time in the history of the French Republic, to the emergence of a self-assertive judiciary habitus defined by its opposition to the political establishment. Collective action bolstered this identity. Many IMs exchanged dossiers and endorsed each other in public. Some worked together on knotty cases. The obstructionism of the ministry of justice, the defensive acts by the legislature, and the prospect of independence combined to foster a common ethos within the French judiciary.

Judicial solidarity crystallized in controversies surrounding the legally shaky actions of the IMs. Magistrates of all ranks, either individually or through the CSM and the unions, rallied around the IMs when they clashed with politicians, ministers of justice, suspects, and their lawyers. A good deal of investigative strong-arming was procedurally problematic and professionally perilous. Yet ministers of justice balked at lodging complaints with the CSM, which was, in any case, loath to go after its own.

There was substantial support from the bench as well. Young judges manning the appeals courts in the eighties and nineties, a large number of whom were former IMs themselves, proved to be very favorably disposed to the probes and at times glossed over procedural irregularities. Trial judges frequently included suspension of eligibility in their verdicts against politicians. Quite a few did not abstain from pronouncing harsher sentences than what the prosecutors sought. Some judges, such as those who presided over the trials of Roland Dumas and Alain Carignon, rationalized prison sentences by moralizing language when incriminating evidence looked inadequate. Aggravation of sentences in appeal became unexceptional in corruption cases.

Executive interceptions only hardened the solidarity on the bench. Many senior judges from the Court of Cassation upbraided high-ranking prosecutors when they seemed to side with politicians. In January 1996, Jean-Francois Burgelin, the newly appointed general prosecutor of the Paris Appeals Court, pointed to the perverse economic consequences of the investigations and entreated restraint. The first president of the Court of Cassation, Pierre Drai, immediately snapped, "A judge is responsible solely to his conscience." In November 2000, the prosecutor of the Appeals Court of Paris decided to discontinue action against the spouse of the mayor of Paris, who was charged with receiving payments for an allegedly bogus administrative report, after a lower court overruled the acts of the IM responsible for the probe. Magistrates were up in arms. In an incident testifying to the new clout of the judiciary, General Prosecutor of Paris Alexandre Benmakhlouf, a political appointee openly accused of protecting the mayor, had to resign.

The antimagistrate rhetoric was mostly associated with the left until 1993. But the suicide of former Socialist Prime Minister Pierre Bérégovoy on May 1, 1993, in the wake of a bribery probe fired up all the French political dignitaries. At the funeral, right-wing Defense Minister François Léotard, who would himself soon be placed under investigation, called the alliance between the magistrates and journalists "a novel form of fascism." Proclaiming the integrity of his former prime minister and elegizing him as a victim of slanderous leaks, President Mitterrand lashed out: "All the explanations in the world cannot justify throwing the honor of a man, and finally his life, to the dogs." Yet even though they did at times make common cause, the political elite were losing the war.[64] Édouard Balladur was reeling in 1994 from the resignation of three of his ministers who had been placed under investigation one after another. It was with chagrin that Mitterrand reportedly reprimanded his frazzled right-wing prime minister in one of his last cabinet meetings:

> Monsieur le Premier ministre, you are the executive branch. I named you in accordance with the constitution. You have been elected by the people. You are the victim of a judiciary riot. You have to fight it. You are not doing so.[65]

The scandals activated the dormant powers of the IMs. Balzac's assessment about them become partially a reality – but only after the inquisitorial penal procedure was explosively fused with the publicity of the investigative process. Beleaguered and baffled, all governments endeavored to revamp the penal procedure in the nineties. All overhaul attempts were, however, slated as schemes to stymie the investigations; they more or less withered on the vine. The proposal of a new penal procedure code on January 5, 1993, stirred a public demonstration by the Association Française des Magistrats Chargés de l'Instruction (AFMI). On February 11, 1993, fifty-six of the sixty-two IMs of the Criminal Court of Paris stated that they were ready to be relieved of their duties in protest. The AFMI was backed by all the other magistrate unions and the media. Judges went on a one-day strike.

In large part due to this mobilization, the 1993 judiciary reform fizzled out and did not go beyond the symbolic terminological replacement of the concept of "l'inculpation" (indictment) with that of "la mise en examen" (placing under investigation). The new right-wing government had scarcely more luck when it laid out its own reform blueprint in 1996. The AFMI announced that the magistrates would refuse to even scout the proposal. Finally in 2001, when the IMs were deprived of their right to detain suspects with the law on the presumption of innocence, two demonstrations took place at Place Vendôme in front of the ministry of justice. And the IMs were not much declawed with the new law. The statistics of January 2001 showed that of the 103 people put by the IMs before the newly established "judge of liberties," 100 had been remanded in custody. It seems that the new judges do little more than rubber-stamp the arrest requests of the IMs.

Despite the growing consensus in France to supersede the inquisitorial penal procedure with the Anglo-Saxon adversarial method, the IMs proved untouchable because of the obloquy heaped on the political elite by the scandals. Politicians tried to fend off the judicial assaults by rescinding the provisions of the law on the misuse of corporate assets.[66] Several bills were introduced in the National Assembly in the nineties to circumscribe the scope of the infraction and impose time limits on it in an effort to preclude the magistrates from ferreting out corruption dating back to the eighties. While these efforts also resonated with the jeremiads of the business community, they all foundered in the face of judicial and media resistance.

It is an important consequence of the corruption scandals of the nineties that the role of the lower-level legal actors distended to the detriment of political appointees. For over a century, the hierarchical power of the ministry of justice over the prosecution had ensured a democratically legitimized, coherent, and unified penal policy. By dint of the disarray and discredit generated by the scandals, however, the ministry's reign over the public prosecutor's department attenuated. The 1993 reform allowed ministers to give only written directives to prosecutors in specific cases and stipulated that these be added to the dossier. Under intense fire, the Socialist Minister of Justice Élisabeth Guigou finally pledged in 1997 to give no directives whatsoever to prosecutors in these situations and announced that she would soon make this promise a constitutional reality.

By the end of the nineties, the unity of the prosecution in corruption cases was in jeopardy. The waning hold of the ministry of justice sapped the hierarchy within the public prosecutor's department. Relations frayed with many prosecutors distrusting their deputies and these, in turn, ascribing all kinds of political motives to the decisions of their superiors. The rank-and-file at times schemed behind the back of the higher-ranking prosecutors.[67] The result was a sometimes acephalous prosecution. For instance, Public Prosecutor of Paris Jean-Pierre Dinthillac publicly argued in 2000 that President Chirac could be heard as a witness in the municipal kickbacks investigation. He thereby contravened both the decision of the Constitutional Council regarding the immunity of the president and the opinion of his superior, the general prosecutor of the Paris Appeals Court.

The powers of the CSM, the disciplinary body of magistrates also responsible for proposing or confirming judicial appointments, became the major stake in the struggle between the judiciary and the executive branch. In November 1990, while the police forces halted a rally by 2,500 legal officials at the gates of the Palace of Justice in Paris, President François Mitterrand was addressing the

Court of Cassation at its bicentennial ceremonies. He roundly disparaged demands for independence, reminded the judiciary of its lack of democratic legitimacy, and lambasted its corporatist leanings:

> What will be the guarantee of your independence in our Republic? The unions? The professional associations? Under the pretext of protecting the judges from the occasional abuses of political authority, which is at any rate under the control of the parliament and public opinion, one would establish the sway of unaccountable powers over the judiciary. Judges, citizens, and justice would all lose. Don't count on me for this.[68]

Three years later, however, in the wake of the scandals that had cost the Socialists the legislative elections, Mitterrand reluctantly ratified the reform of the CSM, which was proposed by the new right-wing government and which created a new disciplinary body composed of twelve magistrates and four nonmagistrates. Whereas the president had appointed all the members of the CSM up to that time, in the new system, the magistrates hail from the different ranks within the judiciary and are elected by their peers. This remodeling shrunk the influence of the executive branch over the CSM; moreover, the election by peers and the representation of all the echelons enfeebled the judicial hierarchy and boosted the leverage of the low-ranking legal actors such as the IMs and deputy prosecutors as well as that of the magistrate unions. Three sitting or former union presidents and four other union members were elected to the CSM in 2002.

The powers of the CSM in judicial appointments were enhanced as well. Before 1993, this body simply suggested names for the first presidents of the appeals courts and gave opinions, which could be discarded by the ministry of justice, for the rest of the bench judges. With the 1993 reform, the CSM secured the prerogative to nominate all the upper level bench judges (including the presidents of district courts) as well as to veto those proposed by the minister of justice. No bench judge can now be appointed in France without the consent of the CSM, which also obtained the right to articulate opinions on prosecutor appointments.

The CSM attempted to extend its appointment privileges to prosecutors. A number of governmental appointments were berated as ill intentioned. Several public polemics broke in 1995 and 1996 when seven of the fifteen unfavorable opinions of the CSM in prosecutorial selections were not heeded by the minister of justice. Uproar followed when Minister of Justice Jacques Toubon appointed his chief of staff to the position of the general prosecutor of the Appeals Court of Paris in July 1995. The CSM chided the ministry of partisanship. The unions contended that the nonavowed motive was to stop the probes of the finances of the RPR, the dominant party of the governing coalition at the time. The next year, after the CSM vetoed Alexandre Benmakhlouf, another former aide of the minister of justice, for the post of the president of the Appeals Court in Paris, the magistrates demanded that the executive branch desist altogether from participating in appointments. On March 6, 1997, the CSM released its annual report, which objurgated President Chirac and insisted on a veto right in the nominations of general prosecutors. The minister of justice of the newly elected left-wing government Élisabeth Guigou succumbed and acquiesced not to appoint any prosecutors nixed by the CSM. The CSM thus acquired effective confirmation privileges in the nomination of all magistrates.

By 1998, the French judiciary had fortified anticorruption enforcement and wrestled considerable independence from the executive branch. The powers of the CSM were widened, and the public prosecutor's department gained some autonomy from the ministry of justice.

## The Limits and Discontents of Scandal

The scandal climate did carry on into the 2000s with several spectacular cases, such as the 2004 trial of former Prime Minister Alain Juppé, who was eventually convicted for creating fictitious jobs, receiving an eighteen-month suspended jail sentence and loss of civic rights for five years. Yet the corruption investigations started during the current decade seem to register much less interest, and those implicated in scandals have been receiving lighter censure. There was scarcely a word from the major dailies and the mainstream parties when President Chirac was accused by the offbeat paper *Le Canard enchaîné* in 2006 of disposing 50 million francs in a secret Japanese bank account. The opinion polls continue to show pervasive political cynicism in France: according to one conducted in 2000, 64 percent of the French population believe that most politicians are corrupt,[69] and there has been a slight surge in the abstention rate during the nineties. Nevertheless, many politicians not only placed under investigation but also actually sentenced have come back and won elections in the 2000s. Henri Emmanuelli's constituency was much less harsh on him than the legal system had been when he ran again for the National Assembly after his civic rights were reinstated; he was elected with a landslide. In March 2001, the French public reelected eight mayors under investigation as well as nine mayors convicted of corruption and related crimes. Finally, despite all the charges of financial fandango swirling around him, President Chirac was elected for a second term the same year. The French grew blasé about corruption in the 2000s.

The combat against corruption has not completely delivered on its promise either. Surveillance agencies such as the Cour des Comptes or the Inspection des Finances still enjoy little autonomy and lack the sinews to monitor effectively the administration and the political class. More important, even though headway was made in the 1990s, the following decade failed to produce the full independence that the French judges were dreaming of. This outcome has much to do with the particularities of scandal as a social form. The following are especially relevant here: a succession of similar scandals obeys the law of diminishing effects; scandals may impose public costs; third parties that are affected by scandals frequently intervene to manipulate their course; denouncers need to be able to signal impartiality to fully profit from scandals; and publicity is often a double-edged sword.

First, the attention that a wave of scandals elicits cannot be sustained indefinitely. A scandal will make subsequent ones with similar content easier to break. At the same time, however, triggered anger or shock will progressively decline until the events dissolve into politics as usual. The alleged transgressors climbed in stature and their transgressions rose in enormity during the nineties to off-set this dynamic, but by the 2000s, the corruption affairs were generating less and less outrage and becoming more and more routine.[70]

There is a second and perhaps more crucial reason why the tide began to ebb. Scandal proved to be a fruitful strategy for French judges in the 1990s thanks to its contaminating effects on the associates and organizations of the accused politicians. But scandals can also exert public costs, which account in part for the fact that the anticorruption crusade in France lost much of its steam during the 2000s. By discrediting the mainstream political parties, the investigations of the 1990s ended up helping actors outside the establishment, particularly the extreme-right National Front. A major turning point was Jean-Marie Le Pen's striking accession to the second round of the presidential elections in 2002. The event forced many to reconsider the benefits of the corruption probes – chiefly because the issue was a big part of Le Pen's popular appeal.[71]

Third, the IMs have been less and less able to master the scandals they create, this making their probes increasingly look like politics. The judges have had to depend greatly on political actors as sources in their probes. At the same time, politicians of all stripes and parties, who often find themselves meshed in the very same scandals as a result of the cross cutting illicit finance ties in France, can and often do manipulate the course of the investigations at every step through recriminations. As a result, probes are either politicized or can at least seem that way. In many instances, politicians have been able to use the judges for their own interests.[72] Politically appointed public officials have at times manipulated the course of the investigations as well. For example, much of the findings of the IM Éric Halphen against President Chirac originated from an anonymous informer in the secret service who later turned out to have been appointed by the former socialist government.[73] There are some indications that the troubles that beset recently Nicolas Sarkozy before he became president (in an investigation that centered on laundered kickbacks from the sale of several frigates to Taiwan) might have to do with the false allegations made by his rival, former Prime Minister Dominique de Villepin. Or consider how the IM of Lyon Philippe Courroye could not have single-handedly brought down Minister Alain Carignon in 1994. The demise of this rising star of French politics in the first half of the 1990s took significant cooperation from sundry politicians. The Ecologists in the Grenoble municipal council acted as *parties civiles* so that the investigation could be opened.[74] More important, the IM relied heavily on the testimony of a former Carignon aide, who had later defected to the rival wing of the center-right party RPR headed by Jacques Chirac.[75]

Politicization can spring from within the state as well. Although the IMs have augmented their role in the judicial process, they still frequently rely on the support, or at least the acquiescence, of political appointees in the prosecution. Yet since the French Jacobin tradition postulates a unified penal policy and does not allow prosecutors to be elected, it has not been possible to render the prosecution fully independent. And, following the example of the IMs, the prosecutors have themselves been resorting to publicity. The second half of the nineties witnessed public run-ins among them. Consider the following episode. President Chirac cited executive privilege upon receiving the aforementioned summons letter from Éric Halphen in April 2001, and the Constitutional Court recognized his immunity while in office. This, however, did not prevent Jean-Pierre Dinthillac, the prosecutor of Paris, to voice his support for Halphen and his difference of opinion with the highest court in France. A wrangle ensued in the press about whether the president should testify. Because one of the prosecutors was appointed by the president and the other by the minister of justice, for many, the affair did not transcend the clash of partisan passions. Citizens are unlikely to withdraw their support from a politician with legal ennuis if they can assume that the latter is the victim of politicking.

A fourth development that has harmed the corruption crusade is the declining ability of the judicial actors to signal impartiality to the public.[76] The effectiveness of a denunciation hinges in part on the apparent motivations of the denouncer – even more so if it alleges more than it exposes. IMs are not appointed by politicians and their targets spanned the entire political spectrum; they could thus appear relatively unbiased during the nineties. But the investigations engendered alliances and dispositions that have come to sabotage the enterprise of the anticorruption judges in the 2000s. The group identity that the crusade required and entailed has not been an unmitigated good. To the extent that a judge is perceived as acting on behalf and for the benefit of a particular group, the effectiveness of the publicized investigations – in terms of corruption control or status enhancement – dramatically decreases.

Many IMs have, however, been cooperating in all kinds of ways with each other, as well as with the other members of the judiciary. We already saw the significance of collusions with deputy prosecutors. The IMs have also often needed the backing of higher judges when their acts were sent on appeal by lawyers or hostile prosecutors on procedural bases. Many bench judges in the chambers of accusations were disinclined to overturn the IM decisions in the early nineties even when they seemed to be in violation of due process. Collegiality and secrecy of proceedings helped. Finally, the magistrate unions saw their differences evaporate during the nineties and started taking common stands in controversies regarding the procedural audacities of the IMs. The visibility of the magistrate unions added to the clout of the judiciary within the state apparatus as the reform of the CSM augmented the syndical representation within it. But prominent and brawny unions hamstring the judiciary's claim to disinterestedness.

Moreover, the dominant magistrate unions have refused the separation between the bench and the prosecution – an issue that was at the heart of all the reform propositions – with the argument that that this would make functionaries out of prosecutors. The French judiciary wants not only to be independent; it wants to be independent as a group. The group formation that had been so central to the successes of the nineties now risks giving the impression that the magistrates might have evolved into a self-righteous interest group with much beef but no democratic legitimacy and accountability. Whether this is true or not, the contestation between the politicians and the magistrates in the political scandals came to be perceived less and less as an opposition between law and wrongdoing but more and more as a settling of scores between two self-regarding groups. A poll conducted by TNS Sofres on August 25, 2000, found that 49 percent of the responders second-guessed the magistrates during the investigation of Jacques Chirac for the illicit finances of his party, RPR – as opposed to 47 percent who thought that the legal officials were acting independently. These figures roughly reproduce the proportion of right-wing and left-wing voters in France. The same study also found that again 49 percent of the respondents considered the allegations about Chirac to be the result of political machinations.

The final element that blunted the anticorruption drive has to do with publicity itself. Publicity can be used by those attacked in scandals as much as by the attackers. This is another reason investigations have come to blemish the magistrates themselves. The years 2000 and 2001 witnessed an increasing number of acquittals in high-profile corruption cases, including the trials of the leader of the Communist Party Robert Hue and of the former president of the Constitutional Court Roland Dumas. These incidents exposed sloppy and overzealous investigative work. After the former minister Dominique Strauss-Kahn was exonerated in 2001, the presiding judge castigated the prosecution and the IMs for the paucity of evidence they brought to court. Some IMs saw their acts quashed. These reversals led to the reform of the penal procedure in 2001, which was supported both by the political elite and the French public – much to the displeasure of the magistrates and their unions. With the Law on Presumption of Innocence, the IMs lost the power to remand in custody.

The very publicity that the IMs exploited so well to fight corruption and enhance their status may eventually come to undercut their official instrument, the inquisitorial penal procedure, the legitimacy of which comes from the secrecy of the investigative process. The publicity of the investigations has unintentionally given politicians and prominent businesspeople in the 2000s opportunities to position themselves as the victims of undue process. The gripes of the French elite are not without basis. Statistics show that, in 2004, 42 percent of all suspects placed under investigation by French IMs were remanded in custody and that this group constitutes 77.2 percent of the prison population.[77] In the same year, close to 2,000 people in

France left prison after charges against them had been dropped or after being absolved. The discontents of the French judicial system, especially the lack of defense rights and the woeful state of prisons, became major issues on the public docket in the 2000s, in great part as a result of the accounts of the CEOs and political figures attacked by the IMs in corruption probes.

# FIVE

# Sex and the American Public Sphere

THE AMERICAN public sphere was "All Monica, All the time" in 1998. The nation spent an entire year engrossed in a lewd narrative about adulterous sex in the Oval Office between President Clinton and a sprightly White House intern. It was a cheap but very lucrative story for the media, which, to keep the plot moving, fed the public daily with a steady stream of fresh allegations – some true, others canards. Show hosts and pundits of all stripes had a field year, every fresh off-color claim about presidential sex stirring novel contro-versy and moral fury – sometimes seemingly sincere, often flagrantly feigned. For most Americans, it was hard not to be interested, not to be amused. The Starr Report, the lurid account of the illicit liaison scribed by the Independent Counsel's office that was investigating the president, was downloaded an estimated nine million times in two days after it hit the Internet.

But the scandal was serious business, too. The revelation of Bill Clinton's affair with Monica Lewinsky and the legal complications that arose thereof plunged the American democracy in a drawn-out constitutional crisis, making the satyrical politician, already embat-tled by a sexual harassment suit, the second impeached president in history and pushed him to the brink of resignation. Recall the general-ized outrage among the political and intellectual elite. Conservatives clobbered Clinton for having contaminated the White House; liberals rejoined that it was precisely the unscrupulous Republican onslaught on the office of the presidency that was responsible for the pollution. And the maelstrom soon implicated numerous third parties in a quite direct way. Newt Gingrich and Bob Livingston resigned one after the other from the position of Speaker of the House – the former as the Republicans lost the House in the November 1998 midterm elections, the latter a month later when he learned that *Hustler* was about to go to press with his own past sexual escapades. The scandal had many repercussions in society too. Take a particularly odd one. The editor of the prestigious *Journal of the American Medical Association* was sacked after he approved the publication, during the impeachment trial of the president, of an unsolicited, peer-reviewed study produced by the Kinsey Research Institute, which found that 59 percent of an undergraduate sample from an Indiana college agreed with Clinton by not regarding oral sex, the main form of physical activity that he indulged in with Lewinsky, to be sex.

The United States has since been blessed with a sexually demure president, and these are sober times of war and terrorism. Public discourse is nonetheless still steeped in sex scandals. Just for a small sample, consider all the sleaze that has been alleged or revealed in public in the recent years about Michael Jackson, Paris Hilton, hundreds of Catholic priests, Arnold Schwarzenegger, former New Jersey governor James McGreevey, former New York governor Eliot Spitzer, the mayor of Detroit Kwame Kilpatrick, television host Bill O'Reilly, former Illinois Senator Jack Ryan, the Duke University lacrosse team, Congressman Mark Foley, and Senator Larry Craig. Some of these incidents were tabloid matters, ludic and diminutive. Not all the allegations that make it to the news are credible or worthy of significant reaction. Few people seem to have much believed a recent book by Edward Klein that makes sexual insinuations about Hillary Clinton[1] – and those who agree have not changed their opinion of her as a result. Nevertheless, there have recently been many sex scandals with consequences, not only on the perpetrators but also on various third parties.

Janet Jackson's "wardrobe malfunction" at the close of the 2004 Super Bowl halftime show – occasioned when Justin Timberlake tore off part of her top and exposed her right breast – seems like the ultimate frothy news item. Yet it led to Congressional hearings, $8 million worth of fines on entertainment companies for indecency violations, and the end of Howard Stern's career on national radio. Jack Ryan withdrew from the senatorial race in Illinois in 2004, ensuring that the GOP would lose a seat, after the *Chicago Tribune* obtained divorce documents divulging that the Republican politician had propositioned his actress wife to have sex with him in a club. Eliot Spitzer resigned in March 2008 from the office of the governor of New York after a federal investigation caught him contacting an expensive prostitute for an assignation. Allegations of pedophilia by Catholic priests peaked in 2003 and 2004, disgracing the entire Church. The revelation of Mark Foley's off-color Internet communications with Congress pages in October 2006 generated cries for House Speaker Dennis Hastert, panned for covering up the congressman's comportment, to resign. The episode was a factor in the Republican wipeout in the 2006 midterm elections. Or take the effects of the sexual abuse scandals that rocked the Catholic Church in 2002. An ABCNEWS/*Washington Post* poll found that, whereas 27 percent of all Americans and 9 percent of Catholics had an unfavorable view of the Catholic Church on February 20, 2002, these figures climbed to 52 percent and 30 percent, respectively, by December 15, 2002.

What accounts for the high frequency of sex scandals in American public and political life? Two different constructivist arguments are usually offered to answer this question: societal puritanism and moral activism by elites. Let us focus on the first one. Many point to a deep-seated, antediluvian puritanical streak in the national psyche. Americans – or at least an appreciable and vociferous portion of them – are simply too uptight about sex, too eager to make a disproportionate fuss of pedestrian peccadilloes. What is more, it is said, a politician's private morality is deemed as revelatory of his or her public virtues in the contemporary United States. There seems be some evidence for this account. Didn't Gary Hart relinquish his presidential bid when his adulterous dalliance with a model was revealed in 1988? And not only Bible Belt Republicans but also some liberals publicly castigated Clinton during the Lewinsky scandal. It was the *New York Times* which wrote that Clinton deserved to be censured by Congress and urged in an angry editorial on December 16, 1998: "For Us, Not Him: Vote No on Impeachment." And didn't Clinton, after he could no longer gainsay his extramarital impropriety, go around abjectly contrite with clergymen asking for forgiveness?

Liberals did despair of American puritanism, which they thought was shamefully anachronistic, during the Lewinsky hullabaloo. But right-wing commentators eventually joined in the lamenting. William J. Bennett bellyached about the languishing vitality of traditional morals[2] as the American public, by and large, proved accommodating of the president and punished the Republicans in the 1998 midterm elections for persecuting him. In effect, although there were moments in the scandal when things looked bleak for Clinton, his popularity and job approval ratings remained, for the most part, high. At any rate, if puritanism was the nub of the Lewinsky crisis, how did Franklin D. Roosevelt and John F. Kennedy get away with their adulteries in a much more austere America while Bill Clinton was impeached in the times of *Sex and the City*?

In any case, how consistent are public attitudes toward politicians ensnared in sex scandals? Those toward Clinton did vary in the course of the Lewinsky crucible, and many American politicians publicly revealed to be adulterers do ride out their scandals. So maybe Americans are not so unambiguously puritanical about sex. Didn't Clinton eventually survive his ordeal while House Speaker-Elect Bob Livingston proved to be the most prominent casualty of the scandal? And, as conservatives did not tire of pointing out, wasn't the cause of Clinton's incubus lying under oath and not just simple adultery?

Finally, it is unclear whether Americans are more straitlaced about sex than others. Let us compare the United States with the permissive land par excellence in the American popular consciousness, France. Despite stereotypes, the Americans and the French do not seem to differ in their reporting of adultery. A recent study found that the vast majority (over 90 percent) among those living in a couple in both countries reported to have been monogamous during the year preceding the survey.[3] Another research result is that although the French are somewhat less intolerant of marital infidelity than Americans, the general stance in both countries is one of strong intolerance.[4] What about attitudes toward adulterous politicians? In a CBS 1992 poll – conducted in the wake of allegations by Gennifer Flowers that she had had sex with the presidential candidate Bill Clinton – only

14 percent of Americans said that they would not vote for an adulterer. This is not high. If you think it is, consider the following. A January 24–25, 2006, poll conducted in France by TNS Sofres for *Le Figaro* found that 17 percent of the Gallic sample would not vote for a presidential candidate guilty of extramarital affairs. It seems that the French are actually somewhat less tolerant of straggling politicians. Yet it is indeed the case that there are fewer sex scandals in France than in the United States.

The puritanism explanation is problematic. It is not the only theory, though. Another common interpretation of the Lewinsky affair laid the blame on those who hounded the feckless president. Wasn't the Lewinsky scandal the concoction of an opportunistic collusion bringing together a prurient media with skuzzy tabloid standards; a biased and rambunctious independent counsel; and hardshell Republicans in Congress hell-bent on withering the president either because of rabid puritanism or simply for political gain?

Let us call this the moral activism argument and assay its validity. Again, on the surface, there seems to be some evidence for it. As we saw in Chapter 3, the media coverage of presidents has turned acerbic since the 1960s, and many thought that its relentless and seedy treatment on the television, press, and the Internet was what fueled the affair. Didn't the talking heads bloviate day in and day out for a year about semen-stained dresses, whether the president's actions with Monica Lewinsky qualified as sex or not, and other tawdry things? It is difficult not to come to the conclusion that the Lewinsky scandal was just another feeding frenzy, the product of the pertinacious post-Watergate media on the prowl for scoop with no respect for the privacy of public figures. The conservative news sources such as Fox and the *Drudge Report* might have aggravated the president's predicament, but wasn't it Michael Isikoff, a reporter working for the presumably liberal *Newsweek*, who first got the dirt on Clinton? And there is evidence that American politics have become more confrontational with proportions of moderates in each party dropping and the ideological distance between the Republicans and Democrats widening since the mid-1960s.[5] Weren't the Republicans particularly pugnacious in their pursuit of the president, so much that in the end their political pugilism cost them the midterm legislative elections in November 1998?

Yet the activist account has problems of its own. Aren't we forgetting that the Lewinsky scandal was foremost a legal affair? Even though the impeachment was a political operation governed by partisan passions, and even if we could attribute ulterior motives to Kenneth Starr, the transgressions that got the president into trouble were legal ones. And we should also remember that a good deal of the media coverage of the scandal simply followed the legal process. It seems that American journalists were scarcely more prurient than American law. In any case, media are neither homogeneous nor omnipotent. Far from it, they are internally fractious and very much constrained by social norms (decency, the notions of "news fit to print," and public interest) and laws (on defamation, privacy, and speech).

It is unclear whether American news sources are exceptionally prurient by disposition. Consider again France. There is no evidence that the French are not interested in the private lives of public figures. President Nicolas Sarkozy's affair with the supermodel-turned-singer Carla Bruni that ended with marriage was closely followed by the French media. The main reason there are few sex scandals in contemporary French politics are the legal protections that Gallic politicians enjoy against the unfavorable publicization of their private lives in the form of tough privacy and defamation laws.[6] The media are cognizant of these protections and act accordingly. The editor of *Paris Match* was fired in 2005 after the weekly magazine published a cover photo of the wife of the then Interior Minister Nicolas Sarkozy and her lover. Former President François Mitterrand could long keep the existence of a daughter born out of wedlock out of the papers despite the fact that many in the tout-Paris were in the swim. The matter was revealed again by *Paris Match* in 1994, just months before he left office – but only after Mitterrand authorized the story. Compared with their French counterparts, the American media are legally much less constrained.

Intensified partisanship in American politics can explain in part the treatment that Clinton received from the Republicans. But the activist account of the Lewinsky affair – and, by extension, of the high incidence of sex scandals in the contemporary United States – is inherently unsatisfactory unless we understand the conditions that make journalistic and political acrimony both possible and profitable. As we saw in the third chapter, this has to do in part with the post-Vietnam and post-Watergate environment, which decreased confidence in the government and thereby made politicians more and more vulnerable to moral attacks from society, law, and each other. This cannot, however, be the whole story, for it does not tell us why so many barbs aimed at politicians of all ranks in the past forty years have been about sexual depravity.

I show in this chapter that a fundamental enabling structural condition of the rise of national sex scandals in the United States has been, paradoxically, the sexual liberalization of the sixties. Sex scandals luxuriate in settings in which the publicity of sex has lost a good deal of its embarrassing, shameful, discomfiting quality for audiences. I call this declining modesty. The relative attenuation of the puritanism of Americans since the early sixties has dramatically lowered the threshold of shame associated with the publicity of sexuality. As a result, sex talk in public has been normalized, indeed banalized. And as Americans lost their modesty, their reticence also declined. A by-product of the relative ease with which contemporary Americans talk about – and especially listen to and read about – sex in public is that the symbolic and emotional costs of public accusations of sexual misconduct both for accusers and audiences have dwindled, even though fewer people are outraged (and somewhat less so) when scandals occur. We have here another instance of a negative relationship between frequency of scandal and its negative effects on the public.

Declining modesty has, furthermore, laid the ground for the politicization of sex by various groups, from feminists to conservatives. Sexual politics is intimately linked to the rise in scandal activity in the American public sphere. It has not only generated novel norms regulating sexual behavior; it has also attacked the privacy that had formerly shrouded sexuality from public view. As a result, public discourse on sexuality has not simply been tolerated but actively encouraged and even legally prescribed.

There are then two proximate causes of the rise of sex scandals in America, and they have both been enabled by sexual liberalization: declining modesty and politicization of sexuality. As I show shortly, the former is, in many ways, the condition of the latter. But let us first make a detour for an exploration of the relationship between sex and scandal.

## Sex and Scandal

What accounts for the close association, since time immemorial, between sex and scandal? Why is sexual wrongdoing from the Trial of the Templars of the early thirteenth century (in which the legendary knights were accused of everything from pedophilia to homosexuality) to the Diamond Necklace affair of the 1780s (which involved aspersions of adultery on the part of the French queen Marie-Antoinette) to the Lewinsky crisis the common fodder of scandal?

Sex, given our biology, is instinctually attractive. The sexual doings of the high and mighty are particularly riveting, for they tend to be less typical than what the hoi polloi experience in their humdrum lives. Hence, a celebrity sex scandal – and contemporary politicians are often celebrities – gratifies on several levels. We are afforded intimate peeks into the lives of important people, whom we often find to be fascinating. We are offered an opportunity to live vicariously through the sexual experiences that are not ordinarily accessible for want of opportunity, moral qualms, lack of imagination, or maybe cowardice. Simultaneously, a sex scandal slakes our all-too-natural resentfulness by giving us a chance to see those, whose better fortunes are frequently unforgivable, to get their comeuppance. And finally, unlike an accounting scandal, a sex scandal is fairly simple and features a cast we can easily identify with or react against. We find it much more natural to adjudicate on sexual matters: the capacity to judge does not call for special expertise because we have all in various ways tackled moral issues regarding our or others' sexual behavior.

There is clearly something to the nonpareil dramatic force of sexual wrongdoing, to the ease with which it obtains attention. It is not a coincidence that adultery has been a standard narrative device in most literature, high and low, Western or otherwise. But I think this is only part of the story, for sex scandals, like all scandals, generate moral outrage. Sex is not just absorbing. It also lends itself readily to moralizing. A good deal of moral regulation in society targets sexual behavior, even in the liberated Western world – consider attitudes toward bestiality, necrophilia, romantic involvements between professors and students, and incest. Sexual behavior that is consensual (like sex with teenagers or even office flings) can very well provoke multifarious legal or social sanctions. Perhaps more important, many sexual norms are supported by a vehement emotion: disgust. So in sum sex has a dual nature. On one hand, it is essential, salient, and attractive. On the other hand, it is very much a moral matter. Despite significant variations, sexual activity is, in almost all cultures, thought to be fraught with perils and is therefore in need of regulation by external prohibitions as well as internal controls such as shame.

The moral regulation of sexuality is not restricted to actual behavior. It extends to the discursive or visual depictions of things sexual in public. All societies differentiate between legitimate and illegitimate ways to represent sexuality. Direct, inappropriate, or excessive public representation is often embarrassing, if not outright shameful, not only for the norm violators but for the audiences as well – even though societies may disagree as to what is direct, inappropriate, and excessive. As we saw in the Victorian case, publicization of sex through talk is deemed in many cultures to have negative consequences for all those exposed to it and is thought to have a corrupting influence.

In other words, sex is closely linked to taboo – regardless of the fact that the strength of the sex taboos varies historically and geographically. I don't intend to furnish a full-fledged theory of taboo here – a thorny subject that would require extensive cross-cultural work. Mary Douglas has argued that it is a moral prohibition springing from a cognitive puzzle and that it refers to things and beings that resist classification. "Taboo is a spontaneous device for protecting the distinctive categories of the universe.... It confronts the ambiguous and shunts it into the category of the sacred."[7] So the dietary restrictions in Judaism target the meat of animals that do not fit in the existing taxonomic systems. Pork is, for instance, taboo because although pigs have cloven hoof like the ungulates, they don't chew cud. Yet not all categorically ill-fitting animals fit the bill. Dolphins are mammals that live in the sea and hence should be unnerving to us. Yet, as Miller points out, there are no taboos against them.[8] Nor is it really possible to understand from this perspective the taboos surrounding sexuality, nudity, and excrement.

Taboo is not a simple social prohibition. Rather, as Douglas herself argues, it tends to refer more specifically to the avoidance of a dangerous entity, which can be an object, idea, word, or even person. It is believed that contact with this entity – or being exposed to its visual or verbal representation – will bring about danger. Thus, as some theorists have noted but not adequately theorized, not only the profane but also the sacred can be taboo.[9] For instance, the name of God is ineffable for Jews. It is perhaps not a coincidence that for the ancient Hebrews the ultimate scandal came from God himself, whose name was the greatest taboo. In the Bible the word "scandal" refers both to "a stumbling block" and to "great havoc." Moses is, for instance, said to have scandalized the Egyptian Pharaoh with the ten plagues.[10] It was also believed that the only one who could scandalize the dwellers of Jerusalem was, however, YHVH, seen as "the unique snare."[11]

By thinking of taboo as a solution to a cognitive conundrum, theorists have also neglected to take into account our consequentialist attitude toward its violations. And a taboo breaking will entail all the more unforeseeable and uncontrollable effects to the extent that it is public. The intention of the transgressor is often immaterial. As we saw in the Victorian case, despite the widespread grapevine about Wilde's transgressions, homosexuality was nevertheless a big taboo in nineteenth-century England. Publicly talking about it, even to denounce homosexuals, would unwittingly bring about dangerous contaminations not only on the speaker but also on the audiences. Or take the racial epithet "nigger," which has acquired taboo status in the contemporary United States since the 1960s. One cannot utter the word in public, even to denounce its use, unless one is black. Even then it remains a dangerous word.[12]

We observe substantial historical and geographical variations in the extent to which sexuality is moralized in taboos. Ancient Greeks were fairly (and shockingly from our perspective) tolerant of pederasty.[13] They did nevertheless disapprove of lesbianism and sequestered their women. Athenians were comfortable with nude male athletes but were outraged by the lightly clad Spartan women participating in sportive activities. When Plato wrote that pederastic love is better left unconsummated, he was implicitly acknowledging its baseness. Moreover, the Greeks believed that sexual sins had vast contaminating powers even when they were committed unknowingly. The city of Thebes was polluted by Oedipus's incest regardless of the fact that the king had not acted immorally – in the sense of intending evil.

A final connection between sex and scandal. A scandal usually breaks with a moral assault of some kind – a public denunciation or provocation. And although we don't have to agree with some radical feminists who think all sexual intercourse is rape, sex undeniably has some kinship with aggression – at least at the symbolic or iconic level. Consider Jack Katz's marvelous phenomenology of road rage in Los Angeles, where frustrated drivers frequently resort to symbolic anal rape by "giving the finger" to avenge their symbolic castration when they are cut off in traffic.[14] It is not a coincidence that vituperation often includes sexual metaphors to degrade the addressee to his or her biological being. Political attack is no stranger to pornographic lexicon and imagery.[15] What the denouncers attempt to expose in political scandals are often the corporeal excesses of public officials at odds with their sublime pretensions to embody the common weal.[16]

## Sex and Politics in the Nineteenth-Century United States

Sex is both captivating and morally dangerous. Yet, while interest in things sexual is more or less constant through time and space, public reserve about sex is socially and historically quite variable.

The level of sex scandal activity is closely affected by this variability. The American experience bears out this relationship.

The early republic witnessed a large number of public attacks on the sexual righteousness of its patrician elites.[17] Both Washington and Adams were accused of philandering and siring bastards. The Hamilton-Jefferson strife, which began when the two dignitaries were members of Washington's cabinet, was played out through denunciations of dissoluteness. Hamilton was blasted for his adulterous entanglement with a married woman in 1796 by a local muckraking pamphleteer named James Callender, who was subsidized by Hamilton's archenemy Thomas Jefferson. Callender got into prison for sedition when he sailed into Adams, but Jefferson pardoned his former hatchet man soon after he became president. The Jefferson-Callender alliance was short-lived, however. Callender soon sidled up to the Federalists and in 1802 trumpeted out in the *Richmond Recorder* the new president's affair with Sally Hemmings, Jefferson's seventeen-year-old mulatto slave, who, according to recent DNA evidence, bore him children. An elated John Quincy Adams printed a satirical ballad in a Boston paper on the scandal:

> Of all the damsels on the green,
> On mountain, or in valley,
> A lass so luscious ne'er was seen,
> As Monticellian Sally.
> You call her a slave – and pray were slaves
> Made only for the galley?
> Try for yourselves, ye witless knaves –
> Take each to bed your Sally.[18]

This was not the last attack on Jefferson. In 1805, Callender exposed in the *New York Evening Post* how the president debauched the wife of a close friend. Here is how the editorial judged him: "He has corrupted the integrity of the nation, has demoralized the American people for the purpose of promoting his personal aggrandizement." He was a "scoundrel," a "scourge," "the outcast of America."[19]

The Jackson and Adams sides walloped each other with allegations of sexual misconduct in the campaign of 1828.[20] The Jackson supporters accused Adams's fiancé of having slept with him before marriage. A journalist excoriated Quincy Adams not only for being a monarchist, but also for acting as a pimp for Czar Alexander of Russia. The other side countered by pointing out that Andrew Jackson's wife was a divorcée and that he had lived with her while she was married to someone else. In addition to being an adulterer and bigamist, Jackson's detractors said, the presidential hopeful had a strumpet for a mother and was the son of a mongrel father.

Things changed little with the establishment of the Jacksonian democracy. Gail Collins reports that almost every presidential candidate in the antebellum era was rumored to be either a bastard or the father of a second family, even though such talk did not always eventuate in significant scandals.[21] Vice presidents were targets, too. Martin van Buren was said to be the illegitimate offspring of Jefferson's vice president Aaron Burr. When van Buren himself rose to the presidency, the opposition press this time buffeted his vice president, Richard Johnson, for having a black mistress and two children from her. Lincoln and Andrew Johnson both tried to clear their mothers' reputation by brandishing birth records. The facility with which presidents and presidential candidates alike could be fusilladed in public for sexual sins, real or imagined, continued until the 1884 campaign when the Republicans harried Grover Cleveland for getting a store clerk pregnant while he was the sheriff of Buffalo. The Democrats responded in kind, by drubbing the Republican candidate James Blaine for his shotgun marriage. They alleged that his wife had given birth to her son just three months after the couple's marriage. Cleveland edged out his contender, but it seems that the scandal hurt him in a campaign that he started as the shoo-in: he won by only 0.3 percent of the vote.

The high level of sexual attacks in American political life until the middle of the penultimate decade of the nineteenth century would not be so curious if things had not changed so fundamentally thereafter. As Summers points out, from 1884 to late 1960s, we would be hard-pressed to find a major politician in office who had to deal with a sex scandal.[22] I already discussed in the third chapter how nineteenth-century presidents lacked institutional protections against normative attacks, something that they acquired in the course of the twentieth century as the office grew ascendant in American political and social life. This cannot be the whole explanation, however. In this period, we see a relative decline in sex scandal activity involving not just presidents but politicians of all kinds. In fact, we seem to find fewer scandals not merely in politics but in the public sphere in general until the 1960s and 1970s. Both Hollywood celebrities and the Catholic Church started to become snared in scandal almost routinely only after the 1960s and 1970s.

The abrasive press of the nineteenth century obviously has something to do with the sex scandals of the time.[23] Coming from a world in which manners were paramount, Tocqueville had much scorn for the down-and-dirty American journalism:

> So generally American journalists have a low social status, their education is only sketchy, and their thoughts are often vulgarly expressed. In all things, the majority makes the law.... [T]he hallmark of the American journalist is a direct and coarse attack, without any subtleties, on the passions of his readers; he disregards principles to seize on people, following them into their private lives and laying bare their weaknesses and vices.[24]

Yet it would be fallacious to attribute all the responsibility to the journalists. Many of them – but not all because an independent and sensationalistic yellow press had made its entrée into the American public sphere in the 1830s – were themselves at the pay of political actors. Politicians themselves did not refrain from dirtying their own hands. Recall the poem that Quincy Adams printed about Jefferson and Sally Hemmings. It is difficult to imagine a high-status nineteenth-century English politician hollering such vulgarities in public. Nor would the respectable classes be the accommodating audience of such ribald discourse. In contrast, American society in general was candid about sexual matters, and both the press and politicians took advantage of this. The nonreticent media were merely part of a society characterized by low modesty – the condition of raffish attacks in nineteenth-century political life, particularly during campaign periods.[25]

Frankness sprang from two sources. The first one is the fiercely egalitarian culture of the New World. Tocqueville saw a connection between the democratic sentiment in Jacksonian America and the crudity of the public discourse. Modesty about things sexual has a lot to do with attention to proper form and with the suppression of things biological as contaminating matter. These attitudes are in part historical: according to Norbert Elias, the nineteenth-century European reserve, epitomized in Victorianism, was the culmination of a gradual "civilizing process," which consisted of an ever-increasing threshold of shame and disgust regarding violence, sexuality, and biological functions.[26] Standards of civility took root in the aristocratic and middle classes in early modernity. As societies differentiated and interdependencies between individuals increased with the rise of the modern state and capitalism, the new norms gradually expanded to the general population.[27] Modesty nevertheless still functioned for a long time as a social marker, differentiating the respectable strata from the rabble. You will recall from the second chapter that the nineteenth-century English working classes were far less prudish than the middle and upper classes. Upward mobility required adopting discursive modesty. In accordance with the same logic, the nineteenth-century American society, which did not have an aristocratic past and boasted of an egalitarian self-image, deprecated fussiness about social niceties as pretentious haughtiness.[28] Americans took a demotic delight in not mincing their words, in proudly calling a spade a spade in all things, including those of a sexual nature.[29]

The second factor underlying the low level of reserve in nineteenth-century America is the communal control of sexuality. Well into the nineteenth century, in many places until the Civil War, a good deal of moral regulation in society was undertaken by the local community.[30] Western Europe urbanized faster and more profoundly, while much of the United States retained – and to a certain extent still retains – its small-town character. According to the Puritan theology, which dominated the colonial period and whose vestiges hued the nineteenth century, the local community was the primary moral agent.[31] Public accusation and confession were thus an integral part of the enforcement of sexual mores; individual and familial privacy interests were often set aside. As long as they publicly made a clean breast of their sins, women convicted of fornication could (re)marry and join the church in the eighteenth century. The communal aspect of sexual regulation carried over well into the next century and motivated the public denunciations of lecherous politicians. Social control through publicity was not limited to prominent citizens, however. Moral reform societies, remarkably busy across the northern states, revealed the names of local adulterers and fornicators to mortify them in front of their community.[32]

## The Rise of Modesty

The public sphere of the antebellum America, an arena of routine mud-slinging, was mostly a local one. Only 4 percent of the population lived in urban settings in 1830. The post–Civil War epoch, in contrast, witnessed the creation of an increasingly anonymous, urbanized, and national public sphere with the growth of print media. As Paul Starr points out, it was mostly after 1870 that metropolitan press with mass circulation evolved into an important force.[33] Various elements attempted to fill the expanded and unified public domain with sexuality. The penny press had been pushing for sensationalistic coverage since the 1830s. Albeit underground, a national market in pornographic material thrived in the 1860s. Capitalists wanted suggestive advertisements for their products. Urbanization, energized by the great flux of immigration from Europe, allowed the expansion of prostitution. Some social reform groups started to demand frank discussions of sex for medical purposes in the last decades of the nineteenth century. Other forces, however, withstood with remarkable resilience so that the resultant national public sphere until the late 1960s was in many ways more reticent than nineteenth-century small-town America.

Strong voices were heard in society, principally from the middle and upper classes, clamoring for modesty. The communal control of sexuality had already, yet gradually, wilted in the nineteenth century. Church courts were abolished in communities, and sins were no longer confessed to the local public but communicated in written form and in secret to religious officials.[34] From the 1840s onward, moral discipline came to center on child rearing.[35] After the Civil War, the regulation of sexuality was mostly left to the confidentiality of the intimate unit. Privacy was becoming critical for families, which attempted as much as possible to control the flow of information between the intimate domestic domain and the expanded, anonymous, and dangerous public realm. The menace of moral depredation for families grew all the more acute with the increasing amount of sexual material in the mass media and with the spreading of urban prostitution during the last decades of the nineteenth century. Higher classes wanted to shield themselves from the leveling effects of democracy by their insistence on reserve about sexual matters. They also wanted to mark their difference from the rough-hewn urban working classes, whose unadorned, prosaic attitude toward sexuality was seen as crass. In this they were partially successful, and the upshot was a belated, somewhat imitative, labored Victorianism among the upper and upper-middle classes that took hold in the last decades of the nineteenth century.

Hence, just as American candidness about sex had to do with democratic egalitarianism, which, of course, did not extend to blacks, the rising modesty was in part linked to the establishment of cultural stratification. During much of the nineteenth century, the public of the mass media crossed socioeconomic lines. A good deal of newspaper patronage was subsidized by political parties, the bases of which transcended class. And the absence of state patronage meant that unsubsidized media products had to resonate with the masses to be economically viable.[36] The post–Civil War era, however, witnessed a differentiation between high and low culture[37] – within literature, entertainment, and the press. Reserve became the very quiddity of high culture, allowing the elite to demarcate themselves sharply from the masses.

The campaign against the publicity of sexuality is synonymous with the name of Anthony Comstock, who, with the help of his well-heeled sponsors in the YMCA, founded the New York Society for the Suppression of Vice in 1873. Thanks to the labors of this organization, a federal antiobscenity bill was passed in 1873 that prohibited the distribution of obscene materials by mail, obscenity here mostly referring to contraceptive and abortive devices and written material about them. The passage of the "Comstock Act" was a milestone for the "party of reticence," in the words of Rochelle Gurstein, who alerts us to the fact that sexual obscenity as a legal category only came about in the course of the nineteenth century.[38] Further, as Paul Starr points out, "A considerable amount of steamy and sensational literature circulated in America in the 1830s and 1840s without exciting Congressional attention, aggressive local law enforcement, or organized demands for censorship."[39] Similarly, information about contraceptive devices had hitherto circulated unimpeded. The decades following the Comstock Act, however, witnessed the ascendancy of state-enforced moral censorship. In their tug-of-war with reformers advocating sex education, those urging reserve had the upper hand. The latter drew their support from various groups. For instance, a gynecologist speaking at an American Medical Association meeting at the turn of the century said that the topic of venereal disease was so "attendant with filth" that "we besmirch ourselves by discussing it in public."[40] In 1906, when the *Ladies Home Journal* was as bold as to run a story on the issue, 75,000 women discontinued their subscriptions.[41]

Even though he was a private citizen, Comstock was authorized by Congress to enforce the obscenity statutes as a special agent of the post office, which he did with vigor and vim. But it would be facile to chalk him up as an anachronistic puritan. His crusade was not so much against immoral behavior as against obscenity. The New York Society for the Suppression of Vice, like many similar associations in other cities, did not target prostitution but obscenity, with a view to protect children from the corrupting influences of the publicity of sexuality.[42] That Comstock was more interested in reticence than complete sexual rectitude can be verified in the Beecher-Tilton affair of 1872.[43] The scandal featured as its main character Henry Ward Beecher, the famous pastor of the Plymouth Church of Brooklyn. Beecher was also an inveterate womanizer, with a record of adulterous relations with numerous women in his parish, including the wife of the founder of the church. Beecher's latest conquest was Elizabeth Tilton, the wife of Charles Tilton, the editor of a well-known liberal newspaper. The husband eventually got wind of the affair, but all the parties involved maintained silence to forefend a scandal. Although others came to learn about the matter as well, it took Victoria Woodhull's publicization of it in her newspaper *Woodhull and Claflin's Weekly* in 1872 for a scandal to erupt.

Woodhull was a voluble advocate of free love and had been nominated for president by the Equal Rights Party. Politicking had, however, marred her political ambitions. Embittered by her former allies who forsook her, Woodhull decided to divulge the secrets of the famous, especially those who had betrayed her, to make a point about the rampancy, and hence the legitimacy, of free love. Although it was she who broke the scandal by revealing Beecher's adultery, Woodhull actually defended him in her story. Respectable society unanimously condemned her for the exposé, and Comstock sent Woodhull to jail on obscenity charges. She was ultimately acquitted, but the reaction that Woodhull faced shows that America had already started to move away from the boisterous times in which sexual scandalmongering was a sport for the elite of the nation.

The reformist era brought about a new concern. Prior to the famous article of Samuel Warren and Louis Brandeis of 1890, which demanded a legal protection for privacy, there had been no real discussion of the notion. The two jurists saw respect for privacy as the indispensable component of human dignity. Their main worry, spurred by Warren's discomfort with the inordinate attention that her daughter's wedding had obtained in the press, was the profanation of the "sacred precincts of private and domestic life," a process they also called "the cheapening of public discourse."[44]

These developments did not fail to produce effects in the political sphere. As Michael Schudson points out, the last decades of the nineteenth century heralded a new, rational political culture.[45] Reformists wanted politics to be less emotional, less interest-driven, less corrupt, and more elevated. The secret ballot was instituted, civil service was established, and political parties were divested of a good deal of their clout in the late nineteenth and early twentieth centuries. As a result, politics, and particularly political campaigns, which had always been the main settings of allegations of sexual wrongdoing, sloughed off their rowdy, carnivalesque character to molt into a civilized, somber matter.

The press heeded the call as well. Once the simple mouthpieces of political parties, many newspapers now not only aspired to independence but also to high-principled reportage. In an editorial that he wrote after acquiring the *New York Times* in 1896, Adolph Ochs stated that his aim was to provide news "in language that is parliamentary in good society." Surely the yellow journalism promoted by newspaper tycoons such as William Hearst and Joseph Pulitzer did not disappear. On the contrary. But, on the whole, the general culture of modesty made the press corps more reticent and charier of libel laws, and the more serious papers defined themselves by their distance from the sensationalist press. Gail Collins points out that the modus operandi of the press corps after the 1870s was that the private lives of political actors was off limits unless something pushed them inevitably into the public sphere.[46] Reserve toward sexual matters (above all when the political elite were at stake) was a strategy by which journalists enhanced their prestige. Sterilizing and sublimating politics, the media members elevated themselves by claiming some kind of parity with what they covered.

Twentieth-century American politicians until the late sixties were thus largely exempt from sex scandals. Journalists ignored the talk about Wilson's relationship with a married woman. Theodore Roosevelt, his opponent, balked at bringing it up during the campaign of 1912. The press exercised much self-censorship during the presidency of Franklin Delano Roosevelt, above all with regard to his mistress Lucy Mercer who resided in the White House for long stretches of time and who was at his bedside when he died. The most blatant case is that of John F. Kennedy. We saw in the third chapter how the symbolic elevation of the office of the presidency shielded Kennedy, who had wads of sexual encounters with all kinds of women. The goatish president's affair with Marilyn Monroe was well known among the press corps, FBI, and Hollywood. No one breathed a word, and not only out of respect for the presidency. After all, stories about Kennedy's sexual appetite were already unpalatable for the press before he ran for the White House. Seymour Hersh recounts the following incident in his biography of the president.[47] When he was a young senator, Kennedy was the target of a letter-writing campaign by a middle-aged housewife named Florence Kater, who was infuriated by his depraved sexual morals. To expose Kennedy, one day she photographed him scurrying out of the apartment of a comely congressional aide at 3:00 A.M. and then mailed a copy of the picture to fifty leading citizens in New York and Washington, D.C., including editors, columnists, and politicians. No one would have anything to do with the story.

The sybaritic Jazz Age was the exceptional decade during this period of modesty, and it proves the point about the positive relationship between sexual liberalism and political scandal.[48] With consumerism ascendant, the middle classes started to embrace lower-class sexual mores in the 1920s. Dating became both increasingly common[49] and more adventurous, thanks in part to the privacy afforded by automobiles and the availability of diaphragms. Women wore low-cut dresses and danced to sensual music. Movies offered licentious material. There was nudity in *Ben-Hur* (1925), suggestive lesbianism in *Morocco* (1930), and some sort of decadence in almost any one of Cecil B. DeMille's sumptuous pictures. And this was also the time when Hearst's papers were imbued with Hollywood smut like the kind exposed during the 1921 trial of the silent film star Roscoe "Fatty" Arbuckle, tried for the manslaughter death of an actress. It is not a fluke that the only major political sex scandal of the period from 1884 to 1969 could break in this decade of relative sexual liberalization, which made sex easier to publicize. In 1927, four years after Warren Harding died in office – and after he had posthumously fallen from grace as a result of the Teapot Dome scandal – one of his mistresses published a tell-all, under-the-counter book on their affair and lovechild.

The Depression put an end to this wild bout. Discretionary income dropped, and the 1920s seemed debauched in retrospect. A period of sexual austerity was ushered in, resulting in a call back to modesty. The Legion of Decency, formed in 1934, threatened to boycott the movie industry for its offensive merchandise. Hollywood was muzzled by the 1934 production code, which set the standard until the 1960s. Almost all explicit content was now verboten. The Supreme Court's *Ulysses* decision in 1933 indicated that artistic intent could be a legitimate justification for publicizing eroticism, but scabrous books such as *Tropic of Cancer*, which appeared first in 1934 in Paris, could not be published freely in the United States until 1961 – when Henry Miller's novel provoked an obscenity trial. Neither judges nor defendants' lawyers regarded literary depictions of sex as a first amendment issue until the fifties.[50]

The second half of 1940s and the 1950s witnessed an ongoing tussle between modesty and frankness. On one hand, the Kinsey Reports on male and female sexuality that were published, respectively, in 1948 and 1953 revealed – or rather claimed because its findings were later found to be inflated by unscientific methodology – that petting, masturbation, and homosexuality were much more widely practiced than what the average American thought.[51] A major discrepancy between private behavior and public norms was thus exposed. The first volume of the report sold 250,000 copies, and Alfred Kinsey made it to the cover of *Time*. Soft-porn magazines such as *Playboy* (which featured partial nudity) and scandal sheets such as *Confidential* (which traded in gossip about the indiscretions of celebrities without, however, naming names) made strides in publicizing sex.

Yet these developments did not go unchallenged. The suburban domesticity of the postwar period made the middle classes skittish about sexual material in the public sphere, even as the surging incomes of the 1950s allowed for a flourishing market for pornography for men.[52] In 1952, Congress authorized an investigation into obscenity in paperbacks, magazines, and comic books. The antiobscenity drive was spearheaded by the Catholic Church, with its branch the National Organization for Decent Literature in the forefront. By the end of the 1950s, fourteen states had stiffened their obscenity laws. There was a noticeable hike in the representation of sexuality in low-status and underground literature, but elites and respectable media kept their high-mindedness. Even the entertainment world, by and large, subscribed to them. Film noir often tested the boundaries of what was morally acceptable, but mainstream American cinema on the whole churned out sexless pictures until the 1960s. Hollywood studios exercised tight control over the public personas of stars, and journalists who were privy to their dirty secrets often did not write about them. Those who strayed in an unavoidably open manner, like Ingrid Bergman, set off scandals,[53] but such cases were few and far in between.

## Sexual Liberalization and the Decline of Modesty

Sexual liberalism emerged in the 1960s as a contending ethic in the United States and, by the end of the decade, had become dominant. Young demographics and the ideology of expressive individualism mingled to defy traditional norms. Sex grew autonomous from procreation and the nuclear family. Only less than a quarter of Americans endorsed premarital sex at the end of the 1950s. By the late 1970s, this was the percentage of those who deemed such activity to be wrong. Age at marriage rose; fertility rates dropped. Divorce and cohabitation rates skyrocketed from the sixties on, debilitating the hitherto unquestioned status of marriage as the normal living arrangement in society. For many baby boomers, free sexuality had even affinities with resistance against authority, political or parental.

We saw in the second chapter that the very repulsiveness of a transgression for a public may cause underenforcement in view of its negative externalities when publicized. Hence, the softening of sentiments toward an offense, by abating the undesirable effects of its publicity, may give rise to souped-up enforcement. This mechanism applies above all to the case of taboo-like transgressions and offers clues into why contemporary American politics is routinely plagued with sex scandals. Far from being the expression of some antiquated puritanism in the American psyche, the phenomenon is, on the contrary, an unintended upshot of sexual liberalization in a context of debased political authority. The relative relaxation of sexual mores since the early sixties made the publicity of sex appreciably less contaminating for much of the national audiences. Liberalization increased the demand for the public presence of sex in visual or discursive form, for serious reasons as well as for sheer fun. The American media cheerfully purveyed, and the law gave the green light. From the 1930s on, the Supreme Court had continually narrowed the definition of obscenity. But until the 1960s, it was usually artistic intent that legitimated the public representation of sexuality. In contrast, the Warren court affirmed sex as apposite for general consumption in its decisions during this decade.

By the end of the 1970s, the media had dropped the use of circumlocution in sex talk, popular music was already sodden with explicit lyrics, nudity was standard staple in mainstream cinema, adult movie theaters were shooting up everywhere in the land, and suggestive advertisement had become commonplace. Sex on television not only was normalized but also took on a recreational character in the 1970s.[54] The successful TV show *All in the Family* tackled outré topics like homosexuality. *Three's Company*, portraying a man with two attractive female roommates, dealt with less risky matter but with much more raciness. Candid shows on television and radio addressing sexual issues with varying levels of levity crowded the airways in the 1980s and 1990s. A recent report by the Kaiser Family Foundation found that there is one sex scene every four minutes on broadcast and basic cable television, and one sex scene every 90 seconds on premium cable.[55]

To get a sense of the drastic decline of modesty in the American public sphere since the early sixties, consider the following. David Brinkley of NBC was prohibited from saying "venereal disease" on the air in 1962.[56] It was too risqué, too embarrassing for Americans. Compare this with the coverage of the Clinton scandals where the public was treated routinely to reports about "the distinguishing marks on president's penis" and "the semen-stained dress." Lest you put the responsibility on the trashy tabloid and cable media, take the following excerpt from a 1997 story published in the *New York Times*, the American newspaper of record, devoted to oral sex practices among adolescents: "'Do you spit or do you swallow?' is a typical seventh-grade question for girls."[57] This was language "parliamentary in good society" for our most highbrow news outlet one year before Clinton's impeachment.

A fallout of the ease with which contemporary Americans talk about, listen to, and read about sex in public is that the individual and collective costs of making accusations of sexual misconduct about political actors have dramatically dwindled. Of course, the relaxation of sexual mores means that fewer people are outraged (and somewhat less so) in the scandals that erupt. But this trend has been far outpaced by the rate at which sex talk has been normalized, if not banalized, both for the accusers and the audiences, liberals and conservatives. The declining modesty combined with the symbolic degradation of political institutions since Vietnam, and the obstacles to publicizing the sexual misdemeanors of American public figures were remarkably lowered.

It is not adventitious that it was in the 1970s that sex scandals made a comeback to the American political discourse. Suddenly national news was inundated with garden variety adulteries of politicians. Congressmen were being caught flat-footed with prostitutes. Consider, among countless other examples, how Congressman Wilbur Mills was eventually ousted out of office in 1974 after the whole world learned about his dalliance with a stripper after a car accident. Mistresses were suddenly outing political lovers – as in the story broken by the *Washington Post* in 1976 about Congressman Wayne Hays and his secretary Elizabeth Ray, who famously admitted, "I can't type. I can't file. I can't even answer the phone." Congressional wives posed nude for *Playboy*. And it was in 1975, in this new zeitgeist, that John F. Kennedy's illicit sex life was thrust into the public sphere. By the 1980s, television stories about sexual wrongdoing by politicians were already unexceptional, women of varying respectability appearing on *Geraldo* and *Larry King* to tell their steamy escapades with Washington types.[58]

The sole national homosexuality scandal with some political connection that broke prior to the sixties was the Newport Affair of 1921, and it is significant that the event did not feature homosexual politicians but questionable techniques by the Navy to prosecute homosexuals. The affair revolved around an undercover entrapment operation by the Navy officials. Sailors were recruited to solicit sex with a view to expose a ring of suspected homosexuals at the naval training station in Newport, a ritzy resort town in Rhode Island. Franklin D. Roosevelt was the Assistant-Secretary of the Navy at the time, even though he would later claim total ignorance. The suspects were going to be dealt with in the usual way, in secret court-martials, so that the U.S. Navy would not be disgraced. Some zealous investigators, however, wanted to extend the operation into the civilian population using the same methods. An Episcopal Rhode Island minister was arrested and tried twice. Although he was acquitted both times, the entrapment procedures were laid bare during the trial as the minister's defense attorney produced undercover operatives who testified about their encounters. The judge and the jury were outraged at the operation techniques, which ipso facto required debauching sailors. Two months later a congressional investigation took place, which produced a report judging the Navy's activities to be "reprehensible." Graphic sexual acts were described in a Senate committee, but the *New York Times* headline was LAY NAVY SCANDAL TO F. D. ROOSEVELT, DETAILS ARE UNPRINTABLE. The story simply referred to the investigation of "immoralities" in the Navy. The scandal had few consequences and soon blew over.

The fifties saw a hardening of the anti-homosexuality norms within the federal government.[59] Yet one would be hard-pressed to find a major scandal involving homosexuality until 1964. That year Walter Jenkins, one of Lyndon Johnson's closest aides, was arrested during the presidential campaign for soliciting in the men's room of a Washington, D.C., YMCA. He agreed to resign, and the press was persuaded not to run a story, but the Republicans wanted to use the incident for political gain. William Miller, the Republican vice presidential candidate, pushed the president for an explanation, saying that "If this type of man had information vital to our survival, it could be compromised very quickly and very dangerously." Miller was basing his assault on the pervasive belief that homosexuals, given their vulnerability to blackmail, should not be entrusted with high positions in the government. Nevertheless, the press coverage was sparse and circumspect. Neither the Republicans nor the press dared say openly why the aide was arrested. This is how the *New York Times* of October 16, 1964, ran the story: "Mr. Jenkins resigned last night after the disclosure that he had been arrested on morals charges last week and in 1959."

In contrast, many politicians were alleged to be or exposed as homosexuals in the eighties and nineties. Some came out themselves. Actual legal sanctions against gays disappeared during this time with sexual liberalism. Sodomy laws were now dead letters, and American society on the whole grew much more tolerant of homosexuality. Incidents did, nevertheless, draw attention and were seen as scandalous by red America: conservative politicians who were revealed to be gay often suffered from the reactions of their constituents.

More important, the declining embarrassment of reading about homosexuality in the papers also made it possible for all kinds of seedy stories to make the news. These featured not only homosexuals but other items such as prostitute lovers, affairs with subordinates or teens, sexual harassment, and drugs. Officially, it was usually these elements that gave offense – even though, given the exceptionally vehement responses some of these scandals obtained, one wonders if there was not some other less politically correct motive lurking behind the outrage. Here are a couple of examples. In the page scandal of 1982, allegations were made that some male pages on Capitol Hill were engaging in sexual activity with their bosses. A cocaine ring was alleged as well. The affair was closely covered by the CBS and the *Wall Street Journal*, so the Ethics Committee of Congress felt compelled to look into the matter. It turned out, however, in the end that that the pages had been fudging stories. In contrast, Garry Studds (D-Mass.) was censured by the House for having sex with a page in 1983. In 1989, the live-in lover of Congressman Barney Frank of Massachusetts was revealed to be running a male prostitution operation from home. Frank was reprimanded by the House. Take also the Mark Foley affair of October 2006, a scandal that took the intensity that it did not only because the gay congressman was as foolhardy as to engage in concupiscent chitchat with pages in an electronic medium notorious for its lack of privacy, but also because few Americans find it inappropriate that such discourse be aired on national television. Many of these incidents would have been handled in a hole-and-corner fashion before the sexual liberation.[60]

Contemporary sex scandals featuring adulterous politicians may seem inconsequential. Yet it was such an episode that ended with Clinton getting impeached. And the effect of decreasing modesty applies to all sexual transgressions, including grievous ones such as pedophilia and pederasty. Philip Jenkins has argued that while the media, political elite, and prosecutors almost conspired to underplay various incidents of sex within the Boy Scouts in the sixties and seventies, the Church was trounced in the 1990s for similar transgressions.[61] His account pinpoints the multiple conditions and processes underlying the scandals that tainted American Catholicism in the 1990s: the declining prestige of the Church during the 1980s, which augmented its vulnerability to attack during the following decade; dissensions within the hierarchy, which led liberal priests to take their grumblings public; the pyramidal structure of the Church, which enabled easy access to all the internal records of accusations and spread responsibility to higher-ups; the reform of the Federal Rules of Civil Procedure in 1968, which expanded the access of litigants to the federal courts; and the crystallizing consensus in American society that sexual offenders are untreatable. These factors underpinned the next and stronger wave of scandals in the early 2000s as well.[62]

Jenkins's analysis is controversial: it is based on the claim that the members of the Catholic Church are not more or less deviant than those of similar organizations. But regardless of the validity of this argument, it is clear that declining reticence played an essential role in the sea change in attitudes toward the Catholic Church. As Jenkins points out, the common wisdom until the seventies shared by psychologists and clergymen alike was that molestation at an early age did not have lasting effects unless the family, law, or society made a big deal out of it. Publicizing the incident was seen as counterproductive. The shame of having been sexually abused was another check on publicity. It was only after these beliefs and sentiments were weakened that sexual abuse scandals could escalate.[63]

Advances in communications technology in the 1990s and 2000s further sexualized the American public sphere. Unlike national television, whose content is regulated to protect children, cable made uncensored (or relatively uncensored) material accessible to a large audience. Raunchy allegations about prominent personalities are ideal to meet the insatiable demands of the 24-hour news cycle. And with the rise of the Internet the publicization costs of such material tobogganed. Perhaps more important, competition from these new sources eroded the boundaries between the respectable and not-respectable media. Whatever misgivings the high-status journalists have had about smut in the public sphere have been minimized as bloggers have come to upend the gate-keeping privileges of higher-status newspapers. Traditionally, it was the low-status tabloid media that handled such contaminating matter. Yet more and more, the elite media, responding to competitive pressures and declining modesty, have begun to run stories started by hitherto infra dignitatem news sources. Also much of scandal coverage tends to take on a somewhat disingenuous dimension such as publishing gossip or running meta-stories about how other media sources are handling allegations. It was a shoddy supermarket tabloid that first released the Gennifer Flowers–Clinton story in 1992, but major networks picked up the news item the following day, and the Clintons appeared on *60 Minutes* to shake off the adultery charges. The public discussion of the matter was thereby legitimated. CNN carried a press conference in which salacious phone conversations between Clinton and Flowers were played.

## The Rise of Sexual Politics

A new factor arose in the seventies that further increased the amount of sexual wrongdoing in the public sphere: sexual politics. Sexuality was not only allowed into the public sphere; it was also pushed there. The declining modesty made it possible for various social actors – including feminists, gay-lesbian activists, along with mainstream and conservative politicians – to publicize sexuality with a view to politicize or legally regulate it. There is an irony here. Sexual politics could not emerge in full force before sexual liberalism had freed the individual from the control of the nuclear family and community and undermined the modesty norms. At the same time, novel rules between individuals have been proposed and instituted by those who politicized sex.

It is impossible to understand the rise of sexual politics in the United States without feminism. The feminists of the 1960s saw public expression of sexuality as the sine qua non of women's liberation. Helen Gurley Brown's *Sex and the Single Girl* and the magazine she ran, *Cosmopolitan*, epitomized this idea. By wearing miniskirts, women would enjoy liberties formerly monopolized by men. Soon most feminists took issue with this equal-opportunity hedonism, however, and targeted domination in private as well as in public. The shibboleth "personal is political" attempted to invalidate the feelings of shame shrouding sexuality so that women could freely and fully discuss and celebrate their biology. Feminists contended that sexual identity is the spring of one's political behavior. Arguing that the intimate world is already a political one, in the sense of being the site of gender domination, feminism also questioned the private-public distinction. Hence, a great deal of interpersonal and domestic life (including their sexual aspects), which was formerly shielded by privacy norms and shame, would now, if necessary, be submitted to public scrutiny and its standards of justice.

An ambivalent attitude to privacy has haunted feminism since the 1970s. Decisional privacy, as in a woman's control over her reproductive functions, is enshrined as a core value.[64] Informational privacy, in the more ordinary sense of immunity from scrutiny,[65] is, however, distrusted, especially when it is extended to the nuclear family. Privacy as such is regarded to be the protective armor of gender domination, a principle that lets abusive practices such as marital rape and sexual harassment to continue unchecked and unquestioned in the private realm.

For feminists like Catherine MacKinnon, a man's domination over a woman had to be understood as the instantiation of men's domination over women.[66] Seemingly interpersonal matters between particulars had to be treated as social issues between genders. What was apparently private had public significance and had to be laid open to scrutiny by all. And feminists argued that gender domination was hardly restricted to the intimate realm but stretched to the workplace and educational organizations. In such settings, sexual harassment meant not only the use of coercion, intimidation, or compensation to obtain sexual favors from women (quid pro quo harassment). It also included any sexual or romantic behavior – or behavior that can be construed as such by women – that would make them uncomfortable and prevent their full participation in public life (hostile environment harassment). Sexual harassment law, which originated in a 1977 reversal by a federal appeals court holding sexual harassment as sex discrimination in employment, was erected on these ideas.

Sexual liberalism provided the conditions for the rise of modern feminism. Yet once the personal was equated with the political – the political understood as power struggle – any kind of sexual relations between unequals in organizations came to be seen as suspicious and even exploitative unless proven otherwise. In the logic of sexual harassment laws, coercion or illegitimate exchange is the de facto assumption. The onus of proving consent on the part of the subordinate (almost always the woman) is on the hierarchical superior (almost always the man). At any rate, consent can never be definitively established: the subordinate party can always retrospectively maintain that what she thought was a consensual relationship was in fact not.

Federal courts progressively expanded the right to sue in harassment cases in the eighties, and many plaintiffs obtained substantial damages. A mounting number of actions were brought against private and public institutions. In response, organizations hastened to sterilize the workplace, not only because they feared liability or wished the symbolic legitimacy associated with such progressive policies but also because it cost them little to do so. Incidents still occur, though, due in part to the vagueness of the hostile environment clause of the sexual harassment law. And when individuals file charges, these are never simply interpersonal matters – they legally concern the whole organization. Corporate accountability gives incentives to regulate and even monitor personal relations between employees and resolve matters internally. But this is obviously not easy, and when people take their grievances to outside agencies – the courts or the media – the prominence of the organizations involved can grant heightened attention to the scandals that result.

A good number of the major political scandals of the 1990s and 2000s had to do with sexual harassment. Some of them were quite momentous. The Republican senator from Oregon, Bob Packwood, resigned in 1995 after a 1992 *Washington Post* report and a thirty-one-month Senate ethics probe found him culpable of making inappropriate remarks to the female members of his staff. The 1991 confirmation hearings of Clarence Thomas witnessed Anita Hill alleging that the nominee to the Supreme Court had sexually harassed her when she worked under him as head of the Equal Employment Opportunities Commission. Hill claimed that Thomas subjected her to talk about sexual acts and pornographic films after she rebuffed his overtures. The nominee denied the allegations and likened the hearings to a lynching.[67] Thomas was eventually confirmed, but the scandal pushed the issue of sexual harassment onto the public consciousness.

In the wake of these scandals, sexual harassment cases more than doubled, from 6,127 in 1991 to 15,342 in 1996, and the monetary awards granted to victims nearly quadrupled, from $7.7 million to $27.8 million, during this period.[68] Assaults against women were alleged in 1995 at the 1991 convention of the Tailhook association, a private group of retired and active-duty U.S. Navy aviators. The secretary of the Navy had to hand in his resignation, and the scandal wounded the careers of fourteen admirals. Republican Mike Bowers's affair with his secretary, when publicized in 1997, set off an uproar during his bid for governor in Georgia. Paula Jones sued Bill Clinton for sexual harassment in 1994. The House Ethics Committee sanctioned many members of Congress following similar allegations in the eighties and nineties.

These scandals aired very intimate and suggestive material. It was thus not just sexual harassment laws themselves but also the atrophy in modesty that enabled their coming about. At another time, Anita Hill, the U.S. senators, and, most important, the American public would have felt too uncomfortable about talk about porn stars and pubic hairs on Coke cans – things, that, according to Anita Hill,

Clarence Thomas would talk about at work – in the hallowed halls of the Senate.[69] Modesty and reticence were weakened not only in the media and Congress but in all public domains. As we will see in the Lewinsky affair, courts have come to demand more and more information from accused parties about their sexual history.

Sexual politics was central to gay rights activism. In recent decades, proclaiming one's sexuality has come to be seen as the most liberating act for the individual homosexual. Coming out also has a political dimension, for it publicizes homosexuality to normalize and celebrate it in the larger society. Gay sexual politics has not always restricted itself to the affirmative; it also includes outing others. Many activist organizations have been routinely outing homosexual celebrities and politicians since the 1990s. The practice is at times motivated (at least officially) by a desire to show that there are prominent homosexuals in all sections of society. Other times, however, there is a punitive impulse: conservative gays are outed so that their "hypocrisy" in not upholding policies like gay marriage is exposed.

All kinds of positive meanings are attributed to publicized sexuality in contemporary America. Media personalities such as Oprah Winfrey sapped the conventional private-public distinction though confessional television. For feminists, coming out publicly to tell one's story of sexual oppression, as in the "bringing back the night" sessions for rape victims on university campuses, became a crucial component of the healing process. Such acts are oriented to fight against the feelings of shame that the victims might still harbor about their victimization. They make it easier for others in the same situation to come out and form a moral community around the shared experience. Abuse advocates have claimed that traumatic events, however distant in the past, had to be reckoned and dealt with, at times in some kind of public setting. Litigation is encouraged by all movements defending victims of sexual violence, including children. There is obviously here a concern with justice. But this is not all. Telling one's story – even if one cannot make a legal case – is itself seen as emancipatory, in the absence of which victims could blame themselves for their woes. And publicizing sexual victimization for curative purposes has created vested interests for psychologists as well. In the 1980s, the therapeutic community claimed the right and capability to recover memories of sexual abuse. A consensus was reached among professional psychologists that traumatic events not only had long-term effects but were furthermore suppressed by victims. This suppression, it has been argued, hinders recovery.[70] Although this theory could be used to generate or legitimate baseless accusations, especially when suggestion and hypnosis were used as recovery techniques, it also helped the explosion of national scandals of sexual abuse, including those that bedeviled the Catholic Church in the 1990s and 2000s.

Sexual politics did not only aim to draw public attention to transgressions in the private realm. It also proposed new definitions of wrongdoing. Sexual harassment law expanded the breadth of behavior to be punished in the workplace and school: some American universities now regard ogling as sexual harassment. Child advocacy groups have successfully argued that being flashed or exposed to sex talk qualifies as sexual abuse, and the category of incest has been distended to cover touching and fondling.[71] As family wilted as the primary agent of sexual control, miscellaneous norm entrepreneurs attempted to establish novel rules. Feminism in particular has been crucial because it argued that even if women were emancipated from communal and familial control, they still faced systemic domination and exploitation in their relations with men in the public sphere. This is why all sexual interaction between those with power differentials (status, age, and rank) has come to be looked at askance and perceived as questionable at best.

Norm entrepreneurs in civil society and professional groups have taken advantage of declining modesty. But politicians contribute to the rise of sexual politics, too. Countless among them exploit the new confession culture to humanize themselves by publicizing their private lives – for instance, through stories of self-redemption. This often entails sharing some part of one's sexual being. A watershed moment was Jimmy Carter's *Playboy* interview in 1976 where he admitted, "I've looked on a lot of women with lust. I've committed adultery in my heart many times." Although publicly pious, Carter was not too persnickety with scurrilous language either, whether his own or others', as his blunt remark to Norman Mailer in the *New York Times Magazine* on September 26, 1976, revealed: "I don't care if people say –." Mailer added, "And he actually said the famous four-letter word that the *Times* has not printed in the 125 years of its publishing life." Another example is Bill Clinton's discussion of his choice of underwear on MTV during the presidential campaign of 1992. Politicians are often accused of publicizing their private beings, but they may have good reasons for doing so: in a time when self-expression and sharing private experience are de rigueur, reticence will seem stuck-up or suspicious.

Moreover, sexual liberalization has paradoxically transformed private morality into political capital. Private rectitude has become a diacritical public marker to be used predominantly, but not exclusively, by conservatives. This has, however, given a pretext to the media and political opponents to hunt for hypocrisy. Politicians who capitalize on private morality are generally fair game, and sex scandals with consequences in the United States are usually not simply about sexual sins but hypocrisy or other transgressions committed to cover them up. Take the Mike Bowers affair of 1997, in which the Republican candidate for the governorship of Georgia admitted to a longstanding affair with his secretary. Bowers had been the unflagging guardian of the underenforced state laws on fornication, adultery, and sodomy as state attorney, so he lost his party's nomination. Similarly, the allegations of an affair between the Republican governor of South Carolina David Beasley and his female communications directors was a factor in his gubernatorial defeat in 1998 only because the politician had been much beholden to the Christian Coalition in his climb to power. In contrast, politicians such as Rudolph Giuliani and John McCain, who did not run on a moral agenda, were usually not hurt when their extramarital affairs came into the open.[72]

## The Making of the Lewinsky Affair

We are now in a better condition to understand the Lewinsky scandal. Let us first quickly review the facts.[73] In 1995, President Bill Clinton started a sexual relationship with Monica Lewinsky, a 21-year-old intern at the White House. The affair was an irregular one, consisting of sporadic, disjointed encounters in 1995, 1996, and 1997. The couple mostly engaged in fellatio but not genital intercourse. After she transferred to the Pentagon in 1997, Lewinsky blabbed the details of the dalliance to a colleague named Linda Tripp, who execrated the Democrats and had once contemplated writing an exposé about the moral corruption of the Clinton administration.

In the meantime, Clinton was being baited by a lawsuit opened in May 1994 by Paula Jones, a former Arkansas state employee, who sued Clinton for having sexually harassed her in 1991 while he was the governor of Arkansas. Jones charged that Clinton forced her to have oral sex with him. Soon Linda Tripp was in communication with both the *Newsweek* journalist Michael Isikoff, who was closely following the case, and the Paula Jones legal team. More important, she had begun furtively to record her telephone conversations with Lewinsky. The Jones lawyers, attempting to establish a behavioral pattern of sexual relations with subordinates on Clinton's part, submitted to the judge on December 5, 1997, a list of women they believed to have been carnally involved with the president. They wanted to depose all of them. Thanks to the tips coming from Tripp, Lewinsky was on the list and would soon be subpoenaed. Clinton informed his paramour of their quandary and let her know that she could possibly avoid a deposition by filing an affidavit. He suggested that she could account for their acquaintance by simply stating that she used to come to the Oval Office to deliver documents. Lewinsky signed an affidavit on January 7 in which she denied that she had had any sexual relations with the president. She also urged Tripp to gainsay any knowledge of the affair if she was ever questioned and gave her a talking points memo.

A couple of days later, Linda Tripp handed over her tapes to Independent Counsel Kenneth Starr, who had been investigating the president for the last three and a half years on sundry matters including Whitewater. Arguing for a "pattern of deception" on the part of the president, Starr asked for permission from the special court overseeing his office to expand the probe to possible obstruction of justice in the Paula Jones case. The independent counsel had learned from Tripp that Clinton's friend Vernon Jordan had been trying to get a job for Lewinsky at Revlon. Maybe the president was trying to buy her silence. And Starr had suspicions, but no proof, that Vernon Jordan had acted in a similar capacity in Whitewater with Clinton's associates in Arkansas. Finally, he thought that the White House was behind the talking points memo that Lewinsky gave to Tripp: the document looked too legalese. Starr got the extension he wanted. On January 17, 1998, the president was questioned in the Paula Jones case about Monica Lewinsky. He denied in his deposition having had sexual relations with the White House intern.

The Lewinsky scandal broke on January 17, 1998. The *Drudge Report*, a Web site specializing in political lowdown, revealed that day that Michael Isikoff of *Newsweek* had a story on Clinton's affair with a young intern that the magazine editors were unwilling to go ahead with. The *Washington Post* picked up the item on January 21 and reported that Kenneth Starr was investigating whether the president had directly or indirectly suborned Lewinsky to commit perjury. In a news conference on January 26, Clinton denied the allegations with might and main. A cornucopia of charges surfaced, and all kinds of speculations were ventured in the press during the winter and spring of 1998. Lewinsky kept her silence in the face of Starr's determination to prosecute her, so it was difficult to know for sure what had really happened. On the Paula Jones front, Judge Webber Wright dismissed the lawsuit on April 1, 1998, ruling that the plaintiff's story, if true, would merely show that she had been subject to "boorish" behavior but not sexual harassment. Jones appealed, but the case would be eventually settled before a higher court could decide on the issue. On July 28, 1998, Kenneth Starr finally offered Lewinsky immunity in exchange for her grand jury testimony. The former intern did more than present her version of things to the prosecutor; she also turned over a navy-blue GAP dress decked with the president's semen. By virtue of incessant leaks, there had been much babble about this garment in the media during the preceding months, but it was only now that the scandal had a smoking gun.

Stumped by this new development, Clinton admitted, on August 17, 1998, in a taped grand jury testimony of an "improper physical relationship" with Lewinsky. In a televised statement the same evening, the president reiterated his admission to the nation and acknowledged that he had misled the American people. He also added, however, that his relationship with Lewinsky was a private matter and chafed about the violation of his privacy. More important, Clinton denied in his grand jury testimony that he had committed perjury in his deposition in the Paula Jones case. The ennui was that Clinton's admission of impropriety contradicted both his deposition and Lewinsky's testimony to Starr's grand jury. The independent counsel therefore maintained that the president had perjured himself. Clinton contended that the definition of sexual relations did not include receiving oral sex. Here he claimed to have been following the definition of sexual relations provided by the judge presiding over the Paula Jones case. The purview of the definition was in fact broad, including oral sex as well as fondling either directly or through clothing. But the president argued that because fellatio was acted on him, and not by him, he could not be seen as having engaged in sexual relations. In her testimony to the Starr Commission, however, Lewinsky had already controverted Clinton's claim of complete sexual passivity, which, in any case, seemed unconvincing, if not preposterous, to most Americans.

Starr completed his 445-page report on September 9 and sent it to the House of Representatives. The independent counsel recommended four possible grounds for impeachment: perjury, obstruction of justice, witness tampering, and abuse of authority. His office had not drafted a dry legal document, however. The text recounted in graphic detail all the sexual encounters between the president and the intern, from the bawdy badinage on the taste of Clinton's cigar after being inserted in Lewinsky's vagina to the number of times the president ejaculated in the Oval Office bathroom sink. Congress voted on September 21 to release the report, as well as material from the grand jury proceedings, on the Internet. Clinton's videotaped testimony showed to the whole world a hangdog president, his fibs and dodges to the questions of the grand jury all too obvious and pathetic, but also not altogether undeserving of sympathy as his tormentors harassed him without respite about what many judged to be his private life. Soon the House of Representatives, controlled by the Republicans, started the impeachment process. The president stood pat on November 27 with his denials of perjury in his responses under oath to the eighty-one questions that the House Judiciary Committee addressed him. A Democratic motion for a censure resolution in lieu of impeachment was quashed on December 8.

The polls were showing that the public did not support impeachment, however, and the House Republicans lost seats in the November elections in significant part due to their anti-Clinton crusade. The Speaker of the House Newt Gingrich resigned from the position in the wake of the defeat, to be replaced by Robert Livingston. On December 12, in party-line votes, the Judiciary Committee voted to charge the president with four articles: perjury before grand jury on August 17, 1998; perjury in the Paula Jones case on December 23, 1997, and January 17, 1998; obstruction of justice in the Paula Jones case; and abuse of high office. The first and third articles were approved, and Clinton was impeached by the House on December 19 along party lines. The same day Livingston stepped down as Speaker-Elect and said he would also resign from the House in May 1999; he had learned that *Hustler* was about to produce evidence of his own marital indiscretions.

At the end of the thirty-one-day Senate trial, Clinton was acquitted. The result was not surprising: the Republicans did not have the necessary two-thirds majority. On April 12, Judge Wright, who had dismissed the Jones case, found the president in contempt for lying in his January 1998 testimony. Clinton eventually agreed to an out-of-court settlement and paid $850,000 to Paula Jones and her lawyers. On January 19, 2001, the day before Clinton left office, the independent counsel who succeeded Kenneth Starr closed the Lewinsky probe. In exchange, the president confessed to perjury in the Jones case, had his law license suspended for five years, and paid a $25,000 fine.

Had Clinton not had licentious morals that led him to succumb to the advances of a perky intern,[74] we would not have the scandal we had. But the sexual misbehavior is hardly the whole story. A lot of American politicians engage in adultery. Few get mired in scandal the way Clinton did.

There were clearly structural factors at play in the making of the president's ordeal–the ones that I discussed in the third chapter. The first of these is the increasing vulnerability of contemporary presidents to attacks, especially through law. This was confirmed by the Special Prosecutor legislation of 1978 and, more particularly in Clinton's case, by the Supreme Court's decision on May 27, 1997, not to grant immunity to the president from civil lawsuits during the term of his office. As a result of the latter, Clinton became the first sitting president to testify as a civil defendant. The second factor is the heightened polarization within the American political elite. The origin of the Lewinsky scandal was the Paula Jones lawsuit, which was given the go-ahead by the Supreme Court and funded by a right-wing organization. Clinton had already been under investigation, since 1994, by two independent counsels with bottomless funds on Whitewater and other allegations. Absent the problematic move of Kenneth Starr, the second prosecutor probing Whitewater, to extend the investigation to Clinton's testimony in the Paula Jones case, there would have been no scandal. And without a radicalized Republican Party, Clinton would maybe not have been impeached for "high crimes and misdemeanors."

Another crucial structural factor is the banality of sex talk in the contemporary United States. Despite feeble outrage, neither the American people, nor American law, nor Congress were much embarrassed by the wide publicity of a document containing the chapter and verse treatment of the sexual relations between the president and the White House intern. The Lewinsky scandal could only happen in a society that could, in a matter-of-fact fashion, publicly discuss for a year whether oral sex is sex.

Yet this clearly is not all there is to the affair. After all, as Republicans pointed out, there would not have been a scandal had Clinton not lied under oath about his illicit sexual relationship. This is true but incomplete. The president would not have had to lie about his adultery had he not been questioned about it under oath. It was pure mischance on Clinton's part that his lie was exposed. If Lewinsky had been more gingerly about her confidantes, things would have turned out differently. But there was nothing accidental about the legal duress under which Clinton found himself in the Paula Jones lawsuit, and the irony is that the president himself was at least in part responsible for it.

The civil case had little merit, and the judge eventually threw it out. Nevertheless, it segued first into an independent counsel investigation and later into a major presidential scandal – a process that is impossible to understand independent of sexual politics in the contemporary United States. It was with the Molinari amendment to the 1994 Violence Against Women Act that plaintiff lawyers were given the right in sexual harassment cases to ask defendants questions about their history of sexual relations in the workplace. It does not matter if there is no evidence suggesting that such relations are not consensual. In fact, defendants have to testify about them so that their consensual nature can be certified by the court. As Jeffrey Toobin points out, the underlying assumption is that all sexual activity between employees is dubious.[75] And paradoxically it was Clinton himself who had signed the Molinari amendment into law. Given this law, Judge Wright could not but allow the Paula Jones lawyers to interrogate the president about any state or federal employees with whom he had, or sought to have, any kind of sexual relations. Even though she eventually ruled that evidence concerning Monica Lewinsky should be excluded from the trial, Clinton had already been questioned about her and had already lied about it – his testimony in this context amounting to both perjury and obstruction of justice.[76]

Clinton only lied under oath because American law required him to publicize his illicit sex life – and, presumably, because he did not want his wife to know. And once his lie was exposed, Republicans went after him. Telling the truth (or taking the Fifth Amendment, however unpresidential that would have seemed) would have probably saved Clinton from getting impeached. Yet it would not have prevented the scandal. If the president or Lewinsky had spilled the beans, the Jones lawyers and journalists would then try to find out if the intern had received benefits in exchange for sex – in accordance with the logic of sexual harassment laws. Lewinsky's protestations to the contrary would not necessarily have been found credible.

The Democrats bemoaned that the scandal was simply the doing of a zealot of a prosecutor, and it is true that the Congressional Republicans did want to maul Clinton in any way possible.[77] When asked in late November 1998 why they were going to impeach Clinton, despite the dearth of public support for it, the former speaker of the House Newt Gingrich simply said, "Because we can."[78] There was much hatred for the president, seen by many Republicans as nothing but a scapegrace who did not deserve to dwell in the White House. Nevertheless, Clinton's opponents would have been helpless without favorable conditions of attack: sexual harassment laws, lack of public modesty about sexual matters, independent counsel legislation, and Supreme Court's refusal of immunity to the president from civil lawsuits. The irony is that it was the Democrats themselves who passed the first two laws, and historically the American left has been more partial to treating presidents like regular citizens. Hence, the Republicans and Starr merely exploited the general culture of distrust vis-à-vis the presidency, something that they did not create all by themselves.

However antagonistic they may have been, the Republicans did not break any laws. As for Starr, once Tripp slipped him the tapes, it was not that extraordinary for the independent counsel to take the matter to the attorney general. And Janet Reno would have run into fierce flak both from the media and the Republicans had she not advised the special division to appoint a prosecutor to look into the activities alluded to in the Tripp tapes.[79] Maybe another prosecutor would not have extended the investigation into the testimony in the Paula Jones case, but the law did allow Kenneth Starr that move. Sooner or later, the tapes would have come out, and there would most certainly have been strident voices in the country ballyhooing for some kind of probe. Recall how the *New York Times* rebuked Kenneth Starr for abdicating his responsibilities in February 1997 when he momentarily envisioned terminating the Whitewater investigation to become the dean of Pepperdine University Law School.

Starr certainly proved to be a bellicose prosecutor. He was in collaboration with the Jones lawyers to entrap Clinton to commit perjury; the taking of the president's deposition on January 17, 1998, was evidently a sting operation. It was overkill to hound the president of the United States in this fashion, especially given that regular prosecutors rarely prosecute perjury about sex in civil cases. Videotaping Clinton's grand jury testimony was unorthodox, too. Starr's justification was that one of the jurors was absent, but one wonders whether he had not already envisioned eventually releasing it to humiliate the president. Starr did exceed the norms with his steamroller methods, but, again, he was simply exploiting the rights that were accorded to him by the special prosecutor legislation of 1978, which was voted by the Democrats and which allowed for unaccountable, quasi-omnipotent prosecutors. Kenneth Starr's office might have leaked confidential grand jury information to the media, but there is no conclusive evidence for this. Leaks could have originated from anywhere, and, in any case, they do not seem to have significantly affected the course of the scandal.

Starr was excoriated for his decision to propose impeachment to Congress, but note that the president had broken several laws. As Richard Posner's dispassionate and judicious dissection of the case shows, Clinton perjured himself in his deposition in the Paula Jones lawsuit, before Starr's grand jury, and in his responses to the questions put to him by the House Judiciary Committee.[80] The president's suggestions to Lewinsky in December 1997 can also be seen as suborning perjury, even though it is not completely clear whether the president asked her to lie. All of these acts were moreover perpetrated to confound the judicial process in the Paula Jones case so they also qualify as obstruction of justice. For most people, these misbehaviors did not come close to "high crimes and misdemeanors," but this term does not have an unambiguous legal definition, and Congress had the constitutional discretion to decide whether it covered the president's actions.

Nevertheless, there was a big attitudinal chasm between Starr and the Republicans on the one side and a vast portion of the American public on the other, and this is why it was Clinton's inquisitors who emerged as the losers in the end. Structural factors I mentioned earlier made Clinton very vulnerable to legal attack and explain in large part how the scandal erupted, but the outcome of the episode would be determined by politics. The impeachment process and the Senate trial, however calqued on a legalistic format, were very much political. It was politicians who first impeached and then acquitted Clinton. As Posner argues convincingly, this was a form of popular justice, its resemblance to legal justice fairly slight.[81] The Republicans had the majority to impeach the president but not the plurality to convict him in the Senate. They hurt Clinton as much as the law allowed – but eventually paid for their ardor in the midterm elections as they failed to persuade the public that his trespasses were impeachment worthy.

Things looked very touch and go for the president when the scandal broke. A CNN poll found, a couple of days after the first allegations of his liaison with Monica Lewinsky, Clinton's job approval rating, which had been in the 60s, going down to 50 percent. According to an ABC poll conducted at the same time, fewer than 50 percent of Americans felt that Clinton had the "honesty" and "integrity" to serve out his term as president. Another poll, commissioned by Clinton's Svengali, the public relations expert Dick Morris, found that 47 percent would want him out of office if he had had an affair with Lewinsky, lied about it, and asked her to lie about it as well. If Clinton pleaded guilty to obstruction of justice, 56 percent would want him out.

Since for the stalwart Republican and Democratic supporters the unfolding of scandal only confirmed their beliefs about Clinton and his detractors, the president's fate mostly hinged on the attitudes of the moderates on both sides and the swing voters. It seems that the response of this group was in the beginning mostly emotional or legalistic. Some were outraged, and many believed that presidents were not above laws. Soon attitudes changed, however, and Clinton's approval ratings climbed up to the high sixties, even though his character scores remained low.

The standard verity about scandals is that cover-ups always backfire. This is patently wrong. Given the first poll figures, Clinton was astute to keep the truth from the public; opinion turned soon after.

The main reason Americans were mostly with Clinton was the economy, which had been doing swimmingly throughout his second term. I argued in the third chapter that in the post-Vietnam and post-Watergate context, the presidency came to command limited respect from the public and the law and hence grew vulnerable to moral attack, in legal or extra-legal forms. This means that scandals break much more easily. But presidents who are popular themselves can also survive them. While some Americans genuinely thought that Clinton was a bad example and had to be chastised, in these times of sexual liberalism, the idea that the president of the country has to be a role model in things carnal was not accepted by the majority. More Americans thought that his resignation or removal from office would be too costly. The stance of the moderates in both parties and the independents was strategic and decisive: if they wanted the president to go, some Democrats in the Senate could have well voted to convict Clinton.

Most Americans did not want Clinton to go, but they did not terribly mind his yearlong humiliation either. Given high media ratings, it even seems as if the public, for the most part, enjoyed the spectacle. This was not only because some thought the legal process had to run its course but much more because the presidential ordeal did not have an effect on the stock market, which did fabulously all through 1998. Besides, with the Republicans lacking the sixty-seven senators necessary to convict Clinton, the exoneration of the president was almost a foregone conclusion. If the investigation and the impeachment process had immediate negative externalities on the public, it seems well-nigh certain that the scandal would have lasted for a much shorter period of time. As the scandal dragged on and eventually palled on the public, most Americans (60 to 70 percent) blamed Starr. The job approval rating of Clinton actually reached 68 percent while Clinton was being impeached, and the Democrats gained five House seats in the 1998 midterm elections.

For the majority of the public, the scandal was primarily about sex. Clinton perjured himself and obstructed justice, but most Americans were not all that outraged by these legal transgressions and, to the exasperation of the Republicans in Congress, refused to see the matter as something much more than lying about sex. From the perspective of sexual harassment laws – again, laws that the president himself had signed into law – Clinton's actions were tantamount to obstructing Paula Jones's recourse to justice. Yet, for most people, the relationship between the president and Lewinsky was consensual (albeit adulterous), and efforts to publicize it by Tripp and Starr seemed like violation of privacy. So it was these two characters that were the most vilified.

Clinton's allies also acted strategically. Feminists would have definitely gone after the president had he not been a Democrat[82] who had done much to advance their agenda. So they took his side even though Clinton's lie technically obstructed the course of justice in a sexual harassment case and even though feminists are highly skeptical about the legitimacy of relationships involving power differentials, however consensual they may be. Feminist activists and politicians were more concerned with the political costs of Clinton's demise than with his individual transgression. And ironically, if the general public had shared the feminist position on sexual harassment and suspicion of workplace romance to the same extent, the president could have very well, much to the dismay of feminists themselves, gone south.

The structural causes of the Lewinsky scandal are thus: (1) the legal degradation of political authority, (2) the heightened political polarization at the elite level, (3) the low level of modesty and reticence about sexual matters, and (4) the advanced state of sexual politics in the United States. As I have argued, the last two factors stem from sexual liberalization. Compare again France with the United States. The reason the Lewinsky scandal could not have happened in France is not the supposed and empirically unfounded Gallic permissiveness. First, thanks to a more entrenched state tradition, French presidents enjoy more legal immunity during their time in office. There are also tough privacy and libel laws protecting Gallic politicians. Second, sexual politics has had much less legal success in France, which has stronger privacy laws and where sexual harassment legislation is restricted to quid pro quo harassment.[83] If he were the French president, Clinton would definitely not have been ramrodded to testify about a consensual relationship under oath. At the same time, it should be underlined that it was the American public's incomplete internalization of the tenets of sexual harassment laws (along with the strong economy) that accounted for the outcome of the scandal. Legally speaking, Clinton did obstruct justice in the Paula Jones case, but for most people, the scandal was still predominantly about sex, and the overall permissiveness of Americans allowed the president to ride out the storm.

It might also be instructive to compare the dénouement of the Lewinsky scandal with the fate of Oscar Wilde. Although both scandals were path-dependent processes, attitudes toward Wilde escalated, whereas attitudes toward Clinton first moderated and then stayed more or less the same. In the Wilde affair, the externalities of the publicity of Wilde's transgression contaminated more and more third parties – audiences, associates, and authorities. No such thing happened in the Lewinsky affair. There was no real or suspected conspiracy, and the transgression was not something over which contemporary Americans were greatly concerned. Moreover, even though the dependence of the general Victorian public on Wilde was little, most Americans thought that removing Clinton would be highly risky for them.

How about the differences in what happened to Clinton and Nixon? There are multiple factors at work here. Clinton's transgressions seemed less serious than those of Nixon to Americans – they certainly looked less impeachment worthy. But this can't be all; despite the fact that most Americans assumed in the course of 1973 that Nixon had been lying about Watergate, they still did not support his impeachment. That the economy was doing wonderfully in 1998 and badly in 1974 mattered. That the power-prestige (to use Weberian terminology) of Nixon's United States had declined with Vietnam, whereas Clinton led the sole superpower in the world was another element. The House of Representatives impeached Clinton despite his high approval ratings, and this seems to be a result of the heightened legislative polarization since Watergate and the increasing tendency in the political elite to not "pander to the public."[84] This does not, however, mean that the Republicans were completely indifferent to public opinion. Many in the House of Representatives may have voted to impeach Clinton only because it was obvious that he would be acquitted in the Senate. However monomaniacal some Republicans were in their crusade, one wonders if the senatorial GOP as a whole would have been so imprudent as to remove a president with such high approval ratings.

These structural factors and Clinton's political acumen allowed him to wriggle out of the sticky situation in which he found himself. Most Americans were not directly affected but amused by the episode. Yet the scandal was hardly inconsequential. The president had to spend a whole year containing a constitutional snafu instead of leading the country. All of Clinton's military acts in 1998 – a cruise-missile attack on suspected terrorist sites in Sudan and Afghanistan just days after his testimony to the grand jury and another one on Iraq four months later – were second-guessed as the Republicans argued that he was trying to distract the public. The Lewinsky scandal had long-term effects, too. Its detrimental potential for governance now fully actualized, the independent counsel law was left to expire in the aftermath of the affair. Paradoxically, one of the unintended consequences of the scandal was that Clinton's successor gained some immunity to judicial attacks.

The scandal was also significant insofar as it threw a sharp light on a central contradiction. The Lewinsky episode revealed the extent to which sexuality is an integral element of the public sphere in the United States. There are at least two ironies here. First, as I tried to show, sexual liberalization – insofar as it decreased modesty and reticence and set the stage for contemporary sexual politics – led to heightened public disputatiousness about sex. In contemporary America, sex norms are not strong enough to make public discussion of sex scandalous, but not weak enough for us to be indifferent to the sexual behavior of others.[85] Although the decline in modesty is largely a consequence of the sexual liberation of the 1960s, once the former came about, it outpaced the latter. This discrepancy has been deepened by sexual politics, which further weakened modesty while attempting, albeit with limited success, to reestablish puritanism in certain domains of life such as the workplace.

Second, despite appearances, there is an emerging consensus in almost all the sections of American society about the validity of sex talk in public, despite bitter quarrels about legitimate content. Whatever their particular positions on the issues, radicals, liberals, and conservatives all participate in sexual politics with equal fervor. The degradation of the public sphere by sex is frequently decried by conservatives and cultural critics. There may be something hypocritical about such complaints: they often only amplify the contamination they denounce. But perhaps it does not matter much. For better or worse, sex talk in public has already become unexceptional in the contemporary United States.

# SIX

# Provocation in Art

I TURN to art scandals in this last chapter. Both rule-breaking artists and those who respond to them often use publicity in strategic ways. At the same time, art scandals are laden with sentiments and discourses throwing into full relief the extent to which aesthetics can acquire a moral dimension in its reception as well as in its making. The strategic and the moral are intertwined especially in modernism and its scandals.

Current art scandals may seem like low-stake affairs. Legal punishments on offenders are rare, social sanctions in liberal democracies on artistic provocateurs are relatively weak, and the public focused on the event is usually fairly limited. That said, transgressive artworks can intensely affect their audiences. The scandals they engender both reveal and affect the norms of the artistic world; they can transform the prestige rankings among artists. Maybe more important, scandal played a key role in art during the nineteenth and twentieth centuries, in great part because of the oppositional self-identity of modernism, by serving as an engine of change for the avant-garde. The revolt of the impressionists, the rise of abstraction, and postmodernism cannot be comprehended independently of the transgressions of these movements. Scandal thus crystallizes the logic of modern and contemporary art beneath its seeming anomie.

The discussion that follows is mostly about painting and other visual arts, but the general points apply to all aesthetic activity. In fact, what I say should improve our grasp of public challenges, from religious heresy to political provocation, in all spheres of life.

## Transgression in Art and Its Effects

Until now I have been considering mostly denunciatory scandals, events in which real or alleged transgressions committed in private are publicized by nonoffenders. One can also create a scandal by communicating one's transgression to a public or by committing it in front of a public. Examples are art scandals, open heresy as well as public occasions in which someone commits a solecism, makes a scene, or offends common values. Here, the transgressor may be challenging authorities or contesting the norms regarding what can be represented in public. Even if the actor does not attempt a provocation, the act might be read as such. Motives are frequently mixed in art scandals: one may well seek fame and formally experiment at the same time. Whatever the real intentions of the transgressor, which may remain unknown or unknowable, public transgressions, granted that they obtain attention, can provoke. I therefore call the ensuing moral disturbances provocative scandals.

These events may obtain actual audiences witnessing the transgression. Provocative scandals can also break by means of mediated publicity – for instance, by a defiant op-ed piece defending a very unpopular opinion. A scandal with a physically present audience can later be disseminated to a larger, virtual public through the mass media as well. Provocative scandals can be quite consequential. Consider how Luther's defiance of the Catholic Church in 1520 destroyed its already crumbling sacrality and emboldened other heretics and doubters to join forces with him to replace the established dogma with a new one. This open heresy was a milestone in the rise of Protestantism: it shook the brittle religious status quo at the right time and the right place.

The art world provides a most propitious setting for public provocation. A scandal is an emotional affair; so is art. They are also both public: however personal, art is typically destined to an audience composed of nonintimates. But consequential art scandals require that people notice the transgressive work and that opinion leaders bother to denounce it. The work can be weak, or it can be strategically ignored, with the result that its offense is resisted or not confirmed.

The status of the artist; the nature of the transgression; the consensus around the value that it attacks (or is seen as attacking); and the incentives of the authorities, audience leaders, or critics to denounce or disregard the offense all combine to determine whether we in fact have a scandal, as well as its size.[1]

Another important factor is the heterogeneity of the public. The Jewish reactions to Mel Gibson's *The Passion of the Christ* (2004) were on the whole antithetical to the Christian ones. Note that the public that is targeted by an artist may diverge from the one that is provoked. Some artists find themselves occasioning scandals inadvertently; others desperately strive to provoke without success. Furthermore, we can differentiate among the serious students of art, the educated elite, and the general society.[2] These subpublics do not have the same cultural expertise, perceptive schemas, expectations, interests, and attitudes toward unconventional art. Too sharp a discrepancy between an artwork and what the public is used to might result in the artist being simply ignored, especially if the piece lacks a sensory punch that would render indifference difficult.

There is frequently an ideational element to artistic offense. Hence Richard Serrano's *Piss Christ* (1987), the photograph of a crucifix submerged in a tank of urine, was, for some, a disgrace to art. There is, however, obviously much more to the piece. The urine not only defiles the most sacred symbol of Christianity; it has a visceral, maybe even nauseating, effect on the believer. Just like its nonscandalous variety, art that is outrageous succeeds by appealing to our senses. And a work that does not assault a social value can still offend us, if we think that it does not merit the title of art. Art is supposed to be something extraordinary, if not magical; pretenses to it can exasperate or anger us if we feel that we could have created the work ourselves. The "artist" can be accused of being a fraud. This is not solely because there is something sacred about art, but also because the title of artist confers exclusive privileges on its bearer.

Ridicule can be alloyed with indignation if one detects a condescending conceit in such artwork. Consider the popular reaction – at least the way it was articulated in the media – to a conceptual piece made by Carl André. *Equivalent VIII* (1966) is a sculpture

Figure 6.1. Carl André, *Equivalent VIII*, 1966. Firebricks, 127 × 686 × 2292 mm. Tate Gallery, London, UK. © Licensed by VAGA, New York, NY. Photo Credit, Tate, London/Art Resource.

that consists of 120 cream-colored bricks, which are placed on the floor in two layers of 60 to form an oblong structure, reproducing, on a larger scale, the proportions of the individual bricks that make it up (Figure 6.1). Tate Gallery purchased the piece for £5,000 and thereby earned the ire of the *Daily Mirror*, which put the following headline on the front page on February 16, 1976. "What a Load of Rubbish." The story ended wryly: "You can buy ordinary household bricks for between £40 and £60 a thousand. The 120 bricks the Tate bought would be enough to build a large fireproof moneybox."[3] The source of discontent is rarely just monetary, however. An artwork will be deemed scandalous if (or to the extent that) its creator seems to be taking the public as fools. Visceral reactions can be ignited – particularly if the artwork is not a sedate conceptual experiment but is all turbulence. Here is a case reported by Jean Cocteau at the première of Igor Stravinsky's *The Rite of Spring*: "Standing up in her loge, her tiara awry, the old Comtesse de Pourtalès flourished her fan and shouted, scarlet in her face, 'It's the first time in sixty years that anyone's dared to make a fool of me.'"[4]

In our epoch, art has become a "contested concept,"[5] something the definition and scope of which are hotly disputed. Yet a great deal of what is typically seen as art still has an emotional appeal – even though cultivation of the senses is necessary for a rich aesthetic experience. Such art is much more likely to scandalize successfully than one that is affectively cool. Since emotions are unbidden physiological states that we find ourselves in rather than actions,[6] engagement with a work of art involves a certain passivity. We accept this state freely when we go to a museum or movie theater. We want to be surprised, moved – maybe even agitated. We may want to respond to the work, but only after it has emotionally affected us in one way or another. This characteristic of the aesthetic experience, however, opens up the possibility of abuse. Artists can thus be charged with being exploitative, for placing us gratuitously and insidiously in unpleasant affective states without any obvious benefit – cognitive, moral, or otherwise.

The word "shock" is often (and all too easily) used to denote the effect of a scandalous work. It has two major forms: the ugly and the immoral. One often sees or constructs an association between them: the ugly is suspected of being immoral, and the immoral is frequently aesthetically repellent. One reason Pablo Picasso's *Les Demoiselles d'Avignon* (1907) generated such an outcry was because it combined the ugly and the immoral in its portrayal of a seedy brothel scene where five prostitutes with angular figures, lopsided eyes, and threatening glances display themselves seductively to an imaginary john, the viewer (Figure 6.2). Take again Stravinsky's *The Rite of Spring*. Depicting the sacrifice of a virgin with brutal rhythms

Figure 6.2. Pablo Picasso, *Les Demoiselles d'Avignon* (*Young Ladies of Avignon*), 1907. Oil on canvas, 8′ × 7′8″. The Museum of Modern Art, New York, NY. ©2008 Estate of Pablo Picasso/Artists Rights Society (ARS), New York. Acquired through the Lille P. Bliss Bequest. Digital Image © Licensed by SCALA/ Art Resource, NY.

and grating dissonances, which apparently aim to incite atavistic urges in the listener, this pantheistic exaltation shocked many. Here is how Jean Cocteau described the resulting hubbub at the work's première at the Théâtre des Champs-Elysées in Paris on May 29, 1913:

> Let us now return to the theatre of the Avenue Montaigne, while we wait for the conductor to rap his desk and the curtain to go up on one of the noblest events in the annals of art. The audience

behaved as it ought to; it revolted right away. People laughed, booed, hissed, imitated animal noises and probably would have tired themselves out before long, had not the crowd of aesthetes and a handful of musicians, carried away by their excessive zeal, insulted and even roughly handled the public in the loges. The uproar degenerated into a free fight.[7]

Of course the piece is only ugly to the uninitiated. As one appreciates the complex and original forms underlying *The Rite of Spring*, as one understands its proper logic, and especially as we yield to its emotional power, it is hard not to be overwhelmed by its beauty. But this does not necessarily make the work less troubling. As Kundera points out, an important reason the work scandalized not only the bourgeois public but a sophisticated critic like Adorno was its nonsentimental portrayal of the beauty of evil.[8] *The Rite* is now a common staple of concert repertoire, although it maintained its shock value in the twenties. Zelda and F. Scott Fitzgerald used to offer their dinner guests two choices: listening to a recording of Stravinsky's famous symphonic work or looking at pictures of mutilated soldiers.[9] Note that even the abstract can generate a physical reaction if it is imposingly ugly. Consider the response of the Cambridge vicar to a public sculpture made by Barry Flanagan titled *Vertical Judicial Grouping* (1972), a work that consisted of four twisted, spiky 18-foot-high fiberglass pillars and a metal goalpost: "I think the thing is quite revolting. It made me feel quite sick when I saw it."[10]

The shocking is not always ugly or just ugly. Sometimes it is the novel and the surprising. Hence it can have a positive quality: in fact, all successful artwork derails expectations, be they moral or aesthetic, in one way or another.[11] Yet what was once shocking will soon be trite if not tedious. The principle of the decreasing piquancy of scandal forces the vanguards to go each other one better to generate the same amount of reaction. Even though scandalous art loses its bite with time and repetition, it normalizes transgressions along the way. Artistic representations numb the taboo around sex. A succession of blasphemous acts degrades religious symbols.

Provocation is an expressive technique that can be deployed in politics as well. Disobeying or sinning in public can encourage others to

imitate the act, lay bare moral fissures within audiences and authorities, and test their commitment to uphold the norm. Provocation
can delegitimize authorities too. The civil rights movement and the
anticolonial movement in India thrived on public defiance, provoking
illegitimate repression almost through a self-fulfilling prophecy. Take
the pragmatics of civil disobedience. First, by public contestation one
displays the courage of one's convictions. And since in all societies
courage is a surefire way to claim honor, defiance morally aggran-
dizes its author in the eyes of neutral observers, sympathetic associates, and even perhaps authorities. Second, civil disobedience is cal-
ibrated to incite the authorities into revealing their "real nature." By
provoking its officials, the dissenter, much like a Weberian in action,
attempts to reduce the state to its violent core. As the British colonial
power discovered to its dismay, civil disobedience can rouse – or
trick – the authorities into an ordeal in which, by being provoked by
the provocateur, they will produce to the whole world the evidence
of their illegitimacy. Violent reaction is at times exactly what the
public offender desires.[12]

The risks and profits of scandal are contextually variable for
artists. It matters quite a bit whether the violation is illegal or not.
So does the general strength of the values that are threatened. Open
blasphemy takes much less audacity and is less of an interesting
event in contemporary America than in medieval Europe or the Middle East. Cultural expectations regarding art mold reactions as well.
Transgressive art can nevertheless be ignored, and there are several
reasons for this. One is protection: indifference or detached amuse-
ment keeps at bay the contagious, sometimes seductive disgrace that
emanates from such art. Moreover, a scandal can end up increasing the status of the offender, and we may not want that. *Esse est
percipi.* To be is to be recognized. Being noticed by a multitude
for a disruptive act is even better, and a public denunciation by a
high-status actor risks establishing the transgressor on a par with the
denouncer by a negative consecration. It is thus not surprising that
many transgressors seek to be denounced. They may well anticipate
that the negative glory with which they will be crowned will trump
the sanctions that they will receive. One conclusion we can draw

from the calculus of provocation is that both too much and too little repression are suboptimal to transgressive artists, either crushing
them senseless or rendering them irrelevant. Medium-level repression
will, in contrast, prove ideal because it both allows the provocateur
to appear courageous and lends salience to his act.

Denouncers of transgressive art can also attempt to enhance their
standing through scandal. By his condemnation of the *Sensations*
exhibit in the Brooklyn Museum of Art in 1999, which featured a
painting by Chris Ofili that used elephant dung and pornographic
images to depict the Virgin Mary, Mayor Rudolph Giuliani communicated the offense to everyone in the city (and the United States),
many of whom had probably not heard of or cared much about the
show. Moves like this can generate paradoxical outcomes if the public is normatively variegated. Both the artist and the denouncer can
gain. The *Sensations* incident shored up the conservative credentials
of the otherwise politically moderate mayor and pushed skyward the
prices of the works of the Young British Artists. Condemnation of
the Saatchi Collection in the name of the values of one part of the
audience only made it sexy in the eyes of the other.

A scandal always risks generating unanticipated consequences, a
hazard from which artists are hardly exempt. They cannot always
envision how authorities, audiences, and opinion leaders will inter-
pret and react to their creations. Powerful denouncers can impose
their own self-interested, authoritative definitions on art that has
ambiguous content. Despite common wisdom, images are not always
more powerful than words; visual arts are particularly prone to produce indeterminate meaning and typically need words (a title, an exegesis by the painter or a critic, an attack by a denouncer, etc.) for their
sense to be stabilized.[13] Since representing something does not necessarily entail taking an unequivocal stance toward it, moral ambiguity
is endemic to art. In 1990, Karen Finley, a feminist artist, daubed
her naked body with melted chocolate in a work of performance
art called *We Keep Our Victims Ready*. She asserted that she was
attacking patriarchy, her smeared body symbolizing the oppressed
status of all women. For the journalist William Novak and some
others, however, insofar as it could not but appeal to wanton lust,

the show was ordinary pornography, regardless of the proclaimed high-minded intentions of the artist. For her critics, it looked like the artist was being hypocritical, wanting both attention and moral high ground, pretending as if the work was noticed not because of its prurient content but because of its political message.

Or consider again Serrano's *Piss Christ*. The first impression of the viewer when confronted with this photograph is a crucifix in a hazy, glowing, translucent liquid; the image itself is aesthetically very pleasing. It is after one reads the title that the artwork turns blasphemous. But even then its meaning is not necessarily fixed. The artist propounded that his work was a critique of how capitalism abases religion. For the believers, however, the immersion of a crucifix in urine is sacrilegious whatever anyone says. The intention of the artist – which in any case may be unfathomable, unclear, or untrustworthy – may well not determine the meaning of an artwork for the audience. Artists such as Jock Sturges may profess all they want to be celebrating the innocence of children in their photographs of naked teens. They cannot help looking like child pornographers, for the images they produce have public meanings and effects independent of their putative motivations.[14]

A similar situation arises when an artist represents something that is abominable without reprobating it in some way.[15] Violent Hollywood movies are seen as less troublesome to the extent that they explicitly condemn the mayhem they detail, or at least to the extent they seem to distinguish legitimate violence from its illegitimate cognate. Gustave Flaubert survived the scandal of *Madame Bovary* partly because his lawyer strategically and successfully argued in the 1857 obscenity trial that the book had to depict depravity minutely before it could condemn it – even though one could argue that it is the very absence of a clear moralizing stance in the novel toward its main protagonist that makes it great literature. Here is a more contemporary example, the British artist Marcus Harvey's *Myra*. The work is an oversized facsimile of the sinister mug shot of a child-murderer, fashioned by the stenciled handprints of her victims. Outraged viewers pelted eggs on the painting in the 1997 *Sensations* exhibit. Many believed that the artist had turned the vicious killer into a celebrity, callously using the innocent children she slaughtered in the process.

Although a scandal will often transcend the intentions of its creator, the latter may receive blame from some quarters in the case of a calamitous upshot. An extreme example is Salman Rushdie's *Satanic Verses*, a fantastical novel that seemed blasphemous to many Muslims because of its portrayal of Prophet Mohammed. The publication of the book eventuated in a death fatwa proclaimed by the Iranian leader Khomeini against the writer. Riots broke all over the world; the Japanese translator of the book was assassinated. Even though the religious edict was universally denounced in the West, some elites still publicly maintained Rushdie should have anticipated that his sensationalism would wreak global havoc and not have published the book.

## Impressionism and Its Scandals

Art scandal precedes modern times in the West. Caravaggio found himself more than once accused of blasphemy and indecency for his naturalism. The Inquisition saw something wicked in Velázquez's *Rokeby Venus* (1648–51), which showcased the buttocks of a nude at its center. Nevertheless, because artistic activity was strongly regulated, scandal was a rare event until the second half of the nineteenth century. And before then, despite occasional mavericks, there were no fundamental disagreements on stylistic and substantive matters among artists, audiences, and authorities. Art was not perceived primarily to be a vehicle for personal expression, and artists, very much dependent on the patronage of political grandees, religious authorities, or wealthy benefactors, did not have an oppositional identity. On the contrary, they frequently painted to praise dogma or to educate the illiterate masses by illustrating passages from the Bible.[16]

Transgression, however, took center stage in nineteenth- and twentieth-century art. There is indeed an elective affinity between transgression and modern art, which achieved independence through a succession of scandals, as artists claimed the right to pick their subjects, contested censorship, and challenged the conventions of representation. The offensive commenced in nineteenth-century France, first, because it was in the hexagon that tradition was most profoundly institutionalized: there was thus something significant to attack. Second, that very institutionalization had boosted the prestige of the artist within French society, with the unintended consequence that the aesthetic spars of the nineteenth century would be incidents of copious sound and fury played out in front of interested national – even international – audiences.[17]

Established in 1648, the Royal Academy supplanted the medieval artist guilds and imposed standards on artistic production in France.[18] Even though norms were not immutable, change was slow and endogenous. The official art of the first half of nineteenth century favored paintings with dark tones and firm outlines. Artists used varnish to remove brushwork: a detailed, smooth finish was de rigueur. Perspective structured the pictorial space. Classical and Christian subjects overshadowed landscapes and still lifes in the prestige hierarchy; everyday themes were eschewed. Noble expressions and gestures were privileged in the representation of human beings. The Academy exercised its control both through École des Beaux Arts, which trained the quasi-totality of artists in the nation, and the Salon, the annual exhibition of approved work. Because dealers were both fairly insignificant and risk-averse, mobility in the art world was contingent on Salon approbation. And this was a bare minimum; every year thousands of works made it to the exhibition each vying for precious wall space. Ambitious artists hoped that their paintings would be displayed visibly and not too high. Medals awarded by the Salon were particularly coveted, for they opened the way for state commissions and official accolades, which signaled to the affluent bourgeoisie the merit of the painter.

Some painters began to question the academic norms in the nineteenth century. Delacroix proclaimed the primacy of color over draughtsmanship and, thanks to his uncontestable talent, had a substantial following. His romanticism marked the mid-nineteenth-century French art. Courbet constituted a bigger threat, however. Finding the elevated subjects and graceful poses required by the

Academy to be both factually and morally false, he drew unwashed peasants and stonecutters in scenes from their rough lives.

Realism was often a contentious force in art until the twentieth century, and Courbet was here following in the footsteps of Caravaggio, the *peintre maudit* of the Baroque who was notorious both in life (he died an outlaw) and in art. This master of chiaroscuro inflected his religious paintings with an earthy character as he irreverently placed sacred moments in plebian Italian settings. He had a prostitute model for his *The Death of the Virgin* (1606), a deeply moving painting of Mary, lying dead on a bed, her legs and feet bare, her features swollen. The work outraged the Fathers of Santa Maria della Scala.[19] His main rival, Baglione, found the representation of the virgin as a coarse peasant woman accosted by vulgar pilgrims with dirty feet in *Madonna di Loretto* nothing short of obscene.[20] But Caravaggio set off his biggest scandal with his *Madonna dei Palafrenieri* (1605–6), a painting that was commissioned for Saint Peter's, the greatest church in the Christian world. The piece portrayed the Virgin, Saint Anne, and Christ on the threshold of a stable (Figure 6.3). In Caravaggio's vision, Mary is again a workaday peasant with her skirt rolled up around her knees and unceremoniously holding a naked and bewildered infant Jesus as she is about to crush a viper with her feet. Critics carped that Saint Anne looked like an old hag. It was his pursuit for the sublime in the rugged and the prosaic, however, that made Caravaggio's paintings so moving. To us – and many others at the time including some important protectors[21] – his naturalism is the very hallmark of Caravaggio's genius. To the high clergy, however, his art was unholy. As they rejected the work, the cardinals solemnly denounced its creator:

> We find nothing in this picture but vulgarity, sacrilege, impiety, and disgust. It would seem to be the work of a painter who knows his craft but whose spirit lies in darkness, who has long been far removed from God and adoration of God, and from all good thoughts.[22]

Courbet could also be difficult to digest. Part of the reason was that his realism, being less perceptual than conceptual,[23] involved

Figure 6.3. Michelangelo Merisi da Caravaggio, *Madonna dei palafrenieri.*
(*Madonna and the Serpent*), 1605–6. Oil on canvas, 292 × 211 cm. Galleria
Borghese, Rome, Italy. Photo Credit: SCALA/Art Resource, NY.

painting things that others did not think worthy of painting. His gloomy *Burial at Ornans*, the mammoth size of which contrasted with the ordinariness of the people populating it, depicted a provincial funeral. He used impasto with muddy and somber colors to create rough surfaces that corresponded to the crude and simple people that his paintings portrayed and in effect championed. He was blithely anticlerical as well: his *Return from the Conference* (1863) showed intoxicated clerics. He participated in the 1871 commune and paid the price for it by spending his last years in exile. Transfigured into an idol for the bohemian left during the authoritarian atmosphere of the Second Empire,[24] Courbet had many disciples. This was the period of the obscenity trials of Flaubert's *Madame Bovary* (1856) and Baudelaire's *Fleurs du mal* (1857), the time of the heroic struggles for the independence of art. Just like Courbet's paintings, these works were skewered for their lack of refinement and their indecency. The painter and his votaries nevertheless found plenty of allies in the cultured world, and, with the rise of French mass media, Courbet acquired a sometimes lucrative infamy. "I have painted the picture so it would be refused. I have succeeded. That way it will bring me some money," said Courbet after his *Return from the Conference* was rejected by the Salon.[25] The painting sold very well indeed.[26] Moreover, the academic system was not as rigid as its detractors would have it.[27] Courbet's realism – like the romanticism of Delacroix – could be assimilated into the official framework. But the establishment would have a harder time dealing with the second wave of nonconformists.

It was a handful of painters that unleashed modernism. They were first called "la bande à Manet;" a mocking critic later christened them "impressionistes."[28] These artists violated most of the norms set by the Academy. Rules of perspective were downplayed or even ignored in their work, which lacked balanced compositions, appearance of finish, and correct drawing. Their brushwork was unrestrained and visible, willfully omitting details. The impressionists strived to capture the ephemeral in vibrant paintings by applying small touches of pure color on the canvas. Arguing that this method offered a faithful rendition of how the human eye actually perceived the world, they defended their formal decisions in the name of realism. The impressionists claimed to be realists in content as well. Brushing aside dignified subject matter, they fixed their gaze on everyday life on the boulevards as well as in the boudoirs, often depicting sundry seedy things in a daringly amoral fashion. They were straying significantly and successfully from the academic norms; their apostasy did not go unnoticed. Their scandals were not only disruptive; they also had long-term consequences insofar as the development of modern art is concerned.

From the 1860s to the 1880s, the impressionist paintings would continually obtain negative reactions of varying intensity. But the first, and probably the most important, impressionist scandal was set off by Manet's *Le Déjeuner sur l'herbe*, a painting that outraged in both what it represented and how it did it. This most infamous painter of his generation had been until then in many respects a conventional artist chasing conventional success.[29] Official responses to his submissions to the Salon were a mixed bag until *Le Déjeneur*. The *Absinthe Drinker* (1859), a saturnine portrait of a tramp, was rejected; his colorful *Spanish Singer* (1861) was bestowed an honorable mention. Bypassing the Salon, he did a one-man show in 1863, but his work was panned as slight and lacking in finish.

The same year, Manet submitted the *Le Déjeuner* (Figure 6.4) to the Salon, a work that stood out with its prodigious size (214 cm × 269 cm). The cynosure of the painting is a naked girl with an unidealized body, sitting on the grass in a woodland dell next to two dandies in modish getup and bleary faces. Her clothes scattered about her, she is looking directly at us, unabashed and nonchalant. In the background, we see another girl, barely clad with a shift and rising out of a small creek. She imbues the painting with an odd Arcadian tincture out of step with its otherwise very topical, this-worldly timbre. Manet rejected the classical forms based on lines in favor of light and paint. In sharp contrast with the smooth surfaces dear to the Academy, he used conspicuous brushstrokes, making the painting look unpolished and sketchy. The softly focused background of the pictorial space dramatically contravenes the harsh lighting of its foreground, lending an unnerving shallowness to the image.

Figure 6.4. Édouard Manet, *Le Déjeuner sur l'herbe* (*Luncheon on the Grass*), 1863. Oil on canvas, 214 × 269 cm. Musée d'Orsay, Paris, France. Photo credit: Erich Lessing/Art Resource, NY.

The Salon jury rejected the painting. Manet was not the only snubbed one, however. There were a soaring number of painters in Paris at the time, some trying new things, most of them not very good, but all seeking fame and fortune. The Academy did not know what to do with this population, and, in the face of surging protests, Emperor Louis-Napoléon decided to hold another exhibition. The public would be able to judge for itself what was good and what was not in the new Salon des Refusés. There was of course something disingenuous about the proposition. The cachet of the Salon was a must for most of the educated public. Even though the 1860s witnessed the emergence of art critics writing mostly in small liberal newspapers and extending their support to the mavericks, a large number of rejected artists, fully aware of the stigma, declined to show in the alternative setting. The Salon des Refusés drew large crowds – in fact, larger ones than the actual Salon – but mostly because it provided an opportunity to cast ridicule at the pretentious and the untalented. *Le Déjeuner* was its main attraction.

The reviewers in mainstream newspapers were ruthless. Attacks mostly focused on form. The painting's apparent sketchiness, deliberately fashioned to give an impression of vibrancy, was read as carelessness and clumsiness. The shallowness of the composition was seen as incontrovertible evidence of ineptitude. Manet's natural feminine figures looked simply ugly to the critics. There was, nevertheless, little direct mention of the blatant sexuality of the painting, as if by broaching the topic one would fall into the trap set by the painter. But it would be naïve to think that the sex was not an important cause of the hurly-burly. After all, other paintings that were better approximations of the impressionist prototype met with less opprobrium.

Manet's painting was inspired by Giorgione's *Fête Champetre* (1508) and Raphael's *Judgment of Paris* (1516), but its sexuality was unambiguously modern. The naked girl, obviously no nymph, gazes at the spectator. To many viewers, the work was matter-of-factly portraying two rakish men about town cavorting with a couple of prostitutes in Bois de Boulogne. In the words of a no-nonsense critic: "A commonplace woman of the demimonde, as naked as can be, shamelessly lolls between two dandies dressed to the teeth. . . . This is a young man's practical joke – a shameful open sore not worth exhibiting this way."[30] The scenario was hardly an improbable one. An influx of young, unmarried women were streaming to Paris at the time from the provinces, and they did not all take on reputable jobs to survive. Yet the banality of the scene did not make things any less ignoble – on the contrary. Since the line between model and whore was a thin one both in perception and in reality, wasn't the painter brazenly celebrating his bohemian lifestyle?

Many Parisians perceived *Le Déjeuner* as pornography pure and simple. We should not be snobbish and call them philistines. They were on to something: the Greek origin of the word pornography refers to whore painting. Manet may well have seen it that way, too. The moral boundary that some educated Westerners now draw between eroticism and pornography (the former tasteful and liberating,

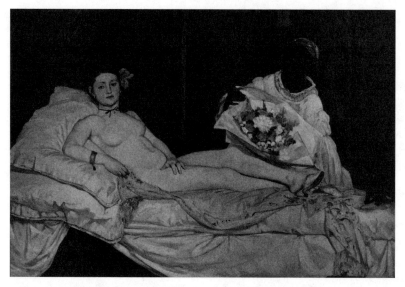

Figure 6.5. Édouard Manet, *Olympia*, 1863–65. Oil on canvas, 130.5 × 190 cm. Musée d'Orsay, Paris, France. Photo credit: Erich Lessing/Art Resource, NY.

the latter vulgar and oppressive) would make little sense to nineteenth-century Europeans. Many painters collected pornographic pictures to help them in their nude studies during this period.[31] Indeed, some of them – not unlike the literary giants of the time such as Baudelaire, Flaubert, and Zola – did cultivate an avid, unapologetic absorption in the abject.

The next major impressionist scandal also blended indecency with aesthetic transgression. In 1865, the Salon accepted Manet's two submissions in an acknowledgment of his talent. One of these stirred another conflagration, however. *Olympia*'s sexuality was even blunter, even more unadorned than that of *Le Déjeuner* (Figure 6.5). The painting features a naked red-haired woman with a flower at her ear languidly reclining on a ruffled bed. Her hand positioned on her pudenda, she shoots a cool, almost cheeky glance at the viewer. Olympia was a common term for a courtesan at the time, and the painting provided shady allusions: the woman's jewels, her sexual confidence, and the posh but not altogether respectable surroundings. Manet's source of inspiration this time was Titian's *Venus of Urbino*

(1538), which depicts a nude in a similar pose and which was once called by Mark Twain "the foulest, the vilest, the obscenest picture the world possesses," one that is "a trifle too strong for any place but a public art gallery."[32]

Twain was too much of a Victorian. In spite of its evident eroticism, Titian's Venus is a coy goddess, her form too perfect, and the painting somewhat allegoric, albeit less so than the typical Renaissance nude. *Olympia*, on the other hand, is very much flesh and blood with bodily hair and imperfections, her unglamorousness granting the demimondaine's sexuality a rawer quality. Manet marshaled the standard tricks in the impressionist toolkit – perfunctory brushwork, stark contrasts, and flattened volumes borrowed from the Spanish masters – to make the nude look as naked, as corporeal as possible. The resultant lack of finish, rough strokes of paint, and wispy contours de-sublimated the nude.

"What is this odalisque with a yellow stomach, a base model picked up I know not where, who represents Olympia?" asked Jules Claretie. Amédée Cantaloube pointed in the same breath to both the lasciviousness and the ugliness of the painting. The Olympia he saw was "a sort of female gorilla," her hands "flexed in a sort of shameless contraction."[33] Another critic wrote, "Art sunk so low doesn't even deserve reproach." Manet was eviscerated for having made himself "the apostle of the ugly and repulsive," for displaying first, "an almost childish ignorance of the fundamentals of drawing, and then, a prejudice in favor of inconceivable vulgarity."[34] Visitors to the Salon mimicked the critics; the painting had to be placed high on the wall to prevent it from being vandalized. Again, few mentioned unequivocally the profession of the naked woman. Manet undoubtedly wanted to provoke. At the same time, his paintings, which used impressionist techniques for realist ends, were denouncing the falsity of the academic nude.

To understand the challenge that Manet posed, we need to make a detour and consider the ambivalent attitude of European art until the impressionists vis-à-vis sexuality. On one hand, the Catholic Church, and later the Academy, found the representation of naked human

bodies to be morally dangerous. For early Christians, the very nakedness of pagan deities bespoke of their diabolical nature.[35] There were,
of course, historical and geographical variations in later stances. The
Italian Renaissance created the *Venus of Urbino*, but Michelangelo's
*David* (1501–4) could ornament the main entrance to the Palazzo
Vecchio only after his sexual organs were veiled with copper leaves.
*Last Judgment* fresco for the Sistine Chapel gave offense to some, and
the representation of undraped genitals in visual arts was outlawed
after Michelangelo's death.[36]

Nakedness could not be altogether avoided in the treatment of
certain subjects and events in Christian iconography, however. Bare
flesh thus had to be transmogrified into de-eroticized nudity. Unlike
the animalistic bodies of Antiquity, Christian art would produce not
objects of lust but perfect figures incarnating ideals.[37] Yet nudes
were naturally not painted solely for religious purposes; there is no
denying the carnal element in Renaissance art. Eighteenth-century
French art similarly had a strong sensual side, as it is evident in the
boudoir scenes painted by François Boucher, Jean-Honoré Frago-
nard, and Antoine Watteau. One solution to the problem was a sort
of hypocrisy regarding erotic consumption. Sensuality was allowed
as long as it was sublimated – or looked sublimated – in some way.
The last approach was particularly favored by the Academy. Take
the luscious odalisques of Ingres, which are not unlike *Playboy* cen-
terfolds in terms of the voyeuristic pleasures they offer,[38] but were
nevertheless usually tolerated by the Academy, for his nudes were
romanticized in an imagined, alien Orient.

Allegorical representations and mythological settings could justify
the nude as well. An example is Delacroix's tempestuous *The Death
of Sardanapalus* (1827), in which the king of Nineveh phlegmati-
cally watches his servants carry out his order to massacre his naked
concubines while he waits for the enemy at his door to do the same
to him imminently (Figure 6.6). The painting raised eyebrows when
exhibited at the Paris Salon in 1828. Still, it was a minor scandal.
In effect, epic paintings – much inferior in caliber to Delacroix's dis-
combobulating fantasy of violence and lust – that illustrated decadent
scenes from Roman history achieved great popularity at the Salon

Figure 6.6. Eugène Delacroix, *The Death of Sardanapalus*, 1827. Oil on canvas, 392 × 496 cm. Louvre, Paris, France. Photo credit: Erich Lesssing/Art Resource, NY.

soon after. It was this kind of double standard that enraged modern artists.[39]

Before the impressionists, Courbet had already assaulted the academic nude. He preferred working with fat models and emphatically pooh-poohed the smoothed-out academic forms. His nudes were seen as ugly as well as lustful, and Courbet did know how to draw attention with them. Louis-Napoléon was so outraged by the vulgarity of Courbet's *La Baigneuse* (1853) that he struck it with his whip. It was Manet, however, who took the realist chutzpah to its pinnacle. *Olympia* was the first painting since the Renaissance in which a nude was placed in a probable setting.[40] Even Courbet's nudes frolicked about implausibly in bucolic locales.

The scandals of the 1860s made the impressionists the laughing stock of the Academy and mainstream critics. Hostile reception, however, braced the solidarity of the rebels, spurring them to undertake collective exhibitions outside the Salon.[41] The first of these took place in 1874. Despite some favorable comments from liberal reviewers, most critical response was blisteringly negative. Jules Claretie of *L'Indépendant* accused them of declaring "war on beauty." To another leading critic, the impressionist exhibition was "a museum of horrors." The auction they organized that year was a total fiasco, interrupted by a hooting crowd. Albert Wolff, the formidable critic of *Le Figaro* and the indefatigable scourge of the impressionists, had the following to say about Renoir's *Nude in Sunlight*: "Try to explain to M. Renoir that a woman's torso is not a mass of decomposing flesh, with green and violet patches signifying that the corpse is an advanced state of putrefaction: you could try, but it would be a waste of effort."[42]

We encounter similar barrages during the next decade as well. In his reaction to the impressionist exhibition of 1886, the critic Joris-Karl Huysmans described a nude of Degas as "real, living, denuded flesh," "debased in her tub, in the humiliating posture of intimate care."[43] With hindsight it is obvious how Degas revolutionized the study of the nude: his bathers evince a natural grace while engaging in the most banal, if not undignified, quotidian actions (Figure 6.7).[44] But for Huysmans these were nothing more than lewd images, reflecting and even glorifying an unregenerate, modern Paris: "Nana washing herself, sponging herself, grooming herself, arming herself for combat, that's the impressionist ideal. Don't forget that the exhibition is two steps from the corner of the boulevard."[45]

The vehemence of the sentiment against the impressionists seems outlandish to us. What is more obvious than the beguiling power of their paintings? Who can resist being moved by *Water Lilies*? Who can look at the urban scenes in a Renoir or Manet and not be charmed by the sophisticated world to which they transport us? The sexuality in Manet or Degas is quite tame by our standards. The impressionist liberties with perspective are hardly disconcerting anymore. There is even empirical evidence that by the 1970s impressionism had been demoted to middlebrow status in France.[46] All this goes to show that the radicalness of its vision eventually became ordinary.

Figure 6.7. Edgar Degas, *The Tub* (*Bathing Woman*), 1886. Pastel on card, 60 × 83 cm. Musée d'Orsay, Paris, France. Photo credit: Erich Lessing/Art Resource, NY.

The élan of modernism could fast transform transgressions into commonplaces, if not orthodoxies.

Yet this is not the whole story. Those who declared impressionism not even worthy of reproach did nevertheless take the trouble to reproach it. The reason is even though it may have posed a threat to some bourgeois values, impressionism was itself already quite bourgeois in other respects. It dealt largely with urban themes. It enjoyed the support of numerous liberal critics and intellectuals. Its influence was spreading fast among artists. The sexuality emanating from the impressionist paintings was regular fodder in literature. So it was in part because of its growing acceptance in many quarters that impressionism needed to be censured. Even though the impressionist painters had to contend with moral opposition, they were also propped up by an expanding demand for art. Astute dealers such as Paul Durand-Ruel and Ambroise Vollard tapped into this market that consisted primarily of the cultured elite of the Third Republic and established lucrative contacts with collectors in the United States, who hailed impressionism as the first democratic art.

Scandals often need congenial conditions to break and be effective. Impressionist scandals could grant the insurgent artists publicity and following precisely because the Salon system, unable to assimilate the swelling painter demographics in Paris and challenged by the dealers and critics who allied with the mavericks, was vulnerable to attack. What is more, paradoxically, it was the Salon system that had unintentionally enabled the impressionist scandals to be as salient as they were by having already magnified the stature of the painters in France during the eighteenth and nineteenth centuries.

By the late 1880s, after five collective shows, the impressionists were no longer that shocking. In part thanks to their scandals, they had made important gains. There had been a modest rise in sales, and the artists commanded much respect within the artistic world. Impressionism had become a lodestar for young painters; Monet was bellyaching about how they were being aped. Already in 1875, critics were saying that the impressionists had imitators even in the Salon. A cartoonist suggested that impressionist paintings would cause pregnant women to miscarry,[47] but publicity reinforced the artists' self-assurance. By the early 1890s, the impressionists were making good money.[48] As one-man exhibitions spawned everywhere in Paris, the Salon lost its hold on the artistic scene and was soon demoted to being just another show, placed under the control of the newly formed Society of French Artists.[49] At any rate, it liberalized its attitudes. Manet was eventually decorated with a medal in 1882, enabling his work to be henceforth admitted to the annual exhibition hors concours. A year before, he had been made a chevalier of the Legion of Honor, thanks to his old friend Antonin Proust, now the minister of fine arts. Renoir would be the second impressionist to receive this highest official tribute in 1900. Manet and his gang had finally arrived.

## The Moral Logics of Modern Art

Modern art further radicalized in the course of twentieth century. Here I consider the thematic provocations of modernism. I then analyze its formal innovations and rejection of mimesis. Modernist radicalization had a lot to do with artistic competition. At the same time, although modern art had a limited elite public, both its production and reception were frequently steeped in contending moral discourses, a characteristic that was brought to the fore in scandals. Modern art mixed sensory salience and moral strife – hence its positive valence to scandal.

## Subversive Content

The impressionist painters had already made forays into thematically risky domains. Modern art – here I refer to Western art until the late 1950s – would only up the ante. Whores became a favorite topic among painters, and nudes grew increasingly violent. Frontiers of indecency were pushed forward as sexuality and all its transgressive modes were represented with a defiant frankness. Consider exhibitionist onanism in Egon Schiele's *Self-Portrait Masturbating* (1911), an unblushing depiction of the scraggy painter himself with withered features and a tumescent penis, casting us a gaze blending angst with lust. Still others attacked the sexual taboos of the time. Take, for instance, the thinly veiled homoeroticism in Paul Cadmus's merry *The Fleet's In* (1934).

Morally ambiguity is central to many modernist masterpieces. The *Guitar Lesson* (1934) of Balthus is a case in point. The painting limns a pubescent girl stretched out on the lap of her female guitar professor. The latter is fondling the student's exposed sex with one hand and yanking her hair with the other, as if she were tuning a guitar and plucking its strings. The transfixed girl is pinching the professor's nipple, her guitar lying on the floor. This is a truly disconcerting image, marked by an uncanny stillness accentuated by the tightness of the composition and the awesome trance in which the tutor and pupil are locked. As many commentators have pointed out, Balthus is quoting as well as profaning a canonical image of Christian iconography: Enguerrand Quarton's *Pietà de Villeneuve-les-Avignons*, in which Virgin Mary and the dead Christ take a pose analogous to that of the musical couple in the *Guitar Lesson*. Yet the reference is

Figure 6.8. Max Ernst, *Virgin Punishing Jesus in Front of Three Witnesses: André Breton, Paul Éluard, and the Painter*, 1926. Oil on canvas, 169 × 130 cm. Private Collection. Photo credit: Private Collection/Superstock.

not a facetious or ironic one, as we would find in surrealist or post-modern works. Balthus recreates the same rapture we find in *Pietà*, even though the latter portrays a most sacred union and the *Guitar Lesson* a most sinister one.

The surrealists, who rose to prominence in the late 1920s and 1930s, were the modern task masters of provocation.[50] As Buñuel put it, their aim was "to explode the social order."[51] They flirted with communism and anarchism, were enthralled with criminals of all types, and slugged nationalist and religious symbols. Some of them were dead serious and righteous in their attacks, others droll. They excelled in irreverent paintings like Max Ernst's *Virgin Punishing Jesus in Front of Three Witnesses: André Breton, Paul Éluard, and the Painter* (1926), a work that depicts a severe Holy Mother slapping the buttocks of the son of God with such ferocity that his halo has fallen on the floor (Figure 6.8). The surrealists believed it was the irrational and the violent that led the way to psychic and political emancipation. Sex would jolt the bourgeoisie out of its complacency. Sodomy, masturbation, exhibitionism, and fetishism thus figured among their favorite topics. Bodily waste, too, acquired a place in the modernist visual vocabulary thanks to them; excrement shocked by contaminating audiences as well as the sublimity of art. The works of Salvador Dali best exemplify the gusto with which surrealism attacked propriety and topsy-turvied symbolic hierarchies. His *Gloomy Game* (1929) brings together a man manually stimulating the penis of another one on a monument; someone resembling the painter in soiled boxers; an anus placed next to a chalice; and vagina-like fissures (Figure 6.9).

Transgressions of this kind were at times met with significant sanctions. A judge publicly burned a sexual drawing by Schiele. In the same trial, the painter was convicted for exhibiting offensive works in a place accessible to children. Balthus's *The Guitar Lesson* could not be shown anywhere until 2001. The Archbishop of Cologne excommunicated Max Ernst because of his aforementioned painting. *Fleet's In* was removed in 1934 from a show at the Corcoran Gallery of Art. Despite such enormities, which sometimes made headlines and turned artists into iconoclasts in the popular consciousness, we observe in

Figure 6.9. Salvador Dali, *The Gloomy Game*, 1929. Oil and collage on carton, 44.4 × 30.3 cm. Private Collection, Spain. ©2008 Salvador Dali, Gala-
Salvador Dali Foundation/ARS, NY. © Archivo Iconografico, S.A./CORBIS.

modern art a negative relationship between thematic transgression and formal innovation. It was usually those who kept their ties to representation who found it easier to scandalize effectively.

The surrealists are a perfect example. Their principle of automatism, which allowed the artist to spontaneously juxtapose cognitively and morally incongruous elements culled purportedly from the unconsciousness, was distinctly modern. Yet the resulting shock was nevertheless anchored in conventional illusionism. The surrealist onslaught on conventional morals required that the figures on the canvas be relatable to actual objects in the world, however disquieting the relation might be. Dali could scandalize as much as he did only thanks to his photographic precision, with which he could make his fantastic perversions as palpable as possible. Furthermore, the exemplary draughtsmanship with which he produced his unsettling images was undeniable evidence of his technical prowess. His work could not be easily ignored. Even after Dali maddened the surrealists themselves with his pecuniary acuity and pro-Franco statements, he still remained indispensable to the movement because of his consummate technique and eccentric showmanship. Most surrealists came to believe that Dali was a degenerate, avaricious reactionary, and some thought that he was merely a craftsman instead of a bona fide artist. Yet Dali's work continued to be showcased in all of their exhibitions well after his banishment from the group. The surrealists were thus not above pragmatism.

It would of course be impossible to reduce the unbridled imagination and humor in surrealist paintings to some social agenda. There was, however, at times a strict, almost Manichean moral impulse behind their trespasses – leftist, anticlerical, and not altogether even-handed vis-à-vis male and female homosexuality. It was not anything goes, as Dali soon discovered after he joined them:

> I was permitted blood. A little crap was all right. But just crap was not on. Depicting genitals was approved, but no anal fantasies. They looked very askance at anuses. They liked lesbians very much indeed, but not pederasts. One could have sadism in dreams to one's heart's content, and umbrellas and sewing machines, but no religion on any account, not even if it was of a mystical nature. And

to dream of a Raphael Madonna, quite simply, without apparent blasphemy, was strictly prohibited.[52]

More important, the surrealists positioned themselves against abstraction, whose formalism they found jejune. Dali announced its demise with glee:

> [*Un Chien Andalou*] ruined in a single evening ten years of pseudo-intellectual post-war avant-gardism. The foul thing figuratively called abstract art fell at our feet, wounded to the death, never to rise again, having seen a girl's eye cut by a razor-blade.... There was no longer room in Europe for the little maniacal lozenges of Monsieur Mondrian.[53]

Such blusterous triumphalism is somewhat misleading, however. Albeit in decline during 1930s, abstraction would reign supreme in the late 1940s and 1950s. Furthermore, abstract painters and their friendly critics were not any less censorious of their modernist brethrens: in their eyes, surrealism was not only passé, but also impure. Dali and company were charlatans using artifice to fool middle-class audiences, who were only too ready to be entertained by threadbare blasphemies. The surrealists sought facile glory from the reactions of the average man and were thus contaminated by the very public they were inciting. Their provocations brought them prominence, but at the cost of trivializing their art.

## Form and Morality

Thematic transgressions could invest the avant-garde with a mystique and confirm the spirit of independence artists claimed for themselves. But modern art is much more than scandalous content. In fact, formal radicalization is what it is mostly about. We could even say that the history of modernism consists of a series of revolutionary ruptures punctuated by brief periods of relative calm and weak consensus as movements proposing new aesthetic models rapidly followed one another. Artists radicalized form in part to experiment with technical possibilities, to expand the domain of imagination, to present their personal vision, and to differentiate themselves from others with as much din as possible. At the same time, moralizing notions of artistic purity and honesty often accompanied or justified aesthetic decisions. When artists were silent, it was critics who often interpreted formal choices as moral ones. Novelty was highly valued, but it was rarely defended as an end in itself; there was often something immoral with the old as well. Unfriendly critics and publics were even readier to resort to moral arguments to contest modern art.

As it is well known, a progressive move away from nature characterizes the formal evolution of modern art. The standard accounts of this dynamic emphasize the importance of the avant-garde ideology.[54] It is true that modernism, in art as in other fields, questioned all conventions. A fascination with the new combined with a single-minded attachment to the notion of progress – at times undergirded by utopian ideologies – and formed the mind-set of modern painters. Mavericks appeared on the scene one after another, with manifestos drafted by themselves or by sympathetic critics, promulgating the obsolescence of former art.[55] Art was synonymous with the act of breaking free from the past. "Only he is alive who rejects his convictions of yesterday," stated Malevich in an apothegm.[56] "In art, one has to kill one's father," Picasso is supposed to have said. Artists were often not content with promoting their own superior visions; they maintained that their very intervention marked the end of art.[57]

Nevertheless, as important as it was in animating artists and legitimating their endeavors, the avant-garde ideology by itself cannot really explain why modern art rejected mimesis. Nor can it explain why form was so often moralized by audiences and artists alike. Another account of modernist élan puts the stress on market forces that pushed artists to seek novelty. Yet commodification of art precedes modern times.[58] In any case, the market for twentieth-century modern art was relatively small when compared with that for conventional works.[59]

Capitalism was nevertheless crucial to the rise of modern art, though in a negative way. Modern art was a reaction to both technology and mass culture, each an offspring of capitalism. It was in large part because photography – and later cinema – did a much better job of recording the factual world than the visual arts that painters recoiled from traditional representation. Through distortion and abstraction, they could differentiate their creations from those produced by the cultural industry and continue to justify their calling.[60] Moreover, representation implied subordination to nature, which was for many modernists simply the aesthetic correlate of a larger thralldom to society, religion, and politics. Necessity was thus turned into a virtue. The defeat to technology would be redeemed into an affirmative steering off from representation and a general rejection of everything extraneous to art. This rejection often took the form of an oppositional morality. Art is not "the slavish copying of an object," said Cézanne.[61] Kandinsky urged a "revolt from dependence on nature."[62] "To approach the spiritual in art, one will make as little use as possible of reality," wrote Mondrian.[63] Once they were freed from the shackles of tradition and from the bondage to nature, painters found that they could focus exclusively on the problems their medium posed. At the same time, the move away from representation eroded settled criteria for aesthetic judgment and made it progressively difficult for a lasting consensus to emerge on the superiority of any style.

Impressionism had an ambivalent position vis-à-vis representation. Manet and his followers warranted their revolutionary techniques on realistic grounds. By dabbing pure blobs of color on the canvas, the colors then merging vividly in the act of perception by the viewer, the impressionists claimed to produce the truthful renditions of our impressions. It was again in the name of realism that these painters eliminated the black shadows and outlines that were dear to the Academy from their work. When they wanted to tackle everyday scenes and unidealized nudes, impressionists were being impelled by a similar imperative as well.

Yet "Manet's gang" originated the antimimetic drive, too. They insisted on the visible brushstroke, which, they thought, was necessary to seize the dazzling force with which the world imposed itself on our senses. As a result, however, their paintings, when descried up close, displayed muddily all their actual making. The strokes of pure color engendered ethereal shapes with an eerie two-dimensionality, especially if they were not seen together from a distance. Embracing a relatively flat pictorial space, the impressionists began to autonomize the canvas from nature. Already pushing the signification process to the fore at the expense of the referent, they inaugurated the drift from the illusionist principles that underlie much of the representational tradition in Western art.

Modern art in the twentieth century jettisoned the phenomenological concerns of impressionism while radicalizing its antimimetic impetus. From Paul Cézanne to Jackson Pollock, verisimilitude worried less and less; indeed, the natural was often seen as an impurity to be avoided. "Retain only what cannot be seen," advised Matisse and added, "I don't paint things. I paint only the relationship between things."[64] Klee's well-known maxim explains the spirit at work: "The intention of modern painting is not to reflect the visible but to make visible."[65] Modern art was thus expressionist in a large sense: instead of slavishly replicating the world, the artists showed or expressed nontangible forces, states, or ideas. Pure abstract art did eventually become hegemonic in the early 1950s with the New York Style. But modernism is not synonymous with abstraction. Distortion was another orientation, and, arguably, a more important one. At any rate, much of modern art melded distortion and abstraction in varying degrees.

Abstract art abandons moorings in the objective world. In contrast, a loose likeness to nature is retained in distortion, but only after a radical transformation. Of course, no painting, modern or otherwise, simply reflects the world. Representation is an interpretative process that involves modification through style and convention; there is obviously no one way to do it. Yet it is only in modernist distortion that representation works by defamiliarizing, by the jolting discrepancy between the painting and the world. This negative representation of the world allows the viewer to see novel beauties or hidden truths, and there is a very strong emotive component to distortion. Emphatic use of color, contorted forms and outlines, and flatness all serve in different ways to express and elicit psychological states.

Increasing distortion characterizes the evolution of modern art. The post-impressionists and synthetists such as Vincent Van Gogh and Paul Gauguin made paintings that were blatantly artificial with exaggerated lines and incandescent colors. Unlike the impressionists, they were much more concerned with the affective potentials of paint than any science of light. Fauvism was the capstone of the kind of distortion that autonomized color from the subject matter; it ignited the first major art scandal of the twentieth century. "Fauves" (wild beasts) was a pejorative designation dubbed by the critic Louis Vauxcelles to Henri Matisse and others around him. With an overall bent for the primitive in the general feel of their paintings, these artists produced works with raw-looking surfaces, used dissonant colors, and drew warped, elongated figures. "Exactitude is not reality,"[66] famously said Matisse: "What I am after, above all, is expression. . . . To express things, you have to evoke them artistically instead of showing them crudely."[67] Matisse wanted to show a reality behind the appearances, a reality that was accessible only to modern art.

Many of his critics ran down his work on a moral plane in the 1905 exhibition of Salon des Indépendants. They said that his colors were brutal and that the distortions in his paintings were symptoms of his self-absorption, a diagnostic that would soon become common currency in the criticism of modern art. In his review of *Woman with the Hat* (1905), the writer Francis Carco, who was otherwise fairly congenial to modernism, intoned: "Nothing about it was physically human. You had the impression that the artist had been much more preoccupied by his own personality than he was by the model's."[68] Even though he sold poorly in the exhibition, the scandal was important in Matisse's rise. His prices soon spiked so high that in 1907 the famous dealer Daniel-Henry Kahnweiler could not sign him up.[69] Attacks on his work did not end, however. Louis Vauxcelles complained about the "cruel coloring"[70] in Matisse's *Nu blue, Souvenir de Biskra* (1907), a painting that was eventually burned in effigy after the Armory Show of 1913 in Chicago.

Cubism was the next major (out)rage in Paris. Following Cézanne, who thought that colorists such as Gauguin were mere decorators, the cubists were obsessed with unity and structure. They broke up objects and reassembled them in unnatural and seemingly haphazard ways on a picture plane divided into cropped geometric facet-planes adjacent to each other. Their paintings often depicted the same object from multiple viewpoints, creating complex and shifting patterns formed of lines, patches, and cubes. The cubist pieces were much more distorted than fauvist work, the chasm between art and its real referent much more gaping and disturbing. Although one could appreciate the allure of the fauvist paintings with their sensual mood and fierce colors,[71] it seemed that the cubists cared little about beauty. Their stuff seemed willfully unsightly.

This dernier cri of the Parisian art scene synthesized maximal distortion with rudimentary abstraction. Cubism was indebted to Cézanne, who strived for orderly compositions independent of inchoate impressions. Yet the structure that the cubist painter aimed at was not to be found in the natural world. In their synthetic phase, cubists pasted all sorts of perishable trinkets such as newspaper clippings, bits of posters, and theatre tickets on the canvas. An artificial universe was fabricated in these collages: objects lost the meanings they had in the real world to acquire new ones by virtue of their constitutive relationships to each other in the pictorial space, conceived as an enclosed system of autonomous signification.[72]

Cubism was not abstraction pure et dure, though. The things that made up a cubist work were figures and objects that had been picked up from the real world. Their provenance could never be quite obliterated, and cubism was most effective when it distorted heavily but noticeably. The most celebrated cubist masterpiece, even though it was completed before the movement came to full flower, is, after all, Les Demoiselles d'Avignon (Figure 6.2). The painting scandalized mostly because of the monstrous mien of the prostitutes parading minaciously in front of the bidder-spectator, a terrorizing ugliness that was the product of Picasso's pugnacity on the feminine figure. The work was genuinely novel: even his close associates like George Braque and Gertrude Stein were shocked. Here is what André Salmon, one of the earliest intellectual champions of the movement, wrote about the painting: "Nudes came into being, whose deformation caused little surprise – we had been prepared for it by Picasso

Figure 6.10. Pablo Picasso, *Large Nude in a Red Armchair*, 1929. Oil on canvas, 195 × 129 cm. Musée Picasso, Paris, France. ©2008 Estate of Pablo Picasso/ ARS, NY. Photo: J. G. Berizzi. Photo Credit: Réunion des Musées Nationaux, Art Resource, NY.

himself, by Matisse, Derain, Braque. . . . and even earlier by Cézanne and Gauguin. It was the ugliness of the faces that froze with horror the half-converted."[73] Braque himself was blanched upon seeing *Les Demoiselles d'Avignon* and fretted to Picasso: "You paint as if you wanted us to eat rope-ends or to drink petrol."[74] His dealer Kahnweiler said, "The picture that Picasso had painted struck everyone as something mad and monstrous."[75]

The emotional power of distortion marks many modernist masterpieces. Consider Picasso's menacingly misshapen nudes (Figure 6.10), Francis Bacon's writhing visages and tortuous naked bodies, or Willem de Kooning's scowling shrews with sagging and swollen features (Figure 6.11). All these brutally contorted figures are figments of imagination; they instigate in us terror and anguish in their aberrations, rather than inspiring any compassion or humility, as do, for instance, Rembrandt's celebrated etchings of old women with all their imperfections and corporal vulnerabilities.[76] This is why modern artists were frequently accused of sadism – when they were not taken to task for not being able to draw or for being portentously tenebrific. Artists or their congenial critics rebutted by saying that they were unflinchingly exposing what was insupportable about the world or ourselves.

Distortion was not always or completely dark. Consider the unmistakable humor in Jean Dubuffet's skull-like portraits made with soil, tar, dust, gravel, and ash as well as paint (Figure 6.12). But expressionism (loosely understood) in modern art did often have a moral nub. A Nazi official came to Picasso's atelier during the occupation in Paris to find out what the whole fuss was about the legendary painter. Noticing *Guernica*, he reportedly asked, "You made this?" Picasso replied, "No, you did this."[77] The painting's wrenched human and animal figures have become almost as emblematic of modern totalitarianism as concentration camps. In a similar vein, a critic reviewing de Kooning's *Women* series (1953), which brought about a scandal when first exhibited at the Sidney Janis Gallery in New York, wrote that the painter was in a battle with "[the] female personification of all that is unacceptable, perverse and infantile in ourselves."[78] Distortion was often seen as the road to purity.

Figure 6.11. Willem de Kooning, *Woman I*, 1950–52. Oil on canvas, 6″3 7.8″ × 58″. The Museum of Modern Art, New York, NY. ©2008 Willem de Kooning Foundation. ARS, NY. Digital Image © Museum of Modern Art/ Licensed by SSALA/Art Resource, NY.

Figure 6.12. Jean Dubuffet, *Portrait d'André Dhotel nuancé d'abricot* (*Portrait of André Dhotel Shaded with Apricot*), 1947. Oil on canvas, 116 × 89 cm. MNAM, Paris, France. Photo credit: CNAC/MNAM/Dist. Réunion des Musées Nationaux/Art Resource NY.

Artists such as Dubuffet embraced primitivism and childlike symbolism to retreat to a primeval state, the simplicity of which would repel only those corrupted by civilization. Klee justified his pseudo-puerile, quizzical reconfigurations of the human figure by saying, "I want to be as though newborn, knowing nothing, absolutely nothing about Europe . . . to be almost primitive."[79]

Abstraction raised somewhat different issues. Allowing art finally to purge itself of all that was extraneous to its nature was seen as the pinnacle of progress in many quarters. The representational element largely evanesced during the 1910s, 1920s, and 1930s in works associated with orphism, constructivism, and neo-plasticism. Robert Delaunay relieved color from any representational function to vouchsafe the integrity of art: "As long as art cannot get free of the object, it will continue to be a description. . . . [and] will degrade itself to become the handmaiden of imitation."[80] Piet Mondrian and Kazimir Malevich drew grids – the archetypal figure of modernism with its flat, sealed-off, structural, unreal, and man-made properties.[81] Wassily Kandinsky fashioned a geometric universe crowded with conglomerations of shapes, spots, and lines. The negation of nature not only aimed to establish the autonomy of art. Some abstractionists of this period were very metaphysical artists and attributed a cleansing otherworldliness to their work. Kandinsky, for example, claimed to be reconstructing numinous harmonies through his pure forms. It was against this staid, salubrious, almost pious formalism that surrealism – with its taste for the sinister and the sanguinary and the sacrilegious – had reacted.

Abstract expressionism took the antimimetic wave to its apex. Its chief hierophant Clement Greenberg argued that, despite its professed rupture, European abstraction had underhandedly clung on to various figurative principles. Kandinsky's compositions, for instance, still evoked natural forms like landscapes for effect and adhered to the conventional ground and figure dichotomy.[82] Much worse, such works were decoration masquerading as art – a cardinal sin in modernist catechism. The abstract expressionist paintings, in contrast, went to extremes in their visual flatness, evidencing their autonomy from nature as well as from other artistic media. The dualities that had structured all preceding art – those between foreground and background, figure and field, line and contour, color and pattern – were all thrown out the window in the works of Jackson Pollock, who conceived the canvas as a homogenous field without any emphases.

The reductionist program of the new frisson attained its acme in the almost empty canvases of color field artists. Barnett Newman simply split enormous expanses of color with a few parallel lines of paint; Clyfford Still and Mark Rothko banished all color contrast in pictorial design. Abstract expressionism was truly hegemonic in the United States during the 1950s. Those odd men out such as Lucian Freud who excelled in figure were reproved as retrograde and struggled just to get exhibition space. Even de Kooning found himself at one point berated for betraying abstraction.

The politics of the new movement was ambiguous.[83] Their anti-mimetic stance and lofty idea of the purity of art enjoined the painters from a direct involvement with politics. They were not all indifferent, however. For some of them, rejecting the beautiful and the natural was a moral decision with political undertones. As Barnett Newman, a painter who defined his art as socialist, said in a 1962 interview, "People were painting a beautiful world, and at that time we realized that the world wasn't beautiful. The question, the moral question, that each of us examined – de Kooning, Pollock and myself – was: what was there to beautify?"[84]

When the abstract expressionists refrained from interpreting their own work in public, friendly critics, who had their own incentives to define and champion the new movement, stepped in – often with moralizing notions. The art historian Meyer Shapiro saw their enterprise as "a counter-attack on the standardization of the twentieth century."[85] Clement Greenberg praised abstract expressionism's honesty: unlike representational art, it did not dupe audiences for effect.[86] He made much of how the New York artists of the post–World War II era rejected perspective and highlighted the glutinous substance of paint by not using any insulating finish. Greenberg thus argued that the abstract expressionists produced an artless art that underlined its production.[87] And unlike surrealism, whose fictional concerns led to ersatz paintings derivative of other aesthetic media, this new art was autonomous and pure.

The abstract expressionists, however, did poach automatism from surrealists, and the most proficient practitioner of this technique was Jackson Pollock. This first American painter of international stature dripped and poured paint (apparently in a spontaneous fashion) on an unprimed canvas stretched out on the floor. Pollock, like many others in his group, strived for a very subjective art in which the inner turmoil of the artist would be projected onto the canvas – in contrast to European abstract art, which was more spiritual and archetypal. Greenberg argued that the spontaneity of Pollock was virtuous as well as therapeutic. For Harold Rosenberg, another famous critic who promoted the gestural work of Willem de Kooning and called abstract expressionism "action painting," the latter was nothing less than a moral struggle:

> In a word, Action Painting is the abstraction of the *moral* element in art: its mark is moral tension in detachment from moral or esthetic certainties; and it judges itself morally in declaring that picture to be worthless which is not the incorporation of a genuine struggle, one which could at any point have been lost.[88]

Abstraction had a moral dimension to less impressed audiences as well. It was indeed a moral problem. Yet there was little agreement on what was wrong with it; its hermetism allowed for a wide gamut of interpretations. Denounced for being elitist and individualistic, abstraction was labeled "bourgeois art" by communist governments and parties all over the world even though its early practitioners many times made common cause with revolutionaries. For some European leftists, abstract expressionism was the cultural tool of American imperialism.[89] The conservative right was hardly more sympathetic. The Republican congressman George Dondero from Michigan called for the withdrawal of governmental aid to modern art as he found abstract expressionists' "distortion, grotesqueness, and meaninglessness" to be un-American.[90] Some of these artists were even suspected of being political radicals in disguise and of encrypting nefarious messages in their paintings.[91] Many people, both in the left and right, saw postwar abstraction as the product of moral decay in modern society.[92] What is more, its defenders and even practitioners – recall the quote by Newman cited earlier – often concurred, but then added that the honest art of an out-of-joint world could not be but out-of-joint itself.

Abstract expressionism was frequently assaulted for being inscrutable, solipsistic, and even supercilious. It was far from obvious that it was art. Misgivings were voiced by cultural simpletons and esteemed experts alike. The *New Yorker* critic Robert Coates did not mince his words about Jackson Pollock's fifth one-man show in January 1948: "I can say of such pieces... only that they seem mere unorganized explosions of random energy, and therefore meaningless."[93] Reviewers of early Pollock likened what they saw to "baked macaroni." It seemed to some that abstract expressionists were simply trying to bamboozle the public. In a podium discussion organized by *Time* in 1948, the curator of graphic art at the Metropolitan Museum dismissed abstract expressionism: "I suspect any picture I think I could have made myself."[94] Modern figurative painters chimed in. Balthus said, "I detest the modern. Today's painters don't know how to make a painterly phrase. Before, at least a minimum of technique was required."[95] Picasso, too, scouted at abstract expressionism. He thought that Pollock's paintings were "meaningless tangles of cordage and smears."[96] According to a *Time* story, "[He] once grabbed an ink-stained blotter, shoved it at a visitor, and snapped, 'Jackson Pollock!'"[97]

Moreover, abstract expressionism was no more exempt from the chargers of decoration than were the European abstractionists. A Yale professor said in the conference mentioned earlier that Pollock's painting *Cathedral* (1947) would make "a pleasant design for a necktie" (Figure 6.13). "It seems to me exquisite in tone and quality. It would make a most enchanting printing silk," pointed out Sir Leigh Ashton, the director of Victoria and Albert Museum in London.[98] And this derision was difficult to chalk up to philistinism or conservatism. It was after all Picasso, the very avatar of modernism, who thought that Pollock's paintings were "panels for wallpaper." Equating pure abstraction with decoration, indeed "with the death of art,"[99] the Spanish painter was always at pains to show his audiences what his figures corresponded to in nature even during his most radical cubist period. His biographer reports: "[He] would object vociferously if anyone told him that one of his paintings was abstract.... Picasso said to me of one work, 'That's a head.' – 'That

Figure 6.13. Jackson Pollock, *Cathedral*, 1947. Enamel and aluminum paint on canvas, 181.61 × 89.06 cm. Dallas Museum of Art, Texas. ©2008 The Pollock-Krasner Foundation/ARS, NY.

thing with the triangle,' I asked. – 'But it's a head, it's a head.'"[100] Abstract expressionist painters and their advocates resorted to decoration charges in their internal scuffles as well. It was Harold Rosenberg who wrote, in a thinly veiled attack on Jackson Pollock,[101] that abstract work lacking "the dialectical tension of a genuine act, associated with will and risk," was nothing better than "apocalyptic wallpaper."[102]

Modern art from its very inception was beset by the Scylla of mimesis on one side and the Charybdis of decoration on the other.

We already saw how mimesis was disdained, but decoration was perhaps even worse. The charge was bandied about among fellow modernists to disparage each other; few were exempt from it. Guillaume Apollinaire, for instance, dismissed the work of the cubist Juan Gris for being too decorative, that of "a shop-window dresser."[103] Cézanne derided Gauguin for simply being "a maker of Chinese images."[104] Autonomy and purity dictated rejecting representation, but nonobjective art could easily look ornamental. Abstract art was thus often grim, even ominous, in its visual outlook and emotional overtones. In a 1943 letter to the *New York Times*, Mark Rothko and Adolph Gottlieb wrote, "only that subject matter is valid which is tragic and timeless." Nevertheless, empirical studies show that most people who own abstract art regard it as decorative.[105]

The very intractability of modern art to the wider public meant that scandals would mostly have an elite audience. To the extent that there was neither a strong nor a durable accord in the art community about the merit or demerit of mavericks (especially if they were new to the scene) nor an academic ideology to be challenged, most twentieth-century scandals looked very much like controversies in exclusive circles. Vanguards could often count on enthusiastic critics, and being attacked by dodos was a badge of honor in the eyes of their aesthetic brethren and the smart set. Scandal, albeit less and less of an extraordinary event, nevertheless remained an essential engine of change. The entrenched incentives to transgress formally and the moral vocabulary used to defend as well to attack art ensured that public debate on modernist work would frequently take the form of scandal, particularly when the artist in question was already famous.

The drift away from mimesis propelled the incredible stylistic momentum of modern art, but it also generated uncertainty regarding what is good. Artworks became what economists call "credence goods," that is, commodities with very-difficult-to-ascertain qualities. The role of things extraneous to works of art was thus magnified in their assessment. Modern art until the 1960s required explanation from either the artists themselves – think of Kandinsky's tracts – or their allies in the world of criticism. A key reason why critics' role expanded in the modern era is the replacement of representation with intertextuality. The more artworks grew autonomous from nature, the more they were ironically bound to each other. A Giotto or a Titian can be appreciated without knowing the place of the painter in the history of art; one would be hard-pressed to say the same for Daniel Buren's stripes, the meaning of which can be grasped only in relation to Piet Mondrian's grids and Robert Ryman's all-white paintings.

Yet expertise was not enough to settle doubts about worth; critics themselves disagreed. Uncertainty – hence the possibility of fraud – made the sincerity of the artist equally important in modern art. Intentions became vital not only in establishing the meaning of a work but also in determining its worth. "Pollock has broken all barriers between his picture and himself. . . . Each one of his pictures is part of himself," wrote the critic Bruno Alfieris and asked despairingly when he was faced with the task of assessing the American artist's work: "What is his inner world worth?"[106] At the same time, given the elusiveness of intentions, moral reputation (the certitude that we are not dealing with a humbug) could be difficult to establish – at least before the artist was canonized by museums.

Modern art appealed mainly to the elite. The ascendance of abstraction, which made painting less emotionally effective especially to the uninitiated, lessened the general appeal of modernism further. Nevertheless, the justification as well as the criticism of modern art by cognoscenti was still undertaken in the name of universal values. Besides, artists derived a good deal of their status from being simply known by the masses. Most people continued to hold on to conventional ideas as to what art should do: they wanted it to represent the world in a way that shows exceptional talent, and they wanted it to move them. It was not always clear whether high modernism did these things. Nonetheless, modern artists beguiled the public. Even those who objected to Picasso's work – finding it ugly or barbarous – could and did think of his paintings as the reflection of an extraordinary person. Or at least this is what they were told to do – in line with the romantic notion, which survived into the modern age, that art is the personal expression of the artist. Jackson Pollock had already started to build a reputation in the art world after the Second World

War. But the 1949 story about Pollock by *Life*, which asked in its title somewhat rhetorically whether he was the greatest American painter alive, was crucial in his climb to iconic status.[107] Most of the letters the magazine received from readers in the wake of the piece were derisive, but becoming a celebrity certainly helped Pollock. The November 1949 show was a triumph. His biographers all mention that he was very proud of the *Life* story. Painters such as Dali who sought attention too openly and too ardently risked losing prestige in the artistic community, but the unction of public fascination was hardly irrelevant for the ambitious.

## The Paradoxes of Contemporary Art

The contemporary art scene – I am referring to the Anglo-Saxon context after the 1960s – presents a stunning heterogeneity. A plethora of styles has gone in and out of fashion.[108] Contemporary art is not unitary; nor does it have a linear history – the kind of narrative that was central to the identity of modernism.[109] Schools coexist: figurative painting experienced a recrudescence after the 1960s, and artists routinely jumble modern elements with classical ones in their works. Maybe more important, the idea of progress, which was second nature to modern art, has few supporters left. It would be impossible for me to review contemporary or postmodern art here. Rather, I limit myself to commenting on two pivotal trends that have altered the moral disputes over art and the use of scandal by artists. One of them is the crisis of the object of art. The other is the return of the real.

### The Crisis of the Art Object

The avoidance of the common and the mass-produced was the very basis of modernist purity. Kitsch, however, encroached into the aesthetic province in the 1960s, mostly thanks to Roy Lichtenstein's oil paintings and Andy Warhol's silk screens. Pop art blurred the distinction between aesthetic objects and artifacts of popular culture: mimetic and even mechanical representations of corn flakes, soup cans, celebrities, or comics demanded artistic status, often with success. Soon after, another wave targeted a second boundary, the one between art objects and real objects. Admittedly, it had not always been self-evident why modernist experimentations should be accorded the title of art. Nevertheless, the idea that artistic objects were ontologically different from things in nature had been central to all aesthetics, modern or not, and was shared by both highfalutin critics and philistine publics.

The notion of the object of art as a unique physical entity created by an inspired act had already been questioned by Marcel Duchamp, who famously sent a ceramic urinal titled "Fountain" to the 1917 exhibition of the Society of Independent Artists under a false signature (Figure 6.14). Duchamp was himself on the jury but resigned when his urinal was rejected. The incident was promptly publicized in the broadsheets the *Blind Man* and *Rongwrong*, kicking up one of the most memorable scandals in the annals of art. Duchamp would later stress in a letter to an old ally that his readymade "was thrown into the public's face in a spirit of defiance."[110] Most found the act meaningless, if not idiotic – mischievous at best. The provocateur himself took pains to emphasize that his readymades were selected randomly with absolutely no rhyme or reason, with no aesthetic impulse: "It is necessary to arrive at selecting an object with the idea of not being impressed by this object on the basis of enjoyment of any order."[111]

Like all provocateurs, Duchamp was constrained by how his audiences were affected by his act and how they defined it. Even those who sympathized with him still wanted to ascribe an aesthetic quality to the urinal. The Dada collector Walter Aremberg thought that it must have been its overlooked luster that set the readymade apart from the other objects in the world and validated its being put on display.[112] Most modernists subscribed to the notion that the raison d'être of art was still, after all, the pursuit of beauty. It did not matter whether beauty was not self-evident. In fact, it was the very mission of the modern artist to reveal novel beauties – for many it was above all this ability that testified to genius. We owe modernism the discovery that the terrible can be awesomely beautiful. Picasso

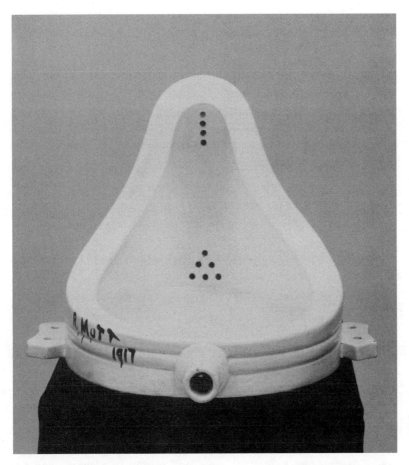

Figure 6.14. Marcel Duchamp, *Fountain*, 1917/1964. Third version, repli-cated under the direction of the artist in 1964 by the Galerie Schwarz, Milan. White earthenware, covered in glazed ceramic and paint, 63 × 48 × 35. Musée National d'Art Moderne, Centre Georges Pompidou, Paris, France. ©2008 ARS, NY/ADAGO, Paris/Succession Marcel Duchamp. Photo: Philippe Migeat. Photo Credit: CNAC/MNAM/Dist. Réunion des Musée Nationaux/Art Resource, NY.

was convinced that people would eventually see the beauty in *Les Demoiselles d'Avignon*, and time has bore him out. If the artist did not create a beautiful object, he or she must then be pointing our attention to the beauty in the world that we ignore. This is what Aremberg assumed in his defense of Duchamp's urinal.

The scandal made some noise but had little immediate or medium-term effect on modern art. Duchamp's severing of artistic activity both from beauty and creation were too much out of step with modernism. He was seen as an eccentric; that was it. Yet the urinal was not forgotten, and Duchamp made a comeback in the 1960s. In fact, his legacy has been immeasurable – so much that, in December 2004, the 500 most important people in the British art world voted his urinal the most influential artwork of the twentieth century. Many artists drew on Duchamp's ideas in the 1960s to go beyond the cul-de-sac bequeathed by abstract expressionism. Andy Warhol's debt to him is evident and enormous. Consider his *Brillo Box* (1964). The work is not a readymade, but rather a replication of plywood Brillo boxes fabricated by another manufacturer, with the logos and lettering silk printed on them by the artist's employees in his "factory" (Figure 6.15). There are no visible differences between a Brillo box and Warhol's facsimile of it. Nonetheless, the work does not simply mimic the banal; it thumbs its nose at our deeply seated notions of aesthetic creation.

Conceptual art, which burst on the scene in the mid-sixties, took things further by declaring that art is fundamentally an ideational practice. Take Joseph Kosuth's *One and Three Chairs* (1965), which features an actual chair, a photograph of this chair, and a photographic enlargement of a dictionary entry for the word "chair" (Figure 6.16). It is the idea behind the piece (that the three chairs are the representations of the universal notion of a chair), and not its factuality or sensory appeal, that makes the work art. Or recall André's *Equivalent VIII*. The actual bricks that the Tate Gallery purchased from André were not the ones that the artist had used when the work was first shown. But apparently the museum curators, unlike the outraged British tabloid media, saw nothing wrong with this. Any brick would do. Conceptual art has had profound and enduring impact, especially as installations have come to replace painting as the paradigmatic aesthetic form. Consider a recent example by Damien Hirst, *The Physical Impossibility of Death in the Mind of Someone Living* (1991), a well-publicized installation which consists simply of a dead shark in 224 gallons of formaldehyde

Figure 6.15. Andy Warhol, *Brillo Box*, 1964. Synthetic polymer paint and silkscreen on wood, 171/8/ × 17 × 14. Private Collection. © Copyright. Brillo Box, 1964. © Copyright 2008 The Andy Warhol Foundation for the Visual Arts/ARS, NY. The Museum of Modern Art, New York, NY Digital Image © The Museum of Modern Art/ Licensed by SCALA/Art Resource, NY.

Figure 6.16. Joseph Kosuth, *One and Three Chairs*, 1965. Wood chair, black and white photograph, and text. Musée National D'Art Moderne, Centre Georges Pompidou, Paris, France. ©2008 Joseph Kosuth/ARS, NY. Photo: Philippe Migeat. Photo Credit: CNAC/MNAM/Dist. Réunion des Musées Nationaux /Art Resource, NY.

Figure 6.17. Damien Hirst. *The Physical Impossibility of Death in the Mind of Someone Living*, 1991. Glass, steel, silicone, shark, and 5% formaldehyde solution, 84 × 252 × 84″. Private Collection. © The artist. Photo: Antony Oliver. Courtesy Jay Jopling/White Cube (London).

(Figure 6.17). Because the corpse putrefied by the time Charles Saatchi sold the work for $8 million in 2006 (it was commissioned for $100,000 in 1991), Hirst had to replace the shark. The buyer, a hedge-fund millionaire, happily defrayed the additional expenses and got himself a fresh fish carcass.

The shift was in part internally generated. Contemporary artists abandoned the oppositional and purist mission with which modernism had identified. They clamored for an art that immediately related to the real world, and those who were tired with the hermetic hubris of high modernism found the new wave refreshing. It is equally possible to see the crisis of the artistic object as the ineluctable upshot of modernist reductionism. All content and form had already been stripped away by the quasi-empty paintings of late abstract expressionists;[113] there was nothing left to attack but the aesthetic object itself.

But the changing relationship between art and other social phenomena was important in the sea change, too. Mass culture of the postwar era was a strong inspiration to young artists. Capitalism molded the art world more directly as well and spurred stylistic dynamism. Art sold at a record rate in the 1960s as avant-garde collecting and speculating became hip for upper-class sophisticates and wannabees. The art market started to display cyclical tendencies, the boom decades of the 1960s and 1980s being stylistically more vibrant than the slump periods of the 1970s and 1990s.[114] In response, from Andy Warhol to Jeff Koons, artists grew unabashedly commercial in their motives, and scandal was often profitable. The political climate of the 1960s and 1970s accentuated the crisis of the traditional understanding of art. A growing number of artists preferred techniques and media that would enable them to produce accessible works. Art that directly thematizes political or personal issues is easier to do through installations, performance art, or photography; the product, whatever the solidity of its aesthetic pretensions, is more immediate and less demanding.

A basic contradiction underlies much of the unease about contemporary art. On the other hand, claims that ordinary urinals, bricks on the floor, or decaying sharks can be art offends conventional aesthetic sensibilities. Consider the public reactions to Damien Hirst, which are typical. When Hirst won Britain's prestigious Turner Prize in 1995 for *Mother and Child Divided*, an installation consisting of a cow and a calf cut into sections and exhibited in a series of glass containers, Brian Sewell of the *Evening Standard* of London noted that the macabre piece was "no more interesting than a stuffed pike over a pub door." Such works are even more scandalous when funded with public monies. Britain's popular press was incensed when it transpired that Tate Gallery had paid £5,000 in 1972 for André's bricks.

On the other hand, no contemporary artist could genuinely wish to obliterate completely the distinction between art and nonart.

Warhol's Brillo boxes might look identical to objects cluttering super-market aisles, but each of his fetches around \$50,000. Although Warhol's work reproduced popular culture icons, it did this in an affectless and ironic fashion – thereby implicitly signaling its superiority over what it mimicked. It did not matter to André or the Tate Gallery which actual bricks constituted *Equivalent VIII*; still, the conceptual artist contended that the work could be forged. Minimalism elevated quotidian objects to aesthetic status; yet, its products looked precious and its asceticism rarefied. Commenting on one of his conceptual animal pieces, Damien Hirst said: "I can't see any difference between going into the butcher's and seeing it in art gallery."[115] But one can well doubt, as many have, the sincerity of the artist given that only his dead animals – and not the ones in the butcher shop – are placed in hallowed museum spaces for everyone to see. The perceived hypocrisy in ridiculing the conventional notion of the artistic object while claiming the benefits associated with the conventional notion of artist is a common complaint in controversies over contemporary art.

Postmodernity has greatly enhanced the uncertainty regarding what art[116] – and especially what good art – is. There was never a robust critical consensus in the modern era, especially with regard to new art. Pollock, for example, had both his backers and his detractors. Nevertheless, since avant-garde works often seemed recondite, expert exegesis was indispensable to artists, and critics played a crucial role in determining worth. Things started to change in the 1960s. "Who needs criticism if anything can be art," lamented the critic Barbara Rose in 1964.[117] Some saw a democratic prospect in this shift. Maybe one did not need these haughty, self-appointed judges. Duchamp had already pointed out in a 1957 lecture the importance of the audience in the artistic process: "The work of art is not performed by the artist alone, but the spectator's point of view affects the all-important transubstantiation of inert matter into art."[118] Note that while art retained its sacrality in this logic, it was no longer just a question of inspiration and its critical confirmation. Rather, spectators joined artists in the aesthetic process.

There is a striking similarity between this theory and the Protestant offensive on the Catholic division between the laity and the clergy.

It is not a fluke that of all Duchamp's readymades, the most famous is a urinal. The transubstantiation he envisioned was thus nothing short of magical: transforming the basest thing (something that one pisses in) into the most sublime (art). It is in a similar spirit that many conceptual artists work with the most mundane (bricks, wires) or the most profane (carrion, excrement, urine, blood). The ritual, nevertheless, requires felicitous conditions. Audience participation presupposes a prior consecration. It is only then that the work will be treated with the indispensable self-fulfilling deference necessary for the transformation. Some contemporary artists argue that art is just a question of artistic intent.[119] Naturally, this sounds arrogant. Furthermore, it is fallacious. One can call oneself an artist and christen all kinds of objects in one's atelier as art. Such a person will not receive attention, and such work will be not transubstantiated unless it is consecrated as art by others and put on public display at the expense of other objects with similar pretensions. Museums had already been important arbiters during modernism, but they remained relatively conservative and usually served to validate a posteriori critical approval. In the sixties, however, dealers, collectors, and galleries together undercut the critic-museum dominance in determining what deserved public attention as works of art. Marketing became essential, the focus of publicity campaigns moving onto the personality of the artist.[120]

The contemporary art scene is a "winner-take-all market,"[121] with the added twist that quality is extremely hard to assess. In this world where attention is synonymous with success, a tiny fraction makes it huge and attains global celebrity not always but often by virtue of clever publicity coups, whereas vast majorities languish in obscurity.[122] Modern artists such as Picasso, Dali, and Pollock all benefited from being celebrities, but, on the whole, their image had followed their success in the art world. From the 1960s onward, however, success became conditional on image. It was Jeffrey Koons's showboating self-promotions (such as self-advertisements in art magazines or photographs of him having sex with his porn-star wife) that enabled his ascent to stardom in the 1980s. If modern artists were quasi-sacred figures understood by a few but revered by many more, postmodern ones are like profane celebrities. As publicity and marketing trumped critical expertise and as demand for art rose in the boom decades of 1960s and 1980s, both commercial success and institutional recognition could come to the lucky few quite earlier in their careers. It took just a couple of years from its inception for pop art to be anointed in a high-profile 1963 exhibition at the Solomon R. Guggenheim Museum. Julian Schnabel's first exhibition sold out before its opening at The Mary Boone Gallery in February 1979. Entrepreneur collectors, such as Charles Saatchi, who single-handedly made the Young British Artists famous, became prime movers.

The idea of art as self-fulfilling prophecy, as a matter of institutional definition, seems aligned with the theories generated by some sociologists and philosophers in the 1970s and 1980s.[123] It is undeniable that art has a social dimension in its production as well as reception and that its very definition can be a stake in discursive battles. Nonetheless, one wonders whether academics were not uncritically buying into the self-serving ethos in the contemporary art world and whether the institutionalist theory can completely capture traditional or even modern art – at least to the same degree. After all, it is hard to disagree with Robert Hughes's pithy observation: "A Rodin in a parking lot is still a misplaced Rodin; *Equivalent VIII* in the same lot is just bricks."[124] That art (and above all great art) transcends its production and institutional context is still a compelling notion. Most people are not interested enough in contemporary art to be strongly miffed at what contemporary artists do. We may even occasionally find their products to be amusing – even more so than traditional art. The *Sensations* exhibit, which combined the outrageous with the grotesque and the macabre with the humorous in inventive ways, drew big crowds. In any case, those who closely follow and care about contemporary art constitute a miniscule minority. Nevertheless, the idea that artworks are things that are unique, physical, and transcendent – and that only those who can create such entities should

Figure 6.18. Piero Manzoni, *Merda d'artista* (*Artist's Shit*) No. *14*, May 1961. Metal, paper, and artist's shit, 1 7/8 × 2½ in diameter. The Museum of Modern Art, New York, NY. ©2008 ARS, NY/SIAE. Rome. Gift of Jo Carole and Ronald S. Lauder. Digital Image © The Museum of Modern Art.

be called artists and enjoy the benefits associated with this honorific title – is one that is difficult to eradicate, and it is recurrently voiced in public disputes about art.

The seeming arbitrariness of what qualifies as art can be frustrating for artists as well – especially for unknown ones. Take the case of Piero Manzoni who, in 1961, filled ninety 30-gram cans with his own excrement to create a work he called *Merda d'artista* (Figure 6.18). The artist had already explored the same theme with pieces such as his thumbprints on hard-boiled eggs or his breath in a balloon. Few took notice of these provocations, which, in retrospect, seem tragic: by age thirty Manzoni had already drunk himself to death.[125] But history would vindicate him in the end. One of the cans was purchased by the Tate Gallery in 1990 for the sum of $68,000 – exceeding the price set by the artist himself, equal to the can's weight in gold, by a hundred times.

## The Return of the Real

The other major trend in the post-sixties era has been the reversal of the antimimetic impulse of modernism. Most contemporary artists dropped their prejudice against representation, which allowed them to produce work that related to or commented on the physical and social world in ways serious as well as ironic. They could thereby provoke in an accessible fashion. A good deal of contemporary art, with its blasphemies and vulgarities, is a throwback to the surrealist program. In addition, art is no longer seen as a negation of the world, and artists have come to forsake the modernist ideology of progress. Some theorists have in consequence announced the end of the history of art.[126] At the same time, the use of performance, readymades, installations, and photography has made it possible for artists to jazz up the level of indecency in their work. Pornographic photographs or sexual acts in public are usually more attention-grabbing than paintings featuring contorted nudes. In the American context, the following factors also contribute to the making of contemporary art scandals: the erosion of the private/public and personal/political distinctions; the glut of artists, each hoping to make a splash by scandal; and the reliance of artists on public funding, which enables conservative opinion leaders to denounce artists, who tend to be liberals, for political profit.

*Guernica* is one of the most famous paintings of the twentieth century, but it is also an outlier. Modernism on the whole shied away from direct political content. In contrast, many contemporary American artists incorporate politics into their work. The adoption of the installment form in the contemporary epoch facilitates subversive attacks against political symbols. Take Kate Millet's *The American Dream Goes to Pot* (1970), simply a flag on top of a toilet seat. Or consider Dread Scott's conceptual piece, *What is The Proper Way to Display a U.S. Flag?* (1988), which consists of a photograph on a wall, a shelf holding an open book, and a flag lying on the floor underneath. The setup is designed to snare the viewers onto walking on the flag, hence unintentionally desecrating it, as they come close to look at the photograph (Figure 6.19). Such works provoke with ease.

Figure 6.19. Dread Scott, *What Is the Proper Way to Display a U.S. Flag?*, 1988. Digital image © The artist.

The exhibit displaying Scott's piece was raided by irate veterans, and President George H. W. Bush called it "disgraceful."[127]

Contemporary art has displayed remarkably little restraint in the realm of sexual representation. Sexual photography, the graphic realism of which makes modernist nudes look vestal in comparison,

284

achieved artistic status after the 1960s. Take some infamous Mapplethorpe photographs, which in 1990 prompted the first obscenity proceeding against an art gallery in U.S. history: a man with his genitals on a whipping block or the artist himself with a bullwhip inserted in his anus. It is not clear if Mapplethorpe's art has a political element. But sexual matters are routinely and openly politicized by contemporary artists, in particular through performance art. Feminism has been at the forefront here. Feminist artists have celebrated femininity and denounced masculine domination in ways they claimed were aesthetic but some others considered thoroughly bawdy. A good example is Carolee Schneemann's *Interior Scroll* (1975), a show which features the artist pulling out a rolled text from her vagina. Performance art gained popularity among artists pursuing gay and lesbian themes as well – again for its provocative potential. The logic of sexual liberalization that we saw in the last chapter, which enabled the politicization of sex by undermining the modesty norms, has been an important factor in the rise of such art.

Bodily waste features heavily in contemporary art too. Warhol made some piss paintings in the 1970s by having some his friends urinate on canvases covered in metallic paint. A couple of these fetched $75,000 cach in the mid-1980s. During the controversy around Duchamp's urinal, the American painter George Bellows had asked disbelievingly: "You mean to say, if a man sent in horse manure glued to a canvas that we would have to accept it?"[128] This is almost what happened in the *Sensations* exhibit when Chris Ofili showed his dung-covered *Virgin Mary*. The effects of real or represented bodily waste are visceral. Yet the intention behind such art is often translucent. The artist can adduce that it is philosophical, but the viewer may well doubt the sincerity of this claim. Take Gilbert and George's *New Testamental Works* (1997), which includes a garish, gargantuan photograph of two large dollops of feces topped with saliva. It is hard not to be disgusted at the sight of the piece, yet the artists have maintained in their public statements that all bodily secretions and excretions contain divine essences.[129] In any case, as corporeal waste increasingly became normal, others moved onto body parts. Striking examples are Rick Gibson's earrings made from human fetuses or his ghoulish performance art from the 1990s in which he ate human tonsils.[130]

The question of what deserves to be called art can become a burning one in the case of publicly funded works. A large number of consequential art scandals in the contemporary United States, those which enlist wide-scale attention and reaction, tend to be about such pieces. And ironically we find that artists or their advocates frequently resort to conventional aesthetic ideologies to defend thematic transgressions if need be. A perfect example is the Mapplethorpe affair, in which the director of the Contemporary Arts Center in Cincinnati found himself arraigned for public obscenity in 1990 for displaying posthumously the famous photographer's sadomasochistic images.[131] The trial hinged on testimony from specialists, who pointed to the formal and classical beauty of the pictures, which, according to one expert, "purifie[d], even cancel[ed], the prurient elements."[132] Commenting on a photograph that showed a man urinating in another man's mouth, a curator lauded the diagonals of the composition. Another stressed formal similarities between a picture depicting fisting and the artist's flower photography. The prosecution could not find any expert witnesses against the photographs, which, for all their blinding indecency, were very glossy and obviously far superior aesthetically to what the members of the jury could produce with their amateur cameras. Mapplethorpe was therefore art. In any case, the war against censorship has been won long ago in the United States. An opinion poll taken during the trial found that 75 percent of the dwellers of Cincinnati, the heartland of red America, opposed all censorship. The scandal was, however, not without effect. It proved a bonanza for the galleries: the price of the Mapplethorpe X portfolio prints climbed from $10,000 to $100,000.

# Conclusion

I suspended normative judgment as much as possible in the course of this book. My main concern was explaining moral conflict in public. Let me nonetheless end with some words on the moral status of scandal itself. The issue is a thorny one. As a social control mechanism, scandal – in its actuality or anticipation – can have salutary effects. Public opinion is often a civilizing influence. And a democratic, free public sphere in which one can denounce iniquities committed by the powerful – especially when legal routes are barred – is a major accomplishment of Western society. At the same time, scandal has disturbing affinities with mob justice. Its guiding principles are guilt by suspicion and guilt by association. The unchecked rule of public opinion with which scandal can threaten us can lead to frenzies and create scapegoats.

Political scandals also have both pros and cons. They can serve as deterrents. There are real social benefits to punishing corrupt politicians, and publicity can disinfect. Political scandals, which do not always require high evidentiary standards, can nevertheless needlessly undermine institutions and weaken public confidence as well. They can thus have direct and indirect, obvious and invisible collective costs that may well outweigh their benefits – although the benefits and costs of a scandal are differentially exerted in a given population, difficult to measure objectively, and, to a certain extent, incommensurable. A profaned presidency completely open to all kinds of attack and limitless scrutiny brings about more accountable presidents, but the scandals that ensue tend to mar the leadership capability at the White House, too. Too much information about presidents and the presidency can cloud our judgment. Excessive familiarity with political actors and institutions can breed contempt – which may be an invisible collective harm, since a certain level of trust in government is a public good. But it is obviously very difficult to know just how much trust is optimal.

We are beset with a similar problem when we make sexuality a contentious public matter through scandal. To the extent that sexual acts have public consequences and are in part legally regulated, they are not always completely private matters. And it is evident how science and art, both of them public practices, can claim a legitimate interest in this elementary dimension of our existence. Finally, sex has always had immense entertainment value. At the same time, however, sex scandals are often unfairly invasive of someone's privacy. They help dissolve the boundary between the private and public, and in the process cheapen both the intimate realm and the polis. Americans are less embarrassed of public talk on sex than their parents were, but they are still uncomfortable with the coarsening that this accompanies. It has become increasingly difficult in the West to differentiate between the private and the public, between the personal and the political. These boundaries are, of course, not fixed: they have been contested and transformed through history. Still, most of us assume and demand some kind of a boundary between these domains; we are offended, upset, or embarrassed in its absence or violation. A certain level of personalization of politics and politicization of personal life is inevitable, and maybe even good. In large doses, however, personalization will level the quality of public debate as politicization will sterilize intimate life and menace individual liberties.

There is a moral ambiguity at the heart of scandal. On one hand, scandals are heavily moral phenomena. Public reaction to them is usually one of indignation – the moral emotion par excellence. Those who publicize transgressions, either others' or their own, are frequently motivated by moral ideals, too. Or they at least (feel they have to) resort to them to legitimate their actions. Public denouncers typically justify their acts in the name of those they appeal to. Public provocateurs, such as artists or heretics, are also often engaged (or claim to be engaged) in a moral enterprise, however incongruous their mode of self-justification might be to that of their audiences.[1]

Even those who try to prevent scandals may have aims that are not selfish. Stonewalling politicians, audiences who ignore provocateurs so that the effects of their misdeeds are not inordinately magnified, or Victorians who underenforce sex norms so that the public sphere would not be contaminated are not always or completely indulging in self-regarding activity.

On the other hand, scandals are profane matter. Highly contagious, they risk polluting all those with whom they come into contact. They have all kinds of third-party effects and unintended consequences that look unjust, immoral, or demoralizing. They can end up normalizing all kinds of transgressions or make them look fascinating by giving them prominence and their authors notoriety. Through scandal the weak can avenge themselves against the strong. But there is something troubling in such vindictive use of morality, which, springing from resentment, tends to succeed only after the powerful are no longer so powerful.

Besides, the very publicity that scandal requires renders the moral status of the behavior of those who take part in them potentially suspect. The salience that denouncers and provocateurs gain can make them look ingenious. Scandal reveals, in an exaggerated form, the dramaturgical paradox of the public sphere: to the extent that that our audiences know that we are aware of their watching us, all our actions, however morally oriented they may be, can always look insincere – especially for malicious eyes. As Hannah Arendt and Erving Goffman saw well, there is something intrinsically shallow about the public sphere. Publicity transforms action into performance and makes each of us a "merchant of morality."[2] Being in public at once compels us to uphold high standards and makes it impossible for us to prove definitively the purity of our motives, even when we are sure that they are pure. Other than courage, there are no moral virtues that can once and for all elude doubt the moment they are displayed in public. Arendt put it sadly: "For it is manifest that the moment a good work becomes known and public, it loses its specific character of goodness, of being done for nothing but goodness' sake."[3]

Denouncers and provocateurs do try to convince publics of their good intentions. They may well succeed. Under certain conditions, scandal is a good way to increase moral standing in the eyes of associates, audiences, and even authorities. Yet any such upgrade is inherently shaky. Things may change. Scandals may get costly or tiresome for the public, and their creators may profit too much and too visibly from them. What once looked virtuous and bona fide may now seem self-promoting and fake. Its ambiguities, however, make scandal an ideal topic if our perspective on morality is a positive one – that is, if we are concerned not with producing normative judgments but with (i) analyzing when and how claims to morality and of immorality are made in different realms of life and (ii) exploring the factors that make such moves more or less likely and successful. This is what I attempted.

# Notes

## One. The Disruptive Publicity of Transgression

1   See inter alia Baker and Faulkner 1993, Biggart 1985, Markovits and Silverstein 1988, Shapiro 1987, and Vaughan 1983.

2   Some of the constructivist sociological works on scandal are Alexander 1989, Becker 1963, Ducharme and Fine 1995, Erikson 1966, Fisse and Braithwaite 1983, Gluckman 1967, Lang and Lang 1983, Larson and Wagner-Pacifici 2001, Lull and Hinerman (ed) 1997, Maza 1993, Molotch and Lester 1974, Randulf 1964, Sherman 1978, and Verdès-Leroux 1969.

3   For such an interpretation, see Alexander's penetrating study of pollution in the context of Watergate and the American civil religion (1989). Alexander, however, also points out that some scandals are failed rituals. Even though his approach is largely Durkheimian, he does not ignore the conflictive dimension of scandals.

4   The term comes from Boorstin 1961.

5   Quoted in Kalb 2001: 243. Another submission was "News for the Millions, Scandal for None." Ochs, however, discarded the result and went with "All the News Fit to Print."

6   Nixon 1978: 972.

7   A very sophisticated work on scandal is J. Thompson 2000. This sociologist builds on Goffman's differentiation of frontstage and backstage and extends Bourdieu's analysis of positions in the political field to study scandal. He sees scandals "as struggles over symbolic power in which reputation and trust are at stake" (2000: 245), and his book contains many incisive points about the rise of "politics of trust" in Western countries. Nevertheless, he exaggerates the role of the media in the making of political scandals at the expense of more structural factors – the ones that I consider in Chapters 3 and 4. Finally, Thompson's model is difficult to generalize to nonpolitical scandals.

8   For the complex etymology of scandal see Dampierre 1954, Rodinson 1970, Thompson 2000, and Verdès-Leroux 1969. "Skandalon," derived from the sanscrite root "skand," referred to obstacles or situations that tested the faith of the Jewish people in the Greek version of the Old

Testament. This understanding of scandal as a "stumbling block" that vitiates religious belief persisted in theological writings until early modernity in the Latin word "scandalum," which was often used to describe the discredit to religion that is occasioned as a result of the immoral conduct of a religious official. Around the same time, "Esclandre" in Old French and the Middle English "scandal" denoted in a more secular fashion defamatory speech (its truth being irrelevant), discreditable events, and improper conduct.

9 For a critique of this tendency, see Williams 1993.

10 For a study of pamphlet discourse, see Angenot 1983.

11 For a phenomenology of public denunciation, see Boltanski 1990: 253–366.

12 Garfinkel 1956.

13 An unavoidable revelation of a transgression to a public can break a scandal, too. Think of a situation à la Jane Austen where a family in a small town finds it impossible to dissemble from the neighbors that the daughter has eloped with a rake because the word is already out and because she is an indispensable part of its public front. The suspected infraction then rapidly becomes the talk of the town. But private talk will not inexorably lead to scandal; the local folk, for various reasons, might pretend, at least in public, as if nothing has happened. This would be more difficult, however, if the daughter returns with a big belly and walks around in public as if there were nothing wrong. I am assuming here a Victorian world in which such things matter both because people care about them and because they are relatively rare.

14 Hitchens 1997.

15 I am indebted to Charles Tilly for this example.

16 The insider-outsider or the associates-public dichotomy is a fractal one (Abbott 2001a). In the eyes of the general readers of the *Post*, the department members (with the possible exception of the denouncer) may look like insiders or even the associates of the alleged transgressor.

17 Chwe 2001.

18 Gluckman 1963.

19 Granovetter 1973.

20 Shibutani 1966.

21 Malinowski 1926: 80.

22 Rousso 1990. On this issue, see also Zerubavel 2006.

23 Tricaud 1977.

24 For a very subtle analysis of blame in personal and public life, see Tilly 2008.

25 Fame does aggravate these contradictions, however. Consider how *Saturday Night Live* tackles one of the aporias of contemporary society, our fascination with and resentment of famous people. On one hand, the show contributes strongly to the celebrity culture: only well-known public personalities, especially those from the entertainment world, are

invited as hosts. In effect, most of the jokes have in recent years come to involve stars and assume an extensive knowledge of tabloid news on the part of the viewers. On the other hand, the invitees are expected to give monologues at the beginning of the show during which they are to let themselves be humiliated in various ways by the cast – this gratifying our grudge at their dubiously acquired high status and the invidious advantages that accompany it.

26 Resentment is the quintessential social emotion in democratic societies (Nietzsche 1998, Scheler 1961, Tocqueville 1969). It springs from the contradiction between the ideological egalitarianism of such societies and the inevitable inequalities they produce. And it is not fortuitous that we use the term "obscene" to qualify big fortunes when they are displayed in public without restraint to those who have less.

27 Shakespeare 1934: 1086.

28 Goffman 1959: 22–30.

29 Posner 1999: 153–9.

30 Goffman 1963.

31 Goffman 1967: 97–112.

32 This idea is captured in the theological differentiation between "active scandal" and "passive scandal." Active scandal refers to the bad example of the one who sins. In contrast, passive scandal is the attitude of the spectator, as well as the denouncer, who, instead of modestly closing his eyes, is given to gratuitous indignation and denounces the vice only to better savor it, becoming in the process the accomplice of the sinner (Verdès-Leroux 1969: 192).

33 The incident is recounted in Julius 2003: 195–6.

34 Douglas 1966: 38; Sartre 1943: 696.

35 On sympathy, see Smith 1976 and Boltanski 1999.

36 This is not the standard response, however. Honor killings are usually undertaken when there seems to be no other legitimate way to repair the breach by the familial unit – for instance, when the daughter cannot be dragooned to marry the man who impregnated her because he is already married or is of a different faith.

37 For the social logic of privacy, see Nock 1993.

38 Jenkins 2001.

39 Kevles 1998.

40 In 1996 an appeals panel absolved Baltimore and his cowriter.

41 Birnbaum 1988, 2003; Verdès-Leroux 1969.

42 Bredin 1986.

43 Bonazzi 1981.

44 A similar but milder situation occurs when an offender owns his transgression in public after being denounced by someone else.

45 Ball 1975; Elster 1989: 109.

46 Molière 1965: 289. The literal translation of the passage captures what I mean even better: "The evil is nowhere but in the brouhaha / It is the

scandal of the world which makes the offense / And sinning in silence is
no sin at all."

47 Kuran 1995.

48 Warriner 1958.

49 Abbott 1983.

50 Hebdige 1978.

51 Thus in Thomist ethics giving scandal is defined not simply as committing
a transgression but as providing occasion for another's fall, intentionally
or not (Thompson 1995: 227n–228n).

52 Birnbaum 1994, Schudson 1992.

53 Sewell 1995.


## Two. The Fall of Oscar Wilde

1 See, for example, Fisher 1995: 136.

2 Pritchard 2001:149.

3 Fisher 1995: 136.

4 Greenberg 1988: 400.

5 Radzinowicz 1968: 330; Gilbert 1977a, 1977b.

6 Ellis 1912.

7 Durkheim 1897.

8 Merton 1957.

9 Black 1976: 11–36; Edgerton 1985: 75–93; Goode 1978: 252.

10 See, for example, Posner 2000: 28. There is, in addition, empirical evidence showing that the high-status and low-status members of groups tend
to be less conformist than those enjoying medium status (e.g., Dittes and
Kelley 1956). Groups tolerate their high-status offenders because they
are thought to contribute more to collective welfare. Furthermore, the
more powerful will be less monitored, will have access to more resources
to cover up their sins, and can induce cooperation from subordinates in
such an endeavor.

11 For costs borne by sanctioners in norm enforcement, see Coleman 1988:
244–5.

12 Lafitte 1958: 16.

13 Greenberg 1988: 338–40; Harvey 1978: 940.

14 Gray 1986.

15 Marcus 1975.

16 The eighteenth century was more latitudinarian of the publicity of sexuality, but obscenity came to be seen as a signal source of moral decay with
the evangelical revival of the 1780s. The panic of contagion caused by the
French Revolution intensified such fears. Nevertheless, it was only in the
course of nineteenth century that we observe a crackdown on obscenity
and public indecency (Starr 2004: 450).

17 Leckie 1999.

18 Terrot 1979.

19  Leckie 1999: 62–111.
20  Himmelfarb 1995: 23–4.
21  Foucault 1980, Weeks 1989.
22  Blackstone 1962: 242.
23  Quoted in Harvey 1978: 942.
24  Quoted in Harvey 1978: 942.
25  Quoted in Hyde 1970: 181.
26  Quoted in Weeks 1989: 103. The 11th amendment of the 1885 Crim-
    inal Law Amendment Act created the new offense of gross indecency
    between male persons in England. This offense, for which Wilde would
    be convicted, covered homosexual acts not involving anal intercourse and
    was punishable by a maximum of two years' imprisonment with hard
    labor. The 1885 legislation, passed ten years before Wilde's conviction,
    has led many to perceive the dramatist to be the prey of the harden-
    ing Victorian puritanism during the last two decades of the nineteenth
    century (e.g., Fisher 1995: 135–66; Foldy 1997; Weeks 1989: 96–117).
    The contention, however, does not comport with the facts. First, it must
    be underlined that the new offense had little effect, for it only included
    acts that were already prosecuted as attempted sodomy. Few prosecutions
    were brought following the amendment (Greenberg 1988: 400). Second,
    homosexuality was not mentioned in the original text of the act and did
    not figure in the agitation for it (Smith 1976). The act was passed as a
    result of the Maiden Tribute campaign headed by the newspaper owner
    William Thomas Stead. The objective of the moral crusade was "to make
    further provision for the protection of Women and Girls, the suppres-
    sion of brothels, and other purposes" (Gorham 1978). Stead opposed
    the 11th amendment and was one of the rare Victorian dignitaries who
    would later display the derring-do to be publicly compassionate to Wilde.
    He lamented, in the aftermath of the Wilde affair, that preoccupation
    with male homosexuality only served to obfuscate the ravages of the
    rampant and much more ruinous female prostitution. Third, the amend-
    ment was proposed by the radical-liberal MP Henry Labouchère, who
    had been critical of the act itself. The intentions of Labouchère, who was
    both a libertarian and Wilde's friend, are nebulous. A contemporaneous
    journalist argued that he aimed to wreck the act by adding an absurd
    amendment (Harris 1959: 144). Others have extrapolated that the law
    simply attempted to extend the aegis that adolescent girls enjoyed to male
    minors (Hall 2000: 38–9). In effect, Labouchère later claimed to have
    calqued his proposal on the French law on the protection of minors of
    both sexes from seduction. Unlike the French counterpart, however, there
    were no age limits in his amendment. The House of Commons passed
    the poorly drafted clause with scarcely any debate in a sparsely attended
    session late at night.
27  Chester et al. 1976, Dockray 1996, Hyde 1976.
28  Quoted in Hyde 1976: 84.

29  Gawthorne-Hardy 1979.
30  Croft-Cooke 1967: 95–118.
31  Hyde 1970: 90–133.
32  Grosskurth 1964: 33–40.
33  *O.E.D.* 1989: 573.
34  For a history of the development of English defamation laws, see Veeder 1903.
35  William J. Bankes, an MP, was prosecuted twice, first in 1833 after being caught in a public lavatory with another man and, second in 1841 for indecent exposure. Acquitted in his first trial, he was allowed to scurry abroad during his second (Hyde 1970: 94). The painter Simeon Solomon was convicted of an indecent offense in a public lavatory in 1873 but only served six weeks (Croft-Cooke 1967: 56).
36  Gilbert 1977a, 1977b.
37  Among others, the bishop of Clogher, MP William John Bankes, Lord Henry, and Lord Beauchamps were granted this option.
38  Radzinowich 1968: 330–1.
39  Roughead 1931: 149–83.
40  Quoted in Hyde 1970: 98.
41  For the English identification of effeminacy with homosexuality in the eighteenth and nineteenth centuries, see Trumbach 1977 and Symonds 1896. The Victorian stereotype of the homosexual described by John Addington Symonds in the 1870s as "pale, languid, scented, effeminate.... oblique in expression" (Symonds 1896: 14–5) matches perfectly the representations of Wilde in *Punch* during the 1880s.
42  Gilbert 1910: 103. To be sure, it is not completely clear whether Gilbert had specifically Wilde in mind when he wrote the libretto that gibed the pre-Raphaelites and aestheticism in general. Nevertheless, the figure of Bunthorne, "walking down Piccadilly with a poppy or lily," was associated so closely with him that most assumed both that Gilbert's line referred to Wilde and that it was founded in reality. Wilde did nothing to falsify the myth. He said that although the act itself would not have been a big feat, to have people think that he had accomplished it was.
43  Ellmann 1988: 136.
44  Wilde 1966: 893.
45  See, among others, Ellmann 1988: 409; Harris 1959: 104; and Marjoribanks 1932: 88.
46  Croft-Cooke 1972: 164.
47  Hamilton 1986: 236.
48  Wilde 1928: 121.
49  Ellmann 1988: 284.
50  Gillespie 1996; Rowell 1978: 104.
51  Gagnier 1986: 81.
52  Gagnier 1986: 56–67. The only one of Wilde's works ever to be censored was *Salomé*. But Wilde was unable to stage the play in London solely

because English law forbade theatrical productions of biblical themes and not due to the content of the work, which had clearly decadent elements.

53 "[R]eviewers then did not criticize the drama as much as they advised the dramatist. Wilde and theater managers were instructed to delete acts, eliminate characters, revise scripts, and modify their own behavior during curtain calls and were generally subjected to the opinions and directorial talents of writers and reviewers who today often seem barely literate" (Gagnier 1986: 52).

54 I am indebted to Randall Collins for this point.

55 Wilde 1928: 95.

56 Wilde 1966: 894.

57 Baker and Faulkner 1993.

58 Nussbaum 2001.

59 On the open-ended quality of scandal, see Blic and Lemiuex 2004.

60 Collins 2004, Goffman 1967.

61 Habermas 1989. Consider, for instance, many of the articles in Calhoun 1992.

62 Arendt 1958, 1982; Goffman 1959.

63 Appearing to do wrong is a wrong both because the public will not have the time and expertise to judge whether there is an offense and because of the potential effect of the appearance on the conduct of others.

64 Queensberry had set out to gather incriminating information on the dramatist upon being sued by Oscar Wilde for libel. Tips from the London thespian world and a prostitute galled of male competition directed his detectives to the lodgings of Alfred Taylor, where Wilde and Douglas had a habit of hooking up with young men.

65 Wilde 1928: 51.

66 Wilde 1928: 54.

67 Wilde 1928: 112.

68 Wilde 1928: 54.

69 Wilde 1928: 52.

70 Wilde 1928: 90.

71 Murray 2000: 208–11.

72 Ellmann 1988: 404–5.

73 Queensberry 1949: 52.

74 Marjoribanks 1932: 204.

75 Wilde 1928: 96–7.

76 This rumor fed from the letters that Lord Douglas was sending from abroad to English newspapers propounding that homosexuality was rife in high places (Foldy 1997: 26–7).

77 Hamilton 1986: 27.

78 Marjoribanks 1932: 230.

79 Healy 1928: 416.

80 The *Daily Telegraph* stated on the morning of April 6, 1895: "The judge did not attempt to silence or reprove the irrepressible cheering in Court which greeted the acquittal of this sorely provoked and cruelly injured father."

81 Quoted in Goodman 1989: 79.

82 According to George Ives, a contemporaneous homosexual rights advocate, the police were no strangers to the sexual predilections of the prime minister (reported in Hall 2000: 55).

83 Quoted in Goodman 1989: 117–8.

84 The nephew-by-marriage of Frank Lockwood, the solicitor-general himself, was one of those cited in Queensberry's plea of justification. A vague reference was made to him in the libel trial, but his name was not uttered in court; it was written on a piece of paper, which was passed on to the judge.

85 Cohen 1993: 145–8.

86 Ellmann 1988: 465.

87 Quoted in Goodman 1989: 132.

88 Quoted in Hyde 1975: 222.

89 Foldy 1997: 35.

90 The procurer, Alfred Taylor, had already been remanded in custody in a raid on a private club in London the year before. He had admitted to having shared his bed with his accusers. The testimony in the Taylor case implicated Wilde, and the procurer's eventual conviction hurt his acquittal chances.

91 Quoted in Hyde 1956: 85.

92 Wilde 1928: 426.

93 Popular fury against Wilde continued for some time after his sentencing. A crowd jeered the infamous convict after the bankruptcy proceedings against him in September 1895. During his transfer from one prison to another, he was spat on by an angry throng (Wilde 1966: 937).

94 Aronson 1994: 181.

95 Croft-Cooke 1963: 274.

96 That the offender's high status can provoke overenforcement is arguably shown by the recent Martha Stewart case. The famous lifestyle and television personality was prosecuted and sent to jail in 2004 for lying in the course of an insider trading investigation. But to prosecute someone for this is somewhat unusual – especially because Stewart lied to congressional staffers not to the police and because she was not under oath. As we will see amply in the fifth chapter, however, under favorable conditions and with the right incentives, legal officials may prefer to concentrate on elite offenders.

97 Ellmann 1988: 536–7.

98 Stone 1977: 680.

99 Bourdieu 1992.

100 Sturgis 1995.

101 For a cogent critique of the variables approach in sociology and a potent plea for the irreducible temporality of social phenomena, see Abbott 2001b.

### Three. The Presidency, Imperial and Imperiled

1 Thompson 2000.
2 Politicians know well that at times responding to such an attack, by drawing attention to the allegations, can bring about a scandal or perpetuate and intensify the one that has already broken. It may be better not to dignify the accusations. Other times, however, when the public is already suspicious or lacks information about the politician, silence can hurt. An example is the travails of Senator John Kerry, whose military record was sandbagged by the "Swift Boat" Vietnam veterans during the 2004 election campaign. The aspersions were false but still crippled the presidential candidate.
3 For this perspective, see Markovits and Silverstein 1988: 7.
4 Darnton 1995, Popkin 1989.
5 The event involved an intrigue concocted by an adventuress called Comtesse de La Motte who bamboozled Cardinal de Rohan, the grand almoner who was out of favor with the queen Marie-Antoinette, into believing that she could regain her regard for him. The countess convinced the gullible cardinal – in a sham interview during which she impersonated Marie-Antoinette – that the queen wished to acquire a diamond necklace with an exorbitant price tag from London and that she had chosen him as her intermediary. Rohan obtained the piece and turned it over to the countess, but a scandal broke when he failed to pay the jewelers. The cardinal was arrested, tried, but eventually acquitted. Much more important, the trial tainted the queen, who already had a bad reputation for profligacy and frivolity. Her enemies calumniously but successfully intimated that she had compassed a plan to obtain the necklace and then refused to pay.
6 Riesman 1942: 735.
7 The data in Figure 3.1 come from the *Statistical Abstract of the United States (1978–2006)*.
8 Pujas and Rhodes 1999, Thompson 2000.
9 See, for instance, Sabato 2000.
10 See, for example, Garment 1991 and Ginsberg and Shefter 1999.
11 See, among many others, Klapper 1960.
12 Schudson 1995: 23.
13 Hallin 1986, Moss 1990.
14 Schudson 1995: 25. The discussion on media in this section is very much influenced by Schudson's brilliant book.
15 But those with low social status can also have less to lose from such attacks, or they may be incognizant of the risks they are taking. In the classical tale of *lèse majesté*, it was a child – someone who is innocently

ignorant of the collective benefits of hypocrisy and the individual costs of truth – who committed the heresy by saying, "The emperor has no clothes." By the same token, however, such nonentities will be easier to discredit if need be.

16 Immunity in the form of high popularity can also create resentment and therefore engender attacks, which will, however, on the whole, be unsuccessful.

17 Presidential power (the capability of a president to impose his or her will on, convince, and deter others in Washington and the country) is not simply a constitutional matter. The constitution itself is equivocal as to the limits of presidential prerogatives. As Neustadt (1991) points out, it stipulates the sharing, rather than the division, of powers among the branches of government.

18 Ginsberg and Shefter 1999: 144–8.

19 Mayhew 2005: 100–35.

20 Dunar 1984.

21 Skowronek 1997. See especially pp. 447–64.

22 Tocqueville 1969.

23 Brace and Hinkley (1992: 94–102) show that the use of force in the international arena by a president is more likely to follow negative dramatic events like presidential scandals.

24 Stone 2004.

25 Schudson and King 1995.

26 I draw here liberally from the magisterial works of Theodore Lowi (1985), Richard Neustadt (1991), Arthur Schlesinger (2004), and Stephen Skowronek (1997) on the American presidency. The conceptualization of the traditional and modern modes of presidential governance is taken from Lowi (1985) with some important modifications.

27 Lowi 1985: 22–43.

28 Tullis 1988.

29 Tocqueville 1969: 182.

30 Summers 2000: 828–30. My discussion of the early republican period owes much to this article.

31 Hofstader 1969.

32 Collins 1998: 25.

33 Quoted in Collins 1998: 25.

34 Wilson 1885.

35 The facts on Tyler come from Crapol 2006.

36 The Johnson impeachment narrative is based on Benedict 1973.

37 Tullis 1988: 87–93.

38 Carman and Luthin 1943, Donald 1961, Skowronek 1997: 197–227.

39 Schlesinger 2004: 127–76.

40 Lowi: 1985: 4–7.

41 Kernell 1997.

42 Kernell 1997: 70.

43  Summers 2000.
44  Woodward 1974.
45  Fine 1996.
46  Neustadt 1997: 194–7.
47  Rozell 2002.
48  Schlesinger 2004: 81.
49  Schlesinger 2004: 84.
50  On the use of executive privilege by the Truman administration, see Schlesinger 2004: 153–5.
51  Quoted in Schlesinger 2004: 158.
52  Rozell 2002.
53  Schlesinger 2004: 158.
54  Safire 1975: 658.
55  Ross 1988: 186–7.
56  Material on Kennedy in this section comes from Hersh 1998.
57  This logic also applied to physical inadequacies. Both Kennedy and Franklin D. Roosevelt experienced few problems in hiding their ailments from the public. The case of Kennedy is particularly revealing as the splendiferous president suffered from venereal and Addison's diseases and was a regular consumer of high dosages of amphetamines.
58  Maltese 1992: 28–116.
59  Rudenstine 1996.
60  Nixon 1978: 112.
61  Clinton 2003: 481.
62  This point is fully developed in Lowi 1985: 176–82.
63  Quoted in Schlesinger 2004: 374.
64  Woodward 2005.
65  Nixon 1978: 872; Ambrose 1991: 156, 309.
66  Brace and Hinckley 1992: 42.
67  Coleman 1988: 191–4; Inglehart 1990.
68  In the 1960s, the public lost its confidence not only in Congress and the executive branch but also in labor and business. In contrast, institutions that seemed above politics, such as the Supreme Court and the military, remained comparatively trustworthy. See Lipset 1983.
69  Nixon 1978: 837.
70  Lang and Lang 1983: 310.
71  Lang and Lang also arrive at a similar conclusion (1983: 135).
72  Various decisions by the Warren Supreme Court following the civil rights movement reflected the new zeitgeist of distrust of political authority. *New York Times v. Sullivan* of 1964 made political actors particularly vulnerable by stipulating that simply publishing falsehood about public officials is not enough to incur a libel judgment and that plaintiffs in defamation cases require proof of actual malice on the part of the journalists. The *Pentagon Papers* decision could also be seen as a product of the rising antiauthority ethos within the judiciary.

73 Lang and Lang 1983: 107.
74 Greenberg 2000; Johnson 2001.
75 Lang and Lang 1983: 83–4.
76 Lang and Lang 1983: 73.
77 Lang and Lang 1983: 77.
78 Lang and Lang 1983: 83.
79 Lang and Lang 1983: 310.
80 Lang and Lang 1983: 91.
81 Lang and Lang 1983: 328.
82 Lang and Lang 1983: 108.
83 Lang and Lang 1983: 112–4.
84 Lang and Lang 1983: 121.
85 Lang and Lang 1983: 117.
86 Brace and Hinckley 1992.
87 Lang and Lang 1983: 126.
88 Bufacci and Burgess 1998, Gilbert 1995.
89 Goffman 1961.
90 Transparency can also undermine the ability to govern. On this point, see Anechiarico and Jacobs 1996.
91 Watergate also stripped the protections of the lower centers of political and economic power in society and created a favorable opportunity structure for the fighters of white-collar crime (Katz 1980).
92 Lipset and Schneider 1983.
93 Lyons 1996.
94 Garment 1991: 52–5.
95 Woodward 2000: 37.
96 Woodward 2000: 30–1.
97 For a trenchant analysis of the capabilities of these legal officials, see Garment 1991: 142–68.
98 Johnson 2001.
99 On this point, see Eastland 1989.
100 Garment 1991: 143.
101 Ginsberg and Shefter 1999.
102 Draper 1991.
103 For polarization, see McCarty et al. 2006.
104 Nie et al. 1976, King 1997.
105 Key 1964, Ginsberg and Shefter 1999.
106 DiMaggio et al. 1996, Alan Wolfe 1998.
107 Grossman and Kumar 1981.
108 Edwards 1996: 234. For the impression management techniques of the Clinton administration, see Kurtz 1998.
109 Heclo 1996.
110 This study has also found that the coverage of individual officials is less negative than that of the political institutions they represent.
111 Council for Excellence in Government 2003.

112 Patterson 1993.
113 Woodward 2000: 168–70.
114 Clayman et al. 2007.
115 For an account of the relationship between the media and the government during the first Gulf War, see Kurtz 1993: 221–44.
116 Drew 2006.
117 Americans have a habit of being sanguine about their own lives and futures while simultaneously decrying the state of the nation (Whitman 1989).
118 Nye et al. 1997.
119 Mansbridge 1997.

## Four.  Investigating Corruption in France

1 Reported in *Le Figaro* on December 1, 1999.
2 Fay and Olivier 2002.
3 Similar anticorruption campaigns transpired in Italy, Spain, and Portugal during the 1990s as well. The analysis offered in this chapter would apply in part to these cases – especially, but not only, because of the similarities in political finance and legal systems.
4 Becker 1963: 155–6.
5 See, for example, Beisel 1990, Clarke 1987, Gusfield 1963, Sherkat and Ellison 1997, and Wood and Hughes 1987.
6 Ellickson 2001, E. Posner 2000, Posner 1998, Sunstein 1996.
7 Sunstein 1996: 909.
8 Elster 1989, Hechter and Opp 2001.
9 On the distinction between legal and popular justice, see Posner 1999: 92–94.
10 Avril 1994, Chalier 1991, Coignard and Wickham 1999, Etchegoyen 1995, Jeanneney 1984, Lascoumes 1996, Lorrain 1993, Mény 1992, Popis 1992, Pujas 2000, Pujas and Rhodes 1999, Suleiman 1993.
11 Becquart-Leclercq 1984.
12 Cohen-Tanugi 1985, Furet 1978, Rosanvallon 1990, Suleiman 1974, Tocqueville 1955.
13 Pujas and Rhodes 1999: 14.
14 Mény 1992.
15 Heidenheimer 1989: 161.
16 Beaud 1999.
17 Doublet 1997: 96. Multiple office holding provides local politicians with access to the central authority, which is, otherwise, given the highly bureaucratic nature of the French administration, often out of reach (Mény 1992). But accumulation of mandates can facilitate corruption as well. For example, a mayor can allocate subsidies from the municipal budget to an association under his or her authority and then siphon money from there for various illegal uses, private or political. Their membership

in the National Assembly also furnishes the municipal officials with relative legal immunity from local administrative controls.

18  Barret-Kreigel 1989, Cohen-Tanugi 1985, Garapon 1996.

19  Only one magistrate refused to pledge allegiance to Marshal Pétain when he inaugurated the anti-Republican Vichy government in 1940. The protestor was deported out of hand. For the history of the relationship between the French judiciary and the executive branch, see Bancaud 1993, Masson 1977, and Larivière 1987.

20  For a sociological treatise of the French magistrates, see Bodiguel 1991. Good overviews of the French judicial system are Cairns and McKeon 1995, Perrot 1995, Rassat 1985, and Ruymbeke 1988.

21  On this scandal, see Derogy and Pontaut 1986 and Garrigou 1989.

22  Lorrain 1993, Loughlin and Mazey 1995.

23  Foucault 1979; Garapon and Salas 1996: 6–11.

24  The 1993 reform of the penal code rechristened *l'inculpation* (indictment) with *la mise en examen* (to be placed under investigation). The stigma attached to the act and the IMs' powers at this stage, however, remained unaltered. For a study of the resistance within the French judiciary against the reform of the penal procedure in the early 1990s, see Lenoir 1992.

25  Tulkens 1992.

26  On the French prosecutors, see Lemesle and Pansier 1988.

27  Both prosecutors and bench judges are called *juges* or *magistrats* in French. To call a prosecutor "judge" is confusing in English. Therefore, I use the term "magistrate" to refer to all members of the French judiciary both on the prosecution and the bench and reserve the term "judge" to those who adjudicate.

28  Balzac 2001: 284.

29  Reported in *L'Express* on 20 April 1990.

30  Quoted in Greilsamer and Schneidermann 1994: 244.

31  Bourdieu 2000: 19–60; Goffman 1967: 239–58.

32  Boltanski 1990: 253–366.

33  Quoted in Laurent Greilsamer and Daniel Schneidermann 1994: 38. Between 1970 and 1990, the number of criminal cases shot from 300,000 to 600,000 a year. The hike especially redounded to the burden of those with low status such as deputy prosecutors and IMs.

34  Roussel points out that the most active IMs of the 1990s came from modest social backgrounds. Moreover, many of them had entered the profession late and had limited advancement prospects (2002: 92–3).

35  Later Jean-Pierre acknowledged in a book that the denouncer was in fact not anonymous (1991).

36  Gaudino 1990.

37  Plenel 1994, Villeneuve 1993.

38  On this scandal, see Gaetner 1998, Le Floch-Prigent 2001, and Lecasble and Routier 1988.

39  Roland Dumas was convicted in 2001 to six months in prison for receiv-
    ing benefits and rake-offs from Elf through his mistress in exchange for
    lobbying for the sale of six frigates to Taiwan when he was the foreign
    minister. His sentence was, however, overturned in appeal two years later.

40  Although not placed under investigation, Prime Minister Lionel Jospin
    also found himself legally implicated in 1999 by allegations about dona-
    tions made during the eighties and early nineties by retail groups in
    exchange for permits to build supermarkets.

41  Source: Author's compilation based in part on Fay and Olivier 2002.
    The high-status politicians include prime ministers, presidents of the
    National Assembly and the Constitutional Council, ministers, deputies
    in the National Assembly, senators in the Senate, and mayors. Many
    high-status politicians hold multiple offices.

42  Renucci and Cardix 1998.

43  For all the tactics used by the public prosecutor's department to thwart the
    investigations, see Bovier and Vogelweith 1997, Vogelweith and Vaudano
    1995.

44  Lowi 1988: viii–ix.

45  Thompson 2000: 61–2.

46  The witness interrogations by the IM of Paris, Eva Joly, in the Elf investi-
    gation were, for instance, announced weeks before in the media. Likewise,
    the indictment date of Henri Emmanuelli was published by *Le Monde* the
    day the Socialist Convention opened in July 1992. This was two months
    before Emmanuelli actually received the official letter from the IM. The
    decision of Eva Joly and Laurence Vichnievsky in March 1998 to place
    Roland Dumas, the head of the Constitutional Council, under investiga-
    tion was also leaked to the press well in advance.

47  This account comes from Gaetner 1992 and Gaetner and Parignaux 1994.

48  Garapon 1996: 22–7.

49  The IM of Rennes, Renaud Van Ruymbeke, for instance, was said to have
    a habit of forwarding copies of the parts of the dossier that he wanted pub-
    lic to all the parties involved in the investigation. These parties included
    not only the suspects and witnesses but also those who were conferred
    the status of plaintiff-victim (*partie civile*) by him. Thus the IMs did not
    need to leak as long as they could establish plaintiff-victims who could do
    the publicizing for them (Zemmour 1997: 106). Civil society associations
    often acquired this status to publicize the contents of investigations. By
    the end of the nineties, 80 percent of all the corruption probes in Paris
    were opened by such private actors. Even some journalists could claim
    the legal status. In his investigation of Alcatel, the IM of Évry, Jean-Marie
    d'Huy, accepted a journalist as a *partie civile* with the rationale that the
    latter owned 10 shares of stock in the firm (Zemmour 1997: 107).

50  Leaking required an alliance between the magistrates and the media
    (Charon and Furet 2000). Frequently censured for genuflecting before

political authority, the French media used the corruption scandals to signal its independence and professionalism (Lemieux 2000).

51 To be sure, if the person under investigation is of high status, it will be almost ineluctable that parts of the case will become known one way or another, thanks to those not compelled to secrecy. In such incidents, however, the norm of the confidentiality of investigation that is imposed on the judge will ensure that allegations will remain merely unsubstantiated claims and not be anointed with the authority of law.

52 Quoted in Roussel 1998: 261.

53 Quoted in Greilsamer and Schneidermann: 103.

54 Quoted in Charon and Furet 2000: 145.

55 Quoted in Greilsamer and Schneidermann 1994: 34.

56 Quoted in Greilsamer and Schneidermann 1994: 34.

57 In January 1992, for example, Renaud Van Ruymbeke orchestrated a raid on the former office of Henri Emmanuelli at the Socialist Party headquarters. Emmanuelli was at the time the president of the National Assembly, constitutionally the third most important person in France. The IM conducted the search on the same day Laurent Fabius moved in as the party's new first secretary, resulting in full-fledged television coverage.

58 Culpability was communicated through unusually high bails, too. Christophe Mitterrand, the son of the former president, was remanded in custody in 2000 by Philippe Courroye in a case involving arms sales to Angola and liberated only after a month with a bail set at 5 million francs. The IM of Paris Édith Boizette defended such practices: "[I demand high bails] in order to prevent them from going to vacations in the sun whenever the fancy takes them. These people have to experience discomfort in their everyday life" (quoted in Greilsamer and Schneidermann 2002: 64).

59 It seemed that the probes were at times structured to defy corrupt solidarities within the state elite. In 1996, President Jacques Chirac named Loïk Le Floch-Prigent, the former chief of Elf who was already under investigation for misuse of corporate assets, to be the head of the National Railways. According to Zemmour (1996: 67), the IM of Paris Eva Joly construed this act to be a disdainful challenge and immediately incarcerated Le Floch-Prigent in response, even though there was feeble legal justification for the injunction.

60 On this scandal, see Decouty 2000 and Giret and Le Billon 2000.

61 The legal immunity of politicians had already been significantly reduced by the abrogation of a law called the privilege of jurisdiction, which had precluded mayors from being indicted by local courts. Pursuant to this law, the moment a mayor was susceptible to be indicted of a crime or an infraction committed while in office, the prosecutor of the republic had to inform the Criminal Chamber of the Court of Cassation so that the latter could designate another IM from a different jurisdiction. The privilege of jurisdiction served many times to slow down the corruption probes

and effectively defuse them. Its suppression in 1993 helped multiply the scandals and bolstered the command that the magistrates exercised over the investigations they initiated.

62 Lascoumes 2001.

63 Quoted in Zemmour 1997: 20. Similarly, Jean de Maillard, the president of the Criminal Court of Blois, said in 2002 to a reporter, "Judges have gotten rid of their inferiority complex vis-à-vis politicians.... There are now more candidates to ENM than to ENA" (quoted in Greilsamer and Schneidermann 2002: 357).

64 To be exact, and much to their detriment, the political elite never quite solved their collective action quandary and waffled between holding unified public stands against the magistrates and exploiting (and at times aiding) the investigations in their internecine savaging. Hence, in the heat of the 1995 presidential campaign, the supporters of Jacques Chirac slipped information to *Canard enchaîné* that revealed the 7 million francs of salary that Balladur received (and never publicly declared) at the head of a branch of Compagnie Générale d'Éléctricité while he was out of office. Soon the Balladur camp retaliated by leaking to *Le Monde* two dossiers on the apartments bought by the Chirac family from the city of Paris below the market price. On how the cohabitation exacerbated scandal mongering, see Balladur 1995 and Carton 2000.

65 Quoted in Zemmour 1997: 130.

66 Lascoumes 1999.

67 On November 6, 1996, Hubert Dujardin, a deputy prosecutor of the Evry Court, opened an investigation on Xavière Tiberi, the spouse of the mayor of Paris. The matter pertained to payments made to Mme Tiberi from the Department of Essonne for an allegedly bogus administrative report. Although Dujardin was the most senior deputy prosecutor of the court, he did not oversee financial cases and was acting on behalf of his superior, the prosecutor of the republic Laurent Davenas, who was vacationing in the Himalayas. Before his departure, however, Davenas had judged the existing evidence against Mme Tiberi to be inadequate and had instructed the prosecution to restrict itself to a preliminary investigation. The deputy prosecutor, on the other hand, thought that Davenas was trying to shelve the matter and appointed an IM to the case. He would openly acknowledge his motives to the press one week later: "I admit that I took advantage of Davenas's absence to take a decision that he would himself perhaps not take." In response, the ministry of interior requested the French Embassy in Katmandu to hire a helicopter to fetch Davenas so that he could invalidate the actions of his subordinate. The operation was mangled; the prosecutor could not be located in the Nepalese wilderness, and the government was mortified when the whole farce was leaked to the press (Davenas 1998).

68 Quoted in Colombani and Portelli 1995: 140.

69 The TNS Sofres poll of August 25, 2000.

70 I am indebted to Randall Collins for having pointed out to me the cyclical element in political scandals in Continental Europe. These are often thrust into the public sphere in the wake of structural transformations that alter the balance of power. In Anglo-Saxon countries, however, scandals are more regularly paced as a weapon in normal politics.

71 Not all the French are happy with the corruption reforms. A recent opinion poll found that while 76 percent of the public supports the ban on business contributions, 50 percent opposes public funding. A more detailed analysis can be found in Adut 2004.

72 By helping the IMs, political actors could also take revenge on their one-time-partners-turned-opponents. An example among many is the revelations of Philippe de Villiers to Thierry Jean-Pierre concerning his former associate, Gérard Longuet of the Republican Party.

73 Merlen and Ploquin 1998.

74 France is one of the few countries in the world where the victims of crimes can participate in the penal process and are eligible for compensation in a criminal trial. A victim has the choice of taking action before civil or criminal courts. The criminal route is typically preferred because in this option the victim will have easy access to all the prosecution documents and have the case dealt with more quickly. The victim will also be spared the expense of separate civil proceedings. Becoming a *partie civile* in criminal proceedings is fairly easy: it is merely contingent on the accord of the dean of the IMs of a given territorial jurisdiction. A 1993 law made the procedure even more enticing by furnishing public funds. As a result, 80 percent of the probes in the financial branch of the Paris prosecutor's department, where many corruption investigations are initiated, were opened thanks to the initiatives of the *parties civiles* in the early 2000s. But it seems that most of the complaints that initiate legal proceedings are made to settle personal or political scores or to attack economic rivals, and 80 percent of such criminal investigations opened by a civil party terminate with the charges being dropped. The corresponding rate for noneconomic crimes is only 24 percent (Greilsamer 2001: 299).

75 On the Carignon scandal, see Avrillier and Descamps 1995 and Bègue and Delattre 1993.

76 For a study of the tension between credibility and self-interest in whistle-blowing, see Bernstein and Jasper 1996.

77 These figures come from Cavarlay 2006 and *Annuaire Statistique de la Justice*.

## Five. Sex and the American Public Sphere

1 Klein 2005.

2 Bennett 1999.

3 Gagnon et al. 2001: 8. Male and female percentages were 92 and 96 in France and 93 and 97 in United States.

4 Saguy 1999. On a scale from 1 (never) to 10 (always), the mean American score was 1.90 and the French 3.69 on the responses to the following question: "Please tell me for.... [the] following statement[s] ("Married men/women having an affair") whether you think it can always be justified, never justified."

5 Jacobs and Shapiro 2000.

6 Sleaze did occupy a place of honor in French politics prior to the establishment of such protections. In October 1968, the bodyguard of the famous actor Alain Delon was found murdered. An investigation uncovered a seamy world of drugs and decadence compromising the members of the French elite. Allegations that Claude Pompidou, the wife of George Pompidou, belonged to this world were leaked to the press by the former prime minister's political foes and senior police officers who worked under their direction. The affair was humiliating for Pompidou and impaired his chances for succeeding de Gaulle. When Pompidou, nevertheless, later became president, he triumphantly weighed in on the National Assembly to pass a law protecting the private lives of political actors.

In any case, reticence about sexual misconduct by politicians might be fading in France. A recent French best-seller titled *Sexus Politicus* documents the adulteries of prominent French politicians (Deloire and Dubois 2006). The authors of the book have, however, withheld many names for legal protection.

7 Douglas 1966.

8 Miller 1997: 44.

9 Douglas 1966, Steiner 1967.

10 Verdes-Leroux 1969: 178.

11 Gandillac 1966: 5.

12 Kennedy 2003.

13 Dover 1997, Halperin 1990. For an economic perspective on the historical and geographical variations in sexual behavior, see Posner 1992.

14 Katz 1999: 18–86.

15 Darnton 1995, Popkin 1989.

16 For the logic of degradation in public accusation, see Luc Boltanski 1990: 253–356.

17 The narratives of early American sex scandals draw from Collins 1998, Ross 1988, Schudson 1977, and Summers 2000.

18 Quoted in Schudson 1976: 44.

19 Quoted in Ross 1988: 34–5.

20 Basch 1993.

21 Collins 1998: 46.

22 Summers 2000.

23 On the press, see Mott 1962.

24 Tocqueville 1969: 85.

25 The publicity of homosexuality remained beyond the pale, however. According to Gail Collins (1998: 51–2), James Buchanan, the fifteenth

president, was probably a homosexual. There was much talk about his sexual inclination in various circles. Andrew Jackson seems to have referred to Buchanan's lover, Senator William King of Alabama, as "Miss Nancy." But no one uttered a word in public.

26 Elias 1982. See also Ariès 1975 and Spierenburg 1984.

27 Elias believed that court society formed the historic nucleus of the civilized world. There is probably an exaggeration. A right to notoriety, a taste for villainy, a contemptuous disregard for conventions has always been the trademark of aristocratic privilege. Moreover, we find a rising concern with etiquette as well as a general squeamishness about things biological among the bourgeoisie during the eighteenth and nineteenth centuries in Europe.

28 Kasson 1990.

29 There is reason to think that this logic operates in different settings as well. Bourdieu and Dumont have shown similar diacritical functions of modesty vis-à-vis things biological in the modern French and traditional Indian contexts, respectively (Bourdieu 1979, Dumont 1967). In contrast, social egalitarianism and intimacy require and are fortified by candidness if not crassness.

30 Flaherty 1972.

31 D'Emilio and Freedman 1988: 3–52. My account of the changing American attitudes toward the publicity of sex in this chapter owes much to D'Emilio and Freedman's wonderful book.

32 Young 2006: 139–42.

33 Starr 2004: 234.

34 D'Emilio and Freedman 1988: 49.

35 Ryan 1981.

36 Starr 2004.

37 Levine 1988.

38 Gurstein 1998: 66. Those familiar with this provocative book will note its difference from the account provided here. Gurstein deserves tremendous credit for advancing our understanding of the public sphere by introducing the concept of reticence and tracing its history in the American context. Nevertheless, her book, which argues for a continuous decline in reticence from late nineteenth century to the 1960s, is marred by an assumption of linearity. Gurstein can account neither for the lack of reserve in America during much of the nineteenth century nor for the strengthening of modesty in many public domains during the first half of the twentieth century. Moreover, her book seems to set the Victorian standards as the norm for the public sphere by using Hannah Arendt's classical – but also idealized – typology of the private-public distinction in ancient Greece.

39 Starr 2004: 236.

40 Quoted in D'Emilio and Freedman 1988: 207.

41 D'Emilio and Freedman 1988: 207.

42 Beisel 1997.

43 For a detailed account of this affair, see Fox 1999.

44  Warren and Brandeis 1890.
45  Schudson 1998: 144–87.
46  Collins 1998: 60–180.
47  Hersh 1998: 107–10.
48  On the decline of modesty in this decade, see, among others, Douglas 1995 and Gurstein 1998.
49  Modell 1989.
50  Gurstein 1998: 179–212.
51  Kinsey 1948, 1953.
52  For the 1950s, see D'Emillio and Freedman 1988: 275–300.
53  A married movie icon with a daughter, Ingrid Bergman got pregnant from an affair with the Italian director Roberto Rossellini during the shooting of *Stromboli* in 1949. Her transgression earned Bergman a harangue on the floor of the U.S. Senate by Edwin C. Johnson. Calling her "a horrible example of womanhood and a powerful influence for evil" as well as "an apostle of degradation," the senator from Colorado proposed legislation requiring that movie performers be licensed based on their morality. The scandal forced Ingrid Bergman to seek exile in Italy, where she married Rossellini.
54  Robert Lichter et al. 1994.
55  Kaiser Family Foundation 2004.
56  Quoted in Sabato 2000: 82.
57  April 5, 1997: 8.
58  For an exhaustive list, see Garment 1991: 169–97. The first major political sex scandal of the low-modesty era was the Chappaquiddick affair of 1969. Senator Edward Kennedy drove his car off a bridge into Poucha Pond. He was able to extricate himself from his vehicle and swim to safety but his young passenger, apparently sexually linked to the senator, drowned. Kennedy waited for ten hours before contacting the police, and then only after consulting his lawyer. Local officials cooperated with the Kennedys to downplay the incident, and the senator got away with a two-month suspended sentence. Even though he was reelected to the Senate in 1970, his presidential prospects were indefinitely darkled. The scandal was a relatively restrained affair. But it also set a precedent.
59  In June 1950, the Senate authorized a formal inquiry into the employment of "homosexuals and other moral perverts" in government. Eisenhower issued in 1953 an executive order that barred homosexuals from all federal jobs.
60  But since they could be made public, reactions to the offenders were also exacerbated by the publicness of the norm enforcement process, during which sanctioners upped the ante to signal rectitude to each other – not unlike what happened to Oscar Wilde. This mechanism accounts for the wrath visited on Mark Foley, whose misconduct, after all, consisted of crass but consensual chatter with nonminor pages, a behavior that is protected by law.

61 Jenkins 1996.

62 Jenkins 2003.

63 Confidence in children's testimonies has not been an unalloyed good; it has spurred frenzies not unlike the historic Salem witch hunt. In 1983, for instance, several teachers in the McMartin Preschool in California were slandered by children. The latter alleged that their teachers abused hundreds of students in sexual rituals to make pornographic movies.

64 Cohen 1997.

65 Nock 1993.

66 MacKinnon 1987.

67 For a narrative of the scandal, see Phelps and Winternitz 1992.

68 The figures come from United States Equal Employment Opportunity Commission Enforcement Statistics.

69 I don't mean that Anita Hill was completely unembarrassed during her testimony, but her anticipated embarrassment was not high enough to prevent her from testifying. More important, most of the public was not greatly embarrassed.

70 McNally 2003.

71 Jenkins 1996: 88.

72 For a long list of such affairs, see Sabato et al. 2000. What about Gary Hart, the Democratic presidential candidate who withdrew from the race in 1988 when the *Miami Herald* published a story about his affair with a model? It seems that the biggest causes of Hart's demise were his denials to journalists who were already inquiring about his sexual life and his challenge to them to prove him wrong.

73 The facts come from Posner 1999, Starr 1998, and Toobin 2000.

74 The Starr Report indicates past doubt that it was Lewinsky who seduced the president, who, however, proved to be a very easy conquest (1998).

75 Toobin 2000: 172–6.

76 Clinton was lambasted for his parsing as to whether what he did with Lewinsky constituted sex, and the president did lie in his testimony when he was asked to state whether he had had sexual relations according to the definition given by Judge Wright. This definition, again drawn from the Molinari amendment, was expansive: it covered any contact with erogenous zones. But it is not impossible that Clinton, who according to the Starr Report heroically withstood Lewinsky's constant cajoling for genital intercourse, did not think at the time that what he was doing was sex. Like most contemporary youth and like most people in his generation, he may have made a sharp distinction between petting and sex.

77 It is not impossible, however, that their animosity was in part fed by the president's lack of cooperation with the prosecutors and the members of Congress.

78 Quoted in Clinton 2004: 824.

79 Posner 1999: 70.

80 Posner 1999: 52–6.

81  Posner 1999: 92–4.

82  It is the ferocious feminist flak on Clarence Thomas during his confirmation hearings that justify this speculation. Anita Hill, who accused the nominee of sexual harassment, did not have a better case than Paula Jones in terms of evidence, and, if true, Clinton's behavior (unzipping his pants and requesting oral sex from a subordinate) should be seen as much more outrageous than Thomas's alleged conduct (talking about pornographic movies and joking about a pubic hair on a coke can with someone working under him) from a feminist perspective.

83  See Saguy 2003 for a comparison of American and French sexual harassment laws.

84  Jacobs and Shapiro 2000.

85  Of course sexual liberalization does not mean increasing tolerance of all carnal behavior. In fact, sexual acts that are not consensual or that involve minors (such as marital rape or pederasty) tend to elicit much less accommodation than what they used to do.

### Six. Provocation in Art

1  This chapter does not deal with public art, but it is obvious that such art, by being already placed in the public sphere, will find it easier to disrupt and scandalize. On the history of American controversies revolving around public art, see Kamnen 2006.

2  Becker 1982: 40–67.

3  Quoted in Walker 1998: 76.

4  Quoted in Brockway and Weinstock, 1939: 599–600.

5  On this concept, see Lakoff 2006.

6  Elster 2000.

7  Quoted in Brockway and Weinstock 1939: 599.

8  See Kundera 1993: 110–13. For Adorno's critique of Stravinsky, see 2006.

9  Oja 2000: 287.

10  Quoted in Walker 1998: 59.

11  Meyer 1956.

12  Some transgressive artists seek antagonism because of the anarchy it could unleash. Luis Buñuel and Salvador Dali, for example, precisely aimed at scandal in L'Age d'or (1930), an avant-garde movie that depicted satyrian Sadians engaging in various acts of blasphemy. The premier set off a convulsion. Indignant spectators splashed ink on the screen; some even shot pistols (Buñuel 1983: 118). On the transformative power of the erotic in surrealism, see Audoin 1973.

13  Barthes 1967.

14  A general discussion of public meanings is found in Swidler 2001: 162–9.

15  This issue is excellently treated in Julius 2003.

16  Baxandall 1986.

17  White and White 1965: 161.

18 The general information on the Academy in this section comes from Boime 1971 and White and White 1965. For a good study of the Salon, see Roos 1996.
19 Hibbard 1983: 204.
20 Lambert 1995: 72.
21 Longhi 1968: 41.
22 Quoted in Lambert 1995: 75.
23 Chu 2007.
24 Clark 1992, Fried 1990.
25 Quoted in Chu 2007: 112.
26 But there must have been a moral cost. This how Courbet had characterized his mission against the powers that be in a 1854 letter: "I hope to live by my art all my life without having ever departed an inch from my principles, without having betrayed my conscience for a single moment, without having made a painting even the size of a hand to please anyone or to be sold" (quoted in Chu 1992: 122).
27 White and White 1965.
28 A great deal distinguished the individual impressionists from each other. Renoir and Monet stressed color and surface forms at the expense of composition, which for Degas and Manet remained the principle preoccupation. In terms of style and general attitude toward painting, Monet, Pissarro, and Cézanne were much closer to each other than to the rest. Although Manet was seen by the press and other impressionists as the leader of the group, he did not exhibit with them. In fact, his paintings lack the outdoorsy feel we associate with the movement, the general formal characteristics of which are arguably better represented in the early works of Monet such as *Impression: Sunrise* (1872). Despite all these differences, however, there was a good deal of communication between impressionist painters, who learned much from each other, and critics, friendly or unfriendly, regarded them as a group. Their very struggle against the establishment soldered these artists with a common ethos and even mission.
29 On Manet see, among others, Clark 1984, Fried 1996, and Hamilton 1954.
30 Quoted in Hamilton 1954: 45.
31 Brettell 1999: 136–8. Prostitutes were one of the most common subjects in late-nineteenth-century French painting (Bernheimer 1989, Clayson 1991).
32 Twain 1996.
33 Quoted in Clark 1984: 94. See also Hamilton 1954 and Fried 1996 for public reactions.
34 Quoted in Hamilton 1954: 71–3.
35 On nakedness and nudity in the European artistic tradition, see Clark 1972 and Mahon 2005.

36 Goya could paint his *Naked Maja* (1797–1800), even though nudes were banned in Spain at the time, because it was the queen's minister Godoy who commissioned the work for his collection. Only someone this influential could defy the dictate of the Church. When Godoy's fortune fell with the ascendance of the new king, Ferdinand VII, to the throne in 1815, the painting was seized. Finding himself in front of the Inquisition, Goya had to render accounts as to why he painted such an obscene work. The Spanish master was exonerated, but the religious authorities decided that he would no longer be allowed to paint for the court.

37 Clark 1972.

38 Hamilton 1961: 42.

39 Another way to make the naked morally palatable was to neutralize it with chastity; sometimes this worked, other times not. Hence the prudish gesture of Titian's Venus, who both bashfully covers her sex and beckons the viewer to it. This strategy allows for an uneasy, but not impossible, conjunction of sexual arousal and celebration of modesty. For the contradictions in attitudes toward nudes in nineteenth-century Britain, see Smith 1996.

40 Clark 1972: 165.

41 Despite maltreatment, most impressionists continued, for a while, to submit their work to the Salon. Renoir wrote in a letter in 1878: "There are scarcely fifteen collectors who can appreciate a painter not approved by the Salon. There are eighty thousand of them who wouldn't buy a single thing if the painter had not shown it at the Salon" (quoted in Mannering 1997: 205).

42 Quoted in Mannering 1997: 150.

43 Quoted in Mahon 2005: 74.

44 For a study of Degas's nudes, see Thompson 1988.

45 Quoted in Dawkins 2002: 68.

46 Bourdieu 1979: 14.

47 Hughes 1991: 113.

48 White and White 1965: 29.

49 On the decline of the Salon, see Maniardi 1993.

50 On surrealists, see Audoin 1973.

51 Buñuel 1984: 107.

52 Quoted in Néret 2003b: 55–6.

53 Dali 1942: 212.

54 See, for example, Bürger 1984.

55 Very frequently innovators took the form of cliques or were lumped into them by critics. Futurists and surrealists were self-forming, self-defining groups, but impressionists, fauvists, cubists, and abstract expressionists were appellations that were given to artists of varying groupness from the outside. These labels stuck and were often proudly accepted by those on whom they were imposed.

56 Quoted in Krauss 1986: 157.

57 Danto 1997.

58 See, for example, Moulin 1967 and Reitlinger 1961.

59 Writing about the 1950s and 1960s, Tom Wolfe argued that there were hardly more than 3,000 people in the art world of New York (1975: 21). Only a dozen galleries in New York dealt in contemporary art in the 1970s (Burnham 1973: 25), even though things had changed quite a bit by the eighties (Crane 1987, Hughes 1992: 387–404).

60 I am, of course, not suggesting that photography is an artless recording of the world. Nor am I saying that modern art was not influenced by photography. For instance, the sharp contrasts in Manet's work as well as the impressionist experimentations with unconventional angles owed much to photography (Gombrich 1972: 523–5). Nevertheless, the move toward a nonobjective art was at least in part a reaction to the rise of photography. In effect, until the seventies, even artistic photography, because of its mimetic character, remained a middlebrow art.

61 Quoted in Elgar 1960: 123.

62 Kandinksy 1977: 46.

63 Quoted in Seuphor 1957: 117.

64 Quoted in Schneider 1984: 22.

65 Quoted in Read 1959: 8.

66 Quoted in Barr 1951: 561.

67 Quoted in Read 1959: 38.

68 Quoted in Spurling 1998: 331

69 Russel 1969: 69.

70 Quoted in Benjamin 1987: 110.

71 In fact, Matisse came to ascribe a positive, soothing objective to his art, which must have nettled his dyspeptic modernist confreres: "What I dream is an art of balance, of purity and serenity devoid of troubling or depressing subject matter, an art which might be for every mental worker, be he business man or writer, like an appeasing influence, like a mental soother, something like a good armchair in which to rest from physical fatigue" (Matisse 1908).

72 Krauss 1999.

73 Quoted in David Britt 1974: 162. This discordance will usually call for some of kind of deciphering or interpreting either by the viewer or by an expert. Nonvisual cues like the title will also serve to direct the gaze of the viewer. However distorted, such modern paintings are nevertheless parasitical on nature – or at least on our conventional capturing of it – in that they derive their meaning and effect from their deviation. The same asymmetry equally applies to the relationship between dissonant music and conventional tonality: the former is constituted by its difference from the latter but not vice versa.

74 Quoted in David Britt 1974: 166.

75 Quoted in Daix 1993: 81.
76 On Rembrandt's approach to the ugly, see Clark 1972: 338–41.
77 Quoted in Warncke 1997: 172.
78 Quoted in Hess 2004: 33.
79 Quoted in Read 1959: 178.
80 Quoted in Partsch 2003: 20.
81 Krauss 1999.
82 Greenberg 1961: 113.
83 Many abstract expressionists like Jackson Pollock and Mark Rothko, who had belonged to the Artists' Union in the 1930s, started out with Marxist sympathies, and the Association of American Abstract Artists was run by Communists in the 1930s and 1940s. By the 1950s, however, abstraction had lost its unitary political identity in the United States.
84 Quoted in Hess 2004: 33.
85 Quoted in Doss 1991: 400.
86 For Greenberg's general theorization of abstract expressionism, see 1961 and 1993.
87 This tendency was not specific to painting but can be observed passim in modernism. For instance, from James Joyce to Alain Robbe-Grillet, avant-garde literature nurtured a growing antipathy toward narration. In like vein, Bertolt Brecht in theater and Jean-Luc Godard in cinema used alienation techniques (e.g., actors addressing the audience/camera, episodic structure undercutting narrative continuity, jump-cuts), all geared to disrupt the artistic illusion and bring attention to how art is a product.
88 Rosenberg 1960: 34–5.
89 Guilbaut 1983.
90 Quoted in Mahon 2005: 160.
91 Such incriminations were not restricted to abstract expressionism. A member of the French National Assembly had denounced cubism in the 1920s for being part of a foreign plot (Blistène 2001: 16).
92 For many critics, the nonmimetic nature of the modern art was both a symptom and a reinforcer of social pathology. Modern literature was also often diagnosed in a similar way by the left. Consider Georg Lukács's well-known stricture of Kafka, Joyce, and Beckett, who, for the Marxist theorist, were the alienated writers of an alienating society, only valuable to the extent that they authentically reflected their times without sugarcoating but nevertheless culpable for not having been able to rise above their social conditions (Lukács 1962).
93 Quoted in O'Connor 1968: 43.
94 Quoted in Life, October 11, 1948.
95 Quoted in Néret 2003a: 76.
96 Quoted in Krauss 1999: 226.
97 Quoted in Greenberg 1961: 69.

98 Both quoted in Solomon 1987: 187.
99 Daix 1993: 152.
100 Quoted in Krauss 1998: 125.
101 On the animosity between the two, see Naifeh and Smith 1989: 704–6.
102 Rosenberg 1960: 34.
103 Quoted in Read 1959: 86.
104 Quoted in Read 1959: 21.
105 Halle 1996.
106 Quoted in Naifeh and Smith 1989: 606.
107 Naifeh and Smith 1989.
108 Crane 1987.
109 Danto 1997.
110 Quoted in Hopkins 2000: 63.
111 Duchamp 1989: 141. He also granted that this is was not easy: "However, it is difficult to select an object that absolutely does not interest you, not only on the day on which you select it, and which does not have any chance of becoming attractive or beautiful and which is neither pleasant to look at nor particularly ugly."
112 Danto 1997: 84.
113 Varnedoe 2006.
114 Visual art became a hot investment in the 1980s. Prices soared – not just of old masters but also of contemporaries with Jasper Johns's *False Start* (1959) setting the record at $17,100,000. The art market depressed in the 1990s, but only to recover in the 2000s.
115 Quoted in Walker 1999: 186.
116 Buskirk 2003, Rosenberg 1973.
117 Quoted in Alberro 2003: 121.
118 Quoted in Hopkins 2000: 41.
119 And some philosophers seem to agree. According to Danto, "A candy bar that is a work of art . . . just has to be a candy bar produced with the intention that it be art" (1997: 185).
120 Alberro 2003.
121 Frank and Cook 1996.
122 Demand for contemporary art increased in the 1960s but was still out-stripped by supply.
123 Becker 1982, Bourdieu 1992, Danto 1997, Dickie 1975, Zolberg 1990.
124 Hughes 1991: 369.
125 Haden-Guest 1966: 41.
126 Belting 1987, Danto 1997.
127 Dubin 1992: 102–20.
128 Quoted in Tomkins 1996: 182.
129 On Gilbert and George, see Farson 1999.
130 Walker 1999: 149–54.
131 For the Mapplethorpe affair, see Meyer 2004 and Steiner 1997.
132 Quoted in Hughes 1993: 183.

## Conclusion

1 For a profound analysis of justification in social life, see Boltanski and Thévenot 1991.
2 Goffman 1959: 251.
3 Arendt 1958: 74.

# References

Abbott, Andrew. 1983. Professional Ethics. *American Journal of Sociology* 88: 855–85.

———. 2001a. *Chaos of Disciplines*. Chicago: University of Chicago Press.

———. 2001b. *Time Matters: On Theory and Method*. Chicago: University of Chicago Press.

Adorno, Theodore W. 2006. *Philosophy of New Music*. Minneapolis: University of Minnesota Press.

Adut, Ari. 2004. Scandal as Strategy and Social Form: The Conditions, Dynamics and Paradoxes of French Political Corruption Affairs. Unpublished Doctoral Dissertation, University of Chicago.

Alberro, Alexander. 2003. *Conceptual Art and the Politics of Publicity*. Cambridge, MA: MIT Press.

Alexander, Jeffrey C. 1989. *Structure and Meaning: Rethinking Classical Sociology*. New York: Columbia University Press.

Ambrose, Stephen E. 1991. *Nixon: Ruin and Recovery, 1973–1990*. New York: Simon & Schuster.

Anechiarico, Frank, and James B. Jacobs. 1996. *The Pursuit of Absolute Integrity: How Corruption Control Makes Government Ineffective*. Chicago: University of Chicago Press.

Angenot, Marc. 1983. *La Parole pamphlétaire: Contribution à la typologie des discours modernes*. Paris: Payot.

Arendt, Hannah. 1958. *The Human Condition*. Chicago: University of Chicago Press.

———. 1982. *Lectures on Kant's Political Philosophy*. Chicago: University of Chicago Press.

Ariès, Philippe. 1975. *Western Attitudes toward Death from the Middle Ages to the Present*. Baltimore: Johns Hopkins University Press.

Aronson, Theo. 1994. *Prince Eddy and the Homosexual World*. London: Murray.

Audoin, Philippe. 1973. *Les Surréalistes*. Paris: Seuil.

Avril, Pierre. 1994. Regulation of Political Finance in France. In Herbert E. Alexander and Rei Shiratori, editors. *Comparative Political Finance among the Democracies*. Boulder, CO: Westview Press, 85–95.

Avrillier, Raymond, and Philippe Descamps. 1995. *Le Système Carignon*. Paris: La Découverte.

Baker, Wayne E., and Robert R. Faulkner. 1993. The Social Organization of Conspiracy: Illegal Networks in the Heavy Electrical Equipment Industry. *American Sociological Review* 58: 837–60.

Ball, Donald. 1975. Privacy, Publicity, Deviance and Control. *Pacific Sociological Review* 18: 259–78.

Balladur Édouard. 1995. *Deux ans à Matignon*. Paris: Plon.

Balzac, Honoré de. 2001. *Splendeurs et misères des courtisanes*. Paris: Adamant Media Corporation.

Bancaud, Alain. 1993. *La Haute magistrature judiciaire entre politique et sacerdoce*. Paris: Librarie Générale de Droit et de Jurisprudence.

Barr, Alfred Hamilton. 1961. *Matisse, His Art and His Public*. New York: Museum of Modern Art.

Barret-Kriegel, B. 1989. *L'État et les esclaves*. Paris: Payot.

Barthes, Roland. 1967. *Système de la mode*. Paris: Seuil.

Basch, Norma. 1993. Marriage, Morals, and Politics in the Election of 1828. *Journal of American History* 80: 890–918.

Baxandall, Michael. 1986. *Painting and Experience in Fifteenth-Century Italy*. Oxford: Oxford University Press.

Beaud, Olivier. 1999. Le Transfert de la responsabilité politique du ministre vers ses proches subordonnés. In Olivier Beaud and Jean-Michel Blanquer, editors. *La Responsabilité des gouvernants*. Paris: Descartes & Scie, 203–34.

Becker, Howard. 1963. *Outsiders: Studies in the Sociology of Deviance*. New York: Free Press.

———. 1982. *Art Worlds*. Berkeley: University of California Press.

Becquart-Leclercq, Jeanne. 1984. Paradoxes de la corruption politique. *Pouvoirs* 31: 19–36.

Bègue, Éliane, and Florence Delattre. 1993. *Le Juge et le ministre. Le face-à-face Courroye-Carignon: Une affaire d'État*. Paris: Robert Laffont.

Beisel, Nicole. 1990. Class, Culture, and Campaigns against Vice in Three American Cities, 1872–1892. *American Sociological Review* 55: 44–62.

———. 1997. *Imperiled Innocents: Anthony Comstock and Family Reproduction in Victorian American*. Princeton, NJ: Princeton University Press.

Belting, Hans. 1987. *The End of the History of Art*. Chicago: University of Chicago Press.

Benedict, Michael Les. 1973. *The Impeachment and Trial of Andrew Johnson*. New York: Norton.

Benjamin, Roger. 1987. *Matisse's "Notes of a Painter": Criticism, Theory and Context, 1891–1908*. Ann Arbor, MI: UMI Research Press.

Bennett, William J. 1999. *The Death of Outrage: Bill Clinton and the Assault on American Ideals*. New York: Free Press.

Benton, Erika Doss. 1991. *Pollock and the Politics of Modernism: From Regionalism to Abstract Expressionism*. Chicago: University of Chicago Press.

Bernheimer, Charles. 1989. *Figures of Ill Repute: Representing Prostitution in Nineteenth-Century France*. Cambridge, MA: Harvard University Press. 1989.

Bernier, Georges, and Monique Schneider-Maunoury. 1995. *Robert et Sonia Delaunay. Naissance de l'art abstrait*. Paris: J.-C. Lattes.

Bernstein, Mary, and James M. Jasper. 1996. Interests and Credibility: Whistleblowers in Technological Conflicts. *Social Science Information* 35: 565–89.

Biggart, Nicole Woolsey. 1985. Scandals in the White House: An Organizational Explanation. *Sociological Inquiry* 55: 110.

Birnbaum, Pierre, editor. 1988. *Un mythe politique, "La République juive": de Léon Blum à Pierre Mendès France*. Paris: Fayard.

———. 1994. *La France de l'affaire Dreyfus*. Paris: Gallimard.

———. 2003. *The Anti-Semitic Moment: A Tour of France in 1898*. New York: Hill and Wang.

Black, Donald. 1976. *The Behavior of Law*. New York: Academic Press.

Blackstone, Sir William. (1769) 1962. *Commentaries on the Laws of England*. Boston: Beacon Press.

Blic, Damien de, and Cyril Lemieux. 2005. Le Scandale comme épreuve: Éléments de sociologie pragmatique. *Politix* 18: 9–38.

Blistène, Bernard. 2001. *A History of 20th Century Art*. London: Thames and Hudson.

Bodiguel, Jean-Luc. 1991. *Les Magistrats, un corps sans âme?* Paris: Presses Universitaires de France.

Boime, Albert. 1971. *The Academy and French Painting in the Nineteenth Century*. London: Phaidon.

Boltanski, Luc. 1990. *L'amour et la justice comme compétence*. Paris: Métailié.

———. 1999. *La souffrance à distance: Morale humanitaire, médias, et politique*. Paris: Métailié.

———, and Laurent Thévenot. 1991. *De la justification. Les Économies de la grandeur*. Paris: Gallimard.

Bonazzi, G. 1981. Pour une sociologie du bouc émissaire dans les organisations complexes. *Sociologie du Travail* 2: 300–23.

Boorstin, Daniel J. 1961. *The Image: A Guide to Pseudo-Events in America*. New York: Harper and Row.

Bourdieu, Pierre. 1979. *La Distinction. Critique sociale du jugement*. Paris: Les Éditions de Minuit.

———. 1992. *Les Règles de l'art. Gènese et structure du champs littéraire*. Paris: Seuil.

———. (1972) 2000. *Esquisse d'une théorie de la pratique*. Paris: Seuil.

Bovier, Jean-Claude, Pierre Jacquin, and Alain Vogelweith. 1979. *Les Affaires, ou comment s'en débarasser*. Paris: Découverte.

Brace, Paul, and Barbara Hinckley. 1992. *Follow the Leader: Opinion Polls and the Modern Presidents*. New York: Basic Books.

Bredin, Jean-Denis. 1986. *The Affair: The Case of Alfred Dreyfus*. New York: George Braziller.

Brettell, Richard. 1999. *Modern Art 1851–1929*. Oxford: Oxford University Press.

Britt, David, editor. 1974. *Modern Art: Impressionism to Post-Impressionism*. London: Thames & Hudson.

Brockway, Wallace, and Herbert Weinstock. 1939. *Men of Music*. New York: Simon & Schuster.

Bufacci, Vittorio, and Simon Burgess. 1998. *Italy since 1989: Events and Interpretations*. London: Macmillan.

Buñuel, Luis. 1983. *My Last Sigh*. New York: Knopf.

Bürger, Peter. 1984. *The Theory of the Avant-Garde*. Minneapolis: University of Minnesota Press.

Burnham, Sophy. 1973. *The Art Crowd*. New York: David McKay.

Buskirk, Martha. 2003. *The Contingent Object of Contemporary Art*. Cambridge, MA: MIT Press.

Byron, Lord. 1943. *Don Juan: A Satiric Epic of Modern Life*. New York: Heritage.

Cairns, Walter, and Robert McKeon. 1995. *Introduction to French Law*. London: Cavendish Publishing House.

Calhoun, Craig, editor. 1992. *Habermas and the Public Sphere*. Cambridge, MA: MIT Press.

Callé, Bernard. 1992. *La Détention provisoire*. Paris: Presses Universitaires de France.

Carman, Harry J., and Reinhard H. Luthin. 1943. *Lincoln and the Patronage*. New York: Columbia University Press.

Carton, Daniel. 2000. *Cohabitation, intrigues et confidences*. Paris: Albin Michel.

Cavarlay, Bruno Aubusson de. 2006. La Détention provisoire: Mise en perspective et lacunes des sources statistiques. *Questiones pénales* 19(3): 1–4.

Chalier, Yves. 1991. *La République corrompue*. Paris: Robert Laffont.

Charon, Jean-Marie, and Claude Furet. 2000. *Un Secret si bien violé. La Loi, le juge et le journaliste*. Paris: Seuil.

Chester, Lewis, David Leitch, and Colin Simpson. 1976. *The Cleveland Street Affair*. London: Weidenfeld and Nicolson.

Chu, Petra ten-Doesschate, editor. 1992. *Letters of Gustave Courbet*. Chicago: University of Chicago Press.

———. 2007. *The Most Arrogant Man in France: Gustave Courbet and the Nineteenth-Century Media Culture*. Princeton, NJ: Princeton University Press.

Chwe, Michael. 2001. *Rational Ritual*. Princeton, NJ: Princeton University Press.

Clark, Kenneth. 1972. *The Nude: A Study in Ideal Form*. Princeton, NJ: Princeton University Press.

Clark, T. J. 1984. *The Painting of Modern Life: Paris in the Art of Manet and His Followers.* Princeton, NJ: Princeton University Press.

———. 1992. *Image of the People: Gustave Courbet and the 1848 Revolution.* Princeton, NJ: Princeton University Press.

Clarke, Alan. 1987. Moral Protest, Status Defense and the Anti-Abortion Campaign. *British Journal of Sociology* 38: 235–53.

Clayman, Steven, John Heritage, Marc Elliott, and Laurie McDonald. 2007. When Does the Watchdog Bark?: Conditions of Aggressive Questioning in Presidential News Conferences. *American Sociological Review* 72: 23–41.

Clayson, Hollis. 1991. *Painted Love: Prostitution in French Art of the Impressionist Era.* New Haven, CT: Yale University Press.

Clinton, Bill. 2004. *My Life.* New York: Knopf.

Cohen, Ed. 1993. *Talk on the Wilde Side.* New York: Routledge.

Cohen, Jean. 1997. Rethinking Privacy: Autonomy, Identity, and the Abortion Controversy. In Jeff Weintraub and Krishan Kumar, editors. *Public and Private in Thought and Practice.* Chicago: University of Chicago Press, 133–165.

Cohen-Tanugi, Laurent. 1985. *Le Droit sans l'État.* Paris: Presses Universitaires de France.

Coignard, Sophie, and Alexandre Wickham. 1999. *L'Omerta française.* Paris: Albin Michel.

Coleman, James. 1988. *Foundations of Social Theory.* Cambridge, MA: Harvard University Press

Collins, Gail. 1998. *Scorpion Tongues.* New York: William Morrow.

Collins, Randall. 2004. *Interaction Ritual Chains.* Princeton, NJ: Princeton University Press.

Colombani, Jean-Marie, and Hugues Portelli. 1995. *Le Double septennat de François Mitterrand. Dernier inventaire.* Paris: Grasset.

The Council for Excellence in Government and the Center for Media and Public Affairs. 2003. *Government: In and Out of the News.* Washington, DC: Author.

Crane, Diana. 1987. *The Transformation of the Avant-Garde: The New York Art World, 1940–1985.* Chicago: University of Chicago Press.

Crapol, Edward P. 2006. *John Tyler: The Accidental President.* Chapel Hill: University of North Carolina Press.

Croft-Cooke, Rupert. 1963. *Bosie: Lord Douglas, His Friends and Enemies.* New York: Bobbs Merrill.

———. 1967. *Feasting with Panthers: A New Consideration of Some Late Victorian Writers.* London: W. H. Allen.

———. 1972. *The Unrecorded Life of Oscar Wilde.* London: W. H. Allen.

Daix, Picasso. 1993. *Picasso: Life and Art.* New York: Icon.

Dali, Salvador. 1942. *The Secret Life of Salvador Dali.* New York. Dial Press.

Dampierre, Eric de. 1954. Thèmes pour l'étude du scandale. *Annales* 9: 328–36.

Danto, Arthur C. 1997. *After the End of Art.* Princeton, NJ: Princeton University Press.

Darnton, Robert. 1995. *Forbidden Best-Sellers of Pre-Revolutionary France.* New York: Norton.

Davenas, Laurent (with Dominique Pouchin). 1998. *Lettre de l'Himalaya. À ceux qui jugent et ceux qui sont jugés.* Paris: Seuil.

Dawkins, Heather. 2002. *The Nude in French Art and Culture, 1870–1910.* Cambridge: Cambridge University Press.

Decouty, Eric. 2000. *Les Scandales de la MNEF.* Neuilly-sur-Seine: Michel Lafon.

Deloire, Christophe, and Christophe Dubois. 2006. *Sexus Politicus.* Paris: Albin Michel.

D'Emilio, John, and Estelle B. Freedman. 1988. *Intimate Matters: A History of Sexuality in America.* Chicago: University of Chicago Press.

Derogy, Jacques, and Jean-Marie Pontaut. 1986. *Enquête sur trois secrets d'État.* Paris: Robert Lafont.

Dickie, George. 1975. *Art and Aesthetics: An Institutional Analysis.* Ithaca, NY: Cornell University Press.

DiMaggio, Paul, John Evans, and Bethany Bryson. 1996. Have Americans' Social Attitudes Become More Polarized? *American Journal of Sociology* 102: 690–755.

Dittes, James E., and Harold H. Kelley. 1956. Effects of Different Conditions of Acceptance upon Conformity to Group Norms. *Journal of Abnormal and Social Psychology* 53: 100–7.

Dockray, Martin. 1996. The Cleveland Street Scandal, 1889–1890: The Conduct of the Defence. *Journal of Legal History* 17: 1–16.

Donald, David Herbert. 1961. *Lincoln Reconsidered: Essays on the Civil War Era.* New York: Random House.

Doublet, Yves-Marie. 1997. *L'Argent et la politique en France.* Paris: Economica.

Douglas, Ann. 1995. *Terrible Honesty: Mongrel Manhattan in the 1920s.* New York: Farrar, Straus & Giroux

Douglas, Mary. 1966. *Purity and Danger: An Analysis of the Concepts of Pollution and Taboo.* New York: Praeger.

Dover, K. J. 1997. *Greek Homosexuality.* Belair, CA: MJF Books.

Draper, Theodore. 1991. *A Very Thin Line: The Iran-Contra Affairs.* New York: Simon & Shuster.

Drew, Elizabeth. 2006. Power Grab. *The New York Review of Books* 53(11): 10–15.

Dubin, Steven. 1992. *Arresting Images.* London: Routledge.

Duchamp, Marcel. 1989. *The Writings of Marcel Duchamp.* New York: Da Capo Press.

Ducharme, Lori J., and Gary Allan Fine. 1995. The Construction of Nonpersonhood and Demonization: Commemorating the Traitorous Reputation of Benedict Arnold. *Social Forces* 73: 1309–1331.

Dumont, Louis. 1967. *Homo hierarchicus: Essai sur le système des castes.* Paris: Galllimard.

Dunar, Andrew J. 1984. *The Truman Scandals and the Politics of Morality*: Columbia: University of Missouri Press.

Durkheim, Emile. (1897) 1951. *Suicide*. Glencoe, IL: Free Press.

———. (1918) 1968. *Les Formes élémentaires de la vie religieuse*. Paris: Presses Universitaires de France.

Eastland, Terry. 1989. *Ethics, Politics, and the Independent Counsel: Executive Power, Executive Vice*. Washington D.C.: National Legal Center for the Public Interest.

Edgerton, R. 1985. *Rules, Exceptions, and Social Order*. Berkeley: University of California Press.

Edwards, George C., III. 1996. Frustration and Folly: Bill Clinton and the Public Presidency. In Colin Campbell and Bert A. Rockman, editors. *The Clinton Presidency: First Appraisals*. Chatham, NJ: Chatham House.

Elgar, Frank. 1960. *Cézanne*. New York: Harry N. Abrams

Elias, Norbert. (1939) 1978. *The History of Manners*. New York: Pantheon.

———. (1939) 1982. *Power and Civility*. New York: Pantheon.

Ellickson, Robert C. 2001. The Evolution of Social Norms: A Perspective from the Legal Academy. In Michael Hechter and Karl-Dieter Opp, editors. *Social Norms*. New York: Russel Sage, 35–75.

Ellis, Havelock. 1898. *Studies in the Psychology of Sex. V. I: Sexual Inversion*. London.

———. 1912. *The Task of Social Hygene*. London: Constable.

Ellmann, Richard. (1984) 1988. *Oscar Wilde*. New York: Alfred A. Knopf.

Elster, Jon. 1989. *Social Norms: A Study in Social Order*. Cambridge: Cambridge University Press.

———. 2000. *Strong Feelings: Emotion, Addiction, and Human Behavior*. Cambridge, MA: MIT Press.

Emmerling, Leonhard. 2003. *Jackson Pollock*. Los Angeles: Taschen.

Erikson, Kai T. 1966. *Wayward Puritans: A Study in the Sociology of Deviance*. New York: Wiley.

Etchegoyen, Alain. 1995. *Le Corrupteur et le corrompu*. Paris: Juillard.

Farson, Daniel. 1999. *Gilbert and George: A Portrait*. London.

Fay, Bruno, and Laurent Olivier. 2002. *Le Casier judiciaire de la République*. Paris: Ramsay.

Fine, Gary Allen. 1996. Reputational Entrepreneurs and the Memory of Incompetence: Melting Supporters, Partisan Warriors, and Images of President Harding. *American Journal of Sociology* 101: 1159–93.

Fisher, Trevor. 1995. *Scandal: The Sexual Politics of Late Victorian Britain*. Phoenix Mill: Alan Sutton.

Fisse, Brent, and John Braithwaite. 1983. *The Impact of Publicity on Corporate Offenders*. Albany: State University of New York Press.

Flaherty, David H. 1972. *Privacy in Colonial New England*. Charlottesville: University of Virginia Press.

Foldy, Michael S. 1997. *The Trials of Oscar Wilde: Deviance, Morality, and Late-Victorian Society*. New Haven, CT: Yale University Press.

Foucault, Michel. 1979. *Discipline and Punish*. New York: Random Press.
————. 1980. *History of Sexuality*. New York: Vintage Books.
Fox, Richard Wightman. 1999. *Trials of Intimacy: Love and Loss in the Beecher-Tilton Scandal*. Chicago: University of Chicago Press.
Frank, Robert H., and Philip J. Cook. 1996. *The Winner-Take-All Society: Why the Few at the Top Get So Much More than the Rest of Us*. New York: Penguin.
Fried, Michael. 1990. *Courbet's Realism*. Chicago: University of Chicago Press.
————. 1996. *Manet's Modernism*. Chicago: University of Chicago Press. 1990.
Furet, François. 1978. *Penser la révolution française*. Paris: Gallimard.
Gaetner, Gilles. 1992. *L'Argent facile. Dictionnaire de la corruption en France*. Paris: Stock.
————. 1998. *Le Roman d'un séducteur: Les secrets de Roland Dumas*. Paris: JC Lattès.
Gaetner, Gilles, and Roland-Pierre Paringaux. 1994. *Un juge face au pouvoir. De la gauche à droite, les secrets de Renaud Van Ruymbeke*. Paris: Bernard Grasset.
Gagnier, Regenia. 1986. *Idylls of the Marketplace: Oscar Wilde and the Victorian Public*. Stanford, CA: Stanford University Press.
Gagnon, John H., Alain Giami, Stuart Michaels, and Patrick de Colomby. 2001. A Comparative Study of the Couple in the Social Organization of Sexuality in France and the United States – Statistical Data Included. *Journal of Sex Research* 38: 24–34.
Gandillac, Maurice de. 1966. Brèves notes préliminaires pour une métaphysique du scandale. *Cahiers Renaud-Barrault* 54: 3–13.
Garapon, Antoine. 1996. *Le Gardien des promesses: Justice et démocratie*. Paris: Odile Jacob.
————, and Denis Salas. 1966. *La République pénalisée*. Paris: Hachette.
Garfinkel, Harold. 1956. Conditions of Successful Degradation Ceremonies. *American Journal of Sociology* 61: 420–4.
Garment, Suzanne. 1991. *Scandal: The Culture of Mistrust in American Politics*. New York: Random House.
Garrigou, Alain. 1989. Strategic Analysis of a Scandal: "Carrefour du Développement." *Corruption and Reform* 4: 159–79.
Gattegno, Hervé. 2001. *L'Affaire Dumas*. Paris: Stock.
Gaudino, Antoine. 1990. *L'Enquête impossible*. Paris: Albin Michel.
Gawthorne-Hardy, Jonathan. 1979. *The Public Schools Phenomenon, 1597–1977*. London: Penguin.
Gay, Peter. 1986. *The Tender Passion: The Bourgeois Experience, Victoria to Freud, Volume 2*. New York: Oxford University Press.
————. 1998. *Pleasure Wars: The Bourgeois Experience, Victoria to Freud, Volume 5*. New York: Norton.

Gilbert, Arthur N. 1977a. Buggery and the British Navy, 1700–1861. *Journal of Social History* 10: 72–98.

———. 1977b. Sexual Deviance and Disaster during the Napoleonic Wars. *Albion* 9: 98–113.

Gilbert, Mark. 1995. *The Italian Revolution: The End of Politics, Italian Style?* Boulder, CO: Westview Press.

Gilbert, W. S. 1910. *Original Plays: Third Series*. London: Chatto.

Gillespie, Michael Patrick. 1996. *Oscar Wilde and the Poetics of Ambiguity*. Gainesville: University of Florida Press.

Ginsberg, Benjamin, and Martin Shefter. 1999. *Politics by Other Means: Politicians, Prosecutors, and the Press from Watergate to Whitewater*. New York: Norton.

Giret, Vincent, and Véronique Le Billon. 2000. *Les Vies cachées de DSK*. Paris: Seuil.

Gluckman, Max. 1963. Gossip and Scandal. *Current Anthropology* 4: 307–16.

Goffman, Erving. 1959. *Presentation of Self in Everyday Life*. Harmondsworth: Penguin.

———. 1961. *Asylums: Essays on the Social Situation of Mental Patients and Other Inmates*. New York: Anchor Books.

———. 1963. *Stigma: Notes on the Management of Spoiled Identity*. New York: Simon & Schuster.

———. 1967. *Interaction Ritual: Essays on Face-to-Face Behavior*. New York: Pantheon.

Gombrich, E. H. 1972. *The Story of Art*. London: Phaidon.

Goode, William J. 1978. *The Celebration of Heroes: Prestige as a Control System*. Berkeley: University of California Press.

Goodman, Jonathan, compiler. 1989. *The Oscar Wilde File*. London: Allison and Busby.

Gorham, Deborah. 1978. The "Maiden Tribute of Modern Babylon" Revisited: Child Prostitution and the Idea of Childhood in Late-Victorian England. *Victorian Studies* 21: 353–79.

Granovetter, Mark. 1973. Strength of Weak Ties. *American Journal of Sociology* 78: 1360–80.

Greenberg, Clement. 1961. *Art and Culture: Critical Essays*. Boston: Beacon Press.

———. 1993. *The Collected Essays and Criticism*. Chicago: University of Chicago Press.

Greenberg, Daniel F. 1988. *The Construction of Homosexuality*. Chicago: University of Chicago Press.

Greenberg, Gerald S., editor. 2000. *Historical Encyclopedia of U.S. Independent Counsel Investigations*. Westport, CT: Greenwood Press.

Greilsamer, Laurent, and Daniel Schneidermann. 1994. *Les Juges parlent*. Paris: Fayard.

———. 2001. *Où vont les juges?* Paris: Fayard.

Grosskurth, Phyllis. 1964. *John Addington Symonds*. London: Longman.

Grossman, Michael, and Martha Kumar. 1981. *Portraying the President: The White House and the News Media*. Baltimore: Johns Hopkins University Press.

Guilbaut, Serge. 1983. *Comment New York vola l'idée d'art moderne: Expressionnisme abstrait, liberté et guerre froide*. Nimes: Éditions Jacqueline Chambon.

Gurstein, Rochelle. 1998. *Repeal of Reticence*. New York: Hill and Wang.

Gusfield, Joseph R. 1963. *Symbolic Crusade: Status Politics and the American Temperance Movement*. Urbana: University of Illinois Press.

Habermas, Jürgen. 1989. *The Structural Transformation of the Public Sphere*. Cambridge, MA: MIT Press.

Haden-Guest, Anthony. 1996. *True Colors: The Real Life of the Art World*. New York: Atlantic Monthly Press.

Hall, Lesley A. 2000. *Sex, Gender, and Social Change in Britain since 1880*. New York: St. Martin's Press.

Hall, Peter A., Jack Hayward, and Howard Machin, editor. 1994. *Developments in French Politics*. London: Macmillan.

Halle, David. 1996. *Inside Culture: Art and Class in the American Home*. Chicago: University of Chicago Press.

Hallin, Daniel. 1986. *The Uncensored War. The Media and Vietnam*. Oxford: Oxford University Press.

Halperin, David M. 1990. *One Hundred Years of Homosexuality and Other Essays on Greek Love*. London: Routledge.

Halphen, Éric. 2002. *Sept ans de solitude*. Paris: Denöel.

Hamilton, George Heard. 1954. *Manet and His Critics*. New Haven, CT: Yale University Press.

Hamilton, Richard. 1961. For the Finest Art, Try Pop. *Gazette* no. 1: 42–3.

Hamilton, Sir Edward. 1986. *The Destruction of Lord Rosebery: From the Diary of Sir Edward Hamilton 1894–1895*. London: Historians Press.

Harris, Frank. (1916) 1959. *Oscar Wilde*. East Lansing: Michigan State University Press.

Harvey, A. D. 1978. Prosecutions for Sodomy in England at the Beginning of the Nineteenth Century. *The Historical Journal* 21: 939–48.

Healy, Timothy Michael. 1928. *Letters and Leaders of My Day*. London: T. Butterworth.

Hebdige. Dick. 1978. *Subcultures: The Meaning of Style*. London: Routledge.

Hechter, Michael, and Karl-Dieter Opp, editors. 2001. *Social Norms*. New York: Russel Sage.

Heclo, Hugh. 1996. Presidential Power and Public Prestige: A "Snarly Sort of Politics." Paper presented at the Presidential Power Revisited Conference. Woodrow Wilson International Center for Scholars, Smithsonian Institute, June.

Heidenheimer, Arnold J. 1989. Perspectives on the Perception of Corruption. In Arnold J. Heidenheimer, Michael Johnston, and Victor T. LeVine, editors. *Political Corruption: A Handbook*. Edison, NJ: Transaction, 149–164.

Hersh, Seymour M. 1998. *The Dark Side of Camelot*. New York: Back Bay Books.

Hess, Barbara. 2004. *Willem de Kooning 1904–1997: Content as a Glimpse*. Los Angeles: Taschen.

Hibbard, Howard. 1983. *Caravaggio*. New York: Harper & Row.

Hichens, Robert Smyth. (1894) 1970. *The Green Carnation*. Lincoln: University of Nebraska Press.

Himmelfarb, Gertrude. 1995. *The De-Moralization of Society: From Victorian Virtues to Modern Values*. New York: Knopf.

Hitchens, Christopher. 1997. *Missionary Position: Mother Teresa in Theory and Practice*. London: Verso.

Hofstader, Richard. 1969. *The Idea of a Party System: The Rise of Legitimate Opposition in the United States*. Berkeley: University of California Press.

Hopkins, David. 2000. *After Modern Art, 1945–2000*. Oxford: Oxford University Press.

Hughes, Robert. 1991. *The Shock of the New*. New York: Knopf.

———. 1992. *Nothing If Not Critical: Selected Essays on Art and Artists*. New York: Penguin.

———. 1993. *Culture of Complaint: The Fraying of America*: New York: Oxford University Press.

Hyde, Montgomery H. (1948) 1956. *The Three Trials of Oscar Wilde*. New York: University Books.

———. 1970. *The Other Love*. London.

———. 1975. *Oscar Wilde: A Biography*. New York: Farrar, Straus & Giroux.

———. 1976. *The Cleveland Street Scandal*. New York: Coward, McCann & Geoghegan.

Inglehart, Ronald. 1990. *Culture Shift in Advanced Industrial Society*. Princeton, NJ: Princeton University Press.

Jacobs, Lawrence R., and Robert Y. Shapiro. 2000. *Politicians Don't Pander: Political Manipulation and the Loss of Democratic Responsiveness*. Chicago: University of Chicago Press.

James, Henry. (1890) 1989. *Tragic Muse*. New York: Penguin.

Jean-Pierre, Thierry. 1991. *Bon appétit, messieurs*. Paris: Fixot.

Jeanneney, Jean-Noël, *L'Argent caché. Milieux d'affaires et pouvoir politique dans la France du XXe siècle*. Paris: Seuil, 1984.

Jenkins, Philip. 1996. *Pedophiles and Priests: Anatomy of a Contemporary Crisis*. New York: Oxford University Press.

———. 2003. *The New Anti-Catholicism: The Last Acceptable Prejudice*. New York: Oxford University Press.

Johnson, Charles A. 2001. *Independent Counsel: The Law and the Investigations*. Washington, DC: CQ Press.

Julius, Anthony. 2003. *Transgressions: The Offences of Art*. Chicago: University of Chicago Press.

Kaiser Family Foundation. 2005. *Sex on TV 4*. Available at: http://www.kff.org/entmedia/entmedia110905pkg.cfm.

Kalb, Marvin. 2001. *One Scandalous Story: Clinton, Lewinsky, and Thirteen Days That Tarnished American Journalism*. New York: Free Press.

Kamnen, Michael. 2006. *Visual Shock. A History of Art Controversies in American Culture*. New York: Knopf.

Kandinsky, Wassili. 1977. *Concerning the Spiritual in Art*. New York: Dover.

Kasson, John F. 1990. *Rudeness and Civility: Manners in Nineteenth-Century Urban America*. New York: Noonday Press.

Katz, Jack. 1980. Social Movement against White-Collar Crime. *Criminology Review Yearbook* 2: 161–84.

———. 1999. *How Emotions Work*. Chicago: University of Chicago Press.

Kennedy, Randall. 2003. *Nigger: The Strange Career of a Troublesome Word*. New York: Vintage.

Kernell, Samuell. 1997. *Going Public: New Strategies of Presidential Leadership*. Washington, DC: CQ Press.

Kevles, Daniel J. 1998. *The Baltimore Case: A Trial of Politics, Science, and Character*. New York: Norton.

Key, V. O. 1964. *Politics, Parties, and Pressure Groups*. 5th ed. New York: Crowell.

King, David. 1997. The Polarization of American Parties and Mistrust of Government. In Joseph S. Nye, Philip D. Zelikow, and David C. King, editors. *Why People Don't Trust Government*. Cambridge, MA: Harvard University Press, 155–178.

Kinsey, Alfred. 1948. *Sexual Behavior in the Human Male*. Philadelphia: W. B. Saunders.

———. 1953. *Sexual Behavior in the Human Female*. Philadelphia: W. B. Saunders.

Klapper, Joseph T. 1960. *The Effects of Mass Communications*. Glencoe, IL: Free Press.

Klein, Edward. 2005. *The Truth about Hillary: What She Knew, When She Knew It, and How Far She'll Go to Become President*. New York: Sentinel.

Krauss, Rosalind E. 1986. *The Originality of the Avant-Garde and Other Modernist Myths*. Cambridge, MA: MIT Press.

———. 1999. *The Picasso Papers*. Cambridge, MA: MIT Press.

Kundera, Milan. 1993. *Les Testaments trahis*. Paris: Gallimard.

Kuran, Timur. 1995. *Private Truths, Public Lies*. Cambridge, MA: Harvard University Press.

Kurtz, Howard. 1993. *Media Circus: The Trouble with America's Newspapers*. New York: Random House.

———. 1998. *Spin Cycle: Inside the Clinton Propaganda Machine*. New York: Free Press.

Lafitte, François. 1958. Homosexuality and the Law: The Wolfenden Report in Historical Perspective. *The British Journal of Delinquency* 9: 8–19

Lakoff, George. 2006. *Whose Freedom?: The Battle over America's Most Important Idea*. New York: Farrar, Straus & Giroux.

Lambert, Gilles. 2005. *Caravaggio*. Köln, Germany: Taschen.

Lang, Gladys, and Kurt Lang. 1983. *The Battle for Public Opinion: The President, the Press, and the Polls during Watergate*. New York: Columbia University Press.

Larivière, Daniel Soulez. 1987. *Les Juges dans la balance*. Paris: Éditions Ramsay.

Larson, Magali Sarfatti, and Robin Wagner-Pacifici. 2001. The Dubious Place of Virtue: Reflections on the Impeachment of William Jefferson Clinton and the Death of the Political Event in America. *Theory and Society* 30: 753–74.

Lascoumes, Pierre. 1996. *Élites irrégulières. Essai sur la délinquance d'affaires*. Paris: Gallimard.

———. 1999. *Corruptions*. Paris: Presses de Sciences Po.

———. 2001. The Fight against Corruption in France. *French Politics, Culture & Society* 19: 55–7.

Le Floch-Prigent, Loïk. 2001. *Affaire Elf. Affaire d'État*. Paris: Le Cherche Midi.

Lecasble, Valérie, and Airy Routier. 1998. *Forages en eau profonde. Les Secrets de "l'affaire Elf."* Paris: Grasset.

Leckie, Barbara. 1999. *Culture and Adultery: The Novel, the Newspaper, and the Law, 1857–1914*. Philadelphia: University of Pennsylvania Press.

Lemesle, Laurent, and Frédéric-Jérôme Pansier. 1988. *Le Procureur de la république*. Paris: Presses Universitaires de France.

Lemieux, Cyril. 2000. *Mauvaise presse. Une sociologie compréhensive du travail journalistique et de ses critiques*. Paris: Métailié.

Lenoir, Rémy. 1992. Champs judiciaire et réforme de l'instruction. In Mireille Delmas-Marty, editor. *Procés penal et droits de l'homme*. Paris: Presses Universitaires de France.

Levine, Lawrence. 1988. *Highbrow/Lowbrow: The Emergence of Cultural Hierarchy in America*. Cambridge, MA: Harvard University Press.

Lichter, Robert S., Linda S. Richter, and Stanley Rothman. 1994. *Prime Time: How TV Portrays American Culture*. Lanham, MD: Regnery Publications.

Lipset, Seymour, and William Schneider. 1983. *The Confidence Gap: Business, Labor, and Government in the Public Mind*. New York: Free Press.

Longhi, Roberto. 1968. *Caravaggio*. Leipzig: Editions Leipzig.

Lorrain, Dominique. 1993. L'Argent et le gouvernement municipal. *French Politics & Society* 11: 65–72.

Loughlin, John P. and Sonia Mazey, editors. 1995. *The End of the French Unitary State?: Ten Years of Regionalization in France (1982–1992)*. London: Routledge.

Lowi, Theodore. 1985. *The Personal President: Power Invested, Promise Unfulfilled.* Ithaca, NY: Cornell University Press.

———. 1988. Foreword. In Andrei S., Markovits, and Mark Silverstein, editors. 1988. *The Politics of Scandal: Power and Process in Liberal Democracies.* New York: Holmes & Meier, vii–xii.

Lukács, Georg. 1962. *The Meaning of Contemporary Realism.* London: Merlin.

Lull, James, and Stephen Hinerman, editors. 1997. *Media Scandals: Morality and Desire in the Popular Culture Marketplace.* New York: Columbia University Press.

Lyons, Gene. 1996. *Fools for Scandal: How the Media Invented Whitewater.* New York: Franklin Square Press.

MacKinnon, Catherine A. 1987. *Feminism Unmodified.* Cambridge, MA: Harvard University Press.

Mahon, Alyce. 2005. *Eroticism and Art.* Oxford: Oxford University Press.

Malinowski, Bronislaw. 1926. *Crime and Custom in Savage Society.* New York: Humanities Press.

Maltese, John Anthony. 1992. *Spin Control: The White House Office of Communications and the Management of Presidential News.* Chapel Hill: University of North Carolina Press.

Maniardi, Patricia. 1993. *The End of the Salon: Art and the State in the Early Third Republic.* New York: Cambridge University Press.

Mannering, Douglas. 1997. *Impressionists.* Bristol: Paragon.

Mansbridge, Jane. 1997. The Social and Cultural Causes of Dissatisfaction with U.S. Government. In Joseph S. Nye, Philip D. Zelikow, and David C. King, editors. *Why People Don't Trust Government.* Cambridge, MA: Harvard University Press, 133–54.

Marcus, Steven. 1975. *The Other Victorians: A Study of Sexuality and Pornography in Mid-Nineteenth-Century England.* New York: Basic Books.

Marjoribanks, Edward. 1932. *The Life of Lord Carson.* London: The Camelot Press.

Markovits, Andrei S., and Mark Silverstein, editors. 1988. *The Politics of Scandal: Power and Process in Liberal Democracies.* New York: Holmes & Meier.

Masson, Gérard. 1977. *Les Juges et le pouvoir.* Paris: Éditions Alain Moreau.

Matisse, Henri. 1908. Notes d'un peintre. *Grande Revue* II: 731–45.

Mayhew, David. 2005. *Divided We Govern: Party Control, Lawmaking, and Investigations, 1946–2002.* New Haven, CT: Yale University Press.

Maza, Sarah. 1993. *Private Lives, Public Affairs: The Causes Célèbres of Prerevolutionary France.* Berkeley: University of California Press.

McCarty, Nolan, Keith T. Poole, and Howard Rosenthal. 2006. *Polarized America: The Dance of Ideology and Unequal Riches.* Cambridge, MA: MIT Press.

McNally, Richard J. 2003. *Remembering Trauma.* Cambridge, MA: Harvard University Press.

Mershon, Caron, and Gianfranco Pasquino. 1995. *Italian Politics: Ending the First Republic*. Oxford: Westview.

Merton, Robert K. (1949) 1957. *Social Theory and Social Structure*. Glencoe, IL: Free Press.

Mény, Yves. 1992. *Corruption de la république*. Paris: Fayard.

Merlen, Eric, and Frédéric Ploquin. 1998. *La Commissaire et le courbeau*. Paris: Seuil.

Meyer, Leonard. 1956. *Emotion and Meaning in Music*. Chicago: University of Chicago Press.

Meyer, Richard. 2004. *Outlaw Representation: Censorship and Homosexuality in Twentieth-Century American Art*. Boston: Beacon Press.

Miller, William Ian. 1997. *Anatomy of Disgust*. Cambridge, MA: Harvard University Press.

Ministère de la Justice. 2007. *Annuaire statistique de la justice*. Paris: Documentation Française.

Modell, John. 1989. *Into One's Own: From Youth to Adulthood in the United States, 1920–1975*. Berkeley: University of California Press.

Molière, Jean Baptiste Poquelin de. 1965. *The Misanthrope and Tartuffe*. Translated by Richard Wilber. San Diego ,CA: Harcourt and Brace.

Molotch, Harvey, and Marilyn Lester. 1974. News as Purposive Behavior: On the Strategic Use of Routine Events, Accidents and Scandals. *American Sociological Review* 39: 101–12.

Moss, George. 1990. *Vietnam: An American Ordeal*. New York: Prentice Hall.

Mott, Frank Luther. 1962. *American Journalism: A History, 1690–1960*. New York: Macmillan.

Moulin, Raymonde. 1967. *Le Marché de la peinture en France*. Paris: Les Éditions de Minuit.

Murray, Douglas. 2000. *Bosie: A Biography of Lord Alfred Douglas*. New York: Hyperion.

Naifeh, Steven, and Gregory White Smith. 1989. *Jackson Pollock: An American Saga*. New York: C. N. Potter.

Néret, Gilles. 2003a. *Balthasar Klossowksi de Rola Balthus*. Köln, Germany: Taschen.

———. 2003b. *Salvador Dali*. Köln, Germany: Taschen.

Neustadt, Richard E. 1991. *Presidential Power and the Modern Presidents: The Politics of Leadership from Roosevelt to Reagan*. New York: Free Press.

———. 1997. The Politics of Mistrust. In Joseph S. Nye, Philip D. Zelikow, and David C. King, editors. *Why People Don't Trust Government*. Cambridge, MA: Harvard University Press, 179–201.

Nie, Norman, Sidney Verba, and John R. Petrocik. 1976. *The Changing American Voter*. Cambridge, MA: Harvard University Press.

Nietzsche, Friedrich. 1998. *On the Genealogy of Morals*. New York: Oxford University Press.

Nixon, Richard M. 1978. *RN: The Memoires of Richard Nixon*. New York: Grosset and Dunlap.

Nock, Steven L. 1993. *The Costs of Privacy: Surveillance and Reputation in America*. New York: Aldine de Gruyter.

Nussbaum, Martha. 2001. *Upheavals of Thought. The Intelligence of Emotions*. New York: Cambridge University Press.

Nye, Joseph S., Philip D. Zelikow, and David C. King, editors. 1997. *Why People Don't Trust Government*. Cambridge, MA: Harvard University Press.

O'Connor, Francis V. 1968. *Jackson Pollock*. New York: Museum of Modern Art.

Oja, Carol J. 2000. *Making Music Modern: New York in the 1920s*. New York: Oxford University Press. *Oxford English Dictionary*, (prepared by J. A. Simpson and E. S. C. Weiner). 1989. Oxford: Claredon Press; New York: Oxford University Press.

Partsch, Susanna. 2003. *Paul Klee 1879–1940*. Köln, Germany: Taschen.

Patterson, Thomas E. 1993. *Out of Order*. New York: Vintage.

Perrot, Roger. 1995. *Institutions judiciaires*. Paris: Montchrestien

Phelps, Thomas M., and Helen Winternitz. 1992. *Capitol Games: The Inside Story of Clarence Thomas, Anita Hill, and a Supreme Court Nomination*. New York: Hyperion.

Plenel, Edwy. 1994. *Un Temps de chien*. Paris: Gallimard.

Pollard, James. 1947. *The Presidents and the Press*. New York: Macmillan.

Popis, Claude 1992. *L'Argent, le batiment, la politique sous la Ve République*. Paris: Albin Michel.

Popkin, Jeremy. 1989. Pamphlet Journalism at the End of the Old Regime. *Eighteenth Century Studies* 22: 351–67.

Posner, Eric. 2000. *Law and Social Norms*. Cambridge, MA: Harvard University Press.

Posner, Richard. 1998. The Problematics of Moral and Legal Theory. *Harvard Law Review* 111: 1637–717.

———. 1992. *Sex and Reason*. Cambridge, MA: Harvard University Press.

———. 1999. *An Affair of State: The Impeachment and the Trial of President Clinton*. Cambridge, MA: Harvard University Press.

Pritchard, David. 2001. *Oscar Wilde*. New Lanark: Geddes & Grosset.

Pujas, Veronqiue. 2000. Corruption via Party Financing in France. Transparency International Working Paper.

Pujas, Véronique, and Martin Rhodes. 1999. Party Finance and Political Scandal in Italy, Spain and France. *West European Politics* 22: 41–63.

Queensberry, Marquess of. 1949. *Oscar Wilde and Black Douglas*. London: Hutchinson.

Radzinowitz, Leon. 1968. *A History of English Criminal Law, Volume IV: Grappling for Control*. London: Stevens.

Raffalovich, André. 1890. *A Willing Exile*. London: F. V. White.

Randulf, Swen. 1964. *Moral Indignation and Middle Class Sociology*. New York: Schocken.

Rassat, Michèle-Laure. 1985. *La Justice en France*. Paris: Presses Universitaires de France.

Read, Herbert. 1959. *A Concise History of Modern Painting*. New York: Frederick A. Praeger.

Reitlinger, Gerald. 1961. *The Economics of Taste: The Rise and the Fall of Picture Prices, 1760–1960*. London: Barrie and Lock.

Renucci, Jean-François Michel Cardix. 1989. *L'Abus de biens sociaux*. Paris: Presses Universitaires de France.

Riesman, David. 1942. Democracy and Defamation: Control of Group Libel. *Columbia Law Review* 42: 727–1123.

Rodinson, Maxime. 1970. De l'histoire de l'antisémitisme à la sociologie du scandale. *Cahiers Internationaux de Sociologie* 49: 143–50.

Roos, Jane Mayo. 1996. *Early Impressionism and the French State, 1866–1874*. New York: Cambridge University Press. 1996.

Rosanvallon, Pierre.1990. *L'État en France de 1789 à nos jours*. Paris: Seuil.

Rosenberg, Harold. 1960. *The Tradition of the New*. New York: Horizon Press.

———. 1973. *The De-Definition of Art: Action Art to Pop to Earthworks*. New York: Horizon Press.

Ross, Shelley. 1988. *Fall from Grace; Sex, Scandal, and Corruption in American Politics from 1702 to the Present*. New York: Ballantine Books.

Roughhead, William. 1931. *Bad Companions*. New York: Duffield and Green.

Roussel, Violaine. 1998. Les Magistrats dans les scandales politiques. *Revue française de sciences politiques* 48: 245–273.

———. 2002. *Affaires de juges: Les magistrats face aux scandales politiques en France (1990-2000)*. Paris: La Découverte.

Rousso, Henri. 1990. *Le Syndrome de Vichy de 1944 à nos jours*. Paris: Seuil.

Rowell, George. 1978. *The Victorian Theatre, 1792–1914: A Survey*. Cambridge: Cambridge University Press.

Rozell, Mark J. 2002. *Executive Privilege: Presidential Power, Secrecy, and Accountability*. Kansas City: University Press of Kansas.

Rudenstine, David. 1996. *The Day the Presses Stopped: A History of the Pentagon Papers Case*. Berkeley: University of California Press.

Russel, J. 1969. *The World of Matisse*. New York: Time-Life Books.

Ruymbeke, Renaud Van. 1988. *Le Juge d'instruction*. Paris: Presses Universitaires de France.

Ryan, Mary. 1981. *The Cradle of the Middle Class: The Family in Oneida County, New York 1790–1865*. New York: Cambridge University Press.

Sabato, Larry J. 2000. *Feeding Frenzy: How Attack Journalism Has Transformed American Politics*. Baltimore: Lanahan.

———, Mark Stencel, and S. Robert Lichter. 2000. *Peep Show: Media and Politics in an Age of Scandal*. Lanham, MD: Rowman & Littlefield.

Safire, William. 1975. *Before the Fall: An Insider's View of the Pre-Watergate White House*. Garden City, NY: Doubleday.

Saguy, Abigail. 1999. Puritanism and Promiscuity: Sexual Attitudes in France and the United States. *Comparative Social Research* 18: 227–47.

———. 2003. *What Is Sexual Harassment? From Capitol Hill to the Sorbonne*. Berkeley: University of California Press.

Sartre, Jean-Paul. 1943. *L'Être et le néant*. Paris: Gallimard.

Scheler, Max. 1961. *Ressentiment*. Glencoe, IL: Free Press.

Schlesinger, Arthur. (1973). 2004. *The Imperial Presidency*. Boston: Mariner Books.

Schneider, Pierre. 1984. *Matisse*. London: Thames and Hudson.

Schudson, Michael. 1976. Sex Scandals. In Sally Banes, Sheldon Frank, and Tom Horwitz, editors. *Our National Passion: 200 Years of Sex in America*. Chicago: Follet, 41–57.

———. 1992. *Watergate in American Memory: How We Remember, Forget, and Reconstruct the Past*. New York: Basic Books.

———. 1995. *The Power of News*. Cambridge, MA: Harvard University Press.

———. 1998. *The Good Citizen: A History of American Civic Life*. New York: Free Press.

Schudson, Michael, and Elliot King. 1995. The Illusion of Ronald Reagan's Popularity. In *Power of News*. Michael Schudson, author. Cambridge, MA: Harvard University Press, 124–41.

Schultz, Jeffrey D. 2000. *Presidential Scandals*. Washington, DC: CQ Press.

Seuphor, Michel. 1957. *Piet Mondrian: Life and Work*. London: Thames and Hudson.

Sewell, William. 1995. Historical Events as the Transformation of Structures: Inventing Revolution at the Bastille. *Theory and Society* 841–81.

Shakespeare, William. 1934. *Collected Works*. London: MacMillan.

Shapiro, Susan P. 1987. The Social Control of Impersonal Trust. *American Journal of Sociology* 93: 623–58.

Sherkat, Darren E., and Christopher G. Ellison. 1997. Cognitive Structure of a Moral Crusade: Conservative Protestantism and Opposition to Pornography. *Social Forces* 75: 957–80.

Sherman, Lawrence. 1978. *Scandal and Reform: Controlling Police Corruption*. Berkeley: University of California Press.

Shibutani, Tamotsu. 1966. *Improvised News: A Sociological Study of Rumor*. Indianapolis: Bobbs-Merrill.

Skowronek, Stephen. 1997. *Politics Presidents Make: Leadership from John Adams to George Bush*. Cambridge, MA: Harvard University Press.

Smith, Adam. 1976. *Theory of Moral Sentiments*. Oxford: Clarendon Press.

Smith, Alison. 1996. *The Victorian Nude: Sexuality, Morality, and Art*. Manchester, UK: Manchester University Press. 1996.

Smith, F. B. 1976. Labouchère's Amendment to the Criminal Law Amendment Bill. *Historical Studies* 67: 165–73.

Solomon, Deborah. 1987. *Jackson Pollock: A Biography*. New York: Simon & Schuster.

Spierenburg, Pieter. 1984. *The Spectacle of Suffering*. Cambridge: Cambridge University Press.

Spurling, Hilary. 1998. *The Unknown Matisse*. New York: Knopf.

Starr, Kenneth. 1998. *The Starr Report: The Findings of Independent Counsel Kenneth W. Starr on President Clinton and the Lewinsky Affair*. New York: Public Affairs.

Starr, Paul. 2004. *The Creation of the Media: Political Origins of Modern Communications*. New York: Basic Books.

Steiner, Franz. (1956) 1967. *Taboo*. Harmondsworth, England: Penguin.

Steiner, Wendy. 1997. *Scandal of Pleasure: Art in an Age of Fundamentalism*. Chicago: University of Chicago Press.

Stone, Geoffrey. 2004. *Perilous Times: Free Speech in Wartime from the Sedition Act of 1798 to the War on Terrorism*. New York: W. W. Norton.

Stone, Lawrence 1977. *The Family, Sex and Marriage in England, 1500–1800*. New York: Harper & Row.

Sturgis, Matthew. 1995. *Passionate Attitudes: The English Decadence of the 1890s*. London: Macmillan.

Suleiman, Ezra N. 1974. *Politics, Power, and Bureaucracy in France*. Princeton, NJ: Princeton University Press.

———. 1993. Politics of Corruption and Corruption of Politics. *French Politics & Society*. 11: 57–68.

Summers, John. 2000. What Happened to Sex Scandals? Politics and Peccadilloes, Jefferson to Kennedy. *Journal of American History*. 87: 825–854.

Sunstein, Cass R. 1996. Social Norms and Social Roles. *Columbia Law Review* 96: 903–68.

Swidler, Ann. 2001. *Talk of Love: How Culture Matters*. Chicago: University of Chicago Press.

Symonds, John Addington. 1896. *A Problem in Modern Ethics*. London.

Terrot, Charles. 1979. *The Maiden Tribute*. London: Frederick Muller.

Thompson, Denis F. 1995. *Ethics in Congress: From Individual to Institutional Corruption*. Washington, DC: Brookings Institution.

Thompson, John. 2000. *Political Scandal: Power and Visibility in the Media Age*. Cambridge: Polity.

Thompson, Richard. 1988. *Degas: The Nudes*. London: Thames and Hudson.

Tilly, Charles. 2008. *Credit and Blame*. Princeton, NJ: Princeton University Press.

Tocqueville, Alexis de. 1955. *The Old Regime and the French Revolution*. New York: Doubleday.

———. 1969. *Democracy in America*. Garden City, NY: Anchor Books.

Tomkins, Calvin. 1996. *Duchamp: A Biography*. New York: Henry Holt.

Toobin, Jeffrey. 2000. *A Vast Conspiracy: The Real Story of the Sex Scandal That Nearly Brought Down a President*. New York: Touchstone.

Tricaud, François. 1977. *L'Accusation: Recherche sur les figures de l'agression éthique*. Paris: Dalloz.

Trumbach, Randolph. 1977. London's Sodomites: Homosexual Behavior and Western Culture in the 18th Century. *Journal of Social History* (Fall): 1–33.

Tulkens, Françoise. 1992. La procédure pénale: Grandes lignes de comparaison entre systemes nationaux. In Mirelle Marty, editor. *Les Grands systèmes de politique criminelle.* Paris: Presses Universitaires de France.

Tullis, Jeffrey. 1988. *The Rhetorical Presidency.* Princeton, NJ: Princeton University Press.

Twain, Mark. 1996. *Tramp Abroad.* New York: Oxford University Press.

United States Bureau of the Census. *Statistical Abstract of the United States (1978-2006).* Washington, D.C.

Varnedoe, Kirk. 2006. *Pictures of Nothing: Abstract Art since Pollock.* Princeton, NJ: Princeton University Press.

Vaughan, Diane. 1983. *Controlling Unlawful Organizational Behavior: Social Structure and Corporate Misconduct.* Chicago: University of Chicago Press.

Veeder, Van Vechten. 1903. The History and Theory of the Law of Defamation. *Columbia Law Review* 3: 546–73.

Verdès-Leroux, Jeannine. 1969. *Scandale financier et antisémitisme catholique. Le Krach de l'Union Générale.* Paris: Editions du Centurion.

Villeneuve, Charles. 1993. *Les Liaisons dangereuses de Pierre Bérégovoy. Enquête sur la mort d'un premier ministre.* Paris: Plon.

Vogelweith, Alain, and Mario Vaudano. 1995. *Mains propres, Mains liées; France-Italie: La Leçon des affaires.* Paris: Austral.

Walker, John A. 1998. *Art and Outrage: Provocation, Controversy and the Visual Arts.* London: Pluto Press.

Warncke, Carsten-Peter. 1997. *Pablo Picasso.* Köln, Germany: Taschen.

Warren, Samuel, and Louis D. Brandeis. 1890. The Right to Privacy. *Harvard Law Review* 4: 193–220.

Warriner, Charles K. 1958. The Nature and Functions of Official Morality. *American Journal of Sociology* 64: 165–8.

Weeks, Jeffrey. (1981) 1989. *Sex, Politics and Society: The Regulation of Sexuality since 1800.* London: Longman.

White, Harrison C., and Cynthia A. White. 1965. *Canvases and Careers: Institutional Change in the French Painting World.* New York: Wiley.

Whitman, David. 1998. *The Optimism Gap. The I'm OK – They're Not Syndrome and the Myth of American Decline.* New York: Walker and Co.

Wilde, Oscar. (1948) 1966. *The Complete Works of Oscar Wilde.* London: Collins.

————. (1911) 1928. *Three Times Tried* (account of the trial in a libel action brought against Lord Queensberry in the Marlborough Street Police Court, London, and the trials of Oscar Wilde and Alfred Taylor held in the Central Criminal Court of London). Paris: Private Print.

Williams, Bernard. 1993. *Shame and Necessity.* Berkeley: University of California Press.

Wilson, Woodrow. 1885. *Congressional Government.* New York: Houghton and Mifflin.

Wolfe, Alan. 1998. *One Nation after All: What Middle-Class Americans Really Think about God, Country, Family, Racism, Welfare, Immigration, Homosexuality, Work, the Right, the Left, and Each Other.* New York: Viking.

Wolfe, Tom. 1975. *The Painted Word.* New York: Bantam Books.

Wood, Michael, and Michael Hughes. 1987. The Moral Basis of Moral Reform: Status Discontent vs. Culture and Socialization as Explanation of Anti-Pornography Social Movement Adherence. *American Sociological Review* 49: 86–99.

Woodward, Bob. 2000. *Shadow: Five Presidents and the Legacy of Watergate.* New York: Simon & Schuster.

———. 2005. *The Secret Man: The Story of Watergate's Deep Throat.* New York: Simon & chuster.

Woodward, C. Van. 1974. *Responses of the Presidents to Charges of Misconduct.* New York: Dell.

Young, Michael. 2006. *Bearing Witness Against Sin: The Evangelical Birth of the American Social Movement.* Chicago: University of Chicago Press.

Zemmour, Éric. 1997. *Le Coup d'état des juges.* Paris: Grasset.

Zerubavel, Eviatar. 2006. *The Elephant in the Room.* New York: Oxford University Press.

Zolberg, Vera. 1990. *Constructing a Sociology of the Arts.* New York: Cambridge University Press.

# Index

Abbott, Andrew, 292, 299
ABC News, 127, 177, 218
*Absinthe Drinker*, 239
Abstract Expressionism, 264–70, 274, 277–8, 315, 317
abstraction, 254, 256–7, 259, 264–70, 317
Abu Ghraib Affair, 74, 126
Adams, John, 88, 89, 186
Adams, John Quincy, 186, 187–8
Adams, Sherman, 97–8
Adorno, Theodore, 230
adultery, American politicians and, 177–8; attitudes in France and U.S., 178; attributed to Marie-Antoinette, 182; of Beecher, 192–3; Carter and, 208; of Clinton, 178, 203, 213–14; of Hamilton, 186, Jackson, 187; of Jefferson, 89; in literature, 41, 183; of Mike Bowers, 209; moral societies and, 190; Victorian attitudes toward, 42
Aestheticism, 69–70, 296
Agnew, Spiro, 102
Alexander, Jeffrey, 291
Alfieris, Bruno, 270
*All in the Family*, 198
*The American Dream Goes to Pot*, 283
ancient Greeks, 14, 185
André, Carl, 226–7, 274, 278, 279
anticorruption, 105, 138–9, 147, 149, 156, 168, 170, 303
anti-Semitism, 30–1
Apollinaire, Guillaume, 269
appearances, 27, 42, 56, 59, 63, 72, 78, 85–6, 103–4, 119, 132, 171, 247, 248, 297
Arbuckle, Roscoe "Fatty," 195

Aremberg, Walter, 272–3
Arendt, Hannah, 289, 310
Armstrong, Lance, 16
art (general), affinities with scandal, 225; art market, 247, 255, 278, 280–1, 318; capitalism and, 233, 255–6, 278; as a contested concept, 228; emotional element in, 228; indeterminacy of meaning in, 232–4; institutionalist theories of, 281–2; moral ambiguity in, 232–3; nudity in, 243–5; as a self-fulfilling prophecy, 281; transgression in, 225–34
art, contemporary, 271–86; crisis of the art object; 271–83; eclecticism of, 271; installations, 274, 278; return to real, 283–6. *See also* conceptual art
art, modern, 238–171; the avoidance of decoration of, 258, 264, 268–70; dissonance, 316; the formal radicalization of, 254; the idea of progress in, 271; intention and, 233–4, 270; intertextuality, 270; moral ambiguity in, 249–50; radicalization of, 254; the rejection of mimesis of, 255–7, 265, 268, 269; the role of critics in, 269–70; subversive content of, 249–254; transgression and, 234–5, 316; uncertainty in, 270; use of distortion in, 256–61. *See also* abstract expressionism, abstraction, cubism, fauvism, impressionism, surrealism
art scandal, 224–34; the decreasing effects of, 230; emotional effect of, 226–7; the ideational element of, 226; motives in creating, 225; provocation in, 231–2; the public of, 226; shock in,

343